PRAY, HOPE
& DON'T WORRY

TRUE STORIES OF PADRE PIO
BOOK II

DIANE ALLEN

Published by Padre Pio Press
P.O. Box 191545
San Diego, CA 92159

ISBN: 0983710503
ISBN-13: 9780983710509

I wish to thank the Lord for having given us dear Padre Pio,
for having given him to our generation in this very tormented century.
In his love for God and for his brothers and sisters,
he is a sign of great hope.

— Pope John Paul II

TABLE OF CONTENTS

INTRODUCTION

G od has raised up different saints in different eras, according to the needs of the Church and the errors of the times. Quite often, they are present in the darkest moments of human history to stand as witnesses to God's loving presence in the world. In the 1st century, St. Paul of Tarsus was chosen to spread the message of the Gospel of Christ. In the 5th century, St. Augustine, as Bishop of Hippo, fought the heretical beliefs that were current at the time, especially Donatism. He also helped bring about the transition from paganism to Christianity with his book, *The City of God*.

St. Benedict in the 6th century established his brand of western monasticism that formed the foundation of monasticism in Europe. St. Bernard of Clairvaux in the 12th century helped establish the Cistercian reform of monasticism and through his writings, gave us true devotion to the sacred humanity of Jesus. His mystical treatises won him the name, "Mellifluous (Honey-Sweet) Doctor of the Church."

St. Charles Borromeo in the 16th century, single-handedly brought the Council of Trent to a successful conclusion and spent the rest of his life in northern Italy and Switzerland putting into effect the decisions of the council through Synods and Visitations. In the Age of Enlightenment, when reason was supreme over faith, God sent an unlettered saint, St. John Vianney, to confound the wise.

In our own time, we have been blessed with the witness of Pope John Paul II and Mother Teresa. Toward the end of his life, Pope John Paul II bewailed the state of the sacrament of confession. He maintained that our culture was losing its sense of sin.

Padre Pio (St. Pio of Pietrelcina) had a special vocation and calling to reach out to the sinful and the lost through the sacrament of confession. He spent many hours each day bringing forgiveness and healing to those who sought to be reconciled with God. People came to him from all parts of the world, seeking his spiritual counsel. As a confessor, St. Pio was unique in many ways, especially for his ability to read hearts and for his profound insights into the human soul.

A lawyer from Milan once made his confession to Padre Pio and told him that he no longer attended Mass. St. Pio then asked him to leave the confessional. The lawyer became indignant, but as time passed, he came to understand that Padre Pio was right. Missing Mass on Sunday was indeed a grave omission. Not only did he return to the sacraments, he became a daily communicant.

Padre Pio's life was completely dominated by his love for God and neighbor. Even so, he was sometimes criticized for his strictness in the confessional. On one occasion, he responded by saying, "I have never lost a single one of my spiritual children. I follow them all with my prayers." And it was true. Padre Pio's prayers, and often his voluntary mortifications and sufferings, brought the lost sheep back into the fold. One is reminded of the first recorded words of Jesus in the gospel of Mark: *The time is fulfilled, the kingdom of heaven is at hand. Repent and believe the good news.*

Today, we hear many beautiful and inspirational stories of Padre Pio's life and spirituality. It seems that they increase with the passage of time. Witness this present book, lovingly compiled by Diane and Ron Allen through their years of contact with individuals who had visited San Giovanni Rotondo and had met Padre Pio.

One last observation. Although Padre Pio had experienced advanced mystical states of prayer, his favorite prayer was the Rosary which he prayed continuously. He once said that he prayed 35 rosaries a day. When asked how it was possible to do so he said, "I am able to do more than one thing at a time."

It is my fond hope that this book will bring many closer to St. Pio, and through him, to God.

Reverend Father Edward Steriti, O.C.S.O.
St. Joseph's Abbey
Spencer, Massachusetts

O my Lord, where can I better serve you, than in the cloister, beneath the banner of the Poor Man of Assisi?

- St. Pio of Pietrelcina

CHAPTER 1

Padre Pio - A True Son of St. Francis

*F*rancesco Forgione (Padre Pio) was born in Pietrelcina, Italy on May 25, 1887 and was baptized the following day. His birth was registered in the town hall in Pietrelcina and signed by two witnesses - the shoemaker and a local farmer. Francesco Forgione's father, Grazio Maria Forgione was present, but could not be an official witness because he was illiterate and was unable to sign his name.

When Francesco was just five years old, he dedicated his life to God. As a child, Francesco was serious, meditative, and above all extremely sensitive to spiritual things. As a youth, he assisted the parish priest in Pietrelcina as an altar server. He was diligent and conscientious in his service to the church.

Francesco's parents, Grazio and Giuseppa Forgione, were both deeply religious and they made a great effort to instill spiritual values in their five children. Later in life, Giuseppa reminisced about Francesco and said, "As Francesco grew older, he never did anything wrong. He was never any trouble and he always obeyed me and Grazio."

Francesco felt the call to religious life at an early age. As a boy, he heard a sermon on St. Michael the Archangel preached by Father Giuseppe (Peppino) Orlando. He was deeply inspired by Father Orlando's words. Later in life, Padre Pio was to say that the sermon was one of the compelling factors that led to his decision to become a priest.

Francesco decided to apply for admission to the Capuchin Order, a branch of the Franciscan Order that strictly adheres to the Rule of St. Francis of Assisi. There was a Capuchin monastery in the town of Morcone. It was only twenty-five miles away from Francesco's home in Pietrelcina but it was considered to be a long distance at the time.

Padre Pio's uncle spoke to the parish priest of Pietrelcina, Father Salvatore Pannullo about the matter. Father Pannullo wrote a letter to the Provincial of the Capuchin monastery in Foggia and learned that the Capuchin novitiate of St. Philip and St. James in Morcone was full. Francesco's uncle then advised Francesco to apply to the Benedictine Order in Montevergine. He also suggested to Francesco that he could apply to the Redemptorist Order in Sant'Angelo a Cupola. But Francesco had his heart set on becoming a Capuchin. He decided to wait until there was an opening in Morcone.

On the Feast of the Epiphany, January 6, 1903, fifteen-year-old Francesco Forgione entered the Capuchin novitiate at Morcone to begin his formal training in religious life. He was assigned to cell number 28 and above the door of his cell were the words from Scripture: *You are dead and your life is hidden with Christ in God* (Colossians 3:3). The words symbolized Francesco's new life. He had chosen to die to the world and all worldly concerns. In the cloister at Morcone, he would remain hidden with Christ. He knew the value of a hidden life. It was what he had been longing for. He was handing over his life to God now. It no longer belonged to him. His ties with the world were being severed forever.

On January 22, he was vested in the religious habit of the Capuchin novice. He exchanged his secular clothing for the brown Franciscan habit with hood and scapular. He would wear the Capuchin habit for the next 65 years. At the time of his investiture, his baptismal name was changed. Francesco Forgione became Brother Pio of Pietrelcina.

The year-long novitiate at Morcone was a testing period and a time when the superiors of the Capuchin community scrutinized the novices to see if they had a vocation to religious life. It was also a time of discernment for the novices as they prayed and meditated about their own calling.

The novices in Morcone studied the Rule of St. Francis, Sacred Scripture, and the Constitutions of the Capuchin Order. In the middle of the night they arose for community prayers in the choir. The Divine Office was recited seven times a day. In the evening after night prayers, the students gathered for meditation before the Blessed Sacrament. Brother Pio always chose the Passion of Christ as the source of his meditation.

Life in the Capuchin novitiate at Morcone was austere and uncompromising. The community followed a literal approach to the Franciscan way of life. Anything that lent itself to poverty of spirit, penance, and self-denial was encouraged. The rigid program was difficult and demanding and it served to separate the weak from the strong. Many of the novices found the rigors of the life too difficult and left on their own accord.

The monastery at Morcone was unheated, and in the winter months the students suffered from the cold. It was not unusual to wake up in the morning to see the water frozen solid in the wash basins. The novices were allowed only one woolen undershirt under their habit and one blanket for their bed. Later in life, Padre Pio would reminisce and say that for him, the cold was the hardest part of the novitiate to endure.

At Morcone, the manual labor and daily chores were performed in strict silence. Although there were several periods set aside during the day when the novices could converse with each other, silence was observed the greater part of the time. A quiet environment was considered to be of great importance in order to preserve the interior spirit of prayer and communion with God. A large sign inscribed with the word *Silence* hung over the doorway in the corridor of the monastery. It was to be a constant reminder to the novices. Brother Pio had always felt an attraction to interior solitude and he thrived in the silence of the monastic enclosure.

In regard to the prayerful silence of contemplative life, one is reminded of the beautiful words of St. Paul of the Cross:

Remember that your soul is a temple of the living God. *The Kingdom of God is within you.* Night and day let your aim be to remain in simplicity and gentleness, calmness and serenity, and in freedom from created things, so that you will find your joy in the Lord Jesus. Love silence and solitude, even when in the midst of a crowd or when caught up in your work. Physical solitude is a good thing, provided that it is backed up by prayer and a holy life, but far better than this is solitude of the heart, which is the interior desert in which your spirit can become totally immersed in God, and can hear and savor the words of eternal life.

Father Tommaso of Mount St. Angelo was the Novice Master at Morcone. He set Brother Pio as a role model for all the other novices. Brother Pio was mature, pious, responsible, and dedicated. Even as a student in the novitiate, he seemed to be advanced beyond his years in the religious life. Father Tommaso said of Brother Pio:

> He was an exemplary novice. He was punctual in his observance
> and exact in all things so as never to give the least motive for reproof.
> He was quite different from the other students.

Father Tommaso worried about Brother Pio's health. He was sickly and very thin. Father Tommaso was also concerned about Brother Pio's poor appetite and insisted that he eat more. In general, the meals at the monastery were quite frugal. Nevertheless, Brother Pio had a hard time eating. Going to the monastery dining room for meals proved to be a real trial for him. It was almost impossible for him to finish the food that was set before him. No one was quite sure why. He often tried to give part of his meals to the other novices and he attempted to do so without letting the superior see.

At Morcone, Brother Pio was assigned to help one of the younger students in the novitiate, Brother Angelico. Every day, for three months, Brother Pio visited the novice in his cell and instructed him in the Rule of St. Francis and the Constitutions. He tried to the best of his ability to help Brother Angelico because he realized that he was wavering in his vocation. The young novice, who was fifteen years old, found it difficult to adapt to the monastic way of life. Brother Angelico wrote:

> I waited with eagerness for the hour set by the Master of Novices
> for Brother Pio to encourage me with the words of a good confrere . . .

I still keep in my heart the memory of the kindness and affability of Brother Pio, who since that time has presented himself to me suffused with a deep and unmistakable piety that is able to win the hearts of others . . . He impressed all of us novices by his faultless behavior and by the attraction that he exerted on all who came into contact with him.

Through the help of Brother Pio, the young novice persevered in his studies. He was eventually ordained to the priesthood and was given the name Father Angelico da Sarno.

Brother Pio also encouraged another novice to persevere, Giovanni Di Carlo. Giovanni had decided that life in the novitiate was too hard, too austere, and was making preparations to leave. Brother Pio spoke to him and encouraged him to stay. He reminded Giovanni that many people had made sacrifices so that he could enter the novitiate at Morcone. He told him to think about his family and the desire they had for him to succeed. "With the help of the Virgin Mary and St. Francis, I know that you will get used to this life," Brother Pio said. Giovanni reconsidered and decided not to leave. After his ordination to the priesthood, he would remember Brother Pio's words of encouragement and feel deep gratitude.

On January 25, 1904, at the end of his one year novitiate, Brother Pio was sent to Sant'Elia a Pianisi where he continued his studies for the priesthood. He had six years of academic classes ahead as he moved through five different monasteries of the Capuchin province. They were years of formation, study, training, and purification. The prescribed curriculum included courses in logic, rhetoric, canon law, sacred scripture, philosophy, ecclesiastical history, and theology.

Father Raffaele, was an aspirant at Sant'Elia a Pianisi when he first made the acquaintance of Brother Pio. They remained in the same monastery together for one year. Later, Father Raffaele reflected on his time at Sant'Elia and said:

Young as I was, I didn't know much about virtue, but I saw in Brother Pio something which distinguished him from the other students. Whenever I met him in the corridors, in choir, in the sacristy, in the garden, he was always humble, recollected and silent and there was no danger that he would speak an unnecessary word.

Although Brother Pio was reserved, he was by no means gloomy. His fellow Capuchins observed that he had a fine sense of humor, and enjoyed participating with them in a good practical joke from time to time. He was also approachable and friendly.

Father Leone looked back on his time as a Capuchin student and wrote:

> While we were students in Sant'Elia, Brother Pio always kept to the genuine spirit of the novitiate . . . I never heard him complain of the poor food, although the friary could have given us something better. He never criticized the actions of the superiors and when others did so he either rebuked them or else left their company. He never grumbled about the cold which was really severe or about the few blankets we were given. However, what struck me most about Brother Pio was his love of prayer.

Father Leone observed that Brother Pio always completed his assigned lessons in a timely manner. He often wondered how Brother Pio found the time to study. It seemed as though he was always praying. Father Leone said:

> Using one excuse or another, I would go to his cell and almost always I would find him on his knees in prayer, his eyes red from weeping. I could say that he was a student of continuous prayer. It was enough to look at his eyes to understand that tears were normal to him.

Father Antonino, one of the teachers at Sant'Elia a Pianisi also noticed that Brother Pio shed tears during the period of prayer. Brother Pio kept a handkerchief with him in the chapel and it was generally wet with his tears. Father Antonino wondered why the good Brother cried. He asked Brother Pio for an explanation but he avoided answering the question. One day, Father Antonino pressed him for an answer. Brother Pio finally said, "I weep for my sins and for those of all men." His fellow classmates were well aware of his tears and some of them teased him about it.

Brother Pio's health steadily declined during his years of formation for the priesthood. He suffered from high fevers, chest pains, headaches, bronchial trouble, dizziness, a chronic and severe cough, intestinal trouble, weakness, and more. Often the symptoms of illness appeared suddenly and then vanished as mysteriously as they had come. The medicines that were given to him did not bring any relief. Neither did the bed rest that was prescribed. His doctors were never able to find a satisfactory explanation or come to any definite conclusion about his sickness. Many years later, Padre Pio confided to Father Agostino Daniele, "My illnesses in my youth stemmed in part from a kind of spiritual oppression."

Brother Pio became so ill that his religious superiors were convinced that he would not live to see his ordination day. "I never wanted to be anything except a priest," Brother Pio said. "But if God is calling me out of this life, I will accept it." Because of his poor health, his superiors frequently sent him back to his home in Pietrelcina for a temporary reprieve. It was hoped that the native air and his mother's tender care might help him regain his strength. During his absence, his teachers and fellow students missed him and waited expectantly for his return.

Brother Pio continued to make a favorable impression on those he came in contact with. Father Bernardino, one of his professors said:

> I had Padre Pio as a theology student at Montefusco. He had an average intelligence. He distinguished himself by his conduct. Among his fellow students who were lively and noisy, he was quiet and calm, even during recreation. He was always humble, meek, and obedient.

While his teachers and fellow students admired Brother Pio for his many virtues, they were not aware at that time of the supernatural dimension of his life. He made an effort to keep his mystical experiences hidden and he evidently succeeded. Later in life, Padre Pio was questioned by Father Agostino regarding his heavenly visions. He told Father Agostino that many of the extraordinary experiences began shortly after he entered the Capuchin novitiate.

When Brother Pio was eighteen years old, he had his first experience of bilocation. At the time, he was assigned to the house of studies in Sant'Elia a Pianisi. One evening he was praying in the monastery chapel when he suddenly found himself at the same time, in a far away city, at the bedside of a dying man. Brother Pio prayed with the man and offered him words of consolation. After a time, he found himself back in the monastery chapel. He was confused by the experience and could come to no conclusion as to what had actually occurred. As time passed, he would grow in understanding. There would be many more experiences of bilocation in the future.

Also, there is evidence that the first documented miraculous healing through Padre Pio's intercession took place during his days as a Capuchin student at Montefusco. It involved the instantaneous cure of Daria Scocca, the mother of Mercurio Scocca, one of Brother Pio's best friends. Daria had known Brother Pio since he was a child and she was also a friend to his family.

Since there were numerous chestnut trees near the monastery of Montefusco, Brother Pio occasionally brought a bag of chestnuts to Daria. Because Daria had such a high regard for Brother Pio, it was her habit to save the bags that the chestnuts came in. One day, Daria had a terrible accident in her home. Some gunpowder that was kept in the house, exploded in her face, burning her chest and head. Daria was in excruciating pain and in a near panic. She ran to get one of the chestnut bags and touched it to her face. Immediately the pain vanished as well as the burns on her skin. After Brother Pio was ordained to the priesthood, there would be many more testimonies as to his gift of healing.

Brother Pio continued to apply himself with great diligence to his studies. Although his health remained unstable, he persevered. On January 27, 1907, Brother Pio made his solemn profession of vows. In so doing, he made his final, permanent commitment to God as a Capuchin Franciscan. He said:

> I, Brother Pio, vow and promise to almighty God, to the Blessed Virgin Mary, to our holy Father St. Francis, to all the saints, and to you, Father, to observe all the days of my life, the Rule of the Friars Minor, confirmed by Pope Honorius, living in obedience, without property, and in chastity.

Many years later, Padre Pio looked back on his calling to follow the Capuchin way of life. He reflected on his vocation to the priesthood and wrote:

> My heart has always been on fire with love for him, my All, and for all men. Innocently and unwittingly, I used to pour out my love on those for whom I cared, then he who always watched over me would

reproach me in a fatherly manner . . . It was the voice of a kind Father who intended to detach his son's heart from everything belonging to earth and the mire, in order that I might devote myself entirely to him. With sweet and tender words, he called me to himself to make me entirely his . . .

He seemed to smile and invite me to a different life. He gave me to understand that my safe haven, my peaceful shelter lay in the ranks of the clergy. O my Lord, where can I better serve you than in the cloister, beneath the banner of the Poor Man of Assisi? Then I felt within me two forces wrestling with each other and tearing my heart asunder: the world that wanted me for itself and God who was calling me to a new life.

Dear God! Who can imagine the interior torment I experienced? Although twenty years have passed since then, the mere recollection of that interior combat makes the blood freeze in my veins. You know, O my God, that I always wanted to obey you and that I would rather have died than refuse to answer your call. You know the state of abandonment to which I was reduced at that time and how you stretched out your strong hand and led me firmly to the place to which you had called me. For this I offer infinite praise and thanks to you, O my God. You hid me away from the eyes of all, but even at that time you had entrusted to your son a very great mission, a mission that is known to you and myself alone.

Twenty-three-year-old Pio was ordained to the priesthood by Most Reverend Paolo Schinosi in the chapel of St. Mary in the Benevento Cathedral on August 10, 1910. It was the feast day of St. Lawrence the Martyr. Padre Pio's mother, Giuseppa Forgione, his Uncle Angelantonio Scocca as well as the parish priest of Pietrelcina, Father Salvatore Pannullo were present for his ordination.

Brother Pio, who, from that time forward, would be known as Padre Pio, returned to Pietrelcina in the afternoon. As he entered his hometown, he was greeted by the citizens of Pietrelcina who had assembled along the streets to await him. In their enthusiasm, they broke out into joyful cheers. A band, which had been hired by his sister-in-law, began to play music in his honor. That evening the celebration continued. Giuseppa lovingly prepared a fine meal for all those who were gathered. For the rest of his life Padre Pio would remember with great joy, the "beautiful day" of his ordination.

Padre Pio's brother Michael and his father Grazio were unable to attend his ordination. They had both emigrated to the United States. Grazio was working there so that he could earn the needed money to pay for his son's priestly education. Padre Pio was always deeply grateful for the sacrifice that his father made for him. He often related the fact to others and said, "My father crossed the ocean twice so that I could study for the priesthood." Whenever he shared the story, his eyes would fill with tears.

Grazio was with his family in spirit on his son's ordination day. He organized a celebration with his friends who worked with him in Jamaica, New York. They played the mandolin, sang Italian songs, and shared their joy together in honor of Padre Pio.

On Sunday, August 14, 1910, Padre Pio said his first Mass at Our Lady of Angels parish in Pietrelcina. Father Agostino preached the sermon that day. As a souvenir of his ordination, Padre Pio passed out holy cards with a sentiment that he had inscribed:

> A souvenir of my first Mass - Jesus, my breath and my life: Today with trembling hands, I elevate you in a mystery of divine love. May I be with you for the world - the way, the truth and the life, and for you, a holy priest, a perfect victim.

The words that Padre Pio wrote on his souvenir card for his first Mass are prophetic. He prayed not only that he would be a holy priest for Jesus' sake but also that he would be a victim, a "perfect victim." We know that Jesus accepted the offering that he made. Just one month later, in September 1910, Padre Pio received the invisible stigmata. He experienced the pain of Christ's wounds for the first time. Sometimes the marks of the crucifixion were visible on his body, but at other times they were not. In 1918, the wounds became both permanent and visible.

Jesus knows that my entire life has been consecrated to him and to his sufferings.

- *St. Pio of Pietrelcina*

Prayer was the key to Padre Pio's existence and the guarantee of his mission. Prayer was his daily activity. He also dedicated many hours of the night to prayer. It was the task which he felt was particularly his own, and which drew upon him the attention of the whole world. At the altar, in his cell, or in the monastery garden, with his hands folded in prayer or holding his Rosary, his world was God - to be contemplated, to be praised, to be entreated, to be propitiated. More than anything else, his was a life of prayer, of uninterrupted conversation with God.

- Father Fernando of Riese Pio X

CHAPTER 2

Anecdotes of Padre Pio - Part 1

When Padre Pio (Francesco Forgione) was a child growing up in Pietrelcina, he and his family lived in a very small house, number 32 on Vico Storte Valle (Crooked Valley Lane). It was a stone house with a reed ceiling, very much like all the other houses in the neighborhood. It was the house of poor people, who often struggled in order to survive.

The Forgiones also had a small landholding in the countryside of nearby Piana Romana. It included a vineyard and several fields. One day, Francesco's father, Grazio Forgione, decided to dig a well on his land in Piana Romana. He dug three meters down but was not successful in finding water. Grazio became more and more frustrated in his attempts. Francesco, who was just a boy at the time, watched his father's futile efforts. Finally Francesco said,

"Father, you are not going to find water there." He pointed to an area a short distance away and said, "But if you dig in this spot, you will find water."

Grazio was doubtful that Francesco's words were true. "Son, why should I believe what you are telling me? How do I know that I will find water there?" "You will see," Francesco replied. Grazio realized that he had nothing to lose, so he decided to follow his son's advice. Soon water started gushing from the exact spot that Francesco had pointed to. "Son, how did you know that water was there?" Grazio asked. "Jesus told me," Francesco said simply. As time passed, the well continued to produce a steady and abundant supply of water, more than enough for the needs of the Forgione family.

———

Shortly after obtaining his license to practice medicine, Dr. Andrea Cardone of Pietrelcina became the family doctor for Francesco Forgione (Padre Pio) as well as the entire Forgione family. In the early days, Dr. Cardone had no idea of the worldwide fame that Francesco would one day receive.

Dr. Cardone remembered that as a boy, Francesco would go to the parish church in Pietrelcina every day. Dr. Cardone sometimes watched young Francesco as he climbed the stairs that led to the church. Even before entering the church, Francesco was already recollected in prayer. He always kept his eyes lowered when he walked through the streets of Pietrelcina on his way to school. Some of the local children were without parental supervision and frequently used bad language. Dr. Cardone remembered that little Francesco would cry whenever he heard their profanities and would run away.

When Padre Pio was a young Capuchin monk in Pietrelcina, Dr. Cardone treated him for his many ailments. Often, Dr. Cardone was at a loss as to how to help him. Padre Pio had a chronic cough and was extremely thin. Many people in the town believed that he had tuberculosis. For that reason, some people avoided him, thinking that his condition was contagious. Dr. Cardone tested him on numerous occasions and was relieved to find out that he did not have tuberculosis. He accompanied Padre Pio to Naples in order to consult with Dr. Castellino, the leading physician of that time. But no matter what remedies were given, his health did not improve. His frequent fevers too, were mysterious. Dr. Cardone confided to a friend that he believed that his fevers were of a supernatural origin.

Dr. Cardone remembered that just before Easter, Padre Pio used to gather the youth of Pietrelcina together at his home. He went over the scriptures that would be read on Good Friday and taught them the songs that would be sung between the Passion prayers.

On one occasion, Dr. Cardone was very ill and burning with a high fever. Padre Pio appeared in bilocation at his bedside. He took Dr. Cardone's wrist in his hand, as though checking his pulse. Dr. Cardone was instantly healed. After that, Dr. Cardone often said, "Padre Pio is a patient who heals the doctor."

In 1910, Padre Pio received the first signs of the stigmata on his hands. He told the parish priest of Pietrelcina, Father Salvatore Pannullo, that he became aware of the painful wounds on his hands at the moment when Jesus and Mary had appeared to him. It was referred to as the "invisible stigmata" because the marks would alternately appear and then disappear. Dr. Cardone was one of the few people who saw the red, puncture-like wounds of the stigmata on Padre Pio's hands at that time. In 1918, when Padre Pio was thirty-one years old, the wounds became permanent. Dr. Cardone also examined Padre Pio's stigmata after it became permanent and left a written statement regarding it. He wrote that the wounds "pierced the palms of his hands completely through, so much so that one could see light through them."

Through the years, Dr. Cardone always felt the beautiful impression of Padre Pio's goodness, his sweetness, his superhuman modesty, and his many other virtues. Like a number of the other citizens of Pietrelcina, Dr. Cardone said that he felt honored to have Padre Pio as a personal friend. He also felt it a great privilege to be his doctor. "We of Pietrelcina are proud of the divine grace which works through Padre Pio and spreads so much good throughout the world," Dr. Cardone said.

————

Due to Padre Pio's fragile health, after his ordination to the priesthood, he remained in his hometown of Pietrelcina for more than six years. It was a great disappointment for him to have to be separated from his religious community, but he did his best to accept it. During his years in Pietrelcina, his reputation for sanctity grew. The citizens of Pietrelcina nicknamed him, "our saint."

Padre Pio found many ways to improve the lives of his fellow townsmen in Pietrelcina. A large number of the citizens who lived there had never had an opportunity to get an education. It was not unusual to see Padre Pio out in the fields with the local farmers and day laborers, instructing them in basic reading and writing. He also taught mathematics to the local people. He organized wholesome games for the citizens to participate in and directed a boys' choir at the parish.

Padre Pio had only been a priest for several years when a local farmer of Pietrelcina summoned him one day. Lice had infested the farmer's crops and fruit trees and all seemed doomed for destruction. The farmer asked Padre Pio if he would be willing to go with him to his fields and bless them. Padre Pio agreed to do so. He made the sign of the cross over the man's land and prayed fervently. Shortly after Padre Pio has blessed the crops, the farmer was amazed to see that the lice had all fallen to the ground. The word spread rapidly among the townspeople. The other farmers decided to ask Padre Pio to bless their land as well. That year the harvest in Pietrelcina proved to be excellent.

In the early days of Padre Pio's ministry, a person once asked Padre Pio to come and bless their family home. Padre Pio agreed to do so. He got as far as the kitchen before he stopped. "I cannot go any farther," he said, and he turned around and walked back out of the house. "The family who lives there spreads rumors," he explained to his companion. "We can have no dealings with them."

Padre Pio knew of a priest who used to visit the family. He warned the priest and said, "I would advise you not to go to that home any more. The people who live there spread lies and rumors about others." On another occasion Padre Pio said, "When you spread rumors about someone, it means you have removed that person from your heart. When you take someone from your heart, Jesus also leaves with them."

———————

Countless people were inspired by the reverence and the intense devotion that Padre Pio exhibited whenever he celebrated Mass. He meditated deeply on every word of the Mass. He often shifted on his painful feet and he paused many times to pray in silence. At the Memento - the prayers for the living and the deceased - his voice sounded weary and strained. At times he trembled and wiped the tears from his eyes with a handkerchief. He once said that during the Mass, the Lord allowed him to mystically see all of his spiritual children - those who were living as well as those who had already passed away.

During the Mass, Padre Pio's eyes remained half-closed. If he opened his eyes at all, it was only to look at the altar. He appeared not to notice the people in the congregation, the lights, or the priests and altar boys who assisted him. On one occasion, he spoke about the Mass he had just celebrated and said, "I almost forgot being in this world."

The mayor of San Giovanni Rotondo, Francesco Morcaldi, once asked Padre Pio to celebrate Mass in front of the town hall. When the local citizens as well as people from the surrounding areas heard that Padre Pio had accepted the mayor's invitation, they were filled with enthusiasm. On the day of the Mass, huge numbers of people descended on the town. The square in front of the town hall as well as the adjacent streets were completely full.

After the Mass, the mayor accompanied Padre Pio back to the monastery. "It was such a wonderful turnout," the mayor said to Padre Pio. "Did you see the crowds who came to attend your Mass? Did you notice that the streets were full to overflowing?" "No, I did not notice the people," Padre Pio replied. "As a matter of fact, I was not aware that I was celebrating Mass in the open air. I became so absorbed in the prayers that I did not notice anything."

———————

There was once a man from Turin, Italy who had a great desire to speak to Padre Pio. He wanted to seek Padre Pio's advice on a personal matter that was of great importance to him. Every time he tried to plan a trip to San Giovanni Rotondo, his way was blocked.

The man was finally able to visit Padre Pio but unfortunately the trip had come too late. "I am so happy that I could discuss my situation with you and receive your advice," the man said to Padre Pio. "But I am sorry to say that time is against me. The information that I discussed with you needs to be received in Turin almost at this very moment. Even if I were to send a telegram, it would not make a difference now. The deadline has come," the man said.

"Don't worry about the deadline," Padre Pio replied. "Write a letter immediately and take it to the post office as fast as you can." The man did what Padre Pio suggested even though he was convinced that it would do no good. Miraculously, the letter was received in Turin in a half-hour's time. The postmark was clearly visible on the envelope. The letter had traveled a distance of more than six hundred and fifty miles in thirty minutes. The man was incredulous and also greatly relieved; the information had reached its destination on time.

On one occasion, one of Padre Pio's spiritual daughters wanted to give him a gift. After thinking about it for some time, she decided to give him two canaries. One day, with her bird cage in hand, she boarded a train to San Giovanni Rotondo so that she could present him with the unusual gift.

When the woman arrived at the monastery door, she was greeted by the porter. The woman told him that the canaries were a gift for Padre Pio. "We are not allowed to keep anything for ourselves unless we have the permission of our superior," the porter explained. "There is a strict rule in place regarding gifts of any kind." "But couldn't you please try to do something to help? I traveled a long distance by train in order to come here and I have a great desire to give Padre Pio these birds." The porter then took the birdcage from the woman. He told her that he would let Padre Pio know about her gift.

The porter took the birds to his own cell temporarily. Soon he heard a knock at the door. To his great surprise, Padre Pio was standing there. "These birds just arrived," the porter said. "A woman brought them for you and she has a great desire that you receive them." Padre Pio went over to the birds and for a few moments began to play with them. "Please do me a favor," Padre Pio said to the porter. "Take the cage over to my cell. I would like to keep the birds for an hour or so." The next day, the porter told the woman that Padre Pio had enjoyed the birds, even though he could not keep them. She was very happy to hear the news and very satisfied.

———————

Alfonso De Rosa was one of Padre Pio's spiritual sons. One day, he had the overwhelming urge to see Padre Pio. He could not stop thinking about it. Alfonso decided to make the journey to San Giovanni Rotondo. He felt blessed that he was able to attend Padre Pio's early morning Mass. After the Mass, he asked the Father Guardian if he could visit Padre Pio in his cell but he was denied permission. Alfonso went back into the church to pray. Later that day, he spoke to the Father Guardian again. For a second time, he asked if it would be possible for him to speak to Padre Pio and for a second time the Father Guardian said no.

Alfonso was very disappointed. He returned to the church once again to pray. He tried to resign himself to the fact that he would not be able to speak to Padre Pio that day. He had done all he could but he had not been able to change the Father Guardian's mind. While he was sitting quietly in the church, a stranger approached him. "Are you the man who has a great desire to see Padre Pio today?" the stranger asked. Alfonso replied that indeed he was. "Follow me then," the man said.

The man led Alfonso to the sacristy of the church. Alfonso was very surprised to see that the gate near the sacristy was unlocked. He proceeded to follow the man through the gate. The door which led to the monks' private quarters was also unlocked. The man opened the door nonchalantly and motioned for Alfonso to follow him. They then entered the corridor that led to the Capuchins' cells. At that point, the stranger disappeared from Alfonso's view. Alfonso simply could not figure out where he had gone. He was there one moment and gone the next.

Two Capuchins who were standing in the corridor looked surprised when they noticed Alfonso's presence. Alfonso knew that they would probably demand that he leave the area at once. He could not allow that to happen. He ran the rest of the way down the corridor to Padre Pio's cell. Padre Pio was standing at the door of his cell, saying goodbye to several American priests who were taking their leave. Padre Pio then saw Alfonso. He welcomed him lovingly and gave him a blessing. It was what Alfonso had been hoping and praying for all day. Alfonso's joy was so great that he could not contain himself. Unashamedly, he began to cry.

———————

Michael Conistabile had often heard people speak of Padre Pio and his remarkable spiritual gifts. He listened but he did not believe. To Michael, the talk about the miracles and healings associated with Padre Pio seemed to be pure fantasy. As far as Michael was concerned, there were a lot of fanatical people in the world with overactive imaginations. He remained skeptical about Padre Pio.

After a time, the discussions that Michael heard about Padre Pio began to arouse his curiosity. In June 1950, he decided to take his wife and his one year old son, Gianfranco, to visit Padre Pio's monastery in San Giovanni Rotondo. He wanted to find out for himself the truth about Padre Pio.

Michael found a hotel for his family about one-half mile from the monastery. The next morning, when Michael and his family arrived at the church for Mass, Padre Pio was already at the altar. When the Mass began, Michael had a chance to look at him closely. "He looks just like any other Capuchin," Michael said to himself. Michael saw nothing singular or special about him. But as the Mass progressed, Michael witnessed something extraordinary.

As the congregation prayed the *Our Father*, Michael noticed that the palms of Padre Pio's hands were shining. The wounds in the middle of his hands were a very bright red, a brilliant red. The brightness dazzled Michael's eyes. He shut his eyes momentarily and then opened them. He looked at Padre Pio's hands once again. He wanted to make sure that what he had seen was not an hallucination. He knew that it was not. The light from Padre Pio's hands continued to shine with great intensity. It was as if Padre Pio's wounded hands were illuminated by a thousand electric lights. Michael lowered his eyes and then knelt down. He felt completely confused by what he had witnessed.

The next day, Michael took little Gianfranco with him to the monastery. He was walking down one of the corridors when, much to his great surprise, he happened to see Padre Pio. With little Gianfranco in his arms, Michael greeted Padre Pio and asked him to give his young son a blessing. "Please pray for my little son so that he may someday become a missionary," Michael said. "But why a missionary?" Padre Pio asked. "Let him be what God wills him to be." He then placed his hand on the head of Gianfranco and blessed him. He gave Michael a blessing as well. He spoke to Michael about the nearby shrine in Monte Sant' Angelo which was dedicated to St. Michael the Archangel. He encouraged him to take his family there for a visit.

Every morning at the monastery, Michael went to the sacristy before Mass and waited for Padre Pio. He helped Padre Pio put on his priestly vestments before Mass. When Padre Pio returned to the sacristy after celebrating Mass, Michael was there to assist him. He and his family were able to spend more than a week in San Giovanni Rotondo. Michael had come as a skeptic. He left as a believer.

Teresita De Vecchi went to San Giovanni Rotondo on one occasion in order to make her confession to Padre Pio. As she waited in the confessional line, she was able to see Padre Pio clearly. She noticed that his customary half-gloves covered his hands completely. Teresita had a great desire to see the wounds in his hands. At the very moment she was thinking about his hands and wishing that she could see them, Padre Pio slowly pulled up one of his gloves so that his entire hand was exposed. Teresita noticed that his hand was very white and smooth. In the center of his palm was a large crust of clotted blood which reached almost to his fingers. After a moment, he slowly pulled the glove back down over his hand.

Teresita made her confession to Padre Pio and before she left the confessional, she kissed his hand. She became instantly aware of a strong smell of carbolic acid. After she left the confessional, it lingered in the air around her for several hours. When she returned to her home, she could not get the thought of Padre Pio out of her mind. She kept thinking about the intensity of his dark and piercing eyes and the terrible wounds in his hands.

Several weeks later, Teresita was on a train trip to the city of Lugano in Switzerland. As she passed through a mountainous region, she looked out the window and saw the town that she had grown up in. A feeling of homesickness swept over her. Her heart was aching as she thought of her dear family. Precious memories of days gone by flooded her mind. Suddenly, she noticed the same smell of carbolic acid that she had perceived when she kissed Padre Pio's hand in the confessional. She knew then that Padre Pio was near and was aware of her sadness.

Not long after, Teresita traveled to San Giovanni Rotondo again. She attended the early morning Mass and afterward she waited in the corridor in order to greet Padre Pio. For some reason, when Padre Pio stepped into the corridor, he looked altogether different from the way he had looked when he was at the altar that morning. He seemed to be much taller. He looked luminous and majestic. As he passed down the corridor, he left a trail of perfume behind him.

On another visit to San Giovanni Rotondo, Teresita obtained a ticket for Padre Pio's confessional. She waited three weeks but still her name was not called. Finally, having a family commitment to attend to, she could wait no longer. She had to return to her home.

Before leaving San Giovanni Rotondo, Teresita decided to go to the monastery one last time and wait below the little window where Padre Pio appeared each afternoon to give his blessing to the faithful. Just as Teresita got to the area below Padre Pio's window, she learned that he had already given his blessing for the day. The little window was closed and locked. "Padre Pio has now retired for the day," Teresita was told. "He will return again tomorrow afternoon to give his blessing." About twenty people were still standing below Padre Pio's window, praying the Rosary together. Teresita decided to stay and pray the Rosary with the group.

As Teresita prayed the Rosary, she sent up her fervent petition to Padre Pio. She prayed, "Padre Pio, soon I have to catch a train and return to my home and my family. I waited three weeks to make my confession to you but I was not able to do so. My number was not called. Before I return to my home, I ask you to give me a blessing, a big blessing!"

The little Rosary group continued with their prayers. About ten minutes later, much to everyone's great surprise, the little window of Padre Pio's cell opened once again. Padre Pio appeared at the window and looked out on the small group. For the second time that day, he gave his priestly blessing.

Afterward, he started waving something in the air. It was not the customary handkerchief that he normally held in his hand each afternoon when he waved to the crowd. It was something much bigger. Teresita looked closely. Padre Pio was waving a bed sheet! The little Rosary group could not believe their eyes. "What on earth is Padre Pio doing?" they said in unison. They began to laugh. But Teresita understood. It was an answer to her petition. It was the "big blessing" she had been praying for.

As time passed, Teresita became aware that Padre Pio was watching over her in countless ways. She had asked him to accept her as his spiritual child and he had agreed to do so. "I will be your father," he said. "Just don't do anything to embarrass me!"

One summer day after visiting the monastery, Teresita was getting ready to walk to town. Without warning, she was suddenly caught in a downpour. Unfortunately, she did not have an umbrella with her. She broke into a run. As she ran toward the town, she felt as though she was in a tunnel. It was raining on both sides of her, but not on her. By the time she got to town, she should have been drenched. But instead, she was completely dry. She had just attended Padre Pio's Mass and had offered her Holy Communion for his intentions.

Teresita knew what a privilege it was to be able to attend Padre Pio's Mass. Once, at Padre Pio's Mass, Teresita felt fortunate to find an excellent seat in the very front of the church. She was able to see Padre Pio clearly. He cried through most of the Mass and he dried his eyes with a white handkerchief that was on the altar. Teresita noticed that the blood from the wounds on his hands had stained the handkerchief. As she looked at the handkerchief, she thought to herself how much she would like to possess it. What a blessing it would be to have a relic of Padre Pio. Several hours later, to her great joy, she was given the handkerchief to keep.

To meet Padre Pio even after his death is to find heaven, because that is where he will lead you.

- Father Joseph Pius Martin

CHAPTER 3

Anecdotes of Padre Pio - Part 2

*P*ietro (Pietruccio) Cugino, of San Giovanni Rotondo was just six years old when his father took him to see Padre Pio for the first time. As time passed, Padre Pio grew to love Pietruccio with a fatherly affection. He gave Pietruccio instructions in the Catholic faith and prepared him to receive his first Holy Communion.

In the early days, farmers brought their sheep, horses, and donkeys to the monastery to be blessed by Padre Pio. Pietruccio often helped herd the animals onto the square just outside the church. When Pietruccio was twelve years old, he contracted an incurable eye disease and lost his sight. Even though he was blind, he still found many ways to assist Padre Pio. He liked picking the special wild herbs that Padre Pio enjoyed in his salad. Twice a day he went to the post office to collect the mail for the Capuchins. He did the shopping for the Capuchins as well. He became so familiar with the monastery and the surrounding area that he did not need a cane to get about. He knew every stone, every turn, every step and incline by heart. He became almost a permanent fixture at the monastery.

Padre Pio once said to some of his friends, "Consider the fact that Pietruccio is indeed fortunate. Because of his blindness, he is not able to see the sinful and evil things in this world." As a matter of fact, Pietruccio used to thank God that he was blind because through it, he felt that he received many extra graces from Padre Pio, graces that were not give to others. He was allowed to go to Padre Pio's cell whenever he wanted to. He would often visit Padre Pio in his cell in the evening and stay until Padre Pio got in bed. Then he would kneel at his bedside to receive his blessing.

Through the many years of their friendship, Padre Pio kept Pietruccio at his side. When he was weak and unsteady on his feet, he used to say to Pietruccio, "You lend me your arm and I will lend you my eyes." He would lean upon Pietruccio's strong arm when he walked from the monastery to the church. When Padre Pio became advanced in years, due to his many ailments, he sometimes had difficulty changing his clothing. Pietruccio counted it a privilege to assist him. Each morning, Pietruccio was given a great honor. He preceded Padre Pio out of the sacristy when it was time for the Mass to begin and was allowed to stand very close to the altar for the duration of the Mass.

For Pietruccio, just to be near Padre Pio was a great, inestimable gift. It filled him with a deep joy, a joy that sustained him in all the ups and downs of his life. Every morning when Pietruccio woke up, he would reflect on the previous day. In his mind, he would go over everything that Padre Pio had said and done. Because he loved Padre Pio so much, he wanted to savor every memory.

The Capuchins trusted Pietruccio so completely that they gave him his own key to the monastery. He usually took his meals with Padre Pio and the other Capuchins in the monastery dining room. A special cell was reserved for him so that in inclement weather, he could sleep inside the monastery rather than return to his home.

Once, Pietruccio told Padre Pio that he had a great fear. "Padre Pio," Pietruccio said. "I feel that as long as you are alive, you will always be near to help me. But because of my blindness, I worry about my future. What will happen to me after your death? Who will take care of me?" "The God who helped us yesterday, helps us today, and will help us tomorrow," Padre Pio replied. "He wants us to abandon ourselves completely into his care."

A few days before Padre Pio died, he said to Pietruccio, "I am sorry but I have to leave you." "What do you mean?" Pietruccio asked. "Let us pray about it," Padre Pio replied. Padre Pio died a few days later.

Pietruccio felt shattered by Padre Pio's death. The thought of never seeing Padre Pio again was almost too much for him to bear. He began to feel, for the first time in his life, the full weight of his blindness. As he reflected on it, he became convinced that when Padre Pio was alive, he had carried the cross of his blindness for him. At that time, it did not seem to Pietruccio that it was a burden to be blind. But after Padre Pio passed away, he truly felt that it was a heavy cross.

———

There was a woman named Michelina who counted herself as one of Padre Pio's loyal spiritual daughters. She had met Padre Pio for the first time when she was twelve years old. Every year she traveled from her home in Pescara to San Giovanni Rotondo to attend Padre Pio's Mass. After Padre Pio passed away, she continued to pray to him and ask for his intercession.

Michelina had experienced many trials in her life. Her husband passed away leaving her a widow at a relatively young age. Her son Alfredo became deeply involved in the dark world of drugs. His life was going from bad to worse. Michelina prayed to Padre Pio every day to intercede for Alfredo and to cure him of his addiction. In her prayers, she told Padre Pio that if he would help her son, she would walk the distance from Pescara to San Giovanni Rotondo to pray at his tomb and offer her thanksgiving.

For six years, Michelina prayed daily to Padre Pio for Alfredo. Finally, one day there was a breakthrough. Alfredo had a fight with one of the drug dealers. He decided to break away from the world of drugs forever. His life underwent a complete transformation and he vowed that he would never go back to his former lifestyle.

Michelina was overjoyed. She had not forgotten the promise she had made to Padre Pio. She set off from Pescara to San Giovanni Rotondo with her walking stick and Rosary in hand. She was fifty-six years old.

When she arrived in the town of Francavilla al Mare, one of her relatives decided to join her on the walk. He made a good effort but he was not able to continue for very long. Michelina passed through the towns of Termoli, Poggio Imperiale, and San Marco in Lamis enroute to the monastery of Our Lady of Grace. By the time she reached San Giovanni Rotondo, she had walked 120 miles. Her knee was swollen and her exhaustion was great, but other than that, she was in good condition. She felt great happiness when she finally knelt at Padre Pio's tomb. She prayed in thanksgiving for Alfredo's deliverance from drugs and for his new beginning in life.

Michelina's relatives, knowing the long and difficult journey she had made, met her in San Giovanni Rotondo. When she finished her prayers and devotions at Padre Pio's tomb, they offered her a ride back home and she happily accepted.

On one occasion, Domenico Savino traveled on business from his home in Velletri to the northern part of Italy. On the return train trip home, he struck up a conversation with one of the passengers, a young man named Victor. Victor's sincerity and goodness were so apparent that Domenico liked him at once.

As the two men talked together, Victor shared some of the burdens that were in his heart. He had used the last of the money in his family's savings in order to travel to Milan in search of work. Unfortunately, he was not able to find a job there. His aged parents were in need of care and Victor was deeply concerned for them. He loved them both very much. Domenico's heart went out to Victor. It seemed that he had more than his share of difficulties.

Not long after, Domenico was making preparations to visit Padre Pio's monastery in San Giovanni Rotondo. On the way to the monastery, Domenico passed through the town of Campania, where Victor lived. He stopped at Victor's home and invited him to accompany him on the trip. "I assure you that you will feel the wonderful spiritual benefits of visiting the monastery," Domenico said to Victor. "You can talk to Padre Pio about your many difficulties and ask him to pray for you," he added. Victor was very happy to accept the invitation.

The trip to Padre Pio's monastery had a transforming effect on Victor. While there, he made many visits to the little church of Our Lady of Grace and spent much of his time in prayer. He felt renewed in body, mind, and soul.

In San Giovanni Rotondo, Victor bought two photographs of Padre Pio. He was going to display one of the photos in his home. He decided that he was going to keep the other photograph with him at all times.

The days passed far too quickly and soon it was time for the two friends to return to their homes. A month later, Domenico received a letter from Victor. He wrote that he had found work in a mine in Belgium and was doing well. He was very happy because he was now able to send money home to his parents. He told Domenico that he made sure that he had Padre Pio's photograph with him at all times. It was a spiritual connection to Padre Pio and it filled his heart with a great sense of peace.

Some time later, Domenico received another letter from Victor. Victor wrote that a terrible disaster had struck the mine where he worked. He and some of the other miners had been trapped underground for many hours when the mine shaft that they were working in collapsed.

During that terrible time of waiting, suspended between life and death, Victor talked to the other miners about Padre Pio. He also had Padre Pio's photograph with him. It took many hours of exhausting work before the rescue crew was able to bring all of the miners to safety. The words that Victor spoke about Padre Pio, and the photograph which he shared, proved to be a great consolation to all the miners.

———

In November 1965, Archbishop Adolfo Tortolo of Parana, Argentina was able to spend several days at the monastery of Our Lady of Grace in San Giovanni Rotondo. The Archbishop attended Padre Pio's Mass and during the celebration of the Mass, he noticed a thin line of fresh red blood on Padre Pio's left hand. After the Mass had ended, he had the opportunity to hold Padre Pio's hands in his own. Padre Pio's hands were so hot that the Archbishop described them as "burning like two lighted coals."

Later on in the day, the Archbishop knelt before Padre Pio in order to make his confession. Padre Pio's face was serene and his dark eyes were deep and very beautiful. "You are a bishop," Padre Pio said. "You must give me your blessing." Padre Pio then took the Archbishop's hand and kissed it.

Padre Pio once confided that the wounds of the stigmata were especially painful to him in the late night hours. Archbishop Tortola learned by experience the truth of Padre Pio's statement. One night, while staying at the monastery of Our Lady of Grace, the Archbishop heard moaning sounds coming from Padre Pio's cell. The next day, he asked the Father Guardian if he knew what the sound could have been. The Father Guardian told him that even when Padre Pio was asleep, he continued to suffer through the night. He never slept more than a few hours, but even then, he was not able to have any relief from his pain.

———————

Giuseppe Bassi, one of Padre Pio's spiritual sons, used to attend Padre Pio's Mass when it was held in the small and rustic 16th century church of Our Lady of Grace. At that time, it was Padre Pio's practice to say his Mass at the side altar of St. Francis.

On one occasion, Giuseppe arrived at the church at 4:30 a.m. and waited in the darkness along with many others for the church to open. While they waited, some of the people who were standing in line near Giuseppe, began to converse together. Giuseppe listened with interest to the stories of Padre Pio that the devotees were sharing. One man explained how he had been healed of a very serious back condition through the intercession of Padre Pio. As soon as he finished his story, another man spoke up and said, "That is a lie! I am certain that you were not healed by Padre Pio or by anyone else!" Giuseppe and the others who were present were shocked at the man's rudeness.

The man who made the unkind remark looked to be about twenty-five years old. His skin had an unhealthy, sallow color to it. From time to time, vulgar words would escape from his lips. He did not seem to feel the slightest sense of shame using profanities in such a sacred place. Giuseppe heard the man say that he was from the town of Romagna. That was as much as Giuseppe wanted to know about him. His sarcasm and his anger caused the others who were nearby to feel the same way as Giuseppe did. The man moved about in a nervous way and his body seemed to jerk when he shifted his weight from one side to the other. Among the devout and prayerful people who were gathered in front of the monastery church, the man seemed very much out of place.

Before long, one of the Capuchins came out and unlocked the doors to the church. Once inside, Giuseppe quickly made his way to the sacristy. Already, about fifty men were gathered there. Because of his previous visits to the monastery, Giuseppe knew the routine well. A few minutes before 5:00 a.m. the sacristy door would open and Padre Pio would appear. He would then make his way to the side altar of St. Francis where he said his Mass.

On that particular morning, as Padre Pio walked into the sacristy, his face was marked by an expression of deep suffering. All of the men who had been waiting to see him, knelt down. Padre Pio dragged his feet as he made his way through the crowd. To some, he would offer his hand, to others, he would not. He had his own reasons for doing so.

When Padre Pio saw the man from Romagna kneeling in the sacristy, he paused momentarily and placed his hand on the man's head. He then gave the man his blessing. From what Giuseppe had already witnessed, the young man certainly needed that blessing. At Padre Pio's touch, the man's entire body started shaking. He began to cry. Everyone present could hear his heartbreaking sobs. "Get up, young man," Padre Pio said to him in an encouraging way. "It is good for you to cry. I know that you are sorry. You must have courage." When the man finally rose to his feet, he seemed to be at peace.

Later on that morning, Giuseppe returned to his hotel. There in the lobby stood the man from Romagna. He had evidently booked a room in the same hotel. He was talking to several people who were standing in the hotel lobby with him. Giuseppe decided to join the conversation. The man from Romagna explained that he had come to San Giovanni Rotondo mainly out of curiosity. One of his co-workers had told him about Padre Pio and he found the information interesting. "As soon as Padre Pio touched me and looked at me with those eyes of universal judgment, I felt terrified. I felt an overwhelming urge to cry," he explained.

Giuseppe noticed that the man's physical appearance looked different. Before, he looked unattractive and unwell. Not anymore. He now had a glow of serenity and happiness on his face. Those few moments with Padre Pio were enough to bring about a remarkable transformation.

———

There was a woman (name withheld) who worked in Italy for an international Catholic organization. Her job responsibilities required her to spend much of her time in Rome, where she was in close communication with the Congregation for the Doctrine of the Faith. In addition, her job required her to travel to many different parts of Italy. It seemed like whatever city she happened to be in, people wanted to talk to her about Padre Pio. They often encouraged her to visit Padre Pio's monastery in San Giovanni Rotondo but she had no desire to do so. San Giovanni Rotondo was a small and impoverished village. Looking at a map, it was found on the "spur" of the Italian boot. It was not one of the towns that her organization required her to visit and she saw no good reason to make a special trip there. She began to feel irritated by the constant talk she heard about Padre Pio. She grew to dislike even the sound of his name.

The woman observed that most of the people who spoke to her about Padre Pio seemed to be overly zealous and even fanatical in their devotion to him. In her estimation, they were on the wrong track. She thought it was a shame that so many people had put Padre Pio on such a high pedestal.

In 1956, troubling developments occurred in the Catholic organization that the woman worked for. Once again, she heard the common refrain, "You should go to San Giovanni Rotondo and ask Padre Pio for advice. He will be able to help you." To her, the suggestion seemed absurd. Padre Pio was a priest who practically never left the seclusion of his monastery. In all probability, he knew nothing about the Catholic organization that she worked for. He would be the least likely person to know how to advise her.

The woman sought the counsel of two priests whom she held in great esteem. They both were very familiar with her organization, having implemented it in their own diocese. Both priests listened with attention as she explained the problems within the organization. They advised her to the best of their abilities. However, her immediate supervisor had a completely different idea as to the solution. The woman, after much thought, finally made her own decision on the best course to take. Nevertheless, she was continually tormented by doubts about the decision she had made.

That year, several of the woman's friends, including one nun as well as a dear friend who was a priest, invited her to spend Christmas in Naples with

them. They knew that she was under a lot of pressure from the many responsibilities at her job. She accepted their invitation with gratitude.

One day, during the Christmas vacation, her friends announced that they
were making a trip to San Giovanni Rotondo. They wanted to attend Padre
Pio's Mass and they also wanted to deliver a number of Mass offerings which
they had received from their friends who were not able to make the trip.

Although the woman had no desire personally to visit the monastery of
Our Lady of Grace or to meet Padre Pio, simply to please her friends, she
agreed to go. Even though she had previously thought that it would be futile
to talk to Padre Pio about her work concerns, she reconsidered. As long as she
was going to be visiting his monastery, if the opportunity presented itself, she
would try to speak to him about the matter.

At 4:15 a.m. the woman and her little group stood outside of the church
of Our Lady of Grace, waiting in the darkness for the doors to open. It was
the middle of winter and bitterly cold. When the church doors opened at 5:00
a.m. everyone rushed inside, hoping to find a good seat close to the altar.
What the woman and her companions had not bargained for, was the conduct
of some of the local women of the area. Without regard for anyone, they
pushed, pulled, and elbowed their way to the best seats in the church. The
kind nun, who was one of the woman's companions on the trip, had managed
to find an excellent seat on the very front bench. Hard to believe but entirely
true, the nun was unceremoniously removed from her seat and knocked to
the ground.

The rude conduct in the church of some of the "locals" had been a dis-
graceful scene to witness. It was almost unbelievable. The woman not only
blamed the locals for their outrageous behavior, she also blamed Padre Pio.
After all, he was the cause of all the frenzy.

After a time, Padre Pio came out of the sacristy. Silence then descended
upon the little church. From his first steps up the altar until the end of the
Mass, he remained completely absorbed in prayer. The woman suddenly
found herself carried into what she described as "another world." Attending
Padre Pio's Mass was nothing like she had ever expected. She found it to be a
"supernatural experience," and she was deeply edified.

The priest who had come from Naples with the woman and her other
companions had been to the monastery of Our Lady of Grace several times

before. He had even visited Padre Pio in his cell. Arrangements were made so that the woman and her party would be able to greet Padre Pio before they returned to Naples. They waited in the appointed hallway so that they could speak to him when he passed from the sacristy to the door that led to the Capuchins' cells.

As it turned out, some of the local women, who had caused so much havoc in the church that morning, had come to wait for Padre Pio in the very same spot. Finally, the door of the sacristy opened and Padre Pio appeared. The woman was close enough to get a good look at him. Padre Pio's face was beautiful. It seemed to her to be the most beautiful face she had ever seen. His large, dark eyes, which registered both love and pain, reminded her of the suffering Christ.

As Padre Pio drew closer, the locals began to press upon him and crowd him. Not wanting to cause him any more discomfort than what he was experiencing at that moment, the woman drew back. She now stood behind the first row of women in the corridor.

Padre Pio then paused and finally stopped in front of the woman's two companions and spoke to them. The woman realized that she was no longer in a good proximity to speak to Padre Pio. If only she had stayed in the front row with her friends, she too would have had a chance to speak to him. The many problems she faced at her place of employment suddenly flooded her mind. For a long time, her work situation had been a source of mental agony for her. She thought of the important decision that she had to make soon. She regretted that she would not be able to speak to Padre Pio about it.

Much to the woman's great surprise, Padre Pio then looked straight in her direction. He smiled at her with great love and held out his hand to her. She had the distinct feeling that he was aware of all the thoughts that were in her mind at that very moment. As she looked in his eyes, she suddenly knew the right course to take regarding her work. Exactly how this could happen, she did not know. The doubts that had plagued her for such a long time, vanished. Without saying one word, Padre Pio had answered her urgent need. A peace, like nothing she had ever experienced before, swept over her. She was assured beyond a shadow of a doubt, that all would be well.

Padre Pio was not a common friar, like all the rest of us, although he tried to appear as such. He had something which was supernatural, which distinguished him and elevated him above everyone else. He had the splendor and the greatness of holiness. Whoever approached him was conquered.

- Father Alberto D'Apolito

CHAPTER 4

Father Alberto D'Apolito

Alberto D'Apolito of San Giovanni Rotondo was a young boy in elementary school when he met Padre Pio for the first time. He and several of his friends had decided to go to the monastery of Our Lady of Grace in order to make their confession to Padre Pio. The year was 1917. At that time, Padre Pio was known as the "holy monk" by the local people of the town. It proved to be very accurate description of the celebrated priest.

When Alberto and his friends entered the church, they saw Padre Pio sitting up in the choir loft. He seemed to be in a deep state of prayer. Padre Pio heard the loud voices of Alberto and his companions and got up and looked down from the balcony to see what the commotion was all about. He then spoke to Alberto and his friends and asked them to state their business. When they said they had come to make their confession, Padre Pio immediately went downstairs. He was friendly to the boys and was happy to hear their confessions.

During Alberto's confession, Padre Pio asked him, "Do you often tell lies?" "Yes, I do," Alberto replied. Padre Pio then became very serious and spoke to Alberto brusquely. Alberto's pride was hurt by Padre Pio's stern manner. Alberto made a supreme effort to hold back his tears and he managed to do so. Padre Pio explained to Alberto that lies, even very small ones, were a great offense to God. Alberto never forgot his words. Perhaps if Padre Pio had been more gentle in his approach, Alberto may never have grasped the important meaning of what he was trying to convey. Padre Pio asked Alberto if he had ever been an altar server at Mass. Alberto told him that he had not. "You must promise me that you will learn how to serve at Mass," Padre Pio said. "I want you to go to Mass often and to always love Jesus," Padre Pio added. Then, Padre Pio placed his hand on Alberto's head and gave him absolution and a blessing.

Shortly after Alberto had made his confession to Padre Pio, he took it upon himself to take instructions in how to serve at the Mass. Young Alberto had been impressed by Padre Pio's encouraging words regarding attending daily Mass. After he received the proper training in altar serving, Alberto got up very early every day and served at the morning Mass at his parish before going to school.

In 1919, Alberto's uncle, Father Clemente Centra, who taught at the Capuchin seminary in Montefusco, visited San Giovanni Rotondo. One day, he took Alberto to Our Lady of Grace monastery with him to see Padre Pio. When Father Clemente and Padre Pio saw each other, they embraced with affection. They had both been in the Capuchin novitiate together in preparation for the priesthood. Father Clemente explained to Padre Pio that Alberto was his nephew. "Would you like to be a Capuchin friar like your uncle?" Padre Pio asked Alberto. "No, I would not," Alberto replied. "Why is that?" Padre Pio asked. "It is because I want to be a Salesian priest," Alberto said. "And why would you prefer to be a Salesian priest?" Padre Pio asked. Alberto explained that he wanted to be a Salesian priest because he wanted to live and study in Rome.

Padre Pio told Alberto that some of the students from the Seraphic Boarding School were in the monastery garden playing games. He suggested that Alberto go over and join them. Alberto went to the garden and watched the students at their recreation. Shortly after that, he returned to his uncle who was still talking to Padre Pio. When it was time to say goodbye, Padre Pio gave Alberto a blessing and said to him, "Someday you will become a Capuchin friar just like your uncle. I await you in our school here at the monastery of Our Lady of Grace."

Alberto was too young to seriously contemplate Padre Pio's words or to truly understand the implications of a vocation to the priesthood. However, when Alberto completed his elementary school studies, he did not enter the Salesian school but rather, he enrolled in the Seraphic Boarding School in San Giovanni Rotondo. At that time, Padre Pio was the spiritual director of the school. He also taught several of the classes. Later, he would become the principal of the school.

The small Seraphic Boarding School was the equivalent of middle school/high school and the students who attended were preparing to enter the Capuchin novitiate when they reached age fifteen. The boys were housed at the monastery of Our Lady of Grace.

The students had a well-rounded education which included academics, religious studies, spiritual formation and recreation. One of the favorite games of the boys was playing with a pinata. Blindfolded and with a stick in their hand, they would try to break a pinata filled with candy. Padre Pio derived great enjoyment from watching the boys at their recreation and had great affection for them. He cared about all of their needs, both great and small, and did not want them to lack for anything. He confided to a fellow Capuchin that he was worried because one of the students possessed only one pair of shoes. The boy was the young son of a widowed mother.

Padre Pio wanted the students at the Seraphic Boarding School to lead good Christian lives and to give a good example to others. He also wanted them to succeed in their academic studies. When the boys misbehaved or when they wavered in their vocation to religious life, Padre Pio suffered. He was prepared to make any sacrifice in order to help them.

Padre Pio's love for the boys and his desire for the spiritual success of the school was expressed in a letter to Father Benedetto. He wrote:

I have a keen desire to offer myself as a victim to the Lord for the perfecting of this school, which is very dear to me and for which I do not spare myself any pains. It is true that I have good reason to thank the Heavenly Father for the change for the better in most of the students, but I am not yet satisfied . . . Jesus will give me the strength to bear this fresh sacrifice.

One day, Padre Pio appeared to be very sad. He was taking a walk with the boys when he suddenly began to cry. "One of you pierced my heart today," Padre Pio said. The boys did not know what to make of his words. Padre Pio then explained, "This morning one of you made a sacrilegious Communion at Mass. I know this to be a fact. I also feel bad because I was the one who distributed Holy Communion." At that moment, one of the boys in the group spoke up and admitted that he was the one at fault. With tears in his eyes, he apologized to Padre Pio and said that he was sincerely sorry for what he had done. Padre Pio asked all the other boys to leave momentarily and he then heard the confession of the young man.

Father Federico of Macchia Valforte attended the Seraphic Boarding School in his youth. He left a beautiful written testimony of his impressions of Padre Pio. He wrote:

Padre Pio was always praying, night and day. His main teaching place for us was the choir, where he spent long hours of the day on his knees as a faithful worshiper of Jesus in the Blessed Sacrament. In our midst he prayed and responded, always holding his Rosary in his right hand. In the refectory, after he had hurriedly and listlessly taken a few mouthfuls, he continued to pray. He used to say "I wish the day had forty-eight hours in which to pray." In fact, he never left the choir until midnight. When he went to bed, we felt him to be always keeping watch. His whole day was a continuous dialogue with God.

On one occasion, during recreation time, nine of the boys who were enrolled in the Seraphic Boarding School asked Padre Pio for permission to climb the mountain that was directly behind the monastery. The superior of the monastery was away at the time and had left Padre Pio in charge. Padre Pio gave the boys permission to climb the mountain on condition that they come straight back to the monastery in the afternoon.

Padre Pio grew worried when the boys were late in returning. They had been gone for more than two hours and already the sun was beginning to go down. Padre Pio wished that the monastery had a telephone so that he could notify the authorities, but at that time, in 1919, the monastery did not possess one. A terrible anxiety gripped Padre Pio's heart and he began to cry. He did not know what to do. He spent the night in front of the Blessed Sacrament, tearfully pleading with Jesus to protect the boys and return them safely to the monastery.

The next day, there was still no sign of the boys. Alberto's uncle, Antonio Centra, was at Our Lady of Grace monastery that morning. When he greeted Padre Pio, he noticed that his eyes were red from crying. Padre Pio then sent one of the Capuchins to the police station to notify the Chief of Police. The Chief of Police sent a telegram to all of the other police headquarters in the surrounding areas. Finally, a telegram arrived in San Giovanni Rotondo saying that the boys had been found. After climbing the mountain, instead of returning to the monastery like they were supposed to do, they had decided to walk to the monastery of Vico del Gargano. They spent the night outdoors on the steps of a church in the town of Carpino. They reached the monastery of Vico del Gargano late the next afternoon.

The event had been so traumatic for Padre Pio that he wrote a letter to Father Benedetto, expressing his deepest feelings. "Only God knows how much I cried and how much I suffered. If I did not go crazy and my heart did not break, it was because of Divine grace." As it turned out, none of the nine young aspirants to the Capuchin order ever completed their studies. Each of them, at one time or another, made the decision to leave the seminary. There were two other young men who did not go mountain climbing with the group that day because they were both ill. They were the only two in the class who would eventually be ordained to the priesthood.

As a student in the Seraphic Boarding School, Alberto counted it a privilege to daily receive Padre Pio's blessing and to kiss his hand. As was the practice of the other boys in the school, Alberto would lift up the edge of the glove on Padre Pio's hand and kiss the wound of the stigmata.

As time went by, Alberto became very close to Padre Pio. Alberto enjoyed running errands for him and helping him in many different ways. He was happy that Padre Pio allowed him on occasion to clean and tidy up his cell. When Padre Pio was sick, Alberto would sit at his bedside to keep him company.

Alberto was visiting Padre Pio in his cell on one occasion when the administrator of the Seraphic Boarding School, Father Romolo Pennisi, stopped by. At the time, Padre Pio was ill and was burning with fever. Father Romolo took Padre Pio's temperature and was shocked to find that it registered a dangerous 114 degrees.

On another occasion, Padre Pio was very ill when Father Michaelangelo visited him in his cell. Padre Pio's condition was so bad that the doctor had to be called in. After the doctor examined Padre Pio, he wanted to take his temperature. "Do not do it," Padre Pio warned. "My temperature is so high right now that the thermometer will break if you attempt to get a reading." The doctor had told Father Michaelangelo on a previous occasion that he wanted one of the broken thermometers to keep as a relic. He took Padre Pio's temperature and the thermometer broke instantly.

At times, Padre Pio felt an intense heat in his body during the celebration of the Mass. He referred to it once as a "fire which burns my whole being." He wrote a letter to Father Benedetto on one occasion and said, "Sometimes at the altar my whole body burns in an indescribable manner. My face in particular seems to go on fire. I have no idea, dear Father, what these signs mean." On another occasion he wrote to Father Agostino and said, "I felt a mysterious fire in my heart which I could not understand. I felt the need to put ice on it, to quench this fire which was consuming me."

On one occasion, when Padre Pio was ill, Father Romolo Pennisi offered to share part of the burden. "Why don't you let me take some of your suffering upon myself? You have had to endure it for such a long time," Father Romolo said. "It is not possible," Padre Pio replied. "If you had even one-hundredth of my suffering, you would die instantly."

One day, Father Romolo approached Padre Pio and said to him, "Padre Pio, we are both almost the same age. Which of us will be the first to pass away?" "We are both going to live a long time, but I will die first," Padre Pio replied. "Will I pass away shortly after you do?" Father Romolo asked. "It has been determined by God that you will be very old when you die," Padre Pio replied.

Father Romolo wanted to be able to impart Padre Pio's priestly blessing to the pilgrims who visited San Giovanni Rotondo after Padre Pio's death. He asked Padre Pio for permission, and was given it. Father Romolo lived to be ninety-five years old. Numerous times each day and for many years, he gave Padre Pio's blessing to the pilgrims. Father Romolo passed away in 1981.

As the spiritual director of the Seraphic Boarding School, Padre Pio used to tell the students that he wanted them all to be "worthy sons of the Seraphic Father, St. Francis of Assisi." He gave conferences to the boys every Saturday evening. The conferences included such topics as the Eucharist, the Passion of Christ, purgatory, devotion to the Blessed Virgin, the spirituality of St. Francis of Assisi, and more.

After the Saturday evening conferences, the boys would go to Padre Pio's cell for confession. Even if the sins they confessed were small, Padre Pio took it very seriously. To him, sin was sin. It was that simple. Padre Pio would go to great lengths to counsel the boys. He explained to the boys that even small sins were displeasing to God and had to be rooted out completely. He encouraged them to attend daily Mass and to pray the Rosary. They would often ask him for a signed holy card after they made their confession and he was happy to give them one.

Once, Alberto was present when Padre Pio chased two boys out of the monastery. They were both wearing shorts. The Capuchin superior called Padre Pio to task about his action. "Do you know who the two visitors were that you chased out of the monastery?" the superior asked. "They were the relatives of a very important ecclesiastical prelate!" Padre Pio was not sorry for what he had done. He insisted that people be dressed appropriately when they entered God's house. "Like the church, the monastery is a sacred place," Padre Pio said to his superior. "It should not be desecrated."

On one occasion, when Padre Pio spoke to the boys at the Saturday evening conference on the subject of purgatory, he shared an experience that had occurred just a few days previously. It happened to be winter time, and Padre Pio had gone to the fireplace in the monastery to warm himself. He was surprised to see four Capuchin priests, sitting on benches around the fireplace, warming themselves. He greeted them but they made no reply. They all had the hoods of their Capuchin habits pulled up on their heads. Padre Pio looked intently at the priests but he did not recognize them. He was certain that he had never seen them before. The expression on their faces was one of sadness.

Padre Pio then went to the superior, Father Lorenzo, and told him that four priests whom he had never seen before were downstairs, seated around the fireplace. Father Lorenzo could hardly believe it. He told Padre Pio that no visitors would be coming to the monastery in such bad weather. Besides, how could they have possibly entered the monastery without any of the Capuchins being aware of it. Father Lorenzo and Padre Pio went downstairs together to investigate. When they got to the fireplace, the priests were no longer there. It was then that Padre Pio understood. The four priests he had seen were actually the souls of four deceased Capuchin priests. They were experiencing their purgatory in the place where they had offended God. Padre Pio stayed up all night, praying for them and begging the Lord to free them from purgatory.

Another interesting story that Alberto heard from Padre Pio regarding the souls in purgatory concerned a young man who took Padre Pio by surprise one evening at the monastery of Our Lady of Grace. On that particular night, Padre Pio was all alone in the church, saying his prayers. Suddenly, he heard footsteps. A moment later, it sounded like the candles that were in the sanctuary of the church were being moved. Padre Pio called out and asked who was there but no one answered. A few minutes later, Padre Pio heard a loud noise. It sounded as though the candle in front of the statue of Our Lady of Grace had fallen to the ground.

When Padre Pio got up from his place of prayer to investigate, he saw a young man cleaning the altar in the semi-darkness. Padre Pio had never seen him before. "What are you doing there in the darkness?" Padre Pio asked. "I am cleaning the church," the young man replied. "Who are you?" Padre Pio asked. "I am a Capuchin novice," the young man said. "I am spending my purgatory here in this church. I need your prayers so that I can be released from purgatory." With that, the young man disappeared.

Padre Pio then understood. Many years before, Our Lady of Grace monastery had been a novitiate for young Capuchins who were studying for the priesthood. Evidently, the novice that Padre Pio had seen in the church had lived at the monastery many years before. Padre Pio prayed for the soul of the young man with great intensity, asking the Lord to release him from purgatory.

Padre Pio eventually became accustomed to such visitations. After a time, apparitions of the dead were no longer disturbing to him. "I have seen so many souls of the dead that they do not frighten me anymore," he told one of his confreres.

On occasion, Alberto and his companions at the Seraphic Boarding School were witnesses to the evil spirits who attacked Padre Pio in cell number five, the cell that he occupied for many years. Alberto and the other boys would sometimes be awakened in the night by strange and eerie sounds within the monastery. At times they heard frightening noises coming from Padre Pio's cell. If the boys had to use the washroom in the middle of the night, they were too frightened to go alone. The washroom was right next to Padre Pio's cell. They would wake each other up and walk down the hall together, trembling all the while. The long hall was lit at night by a small oil lamp. The flickering light of the oil lamp caused shadows to dance on the dark walls, making the walk to the washroom even more frightening.

Father Emilio Matrice recalled that when he was a student in the Seraphic Boarding School, he was once awakened in the night by the sound of jeering laughter and the clanking of chains. Young Emilio was terrified and tried to hide under the bed sheets. The next morning, he noticed that one of Padre Pio's eyes was painfully swollen. When pressed for an explanation, Padre Pio admitted that he had received a beating from the devil the previous night. It happened when one of the students was undergoing a strong temptation. In his great need, the student prayed to Padre Pio for his intercession. Padre Pio stormed heaven for the boy and was relieved that the boy had been given the strength to overcome the hard trial. The devil, who hated to be defeated, had unleashed his fury on Padre Pio.

Padre Pio knew that the boys were often afraid in the night and he felt sorry for them. He told them that the devil would never be able to hurt them and he explained to them that they had nothing to worry about. One of the boys once said to Padre Pio in jest, "Send the devil to me and I will be able to make him leave at once." "I see that you do not understand anything," Padre Pio replied. "If you saw the devil even once, you would die of fright." Finally, one day Padre Pio told the boys that they would never again hear any terrible noises in the night coming from his cell. To their great relief, the boys never heard the frightful sounds again.

Alberto felt that he owed his religious vocation to Padre Pio. Many of the other boys in the Seraphic Boarding School felt the same. The students were deeply inspired by Padre Pio's holy life. He lived in the higher spiritual realms, close to God and in communication with the saints and angels. On many occasions, Alberto was blessed to see Padre Pio when his face became luminous, transfigured with an indescribable beauty.

In 1922, Alberto left the Seraphic Boarding School in San Giovanni Rotondo and entered the Capuchin novitiate in Morcone. There were five other young men who entered the novitiate along with him. Father Gaetano, one of the Capuchins who was in residence at Our Lady of Grace monastery, asked Padre Pio about the future of the young men. "Will all of the six who are now in Morcone become priests?" Father Gaetano asked. "No, only two will be ordained," Padre Pio replied. The six young men all received the Capuchin habit in Morcone. Some of them left during the novitiate. Others left later in their priestly formation. Alberto D'Apolito and Cristoforo Iavicola were the only two who became priests.

During the time that Alberto was in formation for the priesthood, his family decided to move to the United States. The idea of being so far away from his loved ones was very painful to Alberto. He felt a great sadness in his heart and was almost overwhelmed by it. He was free to leave for the United States with his family if he so desired. All of the paperwork was in place for his departure if he chose to go with them. He felt a tremendous struggle in his heart. He decided to visit Padre Pio in San Giovanni Rotondo and talk to him about his inner turmoil.

The visit to Padre Pio proved to be very enlightening. Alberto poured out all the pain that was in his heart. Padre Pio spoke to him lovingly and paternally. Padre Pio said to him, "I ask you in the name of Jesus, to make the sacrifice of your family and meet this trial with detachment and renunciation." Padre Pio assured him of his prayers. After speaking to Padre Pio, peace returned to Alberto's heart. He remained in Italy to continue with his priestly studies.

On occasion, people who were possessed by the devil were brought to the monastery so that Padre Pio could pray for their deliverance. Padre Pio felt very sorry for such individuals. With his prayer book in hand, he would repeat the prayers of exorcism for them. He did not show any fear in doing so. Sometimes it entailed a great struggle, a great battle, in order to free the person from the evil spirits. At other times, all that Padre Pio had to do was to make the sign of the cross, and the person would be delivered.

Alberto was present once during an exorcism in which Padre Pio freed a woman from a demon. On that day, Alberto assisted as altar server for Padre Pio during Vespers and Benediction. At the conclusion of Benediction, Alberto and Padre Pio walked into the sacristy. A woman who was known to be possessed by a demon was standing there. When she saw Padre Pio, she began to shout obscenities at him. As she was screaming, Padre Pio opened the book of exorcism and began reciting the prayers. The woman then let out a very loud scream and was suddenly raised in the air to a height of three feet. All who were present in the sacristy witnessed the frightening scene. Everyone ran away in fear. Padre Pio remained calm and continued with the prayers of exorcism. The woman was finally freed of the evil spirit.

Once, Alberto went to Padre Pio's cell to ask him for some advice. He was just about to knock on the door when he heard Padre Pio having a conversation with someone inside. Alberto left and returned about fifteen minutes later. Just as Alberto approached his cell, Padre Pio opened the door. At once, Alberto was enveloped by a heavenly perfume. He noticed that Padre Pio's face looked beautiful. "What are you doing here?" Padre Pio asked. "I came to ask you for some advice but I heard you speaking to someone in your cell. I also heard someone speaking to you, so I wanted to wait until your visitor left," Alberto replied. "Oh no, nobody was here," Padre Pio answered. "I was praying."

Padre Pio prayed by day and by night. He faithfully prayed for the people from all parts of the world who were sending their petitions to him. "Only through prayer," Padre Pio said, "may I hope to be able to help people. By myself, I can do nothing."

Alberto had witnessed Padre Pio's profound absorption in prayer on many occasions. Often, when Alberto needed to speak a word to Padre Pio, he would find him praying in the choir loft of the church. Alberto would greet him but he would make no reply. Alberto had to tap him on the shoulder or shake him in order to get his attention. It was the same when Padre Pio was praying in his cell. Sometimes two or three Capuchins would be having an animated conversation in Padre Pio's cell. If Padre Pio was praying, he often did not even realize that he had visitors.

Through the years, Alberto shared many meals with Padre Pio in the monastery dining room. It was common knowledge that Padre Pio was a very light eater. It was amazing to Alberto how he was able to survive on such a small intake of food. He ate one meal a day only, at midday. He never ate breakfast or dinner. He rarely ate more than just a few bites of the meal. Just a sip or two of coffee or juice satisfied him completely. He received gifts of cookies, candies, and cakes from the pilgrims who visited the monastery but he never ate them. He gave them all away. He enjoyed saving the candies for the children who came to see him. When questioned about his small intake of food, he always claimed that he felt full, too full to eat.

One might conclude that a person with such a restricted diet would be extremely thin. Not so with Padre Pio. He was robust and hearty in appearance. He stood 5 feet 8 inches tall and weighed 165 lbs. Dr. Pietro Valdoni stated that Padre Pio lost approximately one cup of blood a day from the five wounds of the stigmata. And yet, he never suffered from anemia due to the blood loss.

Padre Pio was nauseated at the sight of food. In the monastery dining room, after the blessing over the food, when the other members of the community began to eat, Padre Pio would continue to pray. The superior of the monastery would have to tell him to unfold his napkin and eat, otherwise he would not do so. Quite frequently, Padre Pio offered his dinner to Alberto who was always happy to accept it. Alberto felt it was a great blessing to receive Padre Pio's meal. After lunch, Padre Pio used to go to the veranda and pray the Rosary before going to the sacristy to hear the men's confessions.

Padre Pio's friends and associates as well as the doctors at the hospital were concerned about his lack of nourishment. Mario Nalesso came to the monastery each afternoon from the Home for the Relief of Suffering to bring Padre Pio some jam that was fortified with vitamins and a glass of orange juice. It was always difficult for Padre Pio to consume it. He could never seem to take more than a sip of the juice. Padre Pio used to hand the orange juice to Alberto who was always happy to finish it off for him.

Padre Pio would often go to the pantry in the kitchen to look for roasted chick peas or hard biscuits. Taking them back to his place at the table, he would chew them very slowly, giving the other Capuchins the impression that he was eating a lot. Alberto often asked him for the roasted chick peas. "Why do you want them?" Padre Pio asked. Alberto avoided the question because he felt sure that Padre Pio would not be pleased with his answer. Alberto gave the chick peas that Padre Pio carried in his pocket to people who were sick.

Knowing full well that Padre Pio possessed the gift of healing, Alberto also knew that people were frequently cured through objects that Padre Pio possessed, even food. A number of people testified to such healings. More than once, people were healed simply by putting Padre Pio's photograph underneath their pillow and praying for his intercession. Relics too, like his handkerchief, his gloves, or the cloth that covered his side wound, had healed the sick on numerous occasions.

While most people felt that Padre Pio was an exceptional priest, outstanding in virtue, not all did. Malicious rumors regarding Padre Pio began to circulate widely in the early 1920's. Many priests were jealous of his popularity and resented the fact that so many people attended his Mass and sought him out for confession. The Italian newspapers and magazines frequently printed stories about him, adding sensationalism in their reports of his stigmata and other mystical gifts. Padre Pio became a controversial figure in the minds of many. The Holy Office in Rome was scrutinizing the situation.

The number of people who attended Padre Pio's early morning Mass continually increased as time went by. Complaints arose regarding the unbecoming conduct of some of the residents of San Giovanni Rotondo who attended his Mass each day. The "locals" often created havoc in the church by their aggressive behavior. They resented the pilgrims who came in growing numbers from many different parts of the world. From time to time, the Carabenieri (Italian State Police) had to be summoned to maintain order.

As early as 1922, the ecclesiastical authorities in Rome ordered the Capuchin superior of Our Lady of Grace monastery to "keep Padre Pio under observation." After making a study of the facts, Rome concluded that there was no evidence of the supernatural in Padre Pio's life and ministry. They discouraged people from visiting his monastery in San Giovanni Rotondo.

Starting in 1923 and continuing for a full ten years, Rome conducted numerous investigations of Padre Pio. Decrees and rulings came one after another which would eventually take away from Padre Pio almost all of his priestly functions. In 1925, a directive came from the Holy Office that forbade visitors to speak to Padre Pio after Mass. Furthermore, he was no longer allowed to bless religious articles or give his priestly blessing to the pilgrims.

No one was allowed to kiss his hand. During that time of restrictions, a man asked Padre Pio to bless one of his religious articles. "I have been told that I cannot bless religious articles at this time," Padre Pio said to the man. "But I have not been forbidden to touch them." Padre Pio then rested his hand on the religious article for a moment. The man thanked him and left, feeling completely satisfied.

In 1931, a decree came from the Holy Office in Rome which prohibited Padre Pio from saying Mass in public. In addition, he was no longer allowed to hear confessions, either of the laity or of his fellow Capuchins. For a period of two years, his Mass would be said behind locked doors, in a private chapel inside the monastery. He was allowed to have an altar server assist at his Mass, but no one else was permitted to attend. He was not to have any communication with the public. He became almost like a person sentenced to solitary confinement. Padre Pio described it as "his imprisonment." This was perhaps the most painful period of his life. Nevertheless, he did not become resentful or bitter. He would not allow the Capuchins to criticize the decisions of the Holy Office and he submitted to the restrictions without a word of complaint. For his part, he would not discuss the matter with anyone.

The Capuchin priests and brothers who lived in community with Padre Pio resented the harsh measures that had come from Rome but were helpless to do anything about it. They lived with Padre Pio on a daily basis, and more than anyone else, they knew his mind and his heart intimately. Padre Pio was a blessing to his religious community as well as to the laity who came to attend his Mass. He led an exemplary Christian life, outstanding in virtue. The Capuchins looked up to him as a spiritual role model for all the members of their congregation. He had never been disobedient in any way to the Church. He had done nothing wrong. "Why was he being persecuted?" his Capuchin brothers wondered, but they could find no answer to their question.

The mayor of San Giovanni Rotondo, Francesco Morcaldi, advised everyone to write letters to the Vatican, in defense of Padre Pio. At the mayor's request, hundreds of letters poured into the Holy Office. Nevertheless, the situation remained the same. Essentially, Padre Pio was under "house arrest."

After Father Alberto was ordained to the priesthood, he celebrated Mass at the monastery of Our Lady of Grace for the first time in 1931. Padre Pio was not permitted to be present for Father Alberto's first Mass because of the restrictions that had been placed on him by the Holy Office. However, he was allowed to greet Father Alberto at the conclusion of the Mass. Padre Pio embraced him and assured him that he would always be with him and that he would remember him in his prayers. In honor of the occasion, Padre Pio gave Father Alberto a beautiful holy card of Our Lady of Grace.

During the time of the restrictive measures, the superior at Our Lady of Grace often asked Father Alberto to assist at Padre Pio's private Mass. At that time, Padre Pio's Mass lasted from two to three hours. Father Alberto noticed that Padre Pio's face underwent visible changes during the celebration of the Mass. At the Consecration, he became pale. All of the color seemed to drain from his cheeks. He looked weak and exhausted. His face reminded Father Alberto of Jesus Crucified. Padre Pio's appearance changed completely at the time of Holy Communion. His cheeks became rosy; his eyes were bright. He seemed completely transformed. After the Mass, Padre Pio went to the choir loft to make his thanksgiving and remained there until noon.

Father Alberto counted it a great privilege to assist at Padre Pio's private Mass during the time of his segregation from the public. But like everyone else, he waited in hope for the day when the restrictions would be lifted and Padre Pio would regain his freedom. People from all parts of the world were praying for Padre Pio.

Several individuals who were close to Pope Pius XI, entreated him to reevaluate the decisions of the Holy Office regarding Padre Pio. The Holy Father decided to act on the advice. In March of 1933, Pope Pius XI sent two personal representatives to San Giovanni Rotondo - Bishop Luca Pasetto and Bishop Felice Bevilacqua. They were to observe Padre Pio carefully and then send a report back to the Vatican. The visitation proved to be enlightening. Both of the bishops were favorably impressed by Padre Pio. They were inspired by his piety and by his humility. They also made positive mention of his good sense of humor. A full report was given to the Holy Father. Upon examining the material, Pope Pius XI became convinced that the Holy Office had been mistaken and misled in the restrictive measures that they had placed on Padre Pio's ministry.

In July of 1933, Pope Pius XI reversed the ban against Padre Pio and he was allowed to once again celebrate Mass in public. The following year he was permitted to resume hearing the confessions of men and several months later, the confessions of women. The Holy Father said, "I was not badly disposed toward Padre Pio, but I was badly informed about him."

In 1939, Father Alberto was sent to serve at the Capuchin novitiate house in Morcone. While there, he became ill with blood poisoning and spent two months in the hospital in Naples. Father Alberto had previously accepted an invitation to give a Lenten retreat in the city of Martano. Many people were looking forward to the retreat with great anticipation. However, when it was time to travel to Martano, Father Alberto was still sick. He feared that he would not be able to give the Lenten talks. He visited Padre Pio in San Giovanni Rotondo and asked him to pray for his recovery. Padre Pio said to him, "My son, there are souls in that parish who are in great need. I will pray to the Blessed Virgin. I know that through her intercession, you will have the strength to give the retreat."

During the Lenten retreat in Martano, the parish of the Assumption was filled to capacity. Father Alberto felt strong and energized throughout the retreat. He was able to give the talks with ease, and in between the talks, he heard many confessions. All of the symptoms of his illness had mysteriously vanished. He knew from experience, the power of Padre Pio's intercessory prayers.

The parish priest of Martano was elated with the success of Father Alberto's mission. He decided that he wanted to do something to show his gratitude and enlisted the help of his parishioners in order to do so. When the final Mass of the mission was over, Father Alberto was surprised to hear the sound of applause coming from the street. As he stepped out of the church, he was greeted by a large crowd of cheering people. At once, a band began to play music. Father Alberto was taken in procession through the main part of town. Large numbers of people on either side of the street, showered him with flowers. He was overwhelmed by the expression of love and gratitude that had been shown to him by the citizens of Martano.

Not long after the mission, Father Alberto decided to go to San Giovanni Rotondo to thank Padre Pio in person for his prayers. He was convinced that his recovery had been a true miracle. When he arrived at the monastery, he told Padre Pio about the success of the mission and how his bodily strength had returned in such a marvelous way. He also described the final procession through the streets. He told Padre Pio about the band that accompanied the procession as well as the incredible appreciation that was shown to him by the people of Martano. "Just look what the Blessed Mother can do!" Padre Pio exclaimed. "But I also believe that you helped me by your prayers," Father Alberto replied. "I only prayed for you," Padre Pio said. "In truth, the Blessed Virgin did it all."

Padre Pio's lifelong devotion to the Blessed Virgin Mary was profound. On one occasion, Father Alberto showed Padre Pio a holy card of the Blessed Virgin. "Look how beautiful she is," Father Alberto exclaimed. "Her face is so sweet and so tender." Padre Pio did not think that the holy card was particularly attractive. "It does not do the Blessed Virgin justice at all," Padre Pio said. "But you have seen the Virgin Mary," Father Alberto replied. "I wish you would tell me what she looks like." Padre Pio told Father Alberto that the Blessed Virgin's beauty was so great that no artist would ever be able to capture it, nor could her beauty be described in words. Padre Pio had total confidence in his heavenly Mother. He used to say, "Let us always pray with trust and wait patiently for our Lord and the Virgin Mary to answer our prayers. If we persevere, our Mother will come to our rescue and answer our deepest needs."

Through the years, Padre Pio frequently spoke to Father Alberto about the Third Order of St. Francis. He asked Father Alberto to make a great effort to promote it. As time passed, Father Alberto successfully organized a number of new Franciscan fraternities in different cities throughout Italy. Padre Pio was very pleased.

For a long time, Father Alberto had a desire to have a relic of Padre Pio. One day, he gathered up his courage and asked Padre Pio for a pair of his gloves. "What would you do with them?" Padre Pio asked. "I would like to wear them on cold days," Father Alberto replied. Padre Pio took some gloves out of the closet in his cell and handed them to Father Alberto. Father Alberto noticed that the gloves looked brand-new. His intention was to have a pair that had been worn by Padre Pio. "Why don't you give me the pair you are wearing right now?" Father Alberto asked. But Padre Pio would not agree to it. "I cannot give you the ones I am wearing. I am not allowed to. The ones I have given you have all been washed," Padre Pio said. Father Alberto took the gloves with gratitude. He knew that he might never have the opportunity again.

On another occasion, Father Alberto was in Padre Pio's cell when he noticed a bloodstained handkerchief on the night stand. Alberto was about to take it when Padre Pio saw him and asked him what he was doing. "I am going to take this handkerchief," Father Alberto replied. "You cannot have it," Padre Pio answered. "I will give you a new handkerchief if you want, but you cannot have that one."

When Father Alberto was living in San Severo, one of the Capuchins, Father Placido of San Marco in Lamis, became critically ill with acute cirrhosis of the liver. His condition was so serious that he had to be hospitalized. The year was 1957. Father Placido had been one of Padre Pio's classmates in the novitiate. It was Father Placido who had taken some of the very first documentation photographs of Padre Pio with his stigmatized hands exposed.

While in the hospital, instead of improving, Father Placido's condition grew worse. One night, he saw Padre Pio standing beside his bed. Padre Pio told him to have patience in his illness and not to worry. He assured him that he would recover. After speaking to Father Placido, Padre Pio walked over to the window and placed his hand on the glass. With that, he disappeared.

The next morning, Father Placido felt much better. His strength and energy had returned. He noticed the imprint of a hand on the window pane in his room and remembered that Padre Pio had put his hand on the window before he disappeared. Father Placido told the hospital staff about Padre Pio's visitation. The word traveled quickly and soon it seemed as though everyone in San Servero had heard the news. Many of the townspeople came to the hospital to look at the hand print on the window. The doctors, who did not believe Father Placido's story, became very annoyed at the constant coming and going of visitors. An attempt was made to remove the imprint with soap and water but it mysteriously reappeared. Finally, after several days, the imprint disappeared.

The hospital chaplain told the superior of the monastery in San Severo, Father Piergiuliano, about the incident. Father Piergiuliano went to the hospital and reprimanded Father Placido. He told him in no uncertain terms to stop telling lies by claiming that Padre Pio had visited him. It was causing a big disturbance at the hospital. Father Placido had no doubt as to what he saw. He would not retract his story no matter how angry his superior became.

Father Alberto soon heard the news and went to the hospital to visit Father Placido. He listened as Father Placido recounted the story, but he was skeptical. He thought that perhaps Father Placido had a dream or even an hallucination. "I assure you that I am telling the truth!" Father Placido said. "If you doubt what I am saying, why don't you go to San Giovanni Rotondo and ask Padre Pio about it," he added.

The next time Father Alberto saw Padre Pio, he told him about his visit with Father Placido in the hospital and relayed the story that Father Placido had shared. "Father Placido was critically ill and he has made what appears to be a miraculous recovery," Father Alberto said. "He told me that you visited him in the hospital in San Severo and that you left the imprint of your hand on the window pane. Many people have come to the hospital to see the hand print on the window. Is it true that you appeared to him in bilocation or was he simply dreaming?" "Yes, what Father Placido told you is true," Padre Pio said. "I visited him in the hospital but I do not want you to tell anyone." Father Placido's health continued to improve and he made a complete recovery from his life threatening illness.

On one occasion, Father Alberto was approached by one of Padre Pio's spiritual daughters, Mrs. Maria Mobilia. Maria told Father Alberto that she was expecting a baby. It was a dream come true for Maria and her husband. After a very difficult pregnancy, Maria's first baby had died shortly after birth. Unfortunately, Maria had just received bad news from her doctor. He told her that he believed that the complications that occurred with the first pregnancy would be repeated with the second. He feared that her baby would not live. Maria asked Father Alberto to speak to Padre Pio and ask for his prayers and Father Alberto assured her that he would do so.

When Father Alberto told Padre Pio about Maria's situation, Padre Pio said that he would pray for her and that he was confident that Maria would have a healthy baby. Two months before Maria's delivery date, the doctor told her to prepare herself for the possibility that her baby might not survive. Maria became alarmed and asked Father Alberto to write a letter to Padre Pio. Father Alberto reminded her that Padre Pio had already said that everything was going to go smoothly. Father Alberto was planning on going to San Giovanni Rotondo in a few days and he assured Maria that he would remind Padre Pio once again to pray for her. "Also, please tell Padre Pio that my husband and I want to have a baby boy," Maria said. Father Alberto did not feel comfortable with the request. "I will ask Padre Pio to pray for a happy delivery and a healthy baby. That will be sufficient," Father Alberto replied. "I don't think I have the courage to tell him that you want a boy," he added. However, Father Alberto could see how important it was to Maria. He finally told her that he would try to relay the message.

Father Alberto spoke to Padre Pio and told him that Maria was in a state of great anxiety regarding her pregnancy. "We talked about this before," Padre Pio said. "I already told you that everything is going to go well." Alberto then gathered up all his courage and said, "Maria wanted me to tell you that she wants to have a boy." "The Lord will make her happy!" Padre Pio answered. When the time came for the baby to be born, there were no medical complications. Maria had a beautiful and healthy boy whom she named Tomasino.

Like Maria Mobilia, many others came to Father Alberto with their own pressing needs and concerns. On one occasion, a priest who was greatly troubled sought out Father Alberto. He told Father Alberto that he had asked Padre Pio to accept him as his spiritual son, and Padre Pio made no reply. The priest asked Padre Pio a second time, and again, Padre Pio seemed to completely ignore him. "Padre Pio must have been able to see something in your life that needs to be corrected," Father Alberto said to the priest. "He did not want to hurt your feelings, so he remained silent." The priest admitted to Father Alberto that when he made his confession to Padre Pio, he withheld the fact that he had a close friendship with a woman. All in all, the priest felt that he had done nothing wrong. The woman was like a sister to him. However, his conscience bothered him because of his strong attachment to her.

Padre Pio always counseled priests to be careful to avoid close friendships with women. "It is always dangerous," he would say. While many considered him to be old fashioned in his thinking, Padre Pio knew that a priest's vocation had to be safeguarded at all times. After talking to Father Alberto, the priest distanced himself from the woman. Padre Pio then received him warmly and told him that he accepted him as his spiritual son.

Father Alberto continually saw miracles both great and small through his contact with Padre Pio. One miracle of grace concerned the building of the Holy Family monastery in Pietrelcina. In many ways, it was an answer to the prayers of the people of Pietrelcina. The citizens of Pietrelcina had always hoped that someday it would be possible to have a Capuchin monastery and parish in their town, similar to the one in San Giovanni Rotondo.

The residents of Pietrelcina were, for the most part, poor farmers and laborers. Although they wanted to have a Capuchin parish in their town, they did not have the financial ability to make it a reality. Knowing that Mary Pyle was a person of means as well as a great devotee of Padre Pio, they spoke to her about their desire for a Capuchin parish and monastery. Mary thought it was an excellent idea and wanted to offer her assistance. She spoke to Padre Pio about it and he was very enthusiastic. "Begin the planning as soon as possible," Padre Pio said to Mary. He told her that he would like the monastery and church to be dedicated to the Holy Family and to be named Holy Family monastery.

The idea for a Capuchin monastery in Pietrelcina had actually been in Padre Pio's mind for years. He made a prophecy regarding the future monastery shortly after his ordination to the priesthood. He was still living in Pietrelcina at the time. One day when Padre Pio and Father Salvatore Pannullo, the parish priest of Pietrelcina, were taking a walk, Padre Pio suddenly heard angels singing and perceived the fragrance of incense. "Do you hear the choir of angels?" Padre Pio asked Father Pannullo. "No, I do not hear anything," Father Pannullo replied. "Someday a church will arise on the very spot we are now standing," Padre Pio said. "Hymns of praise to the Lord, like incense, will rise from this place." Father Pannullo had no idea what Padre Pio was talking about.

Padre Pio's prophecy would materialize more than thirty years later. The generosity of Mary Pyle as well as others, made it possible for the work to finally begin. The Holy Family monastery was built on the exact spot in Pietrelcina where Padre Pio had heard the beautiful choir of angels.

The citizens of Pietrelcina, along with the mayor of the town and other dignitaries, gathered together on the day the first cornerstone for the future Holy Family monastery was laid. That very night, a miracle occurred. A very large and beautiful cross suddenly rose up from the construction site into the night sky. Many people witnessed the miraculous event. For thirty minutes, the luminous cross remained in the sky before it finally disappeared. The townspeople considered it to be a sign of the blessings that were to come to the people of Pietrelcina through the Holy Family monastery.

Teresa Fucci was one of the workers who was hired by the Annunziata de Acerra company to help in the building of the Holy Family monastery. On one occasion, she traveled to San Giovanni Rotondo and made her confession to Padre Pio. At the end of her confession, Padre Pio reminded her that she had missed Mass on the last Holy Day of Obligation. Teresa had completely forgotten about it. She explained to Padre Pio that her supervisor required her to work on Sundays as well as on the Holy Days of Obligation. All of the other employees had to do the same. The company was under pressure to complete the construction of the monastery by a fixed date. In order to meet the deadline, it was necessary for the employees to work on the weekends. "Our family is poor and I need to keep my job," Teresa said. "If I do not do what my supervisor asks of me, I am afraid that I will be fired." "It is a grave offense against the Lord to miss Mass on Sundays and on the Holy Days of Obligation," Padre Pio replied. "It would be better for you to lose your job. Never miss Mass again."

After the Holy Family monastery was completed, many wondered how the ongoing financial needs of the Capuchin community would be met. Certainly, the citizens of the Pietrelcina would not be able to bear the financial burden. One of the Capuchins spoke to Padre Pio and voiced the concerns that many shared. "Do not worry," Padre Pio replied. "God is going to send such providence to Holy Family that it will never lack for anything. There will be an abundance of food, an abundance of resources, an abundance of everything. You will see."

Time proved the truth of Padre Pio's words. The monastery never lacked for anything. The kitchen pantries were always full to overflowing. The bills were always paid on time. Father Alberto was assigned to serve at the Holy Family monastery for six years. While there, he witnessed Divine Providence at work on all occasions.

August 10, 1949 was the 39th anniversary of Padre Pio's priestly ordination. Father Alberto was present at Our Lady of Grace monastery for the joyous occasion along with many other Capuchins. Father Luca, who had been named the first superior of the Holy Family monastery in Pietrelcina, also attended the celebration.

Father Luca had watched with great interest and enthusiasm as the Holy Family monastery was being built. He was very happy to be in residence there and he hoped that he would be able to remain there for years to come. He was worried because he had heard talk that he was going to be transferred.

He spoke to Padre Pio about it and said, "I have watched the development of the Holy Family monastery from the beginning. Now that the work is finally completed, I am afraid that I will be transferred. I have a great desire to stay on at Holy Family." "Don't worry about it, my son," Padre Pio replied. "You will not be transferred. You will never be transferred. You will remain forever in Pietrelcina, even after your death." One month later, Father Lucca contracted typhoid fever followed by meningitis. He passed away the following month.

After the Christmas festivities, Padre Pio's brother, Michael Forgione, was leaving San Giovanni Rotondo to travel to Pietrelcina in order to take part in the olive harvest. Padre Pio asked Michael to take a message to the Capuchin priests and brothers at the Holy Family monastery. "Tell them all that on Christmas night, I saw the soul of Father Luca ascend to heaven in great splendor and glory," Padre Pio said. "Father Luca is now praying for all of us from heaven."

The date for the official inauguration of the Holy Family monastery was set for May 20, 1951. The citizens of Pietrelcina were present for the solemn occasion along with the Archbishop of Benevento as well as numerous superiors from the Capuchin Province. Included in the crowd was Mary Pyle. Mary had contributed most of the funds for the building of the monastery.

After the inauguration, Father Alberto traveled to San Giovanni Rotondo and told Padre about the celebration. "I hope you can visit the Holy Family monastery someday. It is truly a sacred place," Father Alberto said. "But I have been there. I have seen it," Padre Pio replied. Father Alberto knew for a fact that Padre Pio had not traveled to Pietrelcina. He rarely left the monastery. Father Alberto understood by Padre Pio's words that he had visited the new monastery through bilocation. Padre Pio indicated the same to Father Agostino. When Father Agostino asked him if it would be possible for him to attend the inauguration, he assured him that he would be there. He told Father Agostino that he would be present in Pietrelcina and at the same time he would be present in San Giovanni Rotondo.

One of the noted benefactors of the Holy Family monastery in Pietrelcina was a man from the United States. Because of his admiration for Padre Pio, he had been very generous in his financial contributions. He finally made a trip to San Giovanni Rotondo in order to meet Padre Pio. At the monastery, he saw that many of the pilgrims approached Padre Pio, kissed his hand, and received his blessing. He wanted to do the same. Much to his surprise, Padre Pio would not receive him or allow him to kiss his hand. Instead, Padre Pio told him to go away. "I do not know you," Padre Pio said to him. The man was very hurt.

The man went to the Capuchin monastery in San Severo where Father Alberto was in residence and told him about the painful incident. The man had a great desire to see Padre Pio again. He thought about it night and day. He begged Father Alberto to travel with him from San Severo to San Giovanni Rotondo. He thought that if Father Alberto introduced him to Padre Pio, the visit would go better than the previous one had.

Father Alberto was reluctant to agree to the man's request. He knew Padre Pio very well. When Padre Pio withheld his blessing from an individual, he had his own reasons for doing so. However, Father Alberto felt obligated to do the favor that the man asked of him. When Father Alberto had been the superior of the Capuchin monastery in Pietrelcina, the man had been very generous in his financial assistance. His help and his kindness had been greatly appreciated. Because the man had freely given so much, Father Alberto felt that he had to comply with his request.

On the trip from San Severo to San Giovanni Rotondo, Alberto asked the man a number of questions about his life. The man admitted to Father Alberto that he had been unfaithful to his wife. Father Alberto explained to him that Padre Pio had the gift of reading hearts. In all likelihood, Padre Pio knew of his infidelity. That was probably the reason why Padre Pio had been cold to him.

Father Alberto told the man that he did not think the second visit to Padre Pio would go any better than the first. "Under the circumstances, I do not think Padre Pio will receive you," Padre Alberto said. "Based on what you have told me, I believe that when Padre Pio sees us, he will throw us both out!"

When Father Alberto and his friend arrived at the monastery, they stood in the corridor and waited for Padre Pio. Before long, they saw him coming down the hall. When Padre Pio saw Father Alberto and his companion, he paused. He said to the man, "I see you brought your lawyer with you this time!" indicating in a disapproving way that he had Father Alberto at his side. "I want both of you to leave immediately!" Padre Pio said brusquely.

When the two walked out of the church and into the open air, the man burst into tears. Father Alberto tried to console him. The man was planning on going to Assisi before being reunited with his family in the United States. Father Alberto advised him to go to confession while visiting Assisi and to make a firm determination to amend his life. Then, if he so desired, he could stop in San Giovanni Rotondo and see Padre Pio before departing for the United States.

The man did what Father Alberto advised him to do. He made a sincere confession while in Assisi. He had a great desire to see Padre Pio before leaving for the United States but he did not have the courage to go alone. He asked Father Alberto if he would be willing to accompany him one more time to the monastery of Our Lady of Grace. Father Alberto agreed to do so.

When Father Alberto and his companion arrived at Our Lady of Grace monastery, they found Padre Pio sitting on the veranda near his cell. Father Alberto introduced the man formally to Padre Pio and said, "Padre Pio, this man is a noted benefactor of the Holy Family monastery in Pietrelcina. He has also been very generous in financially supporting your other works of charity. His willingness to help has been a great blessing to the Capuchin community."

Padre Pio seemed very pleased and thanked the man for all that he had done. He embraced him and then conversed with him cordially. Finally, he placed his hand on the man's head and gave him his blessing. He told him that he would remember him as well as all the members of his family in his prayers. "I want you to live a good Christian life from this time forward," Padre Pio said to him.

About a year later, the man wrote a letter to Father Alberto and begged him to ask Padre Pio if he could visit him again. Father Alberto asked Padre Pio but his answer was an emphatic, "No!" Father Alberto learned later that the man had begun seeing his girlfriend again. His conduct had deeply hurt all the members of his family. Without being told by anyone, Padre Pio had been aware of the man's actions. Padre Pio was praying for the man but he told Father Alberto that he would not receive him.

A few months later, the man wrote another letter to Father Alberto, saying that he had ended the relationship with the woman, this time for good. When Padre Pio was told, he agreed to see the man once again. Greatly consoled, the man was able to speak to Padre Pio and to receive his blessing. It wasn't long after the man's visit that Padre Pio passed away.

Five months before Padre Pio's death, Dr. Francesco Riccardi spoke to Father Alberto and told him that he had just visited Padre Pio and that the state of his health was alarming. Dr. Riccardi did not think that Padre Pio would live much longer. It had always been Father Alberto's desire to be near Padre Pio when his end approached. As Divine Providence would have it, Father Alberto was transferred to the monastery of Our Lady of Grace in May of 1968, four months before Padre Pio died. During the last four months of Padre Pio's life, Father Alberto was at his side every day.

Padre Pio was worn out by years of ill health, long hours of work, and continuous suffering. Due to chronic and severe asthma, he had difficulty breathing. He often felt like he was suffocating. He had a constant cough and was plagued by many other ailments. He told Father Alberto that he felt that he was ready to go and meet the Lord. He prayed for that intention. Nevertheless, he said that he was frightened at the prospect of standing face to face with his Maker. He was afraid that he had not corresponded well enough to the graces that he had received from God. He asked all the members of his Capuchin community to pray for his soul.

Shortly before Padre Pio passed away, Father Alberto visited him in his cell. He told Padre Pio that he was making a quick trip to Montecatini and asked for his blessing. "But can't you see that I am dying?" Padre Pio asked. Alberto canceled his plans at once. Neither he nor any of the other Capuchins had any idea that Padre Pio was so close to death.

On Saturday morning, September 21, Padre Pio felt too ill to say Mass. He asked that Holy Communion be brought to him in his cell. Father Alberto was present in Padre Pio's cell at five o'clock in the morning, when Father Onorato brought Holy Communion to Padre Pio. Father Alberto propped Padre Pio up and placed the paten under his chin. At that moment, he had the sensation that Padre Pio was burning. After receiving Holy Communion, Padre Pio's face became suffused with a beautiful light.

Father Alberto assisted at Padre Pio's last Mass, on September 22, 1968. The church that morning was full to overflowing. Thousands of people were in San Giovanni Rotondo at the time in order to attend the International Convention of Padre Pio's Prayer Groups. All wanted to be present for Padre

Pio's Mass. Padre Pio was extremely ill that morning and almost fainted at the Mass. In the afternoon, Father Alberto went to visit him in his cell and found him sitting on the veranda in a very deep state of prayer. He was completely unaware of the Capuchins who were there with him.

Padre Pio passed away early the next morning, September 23, 1968. He died as he had lived, with the names of Jesus and Mary on his lips and with his Rosary in his hand. Padre Pio once said, "Let us ask the Lord to send us death when his grace is with us, when we are surrounded by him, his mother and Saint Joseph, after having completed our purgatory here on earth." Truly, Padre Pio had spent a lifetime preparing for the moment when he would pass into eternal life.

In every sick person, there is Jesus himself who suffers; in every poor person, there is Jesus who is languishing; in every person who is both sick and poor, Jesus is doubly present.

- St. Pio of Pietrelcina

CHAPTER 5

Padre Pio's Hospital - The Home for the Relief of Suffering

In July 1916, Father Paolino of Casacalenda, the superior of Our Lady of Grace monastery in San Giovanni Rotondo, traveled to the Capuchin monastery of St. Anne in Foggia in order to preach for the feast of St. Anne. Padre Pio lived at St. Anne's monastery at that time. During his visit, Father Paolino noticed the poor state of Padre Pio's health. He was extremely weak and frail and was unable to keep any food on his stomach. At that time, he was also suffering from the intense summer heat in Foggia.

Padre Paolino invited Padre Pio to visit the Capuchin community in San Giovanni Rotondo, thinking that the change of climate might do him good. Padre Pio accepted the invitation with gratitude. At the time, Padre Pio was twenty-nine years old.

Our Lady of Grace monastery in San Giovanni Rotondo was one of the poorest and oldest monasteries that the Capuchins possessed. It was also one of the most isolated foundations in the province. A profound silence surrounded the old whitewashed monastery and the small church that was attached to it. In the distance, the clang of sheep bells could be heard as shepherds took their flocks to graze on the mountain just behind. People from the town rarely walked up the long dirt path to the top of the hill in order to attend Mass at Our Lady of Grace.

Padre Pio loved the solitude and peace that the monastery provided, saying to one of his confreres, "The silence here is beautiful." He also enjoyed the Capuchin community of priests and brothers who lived at Our Lady of Grace and they in turn enjoyed his company.

Padre Paolino wrote a letter to Padre Agostino who was in residence at the Capuchin monastery in Foggia, giving him an update on Padre Pio's visit. He wrote:

> He is happy with us, with the air, the residence, the quiet, the solitude, and everything. And with the exception of the interior trials with which the Lord tries him, it can be said truly that he is happy . . . We ourselves are very happy with him.

While in San Giovanni Rotondo, Padre Pio felt the beneficial effects of breathing the fresh mountain air. The higher altitude seemed to agree with him and the cooler climate was a welcome break from the hot weather in Foggia. In the eight days that Padre Pio spent there, his health showed a marked improvement.

When Padre Pio returned to Foggia, he asked for permission to make another trip to San Giovanni Rotondo. He wrote to the Provincial and said:

> I am going to ask a favor of you and I ask it because Jesus compels me to. He tells me that I must strengthen my body a bit in order to be ready for other trials to which he intends to subject me. The favor I want to ask is to let me spend some time in San Giovanni Rotondo, where Jesus assures me I will feel better. I ask you not to refuse me this charity. (*Letters I*)

Padre Pio received the permission from his superior and returned to the monastery of Our Lady of Grace in September 1916. He would live with the Capuchins there for the next fifty-two years.

The people who lived in San Giovanni Rotondo were mostly poor farmers and manual laborers. It was hard for them to eke out a living in the impoverished area. San Giovanni Rotondo, which was considered to be one of the most backward regions of southern Italy, lacked even the most basic health care for its residents. If a person had a medical emergency, the only recourse was to go to the small hospital in Foggia, some twenty-five miles away. It was generally a twelve-hour journey by horse and cart on a dirt road that was very difficult to travel. Many sick people died on the way to the hospital.

Padre Pio heard many tragic stories regarding far too many people who lost their lives because of the inadequate health care in San Giovanni Rotondo. One man, who had a terrible accident, was taken to the hospital in Foggia for emergency treatment. Unfortunately, no beds were available at the time he was admitted. He was placed on a cot in the hall and had to wait more than a week before being treated for his injuries. Word got back to Padre Pio about the incident and he became very upset. Unfortunately, the man's story was not unique. Padre Pio knew that something had to be done to remedy the situation. He continuously thought about the need for a hospital in San Giovanni Rotondo.

Along with the help of several collaborators, Padre Pio opened a small hospital in San Giovanni Rotondo in 1925. He named it the St. Francis hospital in honor of his spiritual father, St. Francis of Assisi. With only two wards and twenty beds, the hospital was very inefficient according to modern standards. An earthquake in 1938 caused so much damage to the structure, that the little hospital finally had to close its doors for good.

The lack of adequate health care in San Giovanni Rotondo continued to be a serious problem. As more and more people learned of Padre Pio, they visited Our Lady of Grace monastery in increasing numbers. Many were suffering from serious and often life-threatening illnesses. It was obvious to Padre Pio that San Giovanni Rotondo needed a hospital that would be able to provide, not only for the medical needs of the residents, but also for the pilgrims who visited. Padre Pio felt strongly that the future hospital would have to be large and fully-equipped, with state-of-the-art technology that could handle medical emergencies of any kind.

When Padre Pio discussed his dream of building a hospital in San Giovanni Rotondo, many people scoffed at the idea and considered it to be absurd. A number of reasons were put forth as to why it would not work: Padre Pio's religious community did not have the financial resources for such an undertaking; the population of San Giovanni Rotondo was too small to justify the building of a large hospital; people would not want to come to a hospital in such a remote and isolated location; the rocky and mountainous region, sometimes referred to as a "graveyard" was not suitable to build on; Italy was in the midst of an economic crisis; it was the wrong time and the wrong place to consider such a monumental undertaking. In the minds of many, the hospital project was doomed to failure.

The objections that Padre Pio heard regarding the hospital did not discourage him. If anything, the objections caused him to desire the hospital even more. He knew that if he waited until the "right moment" when everything was in good order, the hospital would never be built. "It is so pressing that we do something for the sick people here in San Giovanni Rotondo," he said to a friend. The need for a hospital was constantly before his mind. "We will do it with the help of God," he often repeated.

One day, Capuchin Father Alberto D'Apolito brought a man who was sick to see Padre Pio. Padre Pio's heart was deeply touched when he met the man. He felt very sorry for him. He gave the man his priestly blessing and assured him of his prayers. After the man left, Father Alberto heard Padre Pio quietly pray, "Oh God, there is so much suffering, so much sickness. Please take away the sufferings of that poor man and give them to me." Padre Pio became ill right after he prayed. Father Alberto learned later that the man had made a complete recovery.

In his own life, Padre Pio knew, not only physical suffering, but spiritual suffering as well. "I endure terrible hours of sadness," he once wrote to his spiritual director. His own trials enabled him to have great compassion for those who were sick, especially children. Sometimes he seemed almost paralyzed by the suffering he saw all around him. He often cried unashamedly for those who were ill.

Padre Pio continued to work out the step by step plans for the hospital. He carefully chose the men and women who would play key roles in the leadership and administration of the hospital. There is reason to believe that

Padre Pio had certain people marked out for the tasks before they had even met him. To the casual observer, his selection of certain individuals seemed on occasion, to be impractical. But time and time again, his judgment proved to be correct.

Dr. Guglielmo Sanguinetti was one of the men who was hand-picked by Padre Pio to play a major role in the construction of the hospital. Dr. Sanguinetti's introduction to Padre Pio came about in an unusual way. One day, Dr. Sanguinetti asked his wife, Emilia, what kind of a gift she would like for their wedding anniversary. Emilia told him that more than anything else, she would like to go to San Giovanni Rotondo to see Padre Pio. Dr. Sanguinetti met the idea with great resistance. "Emilia, please don't ask me to take you there," Dr. Sanguinetti said. "Ask me for anything but that. You know how much I dislike religion!" As a fallen-away Catholic, he made a conscious effort to stay far away from churches and any type of religious gatherings. He especially made an effort to distance himself from priests. But he had asked his dear wife what she wanted for an anniversary gift and he felt that he had to honor her wishes. He finally agreed to take her to San Giovanni Rotondo.

Visiting the church of Our Lady of Grace and meeting Padre Pio turned out to be a far different experience than what Dr. Sanguinetti had expected. He attended Mass and the following day had the desire to make his confession to Padre Pio. He had not been to confession in twenty-five years.

Not long after, Dr. Sanguinetti made a second trip to visit Padre Pio. Padre Pio then told the doctor about his desire to have a hospital built in San Giovanni Rotondo. He urged the doctor to move to San Giovanni Rotondo and help him. "You will be the doctor who will help supervise the building project," Padre Pio said to Dr. Sanguinetti. The doctor was dumbstruck. "But that would be impossible!" Dr. Sanguinetti replied. "I am neither an architect nor an engineer. I am a physician. My study has been the human body, not buildings. I know nothing about buildings." "Don't worry about that," Padre Pio said. "That will all be taken care of." "Still, it is unthinkable," Dr. Sanguinetti answered. "I am a country doctor. I cannot afford to retire from my medical practice in Mugello. I do not have the financial means."

Padre Pio then asked Dr. Sanguinetti to explain to him in detail, the particulars of his financial situation. Dr. Sanguinetti told Padre Pio that he earned a modest salary but had no investments and few assets. Padre Pio made light of his financial situation. "Don't worry. All of those matters will be worked out," Padre Pio replied. "You will soon be receiving a ticket. You will see." Dr. Sanguinetti had no idea what Padre Pio was speaking of when he talked about a "ticket." He gave the matter no further thought.

Dr. Sanguinetti and his wife continued to visit Padre Pio from time to time. Whenever they visited, Padre Pio always asked them when they would be moving to San Giovanni Rotondo permanently. "Never," was the answer that was in Dr. Sanguinetti's mind and heart. He had no intention of moving to San Giovanni Rotondo. The whole idea seemed absurd.

Padre Pio told Dr. Sanguinetti that he would one day practice medicine in San Giovanni Rotondo. He also told him that he would keep very busy with the actual building work of the hospital. He was specific in detail as well, even as to the type of truck the doctor would use while supervising at the construction site. He also told him that he would have a driver who would take him where he needed to go. To Dr. Sanguinetti, they were very strange statements, and he did not know what to make of them. Sometimes it seemed like Padre Pio was joking, and at other times, he seemed perfectly serious.

Even if Dr. and Mrs. Sanguinetti did not always understand Padre Pio, there was no denying that they felt the unmistakable spiritual blessings of being in his presence. They also felt his protection on numerous occasions, especially during the time of the Second World War. During the war, more than fifty bombs had exploded in their town. One day, Emilia Sanguinetti expressed her deep fears to Padre Pio. "You will be protected," Padre Pio said to her. As the war continued, all of the surrounding houses in their neighborhood were either destroyed or badly damaged. Not one bomb ever touched their home.

One day, Dr. Sanguinetti was surprised to get a call from his bank. He was informed that one of his government bonds drew a very large sum of money in the state bond lottery. It happened on the feast of the Immaculate Conception. He remembered that Padre Pio had spoken of a "ticket" that would come to him. Dr. Sanguinetti saw the hand of God in the unexpected financial gain. After he gave up his medical practice, he and his wife moved to San Giovanni Rotondo. Right away he started working in earnest with Padre Pio on the plans for the hospital. Each one of the prophecies that Padre Pio had made to him would be realized in the years ahead.

Dr. Carlo Kisvarday, a chemist from Zara, Yugoslavia, also played a key role in the early development of the hospital. He first learned of Padre Pio when he and his wife Mary were making a trip to Germany to see the famed stigmatist and mystic, Therese Neumann. Therese had a reputation for holiness which drew thousands to travel to her home in the small farming town of Konnersreuth. Her life was dedicated totally to God. Many who met her described her as having a childlike purity and humility that was very uplifting to the spirit.

Therese was making plans to join the Missionary Sisters of St. Benedict when she was struck down by an accident on the family farm. After the accident, her health took a sharp decline and she soon became bedridden. Concerning the tragic turn of events in her life, she showed heroic acceptance of the will of God. Later, she had a vision of Christ kneeling in the Garden of Gethsemane and she heard his prayers. When Christ turned and looked at her, she felt a very sharp pain in her heart. It was the first imprint of the stigmata. Later, she would receive the wounds of Christ in her hands and feet as well. Like Padre Pio, Therese Neumann was a victim soul who offered her sufferings in reparation to the Lord. After her death in 1962, Padre Pio told a friend, John Sienna, that Therese often assisted him from heaven.

Dr. Kisvarday and his wife were very close to Konnersreuth when they made a short detour. A stranger happened to strike up a conversation with them and told them a few facts about Padre Pio. Dr. Kisvarday became so intrigued that he decided to change course and to travel the eight hundred miles to San Giovanni Rotondo. Feeling a kind of urgency, he cut the conversation short and left immediately for his new destination.

When Padre Pio met the doctor, he hugged him and held him close to his heart. Dr. Kisvarday could not explain it but he had the strange feeling that Padre Pio had been expecting him. One month later, Dr. Kisvarday made a second visit to the monastery. "I want you to make your home here," Padre Pio said to Dr. Kisvarday. "I want you here beside me." Dr. Kisvarday ran out of the monastery to tell his wife the good news. "Mary, Padre Pio just told me that he wants us to move here!" Dr. Kisvarday said. "He wants us to live close to him and help him with the hospital!" Mary Kisvarday was just as happy as her husband was. Dr. Kisvarday and his wife were able to build a home very close to the monastery. As time passed, the doctor's love for Padre Pio became so strong that he felt like he never wanted to be parted from him.

Many of those who were chosen by Padre Pio to be the organizers of his great work were willing to leave the security of a good job, a steady income, and a comfortable lifestyle. They were ready to work without a salary on a monumental project that would take years to complete and there was no guarantee that the project would be completed. Why were people willing to give up so much and work so hard? It was because of their esteem for Padre Pio. He had asked for their help and they wanted to help him. They felt honored to be called to the task.

Dr. Mario Sanvico, an industrialist from Perugia, Italy was another one of the pioneers of the hospital. Like Dr. Sanguinetti and Dr. Kisvarday, Dr. Sanvico was chosen by Padre Pio to have an important role in the first beginnings of the hospital. After much discussion with Padre Pio, Dr. Sanvico called a committee meeting on January 9, 1940 to formalize the plans. Padre Pio was named founder of the hospital. It was decided that Dr. Sanvico would act as secretary. Dr. Sanguinetti would be the Technical Medical Director. As time passed, Dr. Sanguinetti also worked as the building foreman, driver, adviser, and editor of a popular publication regarding the hospital. Dr. Carlo Kisvarday was designated to be the accountant and treasurer. The Director of Internal Affairs was Miss Ida Seitz. It was understood that Padre Pio would have to approve all decisions made by the committee before any action could be taken.

Later on in the day, Dr. Sanvico and Dr. Kisvardy visited Padre Pio in his cell and reported to him all that had transpired in the committee meeting. Padre Pio was very happy with the news and said, "This evening my earthly work has begun. I bless you and all those who will contribute to this work." Dr. Sanvico and Dr. Kisvardy knelt as Padre Pio spoke to them. Padre Pio wanted to make the first offering for the hospital. He took a coin out of his pocket and handed it to the two doctors. Pietruccio Cugino, Padre Pio's longtime friend, made the second humble donation. Padre Pio spoke to the men from his heart and said:

To God we owe all our love, which, to be adequate, ought to be infinite . . . We must at least give our whole being to love, to charity . . . To carry out this ideal of Our Lord, we must be quite forgetful of self. Rising above selfishness, we must bow down to the sufferings and the wounds of our fellow men. We must make them our own, knowing how to suffer with our brethren for the love of God. We must know how to instill hope into their hearts and bring back a smile to their lips, having restored a ray of light into their souls. Then we shall be offering God the most beautiful, the most noble of prayers, because our prayer will have sprung from sacrifice.

Shortly after the first committee meeting, Dr. Sanvico asked Padre Pio what name he planned to give the hospital. Padre Pio said that he would think about it. Three days later, he told Dr. Sanvico the name he had decided on - the Home for the Relief of Suffering. During the time of the Second World War, the plans for the construction of the hospital had to be put on hold. But Padre Pio never lost sight of his dream. He waited and continued to pray.

When the war finally came to a close, Padre Pio pressed for immediate action. He urged his good friend, Father Giuseppe (Peppino) Orlando to help him. Padre Pio had known Father Peppino from the early days, when they had both lived in Pietrelcina. Padre Pio used to frequently repeat to Father Peppino, "We must start the work on the hospital now, Father Peppino!" "But we're not ready. We don't even have a blueprint or a design drawn up. Everyone will laugh at us!" Father Peppino would reply. However, Padre Pio was persistent. He would frequently nudge Father Peppino with his elbow and say, "Peppino, when are we going to start the work? We must get started!" Although the amount of money that had been collected for the project was much smaller than hoped for, Padre Pio felt an urgency to begin.

On occasion, Father Peppino would try to avoid Padre Pio, knowing that the future hospital would always be the topic of his conversation. Finally, Padre Pio won out. One day Father Peppino said to him, "Ok, I will do what you have asked me to do. Tomorrow I will begin. I will start work on the road." Father Peppino bought two skeins of string, and gathering twenty laborers together, he began to prepare the road. Each day, Padre Pio watched the workers from his monastery window and was elated to see the progress of the building of the road. In the evenings, when Father Peppino came in from the work site, he was covered in dust. Padre Pio, with great satisfaction, would always make it a point to brush off the dust from his cassock.

Angelo Lupi of Pescara, Italy was chosen to be the chief designer and builder of the hospital. He had been selected over many others who wanted the job. He was talented and hard-working and was considered by many to be a genius in his field. Although he was the principal designer, Angelo Lupi did not have a diploma or a degree in architecture. For that reason, he seemed to be a risky choice. He was frequently doubtful about his ability. He was also worried about the lack of proper equipment and materials for such a huge undertaking. For his drawing board, Angelo used an ordinary kitchen table. He knew that he would have to improvise on many occasions and use all of his creative abilities in order to see the work to its completion.

Angelo Lupi shared his anxieties about the project with Padre Pio who simply listened and smiled. "Padre Pio," Lupi said, "I feel daunted by this huge undertaking. I don't even have a degree in architecture and I am being criticized because of it." Some people had reported Lupi to the authorities because he did not have the appropriate certification. "Do not worry about what people say," Padre Pio told him. "The person who complained about you has received his degree from men. But you have received your degree from God." Padre Pio was always there to encourage him and to dispel his fears. Later, Angelo Lupi was awarded an honorary degree.

One of Padre Pio's spiritual daughters, Maria Basilio, donated the land that the hospital was to be built on. The location was right next to the monastery of Our Lady of Grace. Maria was a wealthy woman who lived in Turin. She met Padre Pio in the early days, shortly after he was transferred to San Giovanni Rotondo. When Maria decided that she wanted to live closer to Padre Pio, he advised her to buy the land that was next to the monastery. It seems certain that Padre Pio was guided, even then, to lay the plans for what was to come in the future. Step by step, he prepared for the "great work" of the hospital, down to the last detail.

Cleonice Morcaldi, another one of Padre Pio's spiritual daughters, once saw Padre Pio standing in front of the desolate mountainside on the spot where the future hospital would one day be built. With deep concentration, he gazed silently at the mountain, and then, touching his fingers to his lips, he blew a kiss to the area.

The designated place where the hospital was to be built posed many problems for Angelo Lupi. For one thing, the Mount Gargano region was greatly lacking in natural resources. The aqueduct of Apulia was tapped for a supply of water. To obtain even more water, Lupi built large cisterns to collect rain water. A homemade power plant was used to produce electricity. A lime kiln was built in order to extract the lime that was needed for the plaster. It was an exciting day for the people of San Giovanni Rotondo when Padre Pio came down to the work site in order to bless the lime kiln. Later a stone-crushing machine was acquired.

Tons of the mountainside had to be blasted with dynamite. For many months, explosions were set off twice each day. At times, as many as 350 men were at work on the mountain under the direction of Angelo Lupi. They shoveled, dug, and broke up the stony ground with their pick axes and sledge-hammers. Farmers, shepherds, former servicemen, and even ex-convicts were hired for the labor-intensive work.

A carpentry area and a mechanical workshop were soon added to the building site. The simple farmers, shepherds, and others, were taught the skills of bricklayers, painters, blacksmiths, and woodworkers. While much of Italy suffered from unemployment, there was no unemployment problem in San Giovanni Rotondo. The poor people in the area were deeply grateful for the steady employment which enabled them to provide for their families. With great joy, Padre Pio continued to watch the progression of the work from his monastery window.

During the years that the hospital was being built, the spiritual development of the construction workers was always provided for. A special Mass was held on the first Friday of each month. At the end of the day, a large bell was sounded and summoned all who were involved with the work for the hospital to the church for Mass.

Difficulties were encountered in all stages of the construction work. But those difficulties paled in comparison to the problem of the lack of money. Dr. Kisvarday, who was in charge of the accounts, felt a growing anxiety. He meticulously recorded all donations in an ordinary school copy book. For the most part, the donations that were received were quite modest. The citizens of the town had little extra money to give, even to such a worthy cause.

Members of the hospital committee tried to think of creative ways to solve the money problem. Lotteries, raffles and other fund-raisers were held. Plays with spiritual themes were presented and the proceeds were given to the hospital. Almost every shop in San Giovanni Rotondo possessed a small donation box for the hospital.

Padre Pio made it clear that he would not consider taking out loans to finance the hospital. He advised that the work should be done gradually, as the money came in. When the donations slowed, so did the work. He always saw the work of the hospital as supported by prayer. "This is God's work," he would repeat. "It is not mine. God will see to the money."

Nevertheless, Dr. Sanguinetti, Dr. Kisvarday, and Dr. Sanvico became deeply concerned about the lack of funds. After much analysis of the incoming donations and the outgoing expenses, they realized that there would not be enough money to build the hospital. It seemed that the whole project was doomed to failure. However, through the blessing of Divine Providence, things were about to change.

Barbara Ward, the British journalist and economist visited San Giovanni Rotondo in 1948. Some of Barbara's friends in Rome had told her about Padre Pio and she had a great desire to meet him. With great interest, she viewed the construction work that was being done for the hospital.

During her visit to the monastery, Barbara was able to speak to Padre Pio briefly. She talked to him about her fiancé, Commander Robert Jackson. "I would like to ask for your prayers. I am engaged to be married," Barbara said. "My fiancé, Robert, is a Protestant and I am a Catholic. I would like Robert to be converted to Catholicism." "If it is the Lord's will, he will be," Padre Pio answered. "But when will it be?" Barbara asked. "If it is the Lord's will, right now," Padre Pio replied.

When Barbara returned to London, she was surprised to find that Robert had already been received into the Catholic Church. He explained to Barbara that he was walking past the Jesuit parish in the city of Mayfair one day when he suddenly felt a great longing to go inside. Once inside, he called for the parish priest and explained that he wished to take instructions in the Catholic faith. This occurred on the day that Barbara had spoken to Padre Pio about her desire for Robert to become Catholic.

Barbara told her fiancé about her visit to Padre Pio's monastery and the important work of the Home for the Relief of Suffering. She asked him if he might be able to find a way to assist Padre Pio. Robert was the deputy director of the United Nations Relief and Rehabilitation Administration (UNRRA). The goal of UNRRA was to give aide for purposes of redevelopment to countries that had suffered from the war. Italy had definitely suffered from the war.

Robert set about to present a summary of the hospital's need for financial aid. The project was brought before the U.S. Congress and was approved. UNRRA designated 400 million lire to the Home for the Relief of Suffering. Of that sum, the Italian government took 150 million lire. Padre Pio was very upset by the government's actions, considering it a great impropriety to take part of the funds that had been designated to the hospital. The hospital received 250 million lire which was still a huge sum of money in 1948. Barbara and Robert stepped in at the right time. With the grant, the work would be able to continue until the hospital was completed.

In consideration of the large gift that had been given, UNRRA requested that Padre Pio name the hospital, the *Fiorello Henry La Guardia Hospital*. Fiorello La Guardia, who had died a short time before, had been UNRRA's Director General and was considered to be one of its most outstanding benefactors. Padre Pio had already decided on the name that he wanted for the hospital and he would not agree to change it. He did however, have a large plaque with an inscription of gratitude and a dedication to Fiorello LaGuardia erected in the Home.

In 1950, when Barbara visited San Giovanni Rotondo again, she was delighted to see how the work had progressed and how the grant funds had been used. A big surprise awaited her when she went into the hospital's chapel. There, in one of the beautiful stained glass windows, the artist had etched Barbara's face to portray the face of the Blessed Virgin Mary. Barbara's lovely face, which revealed kindness and great compassion, was the perfect model for the chapel's Madonna window. Because of her very important financial assistance, Barbara Ward was frequently referred to as the "godmother" of the hospital.

Not everyone who learned of Padre Pio's great work had the exemplary qualities that Barbara Ward possessed. One family in San Giovanni Rotondo decided to raise funds for the future hospital. However, their intentions were far from honorable. Instead of turning the donations over to the hospital, they used the money to build a home for themselves. Soon Padre Pio was informed about the matter. The next day, their brand-new house collapsed on its foundations.

On one occasion, a very wealthy man sent a telegram to Our Lady of Grace monastery with a prayer request. He explained that his wife had a terminal illness. He wanted Padre Pio to pray for his wife's healing. If his wife was cured, he intended to give a large sum of money to the Home for the Relief of Suffering. Upon hearing the man's proposal, Padre Pio became upset. He would never accept a donation with strings attached. "One does not bargain with the Lord," Padre Pio said.

A great effort was made to make the Home for the Relief of Suffering look cheerful and welcoming so that the patients would feel comfortable for the duration of their hospital stay. Fresh and fragrant flowers graced the rooms and care was taken to remove the unpleasant antiseptic and medicinal odors common to hospitals. It was never to be referred to as an institution or a clinic or a hospital. It was to be called a Home.

At the request of Padre Pio, the hospital furnishings were chosen with great care to counteract the typical hospital "look" which is often severe and depressing. "Make it beautiful," Padre Pio said to the designers. There were to be no wards, but instead, rooms which had plenty of large, sunny windows. Soft pastel colors were chosen for the interior. The attractive mosaic floors were laid down by some of the local girls of San Giovanni Rotondo. The exterior of the hospital was faced with beautiful pale rose Trani stone. Green marble was chosen for the stairways and red Carso marble for the foyers. There was a large library as well as an auditorium which was equipped to show movies. Terraces and gardens contributed to the overall beauty of the Home.

Dr. Sanguinetti was instrumental in having a parcel of land near the hospital designated as a farm. It would provide the patients with fresh fruit, vegetables, meat, milk, cheese, and eggs. He also had hundreds of tons of rich soil hauled up the slopes near the hospital on the backs of mules. He planted 10,000 trees, mostly pines and cypress, on the side of the mountains. Truly, in San Giovanni Rotondo, the desert had flowered. Through Padre Pio's efforts, it flowered charitably, scientifically and also spiritually.

Dr. Carlo Kisvarday told Padre Pio on one occasion that too much money was being spent on nonessentials, in other words, items to enhance the Home's outward beauty. Padre Pio responded, "No, that is not true. If it were possible, I would make the Home out of pure gold. Nothing is too good or too beautiful for the sick and suffering because in reality the sick person is Jesus." And to a priest who made a critical remark because he thought that the Home looked too luxurious, Padre Pio responded, "Too luxurious? Not at all. A hospital is a tabernacle. Christ is in the sick."

As the days drew closer to completion, Padre Pio could hardly contain his joy. Everything seemed to be falling into place. Twenty-four doctors had put in their applications to work at the Home. A man brought his paralyzed son to the monastery to see Padre Pio. Padre Pio greeted the man with great kindness and said to him, "Do not give up hope. The hospital will be opening in just a few months. You will be able to bring your son to the children's clinic for medical treatment." Padre Pio made it clear that no one who was in need of care was to be turned away due to lack of money.

People with serious illnesses came regularly to the monastery of Our Lady of Grace to ask Padre Pio to pray that their health would be restored. Many of the people who came to see him had cancer. As he formulated the plans for the Home, he expressed his desire for the establishment of a cancer-research center.

The official inauguration ceremony for the opening of the Home for the Relief of Suffering took place on May 5, 1956, sixteen years after the first committee meeting. At the inauguration, Padre Pio offered Mass at an altar that was set up between the two pillars of the hospital entrance. An estimated crowd of 15,000 people was present. During the inauguration, the choir sang the beautiful hymn, *Where There is Charity and Love, There is God.*

Dozens of bishops and priests were in attendance as well as the Minister General of the Capuchin Order, numerous prelates from the Vatican, the president of the Italian Senate, the Minister of State, and other dignitaries of the Italian government. In the crowd were nine hundred representatives from the Padre Pio prayer groups in Europe, South America, India, the United States and other countries. World famous doctors from many parts of Europe were also in the audience. Dr. White, the personal physician of the President of the United States, at that time President Eisenhower, was there to represent the United States.

The new hospital looked magnificent. Three hundred flags of the nations were displayed across the front of the hospital. The American flag was in the center and flew beside the flag of Italy. Cardinal Giacomo Lercaro, the archbishop of Bologna was the Pope's official envoy for the occasion. He spoke to the huge gathering and said:

I have been reminded of the words of our sacred liturgy, *Where charity and love dwell, God is there.* It is equally true that where God is, there charity and love are found together . . . Have you not noticed it here in San Giovanni Rotondo? Yes. The whole world has noticed it!

A message from Pope Pius XII was read by the Minister General of the Capuchin Order. The Holy Father also sent his apostolic blessing. During the ceremonies, military airplanes from the nearby Amendola air field repeatedly flew over the hospital as a sign of greeting and good will.

Padre Pio rarely spoke in public but he did so on the occasion of the inauguration. Deeply and visibly moved, he addressed the huge crowd at the conclusion of the Mass and said:

The Home for the Relief of Suffering is complete. I thank the benefactors from every part of the world who have contributed to its construction. This is what Providence, also with your support, has created. I give it to you. Admire it and bless it together in the name of God.

A seed has been placed in the earth which he will warm with his rays of love. A new army formed through sacrifice and love is about to rise up to the glory of God, and to the comfort of sick souls and bodies. Do not deprive us of your help; collaborate with this apostolate for the relief of human suffering, and the Divine Charity which knows no bounds and which is the very light of God and the Eternal Life, will accumulate for each one of you, a treasure of graces, to which Jesus made us inheritors on the Cross . . . May this work become a center of the Franciscan spirit in action, a place of prayer and science where the human race can be united in Christ Crucified, as a single flock under one Shepherd . . .

May God bless those who have worked, are working, and will work for this Hospital. May he recompense you a thousand times in this life and with eternal joy in the next life. May the Blessed Virgin of all Graces and our Seraphic Father, St. Francis in heaven and the vicar of Christ on earth, the pope, intercede for us that our wishes may be granted.

Padre Pio, together with Cardinal Lercaro, then cut the traditional ribbon leading into the hospital. Together, they went inside and blessed the various rooms and departments.

While the inauguration day was a day of tremendous joy and celebration, it was also bittersweet. Dr. Sanguinetti and Dr. Sanvico, who had labored tirelessly from the very beginning to help Padre Pio accomplish his dream, were not present. Both had passed away before the Home was completed. Dr. Kisvarday, who had worked closely with Dr. Sanguinetti and Dr. Sanvico for years, was overcome with emotion during the inaugural ceremonies. He sat close to Padre Pio and cried through most of the Mass. Angelo Lupi, whose skill and genius had created the magnificent structure, would die in the Home in 1969.

On May 6, 1956, the day after the inauguration, Padre Pio spoke briefly to the doctors who assembled at the hospital for the International Seminar of the European Society of Cardiology. He said:

You have come into the world as I have, with a mission to fulfill. Take note. I am speaking to you about duties, at a time when everyone speaks only of rights. I, as a religious and a priest, have a mission to accomplish. As a religious and a Capuchin, I am bound to the perfect and strict observance of my Rule and vows. As a priest, mine is a mission of atonement, of propitiating God for the sins of mankind.

All this may come to pass if I am in God's grace . . . You have a mission to cure the sick. But if you do not also bring love to the patient's bedside, I do not think that your medicines will be of much use. I can prove this from my own experience. During my illness in 1916 -1917, my doctor, while treating me, first expressed words of comfort to me. Love cannot do without words. And you yourselves, how can you, other than by words, bring spiritual comfort to a patient? . . . Bring God to your patients; that will help them more than any other cure.

The first sick person was admitted to the hospital on May 10, 1956. More were admitted during the month of May, but the numbers were much lower than expected. It was a deep concern to the administrators. On the feast of

Corpus Christi, 1956, Padre Pio went to the hospital and carried the Blessed Sacrament in procession through all of the wards. Right after that, the hospital started to fill up. After only three years, the Home had to be enlarged and a new wing had to be added in order to accommodate the growing numbers of the sick.

Dr. Carlo Kisvarday gave more than twenty years of his life to serving the Home. His esteem for Padre Pio was so great and his dedication to the work was so total that he knew he would never leave San Giovanni Rotondo. His workday began at 5:00 a.m. and rarely ended before midnight. He felt a compelling force, always urging him forward in his efforts. His one fear was that old age and declining health might someday force him to cut back on his working hours.

One day Padre Pio said to Dr. Kisvarday, "Carletto, the Lord has established the date of everyone's death. He alone knows the length of time each of us has on this earth. I am praying for you so that the Heavenly Father might give you one added year of life." The doctor did not know quite what to make of the mysterious comment. Shortly after that, Dr. Kisvarday had a health crisis. He was unconscious when he was taken to the Home for the Relief of Suffering. He remained in a coma for three days.

When Dr. Kisvarday was out of danger and on the road to recuperation, he told his nurse that Padre Pio had come in bilocation to his bedside and had spoken to him. Almost a year later, Dr. Kisvarday passed away. He had been given one extra year of perfect health, thanks to the intercession of Padre Pio.

Padre Pio asked Father Innocenzo of Campobasso to assist as the full-time chaplain at the Home. Father Innocenzo said Mass in the hospital chapel, heard confessions, and visited the sick. He also gave spiritual direction to the nuns who worked at the hospital. He made a holy hour every day in front of the Blessed Sacrament on behalf of all the patients. He served as the chaplain at the Home for 40 years.

Through the years, Father Innocenzo had many beautiful experiences in his capacity as chaplain. He used to enjoy telling Padre Pio about his encounters with the patients. Padre Pio always loved to listen to the stories that Father Innocenzo shared with him.

Once, a woman greeted Father Innocenzo and told him how much his spiritual counsel had helped her when she was a patient in the Home. During her hospital stay, she became desperate when she was told by the doctors that she would never recover. "Father Innocenzo, I have never forgotten your words to me, words that changed my life," the woman said. "And what did I say to you?" Father Innocenzo asked her. "You told me that Jesus continues to suffer in the sick," the woman replied. "Since then, I have been able to accept my condition. Thanks to you Father, I now pray and meditate every day and I am content to suffer."

The patients in the Home felt blessed that Father Innocenzo was there to pray with them and to administer the sacraments. On one occasion, there was a man who spent many months in the Home with a very serious illness. Finally, one day he asked for Father Innocenzo. He then made a sincere confession. The very next day he went into a coma and received the Last Rites. Later that day, the man regained consciousness. When he opened his eyes, he saw Father Innocenzo sitting beside his bed. "Father, what a beautiful thing you did for me!" the man said. "I am so grateful that you heard my confession." Right after that, the man lost consciousness and he died within the hour.

There was another patient at the Home for the Relief of Suffering whom Father Innocenzo visited regularly. Day after day, the man put off making his confession. Finally, one day he decided that he was ready. After he made his confession, he felt such a sense of happiness that he began to cry. From that time forward, every time he saw Father Innocenzo, he expressed his gratitude to him. "I have found life again here at the Home for the Relief of Suffering," the man said. "I must thank God and I must thank Padre Pio that I was able to come here."

Father Innocenzo once told Padre Pio that he believed that those who were sick had an opportunity through their illness, to receive abundant graces from the Lord. "Many graces indeed come to the sick," Padre Pio said. "In the Home for the Relief of Suffering, there flows a grace that sustains, comforts, and gives strength to the sick. It is a grace which flows silently, secretly. Of course, there are always a small number who resist the mercy of God, but even among those, I believe that grace usually triumphs in the end."

Someone suggested to Padre Pio that it would be a blessing to invite an order of nuns to work at the hospital. Several different religious congregations were put forward to him as possibilities. Padre Pio said that the Lord had let him know many years before which nuns to invite. Padre Pio chose the Missionaries of the Sacred Heart of Jesus, a nursing order of nuns.

The Missionaries of the Sacred Heart of Jesus had served in San Giovanni Rotondo from 1909 to 1920. They assisted in a training school, a school for girls, and a home for the elderly. In 1920, the nuns were called away from San Giovanni Rotondo to serve in another area. When they went to say goodbye to Padre Pio, they felt a sadness in their hearts. He had been their confessor since the time of his transfer to the monastery of Our Lady of Grace.

Padre Pio told the nuns that he was sorry to see them leave but he was certain that they would return someday. He pointed to a nearby mountain and said, "When you return, you will work in a big hospital that will be erected where that mountain now stands." Padre Pio's prophecy was fulfilled thirty-five years later, when the Missionaries of the Sacred Heart of Jesus returned to San Giovanni Rotondo to work at the Home for the Relief of Suffering.

Sister Miriam Brusa was one of the nuns of the Missionaries of the Sacred Heart who worked at the hospital. She used to say that the Home was built on Padre Pio's tears. Father Agostino also expressed the same thought. He wrote in his diary, "Padre Pio always suffers for the hospital." Indeed, it was true. No one knew the difficulties and setbacks that occurred regarding the hospital better than Padre Pio.

Once, when Sister Miriam was taking care of the hospital bookkeeping, she noticed that there was a shortage of five million lire for the monthly expenses. She was worried that the employees might not be able to receive their paychecks on time. Sister Miriam decided not to tell Padre Pio about it. Knowing that he had many other difficulties to deal with, she tried to protect him from the day to day problems of the hospital. Sister Miriam determined not to tell anyone about the worrisome matter just yet. Padre Pio always called the Home a work of "Divine Providence." Sister Miriam would place her trust in Divine Providence and petition God through prayer for a solution.

In just a matter of days, Sister Miriam received the exact amount of money that was needed for the monthly expenses. Angela Lazzarini, who played a part in the acquisition of the needed funds, explained to Sister Miriam the details of how the generous donation came about. "I was very surprised when Padre Pio told me that he needed money," Angela said. "As you know, Padre Pio never asks for anything. But he explained to me that the hospital was in need, although he didn't specify the amount. I did not have the money myself so I asked a friend to write a check. When my friend asked me the amount to write, for a reason that I cannot explain I felt urged to say, 'five million lire.' My friend wrote the check for that amount and I took it to Padre Pio. When Padre Pio looked at the check, he told me that it was the exact amount that the hospital needed." It was then that Padre Pio had the money delivered to Sister Miriam. That month, the workers were paid on time, the bills were paid, and all was well.

John McCaffery (see Chapter 14), who enjoyed Padre Pio's friendship for many years, was well aware that the Home was a work of God and a gift of Divine Providence. John said:

> If one thinks just for a moment of what is implied by the setting up of a modern four hundred bed hospital, the immensity and complexity of the task is evident. Situate it then, in the middle of nowhere; make all its prodigious running costs dependent more or less on haphazard charitable donations; consider that it was so constructed as to be capable of harmonious expansion to its present number of a thousand beds. And then ask what force created it.
>
> No amount of thought and planning or even of human blood, sweat, and tears, ever produced that vast and continuing phenomenon. It took a vision not of this world to foresee it all, and a powerhouse of prayer and suffering to bring it to fruition.

Through the years, Padre Pio visited the Home for the Relief of Suffering to pray at the bedsides of the seriously ill and on special feast days, he would occasionally say Mass in the hospital chapel. He took part briefly in the Catholic Doctors Convention that was held at the Home in 1957. At Christmas time, he loved to view the large and impressive Christmas Crib that was displayed on the third floor of the hospital. At times, he attended special meetings of the Third Order of St. Francis at the Home. He also enjoyed attending the religious plays that were held in the hospital auditorium. He was there to bless the first stone which marked the work of enlargement and expansion of the hospital. On one occasion, when Padre Pio was ill, he was admitted as a patient to the Home.

On the 10th anniversary of the Home for the Relief of Suffering, May 5, 1966, Cardinal Giacomo Lercaro, as distinguished guest of honor, celebrated

Mass on the portico of the hospital. In his homily that day, he spoke beautiful and inspiring words about Padre Pio's great work of charity. He said:

> *I was hungry, says the Lord, and you gave me to eat: I was thirsty, and you gave me to drink: I was naked and you covered me: I was in prison and you came to me, sick and you visited me. Lord, when did we see you hungry, thirsty, sick and we aided thee? As long as you did it to one of these my least brethren, you did it to me.* Christ, therefore, is present in suffering. It is he who receives our attention, our generosity, our charity, who implores it. It will be he who will reward it one day, on the great day of his return in glory. It will be he who will reward it, and will reward it with a kingdom, not a human, fleeting one, but one prepared by God . . . .From this presence of Christ in a brother who suffers is born for each of us, the duty to bring relief for suffering . . . The Home which rises here and which we inaugurated ten years ago has interpreted and interprets well, in the wealth of resources, scientific and technical, and in the decorum of the construction, this spirit of devout service to the suffering members of Our Lord.
>
> We cannot offer Christ the crumbs which fall from the table of one who is satiated. The crumbs, in the words of the Gospel, are for the dogs. But when he who hungers is Christ, when the homeless one is Christ, what would we not do for him, and what can ever be worthy of him no matter what we do?

Padre Pio was present along side of Cardinal Lercaro for the 10th anniversary celebration. He spoke briefly to the large crowd that day and said:

> Infinite thanks to the Lord and to the Blessed Virgin, and blessed be those that in any way have cooperated with the Word. My mind and my paternal thoughts go in a special way to the Prayer Groups, now spread all over the world and here today for the celebration of the 10th anniversary of the Home for the Relief of Suffering and for their second International Convention. Together with the Home for the Relief of Suffering, they are the advanced guards of this citadel of charity, alive with faith, centers of love, in which Christ himself is present every time they meet to pray and to celebrate the Eucharist under the auspices of their pastors and spiritual directors.

It is prayer, this united strength of all good people, which moves the world, which renews minds, which sustains the Home, which comforts the suffering, which heals the sick, which sanctifies work, which elevates medical assistance, which gives moral strength and Christian resignation to human suffering, and which spreads the smile and benediction of God on every languor and weakness.

Pray a lot my children. Pray always, without ever tiring, because it is to prayer that I entrust this work, which God has wanted and which will continue to progress and prosper thanks to the help of Divine Providence and the charitable and spiritual contribution of all those who pray. May the almighty and merciful God, who accepts for himself every good that is done to our suffering brethren, recompense you a thousand times over, in the fullest and most abundant measure.

Padre Pio's plans to further help the people of San Giovanni Rotondo included a number of other charitable works. He outlined his desires but did not live to see all of them realized. He wanted to build a home for the elderly, a home for retired priests, day care centers and nursery schools, a clinic for spastic and retarded children, a center for the prayer groups, a retreat house for the clergy, a retreat house for the laity, a Way of the Cross, a nursing school, and an international center of studies for doctors. He said, "We are building not only the Home for the Relief of Suffering, but also other facilities on the whole mountain . . . They are not only my works, but God's, just as he shows me."

When Padre Pio made out his last will, he donated the Home for the Relief of Suffering to the Holy See. He wanted to make sure that his great work of charity would be secure and would continue for future generations. The Vatican became the owner of the largest and finest hospital in Italy. Padre Pio said:

Notice that I made a will leaving everything to the Church, for I am a son of the Church. And when I no longer manage anything, my Mother will have to answer for all the offerings, even the coins, that souls from all over the world donate to the Home for the Relief of Suffering.

Padre Pio remained the administrator of the Home for the Relief of Suffering until his death. Some predicted that after Padre Pio's passing, his hospital would diminish and eventually close. How wrong they were. It has continued to grow and expand through the many years since his death. Although Padre Pio has gone to his eternal reward, his spirit lives on in the Home for the Relief of Suffering. In the bright corridors, in the lovely gardens, and in the quiet chapels, one can pause and sense that Padre Pio is very near. He is still present, still working for the higher good.

Pope John Paul II visited the Home for the Relief of Suffering on May 23, 1987. He greeted the medical personnel, toured the various departments, and also visited the patients. He spoke to all who were gathered and said:

> Padre Pio's great insight was to unite science in the service of the sick, with faith and prayer: medical science in the always advancing fight against sickness; faith and prayer to transform and sublimate that suffering, that despite all the progress of medicine, will always, to a certain measure, remain an inheritance of life in this world.

Padre Pio, from the very beginning, put his Home under the protection of the Blessed Virgin Mary. He promised that Mary would always be present in his "hospital city" where countless lives would be helped and saved. Padre Pio said:

> May Our Lady of Grace, who is the Queen to whom every day and many times in the day, we manifest our love, and of whom we ask her maternal assistance, reign always in the city that will rise here, and may she assist all of you. May the Madonna intensify the love of her children for the Vicar of Christ on earth, and one day may she show us Jesus in the splendor of his glory. Amen

> *O Mary, Health of the sick, help, protect and make blossom, my poor work which is yours, the Home for the Relief of Suffering, for the glory of God and for the spiritual and material advantage of those who suffer in body and soul.*
> *- St. Pio of Pietrelcina*

Only in heaven will we know to what extent the Home for the Relief of Suffering owes to the prayers of Padre Pio. And now we can add - and to the intercession of Padre Pio.

- Pope John Paul II

CHAPTER 6

Anecdotes of the Home for the Relief of Suffering

Francesco Lotti was just a teenager when he met Padre Pio for the first time. After Francesco's father had passed away, he and his mother traveled to San Giovanni Rotondo from their home in the north of Italy. During the visit, Padre Pio said to Francesco, "I will now be your new father." On another visit, Francesco noticed that Padre Pio was looking out the monastery window and seemed to be deep in thought. Padre Pio then pointed to the mountain and said to Francesco, "Someday a large hospital will be built on that mountain. You will be one of the doctors who will work there." But Francesco did not believe that would ever happen. He had already made a decision to pursue a career in the military. However, later he changed his mind and decided to study medicine. Eventually he became the head physician in Pediatrics at the Home for the Relief of Suffering.

For a time, Francesco Lotti was Padre Pio's doctor. Even so, Dr. Lotti never saw his stigmata. Padre Pio never mentioned it, nor the suffering it caused him. Nevertheless, Dr. Lotti was very much aware of the suffering that Padre Pio endured because of the stigmata. Sometimes he saw the painful expression on Padre Pio's face when someone shook hands with him. The only time that Dr. Lotti ever saw the stigmata was when Padre Pio's hands were exposed at Mass.

By living and working in San Giovanni Rotondo, Dr. Lotti learned many things about Padre Pio. For one, he became aware of Padre Pio's unusual eating habits. He came to the conclusion that Padre Pio's daily intake of food was insufficient to sustain life. Padre Pio had his own theory about it. He likened the body to soil. Some soil needed a lot of fertilizer in order for crops to grow. There was other soil that was so rich, it needed no fertilizer at all. Padre Pio said that his body was like the latter. He remarked that on one occasion he was unable to eat for three days due to an intestinal problem. At the end of the three days, he had gained six pounds. "That is what I mean by fertile ground," he remarked.

It was certainly true that Padre Pio's physical constitution seemed to defy science. As impossible as it sounds, at times his heart rate would not be synchronized with his pulse. Padre Pio once told Dr. Lotti that he needed only half the dosage of medicine that is prescribed to a child. On one occasion, when Padre Pio was suffering from bronchitis, he had to be seen by a new doctor because Dr. Sanguinetti, his regular doctor at that time, was out of town. The medicine that Padre Pio was prescribed made him ill. When Dr. Sanguinetti returned and heard what had happened, he was upset. "That would never have happened if I had been here," Dr. Sanguinetti said. He felt that he understood Padre Pio's unique constitution and knew how to treat him for illness.

———

In 1950, during the time that Padre Pio's hospital, the Home for the Relief of Suffering was being built in San Giovanni Rotondo, a small office was set up near the monastery. The purpose of the office was to collect donations for the hospital. People who visited the office could also subscribe to a small publication that the Capuchins made available. The publication kept people informed about the progress and the development of the construction of the hospital. The money that was collected from the subscriptions was given to the hospital.

On one occasion, a woman visited the office and asked that her name be removed from the subscription list. She no longer wanted to receive the hospital publication. While she was talking to the office clerk about her subscription, she showed him a lovely religious article which she had recently purchased as a gift for Padre Pio. She was planning on going to the monastery that very day to give it to him. The obvious question in the office clerk's mind was why the woman wanted to give a gift to Padre Pio if she felt so strongly about not receiving the publication about his hospital. It did not seem to make sense.

Not only had the woman decided to withdraw her support from the hospital, she went so far as to try to persuade others to do likewise. On one occasion, the woman had discouraged one of her friends from making any contributions to Padre Pio's hospital. She told her friend that it would be much better for people to give their money to their home parishes rather than to the hospital fund.

A little later on in the day, the woman returned to the office. The clerk noticed that the woman had tears in her eyes. "Please put my name back on the subscription list for the hospital publication," the woman said. She explained the reason. When she went to the monastery, she happened to see Padre Pio standing in the corridor. She went up to him to greet him but he would not acknowledge her presence. She presented the gift to him but he looked at it with an expression of great consternation. He refused to accept it. It then dawned on the woman that her prior actions had been wrong. She had no business discouraging people from helping such a worthy cause as the Home for the Relief of Suffering. She got the message loud and clear.

During the Holy Year of 1950, Dorothy Gaudiose and her two sisters, Helena and Carmelita were making preparations to travel to Rome. When Dorothy read an interesting article about Padre Pio in the newspaper, she decided to add San Giovanni Rotondo to the itinerary.

When they arrived in San Giovanni Rotondo, they saw many pilgrims both inside and outside the church. At that time, the wait to go to confession to Padre Pio was ten days. Dorothy told one of the Capuchins at the monastery that she and her sisters were hoping that they could have a word with Padre Pio. The Capuchin told her that Padre Pio would soon be passing from the corridor of the church into the monastery. They could wait for him in the corridor but they would need a ticket in order to do so.

With their tickets in hand, Dorothy and her sisters waited in the corridor. A large crowd of women and children had already assembled there. When Padre Pio appeared, the women became very excited. Many of them tried to press toward Padre Pio and to touch him. Padre Pio was patient and humble and did not show any annoyance.

When Padre Pio saw Dorothy and her two sisters standing with the others, he smiled and spoke to them briefly. He asked them where they were from. He was happy to learn that they were Americans. Dorothy immediately felt the strength of his character as well as his deep piety. Then he surprised Dorothy and her sisters by making a humorous remark. All of the other women who were in hearing distance began to laugh.

Dorothy and Helena began to visit San Giovanni Rotondo every summer. Since they were both teachers who had extended summer vacations, it worked out well. In 1961, Dorothy and Helena took a sabbatical from their teaching positions and spent one full year in San Giovanni Rotondo. They were able to attend Mass each day and also felt blessed to be able to make their confession to Padre Pio. Once, Helena confessed that she had missed Mass on Sunday. To her great surprise, Padre Pio told her that she had already confessed that sin. It was true. While in Rome, she had gone to confession and mentioned it at that time.

During that year, Dorothy and Helena became good friends with Mary Pyle. They helped her sort the tremendous amount of mail that came into the monastery. It was usually an all day project. Mary shared many incidents from Padre Pio's life with Dorothy and Helena. She told them that on occasion, when the doctors at the Home for the Relief of Suffering had a difficult surgery to perform, they would first go to the monastery to see Padre Pio and ask him to bless their hands.

Dorothy and Helena were both fluent in Italian as well as English. When Mary Pyle was occupied with other matters, she often sent them in her place to assist as Padre Pio's language translators. When the English-speaking pilgrims were visiting with Padre Pio, Dorothy and Helena would translate for them.

Dorothy felt the graces of being in such close contact with Padre Pio. She told him that she was considering a permanent move to San Giovanni Rotondo. "No," he answered. "That would not be a good idea. You will do many good works in the United States. You must return."

One day Helena asked Padre Pio if there was any other way that she could help him in his important apostolate. "Yes, there is," he answered. "Try to do something for the Home for the Relief of Suffering, even if you have to make sacrifices in order to do so." Helena thought about his words and finally decided what she wanted to do. She told Padre Pio that she owned a home in the U.S. which she had decided to put up for sale. Once the house sold, she wanted to donate the money to the hospital. She was a widow and she had no children. She was also secure financially. Padre Pio asked her three times if there was anyone in her immediate family, like a brother or a sister, who might need her property. Helena told him that none of her relatives needed it. Finally, he said that he would accept her gift and he expressed his gratitude to her for her generosity. He also predicted accurately the price that the house would sell for.

Dorothy too wanted to do something more to help Padre Pio. Unlike her sister, Dorothy did not have any property that she could donate. She wondered what she could do to help. The thought occurred to her that she might be able to write a biography of Padre Pio's life. She worked as an English teacher in a public school and through the years, she had taken many courses in creative writing. She knew that she had the ability to write.

Dorothy spoke to Padre Pio about her idea. She told him that when the book was completed, she wanted to donate half of all the royalties to the Home for the Relief of Suffering. Dorothy was certain that she would encounter many difficulties along the way. She believed that finding a publisher might be the greatest challenge of all. She asked Padre Pio to be with her in her endeavor and to help her find a publisher. Padre Pio replied with a single word, "Spera" (Have hope).

Altogether, it took six years before Dorothy's book was made available to the public. During the very difficult time of trying to find a publisher, she remembered Padre Pio's words. She waited in patience and never lost hope. Her interesting and well-researched book, *Prophet of the People* became very popular. Many people told Dorothy that the book proved to be a great help to them in their spiritual journey.

At home in the United States, Dorothy did much to spread the message of Padre Pio. She gave talks on his life and spirituality at churches, on university campuses, and even at prisons and detention facilities. Everyone was interested in what Dorothy had to say.

After Padre Pio's death, Dorothy became one of the promoters of his cause for canonization. She circulated a petition and collected signatures from individuals, requesting that the formal proceedings begin in regard to his cause. She asked a number of bishops if they would be willing to sign the petition and many of them agreed to do so. Other bishops said that they could not sign the petition because they did not know anything about Padre Pio. Dorothy then sent a gift copy of her book to 300 bishops. She also wrote fifty letters and sent them to bishops in each of the fifty states in the United States. Included with an offering was a written request that the bishop say a Mass for her special intention. Her special intention was that Padre Pio's cause for canonization would proceed smoothly and successfully.

———

Mr. Valentino, of Milan, Italy, used to take his wife to San Giovanni Rotondo so that she could attend Mass and make her confession to Padre Pio. His wife was a person of deep faith and piety. In many ways she was just the opposite of her husband. She had a reserved and gentle nature and was respectful and polite. Her husband, on the other hand, was an arrogant and proud man who had an open hostility toward religion. He especially felt a strong dislike for Padre Pio. Mrs. Valentino prayed continually for the conversion of her husband.

Whenever they made the trip to San Giovanni Rotondo, Mr. Valentino refused to step inside the church of Our Lady of Grace. Instead, he waited for his wife in the square just outside where he drank coffee and smoked cigarettes. He was not afraid to tell people openly that Padre Pio was not the holy man they thought him to be.

One icy and windy day when Mr. Valentino was waiting for his wife in the square, the cold temperature made him so uncomfortable that he felt compelled to go inside the church in order to warm up. When he entered the church, he happened to catch a glimpse of Padre Pio. Their eyes met for just a moment. Mr. Valentino was so taken by the experience, that he had a sudden and dramatic change of heart. He knew then that he had been mistaken in his estimation of Padre Pio.

From that day forward, Mr. Valentino attended the various prayer services at Our Lady of Grace while he waited for his wife to make her confession. He never missed a single prayer service that was offered. He was able to make his confession to Padre Pio as well. Feeling a deep sense of gratitude for the blessings he had received, he wanted to do something to help Padre Pio and wondered what he could do. At the time, Padre Pio's hospital was still under construction. Mr. Valentino bought the first pine trees that were planted at the Home for the Relief of Suffering.

———

In 1956, Dr. Vito Tricarico, an Orthopedic Specialist, was hired to work at the Home for the Relief of Suffering. One of the first people that Dr. Vito met after moving from Rome to San Giovanni Rotondo was Carlo Campanini. One day, Carlo took Dr. Vito over to the monastery and introduced him to Padre Pio. During the conversation, Padre Pio asked Dr. Vito about his family. When he told Padre Pio that his parents were both farmers, Padre Pio seemed genuinely pleased. Padre Pio then told a joke that made everyone laugh. He embraced Dr. Vito and sent him off with his blessing. For the next eight years, Dr. Vito would see Padre Pio almost every evening. He and the other doctors met with Padre Pio in order to discuss important matters dealing with the new hospital. They also discussed various clinical cases with him.

In 1961, Dr. Vito's wife was admitted to the labor and delivery ward of the Home for the Relief of Suffering. Because Dr. Vito was their colleague and because it was his wife's first baby, the doctors on duty in labor and delivery felt somewhat nervous. Dr. Vito was nervous as well. His friend Carlo Campanini told him that they should go and have a word with Padre Pio. Perhaps it would calm Dr. Vito's nerves. Dr. Vito agreed to go. When they arrived at the monastery, they found Padre Pio reading the Bible. Padre Pio was happy to learn that Dr. Vito was about to become a father. He said to Dr. Vito, "If you want to form a good Christian family, you must start with a daughter. Congratulations. Everything went well!" When Dr. Vito walked back over to the hospital, he learned that his wife had just given birth to a baby girl. He was informed that "everything had gone well." They named their beautiful new daughter, Chiara Pia.

———————

On many occasions, Padre Pio demonstrated that he was intuitively attuned to the needs of the Home for the Relief of Suffering. An incident involving his spiritual daughter, Amalia Pagani, is one case in point. One day when Amalia was in the church of Our Lady of Grace, Padre Pio looked directly in her eyes and said to her, "Go outside!" Amalia could not understand why Padre Pio would say such a thing. Three times he repeated the words to her. Feeling hurt and rejected by his strong command, Amalia was in tears as she left the church.

As soon as Amalia stepped outside, she saw one of the Capuchins who was walking toward her and appeared to be in a hurry. "Why are you crying?" he asked. Amalia repeated what Padre Pio had told her in the church. "Would you be willing to follow me quickly over to the hospital?" the Capuchin asked. "There is a little boy in the emergency room and he is fighting for his life. The doctors are working on him at this moment and he is in need of blood. We are searching for a blood donor who has his blood type," the Capuchin explained. Amalia was happy to agree to the Capuchin's request and quickly followed him over to the hospital. As it turned out, Amalia had the exact blood type that was needed. She was very glad that she had been able to help the young boy. She then understood why Padre Pio had insisted that she leave the church immediately.

———————

Dr. Luigi Pancaro was one of the doctors who worked at the Home for the Relief of Suffering. He was also the doctor of many of the Capuchins who were in residence at Our Lady of Grace monastery, including Padre Pio. Dr. Pancaro usually went to the monastery each day at noon in order to join Padre Pio as he recited the Angelus in front of the church.

Living in San Giovanni Rotondo, Dr. Pancaro heard many amazing stories about Padre Pio. A number of people told Dr. Pancaro that they were miraculously healed by Padre Pio. Others spoke of his gifts of bilocation, reading of hearts, and perfume. Dr. Pancaro always had doubts about such stories, believing them to be pure fantasy. He would sometimes say to himself, "If these astonishing things that I hear about Padre Pio are actually true, why doesn't he remove the strong doubts from my mind?" But the doubts held on and would not leave.

Dr. Pancaro had read a number of articles in newspapers and magazines about Padre Pio's charismatic gifts. Much of what was written about Padre Pio seemed to be pure sensationalism and he remained skeptical about such stories. Dr. Pancaro held Padre Pio in the highest esteem. He admired him for his great piety and for his compassion for the poor and the sick. In his estimation, those were the true marks of spirituality.

May 28, 1958, was to be an important day for the Pancaro family. Dr. Pancaro's daughter, Caroline, was to be married on that day at Our Lady of Grace church. Padre Pio had agreed to perform the wedding ceremony. The morning of Caroline's wedding, the Pancaro family attended Padre Pio's 5:00 a.m. Mass. During the Mass, Dr. Pancaro's mind was filled with doubts about the Catholic teachings on the Eucharist, especially the transubstantiation. To Dr. Pancaro, the theology of the transubstantiation seemed ridiculous. He simply did not believe it. He made an effort to banish his negative thoughts during the Mass but he did not succeed.

After Mass, Dr. Pancaro greeted Padre Pio and tried to kiss his hand but Padre Pio would not allow him to do so. Padre Pio whispered in his ear, so that no one else could hear, "My son, what bad thoughts you had at Mass this morning! When are you going to stop thinking like that?"

The next day, the doctor had an opportunity to speak to Padre Pio once again. "Now listen to me attentively," Padre Pio said. "I am not at all offended by what you think of me. But to doubt the great mystery of the transubstantiation is the greatest offence you could commit against God!" Padre Pio looked deep into Dr. Pancaro's eyes. "Now are you convinced?" Padre Pio asked. And yes, at last Dr. Pancaro was convinced.

————

On one occasion, Father Eusebio Notte, who lived in residence at Our Lady of Grace monastery, was invited by one of the doctors at the Home for the Relief of Suffering to be present during an operation, a simple appendectomy. Father Eusebio agreed to observe the surgery.

Everything seemed to be going along just fine with the surgery when suddenly complications arose. It was obvious that the doctor in charge was very worried. Father Eusebio began to pray with great fervor to Padre Pio, begging him to intercede. The patient's condition did not improve. Father Eusebio continued to lift up his prayers to Padre Pio with even greater intensity. Finally, the doctor breathed a sigh of relief. From that point on, everything went well. The crisis had passed and the patient was out of danger.

Father Eusebio went quickly back to the monastery to tell Padre Pio the news. "Thank you so much, Padre Pio, for interceding and for answering my prayers," Father Eusebio said. "I did not have much choice," Padre Pio answered, "You deafened me!"

————

A woman named Estelle Hartnett was once admitted to the Home for the Relief of Suffering in very serious condition. Estelle and her mother had been traveling in Spain when Estelle contracted amoebic dysentery. However, believing that she would soon feel better, she did not seek medical help. Ten days later, she and her mother visited San Giovanni Rotondo in order to attend Padre Pio's Mass. It was there that Estelle's illness grew much worse and she had to be admitted to Padre Pio's hospital.

Estelle was in a great deal of pain and was suffering from chills and a high fever. She was put under the care of Dr. Pietro Melillo. Unlike many of the doctors on staff who spoke only Italian, Dr. Melillo spoke English. Fortunately, there was no language barrier between Estelle and her doctor. Other doctors on staff at the Home for the Relief of Suffering also examined Estelle.

Tests revealed that she had a liver abscess. It was believed that it was brought on by the amoebic dysentery.

One day, Dr. Melillo became alarmed at Estelle's condition. She had a very high fever and only a faint heart beat. Later on in the afternoon, Estelle's condition showed a sudden and dramatic improvement. She felt a sensation which she described as "a fresh, cool breeze" which passed over her body. At once, her fever vanished. She called for Dr. Melillo. He examined her and noted the remarkable change in her condition.

Dr. Melillo told Estelle and her mother that he had feared the worst when he saw Estelle's grave condition earlier that day. He felt helpless as to how to assist her. He wasted no time, but went quickly over to the monastery to discuss her condition with Padre Pio. He asked Padre Pio for permission to touch the wound in his side. He explained that he wanted to touch Estelle with the same hand that had touched his stigmata. Padre Pio said that he would permit it. Without telling Estelle or her mother, he had come back immediately from the monastery and placed his hand on Estelle, the hand that had just touched Padre Pio's side wound. The doctor as well as Estelle and her mother were convinced that Estelle's sudden recovery was a direct result of that touch.

———————

Maria Ugliano and her husband Francesco were elated when they learned that they were going to be parents. Tragically, their baby daughter died shortly after birth. Maria was inconsolable. She was in a constant state of tears and was not able to cope with the sadness of losing her baby. She sank into a deep depression. When she learned about Padre Pio, she decided to visit San Giovanni Rotondo. She attended Padre Pio's Mass and made her confession to him. After spending three days near the monastery of Our Lady of Grace, she felt that she had received the strength to go on living. She and Francesco put themselves under Padre Pio's protection and asked him to accept them as his spiritual children.

In March 1957, Maria became pregnant once again. She and Francesco decided that the new baby would be named either Pia or Pio. When Padre Pio was told that Maria's baby was going to be delivered at the Home for the

Relief of Suffering, he said that it was a good decision. As time passed, Maria became more and more anxious. She hoped and prayed for a healthy baby.

Maria, Francesco, and Maria's mother left their home in Cava dei Tirreni when it was close to the time for the baby to be born. When they arrived in San Giovanni Rotondo, Maria was admitted to the Home for the Relief of Suffering. Francesco went to Our Lady of Grace monastery and told Padre Pio that Maria was in the hospital and asked him to keep her in his prayers. Padre Pio told Francesco that everything was going to be fine.

The next evening, to everyone's great joy, a healthy baby boy was born. Soon afterwards, Maria suffered a very serious hemorrhage. The doctors tried every means at their disposal but could not arrest it. Maria's condition deteriorated quickly. Sister Laura, the nursing nun who was attending Maria, was so worried that she asked the hospital chaplain to give Maria the Last Rites.

Dr. Greco, the attending physician, informed Francesco about Maria's critical condition. "The baby is doing well," the doctor said to Francesco, "but your wife is not. She is in a semiconscious state and in need of a blood transfusion. We have not been able to stop the hemorrhaging. We want you to understand that it is very serious." "But I just went to the monastery and talked to Padre Pio about Maria," Francesco replied. "He told me that she would be fine." Dr. Greco had full confidence in Padre Pio. "If Padre Pio told you that she would be fine, then you have nothing at all to worry about," the doctor said to Francesco.

Francesco then looked at the crucifix that was hanging on the wall in the hospital. With tears in his eyes he prayed, "Dear God, Thy will be done. Remember that Padre Pio told me just today that all would be well. Dear God, promises must be kept. Please save Maria!"

Shortly after that, Maria's condition began to improve. The crisis passed and Maria made a full recovery. Francesco went back to the monastery to thank Padre Pio. Padre Pio took Francesco's hand in his own, blessed him and gave him words of encouragement. Before they parted, he said to Francesco, "Son, always be good and always do good."

———

Giuseppe Scatigna of Palermo, Sicily discovered a lump near his abdomen that grew increasingly painful as time went by. Giuseppe's doctor believed that it was an impacted gland. He treated it with cortisone injections, topical medications, salves and compresses. However, the swelling soon increased and the area became even more painful.

In October 1968, further tests revealed that Giuseppe did not have an impacted gland but rather a very large tumor that was malignant. Giuseppe had a deadly form of cancer called metastatic melanoma. He had surgery, but unfortunately the surgery was not successful. The cancer was in the last stages. The family received the grim news from the doctor that there was no hope of recovery. Giuseppe's wife suggested that they take a trip to San Giovanni Rotondo to pray at Padre Pio's tomb for a miracle.

In San Giovanni Rotondo, Giuseppe became so ill that he was admitted to the Home for the Relief of Suffering. Dr. De Luca examined him and ordered a full battery of tests. When Dr. De Luca saw the test results, he determined that there was nothing more that could be done for Giuseppe other than to try to ease his pain and keep him as comfortable as possible. It was out of the goodness of the doctor's heart that Giuseppe was allowed to stay on at the Home for the Relief of Suffering. Usually, those with a terminal condition were sent home and put on hospice care.

Giuseppe's wife was so distraught that she cried constantly. She was either at the monastery, praying at Padre Pio's tomb, or sitting at Giuseppe's bedside at the hospital. One afternoon when she was praying at the tomb of Padre Pio, Giuseppe had a vivid dream. In his dream, he saw Padre Pio attempting to lift up a huge bolder, but it proved to be impossible. When he woke up, he thought long and hard about the meaning of the dream. He believed that it meant that he was in an "impossible" situation. He needed to pray for a miracle because it was apparent that only a miracle could save him.

One day, Giuseppe's wife saw Father Carmelo, the superior of Our Lady of Grace monastery, and told him about Giuseppe's desperate condition. Father Carmelo's heart was very touched. He felt so sorry for Giuseppe that he did what he normally would not do. He went upstairs to Padre Pio's cell and took a relic from his room. It was a piece of cloth which Padre Pio had used to cover his stigmata. "I want you to know that it is strictly forbidden for me to take this relic out of Padre Pio's cell," Father Carmelo said to

Giuseppe's wife. "You must not tell anyone that I have given this to you. Lay it on your husband's body where the cancer is. We will continue to pray to Padre Pio." Giuseppe's wife returned to the hospital and laid the relic on Giuseppe's incision.

Dr. De Luca believed that Giuseppe would not live more than two or three days at the most. Even so, more tests were ordered. When Dr. De Luca looked at the results of the tests, he saw that everything was normal. He couldn't understand what had happened. He went to Giuseppe's room and examined him. He asked him how he felt. Giuseppe said that his strength had suddenly returned and that he felt fine. There was absolutely no explanation for it. Dr. De Luca then asked Giuseppe if he thought he was strong enough to get out of bed. Giuseppe was able to get out of bed easily and to walk about with no trouble at all. His healing was instantaneous and permanent.

Upon being released from the hospital, the first thing that Giuseppe did was to go to the monastery to thank Father Carmelo. Father Carmelo told him that he had received a true miracle from Padre Pio. Giuseppe returned to his home in Palermo and to his work on the farm. It was hard and taxing labor but Giuseppe was able to do it without any problem. He praised God for the miracle he had received through the intercession of Padre Pio and he enjoyed good health from that time forward.

————

The night before Marita Leonor was scheduled for cancer surgery, she had a remarkable dream. In her dream, she was with the Virgin Mary. The Virgin Mary told Marita that there was a saintly priest named Padre Pio who was a healer. "This is his hospital," the Virgin said. She then showed Marita a very large and attractive hospital. With that, the dream ended. Marita often thought about the unusual dream and pondered the meaning.

After Marita had her surgery, she was scheduled to undergo chemotherapy treatments. She decided to go on a pilgrimage with her mother before the treatments began. On the tour bus, the pilgrims were shown a number of spiritual videos. One of the videos was a documentary of Padre Pio. Among other facts about Padre Pio's life and ministry, the video showed the hospital he had built, the Home for the Relief of Suffering. It looked exactly like the beautiful hospital that Marita had seen in her dream. Marita completed her chemotherapy treatments and her health continued to improve.

May the Home for the Relief of Suffering grow. May it heal bodies and sanctify souls. For those who collaborate, may the good Lord reward them a hundred times over in this life and with eternal life in the next.

- St. Pio of Pietrelcina

The Home for the Relief of Suffering depends on the financial support of generous people in order to continue its mission to serve the sick. The address is:

Home for the Relief of Suffering

71013 San Giovanni Rotondo Foggia (Italy)

Padre Pio had a human aspect. He appears like others in the civilian registers. He is a fellow countryman and a contemporary of our own, born into a certain family, into a certain society, which gives him an identity card like any other citizen. But on the other hand, he appears as one destined to serve a divine purpose, sent as it was, to be a lightning conductor to protect us, as one who is merely lent to us here below to attend to the matter of our salvation.

- Ferdinando Gambardella

CHAPTER 7

Padre Pio and his Gift of Bilocation

*B*ilocation is the phenomenon in which a person is in one place at a given moment and is in another place at the same time. Although bilocation is indeed rare, instances of it in the lives of the saints are well-documented. Nevertheless, it remains a mystery that cannot be fully explained, and in many ways it seems to be beyond the limits of human understanding.

There is little doubt that Padre Pio had the extraordinary gift of bilocation. During his lifetime, although he remained inside the monastery of Our Lady of Grace in San Giovanni Rotondo, he was observed at times, in many different parts of the world. He was reportedly seen at the canonization of St. Thérèse of Lisieux in Rome in 1925 as well as at the canonization of St. John Bosco in 1934. He also hinted that he sometimes went in spirit to the Holy House of Loreto, one of the most revered Marian shrines in the world. The

Capuchins who lived with Padre Pio often wanted to question him about his gift of bilocation, but were reticent to bring up the subject.

Although Padre Pio was never known to speak at length about bilocation, from time to time he made brief comments about it. One time, the Capuchins were talking about St. Anthony of Padua's ability to bilocate. One of the Capuchins said that he wondered if a person who bilocated actually knew that he was doing so. "Of course the person knows," Padre Pio replied. "He might not know if it is his body or if it is his soul that is bilocating, but he is very conscious of what is happening and he knows where he is going."

In 1931, Father Agostino presided at a ceremony for religious profession at a Carmelite convent in Florence. One of the nuns who lived at the convent told Father Agostino that Padre Pio had appeared to her in bilocation. Father Agostino, who was very close to Padre Pio, decided to ask him about it. "Do you sometimes take short trips to Florence?" he asked. "Sometimes I do," Padre Pio replied. The nun also told Father Agostino that she begged Padre Pio to make a visitation to one of the other Sisters in the convent, Sister Beniamina. "No, I cannot visit her," Padre Pio replied. "I do not have God's permission." When Father Agostino asked Padre Pio if he had made such a statement to the nun, he admitted that he had.

Father Eusebio Notte was Padre Pio's personal assistant for five years. Father Eusebio had an outgoing and engaging personality and a good sense of humor. When Padre Pio was feeling unhappy or ill, Father Eusebio was almost always able to cheer him up and bring a smile to his face. He always seemed to know just the right words to say. The other Capuchins marveled at the wonderful rapport that Father Eusebio had with Padre Pio.

In the evenings, when Father Eusebio helped Padre Pio get ready for bed, he would sometimes tease him by saying, "bon voyage." He was referring to Padre Pio's reported "night time travels" through bilocation. On one occasion, when Father Eusebio was biding Padre Pio goodnight, he said to him, "I would like you to take me with you tonight. I will fasten my belt to yours and we will fly together." "But what if your belt becomes loosened when we are up in the air?" Padre Pio asked. Padre Eusebio then smiled at him and said, "Well, perhaps it is better for me to stay in the monastery tonight."

Padre Pio appeared in bilocation to his personal physician, Dr. Andrea Cardone of Pietrelcina, on several occasions. Dr. Cardone left a written testimony regarding the details. One of the visitations occurred on September 23, 1968 at six o'clock in the morning. Padre Pio had passed away approximately four hours before.

Padre Pio once told Father Alessio Parente, "I only know one thing, I go wherever God sends me." On another occasion, he said to Father Pellegrino Funicelli, "All I can tell you is that I always try to remain attached to the thread of God's will." Through the gift of bilocation, Padre Pio was able to visit many of his spiritual children who were in great need of his help. He comforted those who were bereaved, came to the rescue of those in danger, and assisted the dying. It was part of his mission to souls. He truly remained conformed to the thread of God's will.

———

Padre Pio was a seventeen-year-old Capuchin student residing at the monastery of St. Francis of Assisi at Sant'Elia a Pianisi when he had his first experience of bilocation. It happened on the evening of January 18, 1905. He was praying in the choir loft of the monastery church at eleven o'clock in the evening with a fellow Capuchin, Brother Anastasio. Suddenly, Brother Pio found himself in a large and beautiful estate in a far away place. There, he ministered to a man who was dying. At the same time, a baby girl had just been born.

The Virgin Mary then spoke to Brother Pio and said, "I entrust this child to your care. She is a precious jewel. I want you to polish her and make her as brilliant as possible because one day I want to adorn myself with her." "But how can I do that?" Brother Pio answered. "I am a simple Capuchin Brother. My future is uncertain. I do not even know if I will be ordained. And besides, how could I take care of a child?" "You will see," the Virgin replied. "She will come to you. You will meet her at St. Peter's Basilica in Rome." The Virgin then vanished and Brother Pio found himself once again seated beside Brother Anastasio in the church.

Brother Pio knew that he had not fallen asleep in the monastery chapel and dreamed about the incident that had just occurred. He also knew that the experience had not been a product of his imagination. Nor was it an hallucination. But as to what had really happened, he did not know. The experience was so unusual that he decided to write down all of the details. He gave his written testimony to Father Agostino.

As it turned out, the beautiful estate that Brother Pio suddenly found himself in was the home of Giovanni Rizzani. It was located about three hundred and fifty miles away in the city of Udine, in northern Italy. Giovanni had been suffering for many months from a terminal illness. The night of Brother Pio's visitation, Giovanni was on his death bed.

During Giovanni's illness, he had informed his wife Leonilde that he did not want a priest to come to visit him. Giovanni had a great hostility toward religion. His friends kept watch to make sure that no members of the clergy approached the house.

Leonilde Rizzani was a fervent Catholic. Her greatest desire was that her husband make peace with God before his death. She prayed to God and asked him to change her husband's heart. When Giovanni seemed to be near the end, Leonilde begged the Lord for her husband's salvation. As she was praying, she suddenly saw a young Capuchin monk. She could not understand what was happening because he appeared and then he seemed to disappear right before her eyes.

Leonilde, at that time was pregnant. In those anxious moments, she went into premature labor. Soon she gave birth to a baby girl. A friend of the family noticed that a Capuchin monk was standing in the darkness just outside of the Rizzani house. He insisted that the Capuchin be allowed inside. He knew that Giovanni had given specific orders against letting any clergy members in the house. However, it seemed only right to allow the Capuchin to come inside and baptize the newborn baby.

As soon as the Capuchin stepped inside the house, he went directly to Giovanni's room. No one tried to stop him. He spoke to Giovanni privately. Before the visit was over, Giovanni asked for forgiveness for his sins and made his peace with God. He died later that night.

After Giovanni passed away, Leonilde decided to move with her new baby, Giovanna, to Rome. In 1922, when Giovanna was a teenager, she visited St. Peter's Basilica in Rome. At the Basilica, Giovanna was hoping to have the opportunity to go to confession. She had been having many doubts about her faith and she felt that her spiritual life was in a precarious state because of it. She wanted to talk to a priest and ask for advice. However, St. Peter's was about to close so she realized that she would have to wait for another opportunity.

Giovanna was just about to exit the church when she saw a Capuchin priest standing near one of the confessionals. She asked him if he would hear her confession and he agreed to do so. The priest gave her excellent spiritual counsel regarding her doubts about the faith. After Giovanna left the confessional, she told the sacristan that she wanted to wait for the priest to come out so that she could ask him his name. Giovanna waited but the priest did not come out. Finally, the sacristan looked in the confessional and was surprised to find that it was empty.

The following year, Giovanna made a trip to San Giovanni Rotondo. She stood in a crowded corridor with many others who were waiting to greet Padre Pio. When he passed through the corridor, he saw Giovanna and said to her, "Daughter, I know you. On the very day that your father died, you were born." Giovanna did not know what to make of his words.

The next day, Giovanna returned to the church and was able to make her confession to Padre Pio. Lovingly, Padre Pio told her that he had been waiting for her for many years. Giovanna thought that he had mistaken her for someone else. Padre Pio went on to explain to her that he was the priest who had heard her confession the year before in St. Peter's Basilica. "You belong to me, daughter. You have been entrusted to me by the Madonna," he said. Giovanna was later able to read the statement that Padre Pio had written and had given to Father Agostino regarding his experience of bilocation on January 18, 1905, her birthday. Giovanna noted that everything in the written statement was accurate according to her family history.

Padre Pio told Giovanna that he wanted her to visit San Giovanni Rotondo often. Through the years she was able to attend Padre Pio's Mass on many occasions and to make her confession to him. He encouraged her to enroll in the Third Order of St. Francis and she did so. He truly took care of her soul.

A short time before Padre Pio's death, Giovanna felt in her heart that he was calling her to come to San Giovanni Rotondo. Just four days before he passed away, she was able to talk with him. "You will not see me again," he said to her. She then understood that it was to be their last visit. Giovanna knew that for many years, she had been spiritually guided by a saint. She had done nothing to deserve such a grace and she would be forever grateful. "I will be able to help you much more when I am in heaven," he frequently repeated to his spiritual children.

———

In 1905, Father Benedetto Nardella was Padre Pio's professor of philosophy at the Capuchin monastery in San Marco La Catola. At that time, Padre Pio was a student in formation for the priesthood. Father Benedetto was a popular and gifted teacher as well as an author, theologian, and preacher. His preaching ability was so outstanding that he was in great demand in many parts of Italy. He was also an extraordinary spiritual director. He was eventually elected Minister Provincial of the Capuchin Order.

Father Benedetto was to become Padre Pio's first spiritual director. He accompanied Padre Pio step by step on his spiritual journey and helped him in incalculable ways. Padre Pio often said that Father Benedetto understood his soul like no other. He considered Father Benedetto to be his "true teacher" in the ways of the spirit.

After Padre Pio was ordained to the priesthood, he too became a spiritual director to many who were seeking a closer union with the Lord. Whenever he was praised for his ability to direct souls, he referred all the credit to Father Benedetto. He used to tell people that he had received his training from Father Benedetto.

In 1922, Padre Pio's fame as the "priest with the stigmata" was spreading rapidly. That year, many severe restrictions were placed on his ministry by the Holy Office in Rome. One directive called for the dismissal of Father Benedetto as his spiritual director. No clear explanation was ever given as to the reason for the decision. The two Capuchins were ordered to cease all communication with each other.

Father Benedetto had been Padre Pio's spiritual director for twelve years. The news was a crushing blow to both priests but especially to Padre Pio, who depended on Father Benedetto's excellent spiritual counsel. Nevertheless, the two priests obeyed the directive without a complaint.

In the years that followed, whenever Father Benedetto passed through San Giovanni Rotondo, he would mentally send Padre Pio his blessing. Always obedient to the voice of the Church, he made no attempt to visit him.

Father Benedetto was living at the Capuchin monastery in San Severo in 1942 when he became gravely ill. Father Aurelio, who was the superior of the monastery at the time, stayed at his bedside during what proved to be his final illness. He asked Father Benedetto if he would like him to send for Padre Pio. Under the circumstances, it could be easily arranged. It had been twenty years since Father Benedetto and Padre Pio had last seen each other. "There is no need to send for Padre Pio," Father Benedetto replied. "He is right here beside me." Shortly after saying that, Father Benedetto passed away.

———

In 1928, Alberto D'Apolito (see Chapter 4) was a student in the Capuchin seminary, taking the required courses in preparation for ordination to the priesthood. During a few days of vacation time, he had the chance to visit Padre Pio in San Giovanni Rotondo. One day, Alberto noticed Padre Pio staring out the monastery window at a mountain in the distance. He appeared to be deep in thought. Alberto greeted Padre Pio, but there was no response. When Alberto drew closer, he realized that Padre Pio was not even aware of his presence. Alberto tried to kiss Padre Pio's hand but he noticed that it was completely rigid. He heard Padre Pio say, *Ego te absolvo a peccatis tuis.* Padre Pio was pronouncing the words of absolution, just as he did when he was hearing someone's confession.

Alberto ran to get the superior of the monastery, Father Tommaso. Father Tommaso rushed to the window where Padre Pio was standing. Padre Pio was still in the process of repeating the words of absolution when Father Tommaso approached him. Suddenly, Padre Pio shook himself, as though he was waking up from a deep sleep. He looked at Alberto and Father Tommaso and greeted them. "Oh, I was not aware that you were standing here beside me," Padre Pio said. "I was looking out the window at the mountains."

A short time later, a telegram arrived for Father Tommaso from the city of Turin. It was from the relative of a man who had just passed away. The relative sent the telegram in order to thank Father Tommaso for allowing Padre Pio to leave the monastery and assist the dying man. It confirmed to Father Tommaso and Alberto what they had already suspected. Padre Pio had gone in bilocation to hear the man's confession and to assist him in his last moments.

Maria Pompilio, who was one of Padre Pio's faithful spiritual daughters, worked as a school teacher in San Giovanni Rotondo. She attended Padre Pio's Mass every morning and went to confession to him regularly. Through the years, she had received many graces through Padre Pio's intercession.

Once, on Christmas Eve, Padre Pio had gone to the sacristy of the church about 8:00 p.m. to hear the men's confessions. It happened to be a very cold night. Because there was no heating in the monastery at that time, a stove had been placed in the sacristy to take the chill off.

While Padre Pio was hearing the men's confessions, Maria Pompilio and several other women stayed in the church to pray. After the confessions were over, Maria and her companions went into the sacristy to greet Padre Pio and to kiss his hand. Maria noticed that Padre Pio's hand was ice cold. Padre Pio greeted his spiritual daughters and said to them, "May the Child Jesus make you feel his mercy and his tender love." "It is so cold tonight, Padre Pio," one of his spiritual daughters said. "Please speak to us for a while. Tell us more about the Infant Jesus and fill us with the warmth of his love."

Padre Pio then took his spiritual daughters to the visitors' room in the monastery. There was a long table in the room with enough chairs for everyone to be seated comfortably. Padre Pio spoke about the Christmas Mysteries and said, "Daughters, let us meditate on the words from the gospel of John. John, the beloved disciple said, *And the Word was made flesh and dwelt among us.*" Tears filled Padre Pio's eyes as he quoted the words from scripture. He paused for a moment to dry his eyes and then continued. He reflected on the privations of Jesus' birth and infancy. He spoke of how Jesus was born in the winter, the coldest season of the year, in the depth of the night. There among the animals, he was laid in the manger. Mary and Joseph attended him lovingly while the angels in heaven rejoiced.

Suddenly Padre Pio closed his eyes and became silent. "Padre Pio has fallen asleep," one of the women whispered. "He heard confessions all day today and he is exhausted. Let's be very quiet and use the time to pray until he wakes up." "I do not think he is asleep," one of the other women said. "This is Christmas Eve. I believe that Padre Pio is in deep communion with Jesus at this very moment. It is truly a privilege for us to be sitting here with him."

After about thirty minutes, Padre Pio opened his eyes. One of his spiritual daughters then said to him, "Padre Pio, you were silent for a long time. Since it is Christmas Eve, we were wondering if you were with the Baby Jesus?" Padre Pio made no reply. Another said, "Padre Pio, please tell us what you experienced as you sat with your eyes closed." "If you promise not to say a word about it until after my death, I will tell you," Padre Pio replied. "We give you our word that we will tell no one," the women said in unison.

Padre Pio then said to the women, "The Lord permitted me to wish a happy Christmas to my brother Michael who is in America and also to my sister, Sister Pia, in her convent in Rome. Then Jesus showed me all of my spiritual children who have passed on to eternal life and I saw their dwelling places in heaven." The women were deeply inspired by his words.

Before long, it was time for Padre Pio to prepare for the celebration of the Christmas Midnight Mass. Softly glowing candles illuminated the little 16th century church of Our Lady of Grace. When the Mass began, Padre Pio, who held a small statue of the baby Jesus in his arms, processed solemnly down the isle toward the Christmas crib. Together with the choir, the Capuchins and the entire congregation sang Christmas carols and hymns of praise to God. All hearts seemed to glow with the fire of God's love.

After the midnight Mass, before retiring to his cell, Padre Pio spoke to his spiritual daughters for the last time that evening and said, "Tonight heaven opened and many graces came down into your souls." Truly, they had all been blessed.

———

Father Carmelo Durante of Sessano used to go to Padre Pio's cell in the evening to say goodnight to him. One time, as he bid Padre Pio goodnight, Padre Pio said to him, "I am in a hurry because I must make a long journey tonight." "Where are you going?" Father Carmelo asked. Padre Pio made no reply. There was a moment of silence and then Padre Pio added, "To make this journey, I do not need the permission of my superior." At the time, Father Carmelo was the superior of Our Lady of Grace monastery. So it was that Padre Pio, with a bit of humor, hinted to Father Carmelo that he was going to visit someone through bilocation. He would say no more.

Once, in the refectory where the Capuchins took their meals, Father Carmelo was speaking to his confreres about the marvels of air travel. "Do you know that a nonstop flight from Rome to New York takes less than twelve hours?" Father Carmelo said. The information seemed incredible to all of the Capuchins. But Padre Pio was not impressed. "That is a long time!" Padre Pio remarked. "It only takes a second when I travel!" he added.

In 1954, Father Carmelo was making a detailed study of Padre Pio's first years in San Giovanni Rotondo. In order to gather information, he organized some meetings with Padre Pio's spiritual children who had been with him from the beginning. He met with Rachele Russo, the Ventrella sisters, the Pompilio sisters, Filomena Fini, Rosinella Gisolfi, Nina Campanile and others.

During the first meeting, there were ten people in attendance. While the meeting was in progress, Rosinella Gisolfi whispered that she could see Padre Pio in the room. Rosinella, who had received spiritual direction from Padre Pio through the years, was a very devout woman. Father Carmelo was certain that she was telling the truth. He had no reason to doubt it. However, he wanted confirmation regarding Rosinella's claim.

Father Carmelo did not want to ask Padre Pio directly about the bilocation incident. When he returned to the monastery, he asked the Capuchins about Padre Pio's activities that evening. They told him that Padre Pio had conducted the Benediction service in the church just like always and that he had spoken to some of the visitors. After that, he went to bed.

At Father Carmelo's second meeting with Padre Pio's spiritual children, Rosinella saw Padre Pio once again. Father Carmelo decided to speak to Padre Pio about it. One day he gathered up his courage and said to Padre Pio, "Rosinella said that you . . . " and then he trailed off. He lost his nerve midway through the sentence. "What did Rosinella say?" asked Padre Pio. With a great effort, Father Carmelo was finally able to blurt out the words, "Rosinella said that you are present at our meetings through bilocation." "Well, don't you want me to come to those meetings?" Padre Pio asked. As usual, his words were evasive.

Rosinella told Father Carmelo that Padre Pio was present at their third meeting. As time passed, speaking to Padre Pio about bilocation became easier. When Father Carmelo questioned Padre Pio about being present at their third meeting, he confirmed that it was true. "Yes, of course I was at the meeting," Padre Pio exclaimed. Several weeks later Padre Pio said to Father Carmelo, "You never ask me anymore if I attend your meetings. Don't you want to know?" "The reason that I don't ask is because I am now convinced that you are always there," Father Carmelo replied. "Yes, it is true," Padre Pio said. "I accompany you always and everywhere."

Pope Pius X was a man who possessed countless saintly virtues - apostolic zeal, deep humility, piety, simplicity, and more. He has often been called "The Pope of the Eucharist." He advised all to receive Holy Communion frequently and if possible daily. He used to say, "Holy Communion is the shortest and safest way to heaven."

Pope Pius X was distinguished by his extraordinary charity, especially his habitual generosity to the poor. At his own expense, he filled the Vatican with refugees from the devastating earthquake of 1908 in Messina, Sicily. His decision to help the displaced people came long before the Italian government had decided on an action plan.

Pope Pius X, who had a lifelong devotion to the Virgin Mary, became ill on the Feast of the Assumption of Mary (August 15) in 1914. He died five days later. The world mourned the death of the gentle and humble prelate who had remained a country priest at heart throughout his long life. His last will and testament gave a remarkable insight into his character. He said, "I was born poor, I lived poor, I want to die poor."

Pope Pius X was buried in a simple and unadorned tomb in a crypt below St. Peter's Basilica in Rome. Shortly after his death, the faithful began to make pilgrimages to his tomb. Accounts of miraculous favors and cures were soon reported. Healings and miracles had been reported during his lifetime as well. On May 29, 1954, Pius X was canonized by Pope Pius XII.

Padre Pio always had a great love for Pope Pius X. He spoke of him often and with profound reverence. It was common knowledge that Padre Pio did not leave the monastery of Our Lady of Grace in San Giovanni Rotondo. However, on a number of occasions, people reported that they saw Padre Pio praying at the tomb of Pope Pius X in Rome. Pope Pius XI had heard the reports on more than one occasion and did not know what to make of them. He decided to ask the saintly priest, Father Luigi Orione, for his opinion on the matter.

Father Orione (who was canonized in 2004 by Pope John Paul II) was held in great esteem by Pope Pius XI. Members of the clergy as well as people from all walks of life were aware of his great spiritual stature. One day Pope Pius XI asked Father Orione if he believed that Padre Pio came in spirit to pray at the tomb of Pope Pius X. "It is true what the people have said," Father Orione replied. "Padre Pio does indeed visit the tomb of Pope Pius X." "I trust your word," the pope replied. "If you say it is true, I also believe."

———————

Brother Costantino was a lay brother who lived at the monastery of Our Lady of Grace in San Giovanni Rotondo. Padre Pio admired him for his Franciscan humility and simplicity and for his strong faith. Every day Brother Costantino went to town to collect donations for the monastery. Many times, people asked him to carry a message to Padre Pio and he was always glad to do so. By the same token, when he returned to town, he was usually able to bring a reply from Padre Pio.

In 1958, Brother Costantino became ill and was admitted to the Home for the Relief of Suffering. He had just recently celebrated fifty years of religious profession. Padre Pio had presided at the ceremony in which Brother Costantino renewed his vows to the religious life.

One day, a man who had visited Brother Costantino at the hospital spoke to Padre Pio and said, "I think Brother Costantino would be very pleased if you would go to the hospital today and visit him. It would mean so much to him." Padre Pio told the man that he had already been to the hospital to visit Brother Costantino.

Father Giovanni, one of the Capuchins, happened to be standing nearby and overheard the conversation between the man and Padre Pio. He was certain that Padre Pio had not been over to the hospital that day to pay a visit to Brother Costantino. Because of Padre Pio's popularity, it was an "event" whenever he left the monastery. Everybody seemed to know about it.

Father Giovanni went to the Home for the Relief of Suffering and spoke to Brother Costantino. "Has Padre Pio been here to visit you since your hospitalization?" he asked. "Oh, yes," Brother Costantino replied. "He comes two or three times every day to see me. It is a great blessing to have him at my bedside. He gives me resignation." Padre Pio loved Brother Costantino very much. Through bilocation, he was able to console his Capuchin Brother and to help him prepare for death.

––––––––

In 1966, Father Jean Derobert made a trip to San Giovanni Rotondo in order to see Padre Pio. Padre Pio told Father Derobert that he wanted him to start a prayer group in Paris. At that time, Father Derobert was the chaplain of a college that was located on the outskirts of Paris. He was very apprehensive about the idea of starting a prayer group. For one thing, he did not know many people in Paris. Without an ample number of contacts, he did not see how he would be able to interest people in the idea. Just the thought of organizing a prayer group filled him with fear.

Padre Pio, however, was not the least bit dismayed at Father Derobert's concerns. He simply smiled at him and said, "I will help you." When Father Derobert returned to France, he told a friend about his conversation with Padre Pio. His friend was excited at the prospect of having a prayer group in Paris. "Padre Pio has sent me here to help you," the friend replied. "I feel certain of it." Father Derobert could not have been more surprised.

Father Derobert and his friend soon found a beautiful chapel in Paris where they received permission to hold monthly prayer meetings. From the very beginning, a number of people showed great interest and attended regularly. Everything was moving forward in a wonderful way.

A year later, Father Derobert returned to San Giovanni Rotondo. As soon as Padre Pio saw him, he wanted news about the prayer group. He listened with great interest as Father Derobert gave him a full report. Padre Pio then said, "I know the group well. There are some very beautiful souls who attend. I go there often." He then proceeded to describe in detail, the lovely chapel where the group met each month. As a matter of fact, many of the members of the prayer group had told Father Derobert that they often felt Padre Pio's presence at their monthly meetings. Before Father Derobert returned to Paris, Padre Pio gave him some words of wisdom. "Do nothing but pray," he said.

Monsignor John Gannon was acquainted with a retired navy man who lived in Washington, D.C. The man had attempted suicide on two different occasions. Monsignor Gannon advised the man to pray to Padre Pio and to ask for his intercession. He gave the man a prayer card of Padre Pio. The man followed Monsignor Gannon's advice and frequently repeated the prayer to Padre Pio.

One night, the man went to a bar, and feeling a great sense of hopelessness and despair, he began to think once again about ending his life. There was a man at the bar with a beard who came over to him and said hello. "I know what you are planning to do tonight. Don't do it!" the man said emphatically. Monsignor Gannon's friend then asked the stranger for his name. He could not understand him completely but his name sounded something like "Pio." There was no suicide attempt that night, thanks be to God. The man was convinced that Padre Pio paid him a visit and interceded for him in his darkest hour.

Giuseppe Massa was studying theology in Rome in preparation for the priesthood when he became ill. His mother was very worried about his condition. One day his mother, who lived in San Giovanni Rotondo, spoke to Padre Pio about Giuseppe's illness and asked him for his prayers.

Giuseppe soon recovered and was able to continue his studies for the priesthood. It was a great day for the entire Massa family when Giuseppe was ordained a Salesian priest. On the occasion of his ordination, Padre Pio wrote him a personal note and said, "I pray that you will be a holy priest and a perfect victim." Father Giuseppe treasured the handwritten note from Padre Pio. Shortly after his ordination, Father Giuseppe became ill once again. He was finally diagnosed with a kidney disease and was told that he would have to have surgery.

The doctor spoke to Father Giuseppe's mother and told her that it was advisable that she travel to Rome and stand by at the hospital during the time of her son's surgery. Mrs. Massa knew that it would be very difficult for her to make the trip to Rome. Because she could not decide what to do, she went to the monastery and asked Padre Pio for his advice. "You already have five other children to care for. You should not make the trip to Rome," Padre Pio said. "But I think Father Giuseppe will want me to be there when he is having the operation. How will he manage without me?" Mrs. Massa replied. She then began to cry. Padre Pio felt sorry for Mrs. Massa. "If you don't think I should go to Rome to be with my son, then I want you to go in my place," Mrs. Massa said. "Oh, all right then," Padre Pio replied, "I will go."

After Father Giuseppe had his surgery, his health steadily improved. Later, he told his mother that while he was in the hospital, Padre Pio had come and had stood at his bedside. When Father Giuseppe had the opportunity, he traveled to San Giovanni Rotondo and thanked Padre Pio for the visitation he had made to him in his hour of need.

Father Giuseppe continued to gain strength. He would live for fifty more years. Dedicating his time and effort to the religious education of youth, he helped countless souls through his priestly ministry. He truly became the holy priest that Padre Pio prayed that he would be.

————————

Martha Gemsch (see Chapter 8) had been devoted to Padre Pio for many years. Martha had a sister named Lisa who was planning to make a trip to the missions. Lisa, who was an x-ray technician, had great compassion for others. She wanted to bring the technology of her profession to India as well as to other third world countries. She talked to Padre Pio about her plans and he advised her against it. However, she could not be swayed by his words and was determined to follow her heart. Before she made the trip, Padre Pio inquired about her and asked if she had left yet.

Lisa was in the city of Dar es Salaam on the coast of East Africa when she was involved in a terrible auto accident. She died in the hospital the day after the accident. The day that Lisa died was the first day that Padre Pio had resumed hearing confessions after a long absence due to illness. That day, Martha, Lisa's sister, was at the monastery of Our Lady of Grace. She noticed that Padre Pio didn't seem like himself. He was unusually quiet all through the day and seemed very unhappy.

According to Lisa's doctor, Lisa died peacefully and with a smile on her face, even though she died alone and without the support of family or friends. One of the nuns who worked at the hospital, spoke to Lisa's sister, Martha. The nun told her that Padre Pio had come in bilocation to the hospital. Padre Pio said to the nun, "I feel so sorry about what happened to Lisa, but I was here to assist her." Martha was greatly consoled to know that her sister was visited by Padre Pio at the time of her death.

———————

Twenty-year-old Tony Collette of Houston, Texas had a rare and incurable disease that affected his muscles and nervous system. He lived in a constant state of pain. He wore braces on his legs and had metal supports for his weak back. Even with crutches, it was very difficult for Tony to walk. He had several operations, but his condition did not improve. The doctor finally told Tony that nothing more could be done for him.

In 1973, Tony saw a Capuchin monk enter his room at St. Joseph's Hospital. He recognized him at once as Padre Pio. Tony had a great devotion to Padre Pio and had prayed to him many times through the years. Padre Pio smiled at Tony and said, "I want to help you. I will try to help you. Do not be afraid." At that moment, Tony felt a tremor course through his entire body. He felt the presence of God in the room. Padre Pio then disappeared. Tony suddenly realized that he was free of pain. Tony was permanently healed from his debilitating illness. His doctors, nurses, family, and friends were amazed at his instantaneous recovery. Seeing Padre Pio and being healed by him, was something that Tony had never imagined would happen. The experience changed my whole life," Tony stated.

———————

Giovanni Gigliozzi, was a famous journalist, radio broadcaster and writer who lived and worked in Rome. Giovanni had a great love for Padre Pio and Padre Pio in turn, had a great love for him. Giovanni's beautiful spiritual reflections and writings were presented in some of the earliest publications put out by Our Lady of Grace monastery in San Giovanni Rotondo. Giovanni always looked forward to attending Padre Pio's Mass and he did so whenever his schedule would allow him to.

For a long time, Giovanni had suffered from migraine headaches. On one occasion, shortly before he was scheduled to go on the air at his broadcast studio in Rome, he had a severe migraine headache. He knew from experience that the terrible headache would probably last for a long time. He told the director of the show that he would not be able to do the program that day. "But you have to do the program!" the director said. "We have no one who can substitute for you." The director led him to one of the offices that had a couch. He told him to lie down and rest and perhaps the headache would go away. Giovanni followed his advice. He stretched out on the couch, closed his eyes and tried to relax.

Lying on the office couch, Giovanni suddenly heard a strange sound; it sounded like the clicking of Rosary beads. Next, he heard footsteps. He opened his eyes and to his utter surprise, he saw Padre Pio standing beside the couch. He was staring intently at Giovanni. Giovanni was so startled and so frightened by the unexpected appearance of Padre Pio that he let out a scream. The thought occurred to Giovanni that perhaps he was about to die and that Padre Pio was there to usher him into the next world. Padre Pio smiled and put his hand on Giovanni's head in a blessing. Right after that, he disappeared. Giovanni then realized that his migraine headache had vanished. He was able to continue with the scheduled broadcast that day.

The next time Giovanni visited the monastery of Our Lady of Grace, Padre Pio greeted him and said, "By the way, how are those headaches doing?" "I am feeling very well now," Giovanni replied. "And I thank you for assisting me." Padre Pio then smiled at him and said, "My goodness, those hallucinations!" It was Padre Pio's way of confirming to Giovanni that he had come to his aide.

Though I was honored by his friendship for such a long time, I understood practically nothing about Padre Pio . . . And if I have not understood him, believe me, it is not all my fault. Padre Pio had a special talent for hiding himself. He was humble, but with cleverness, I dare say, with merriment. Although he had so many virtues, he never let them weigh on those who were around him.

- Giovanni Gigliozzi

Jesus, our dear Mother, my little angel, St. Joseph, and our father, St. Francis, are almost always with me.

- St. Pio of Pietrelcina

CHAPTER 8

Padre Pio's Love for the Angels

The word angel is derived from the ancient Greek word *aggelos* which means messenger. The angels are God's instruments or messengers whom he uses to communicate his will. References to the celestial or non-corporal beings better known as angels, are mentioned more than 100 times in the Old Testament and more than 150 times in the New Testament. From the first book of Genesis to the last book of Revelation, scriptures speak of the existence of angels.

In the book of Genesis, the three men who appear to Abraham are angels who have taken human form (Genesis 18:2). An angel of the Lord appeared to Moses (Exodus 3:2) in order to lead the Israelites from captivity in Egypt to the Promised Land. The birth of Jesus was foretold by angels (Luke 2:14). An angel ministered to Jesus when he was tempted in the desert (Matthew 4:11) and an angel comforted him in his Agony in the Garden (Luke 22:43). An angel rolled back the stone at the empty tomb of Jesus (Matthew 28:5) and the Resurrection of Jesus from the dead was announced by an angel. In the book of Acts, God sent an angel to free the Apostle Peter after he was jailed by King Herod (Acts 12:7).

Among the angels that are mentioned in Holy Scripture, St. Michael the Archangel is described as "one of the chief princes" and the leader of the heavenly hosts. His name means, "One who is like God." St. Michael has been honored and invoked as patron and protector of the Church since the time of the Apostles. The Greek Fathers of the Church placed St. Michael over all the other angels as "prince of the Seraphim."

In an address to American pilgrims on October 3, 1958, Pope Pius XII spoke eloquently of the holy angels and said, "The angels are glorious, pure and splendid. They have been given to us as companions along the way of life. They have the task of watching over you all, so that you do not stray away from Christ, your Lord."

Pope John Paul II emphasized the important role of angels when he gave six General Audiences in Rome from July 9 to August 20, 1986 entitled "Angels Participate in the History of Salvation." In his catechesis on the holy angels, Pope John Paul II expressed the hope that all people would come to the realization of the reality of angels. In January of 2009, Pope Benedict XVI stated, "In the face of the challenges of our times and the tribulations which every individual experiences in his life, it is salutary to recall the powerful help and solicitous guidance of the holy angels who work together for the benefit of us all."

Among the angelic beings, the role of the guardian angel is one of great importance. The Church teaches that the special work of the guardian angel is to guide an individual on his journey toward God and to protect him from harm during his earthly pilgrimage. The Church celebrates the feast of the Guardian Angels each year on October 2.

Padre Pio had an especially tender love and devotion for his guardian angel. From the time that he was five years old, he was able to see and converse with his guardian angel. In his childlike simplicity, he assumed that everyone had the same experience. Enjoying an intimate friendship with his angel, Padre Pio referred to him as the "companion of my childhood." The loving relationship continued throughout Padre Pio's life. For Padre Pio, his angel was his support, his protector, his teacher, his brother, and his friend. At times, Padre Pio's guardian angel acted as his secretary as well as his heavenly "postman" carrying messages to his spiritual children.

Padre Pio's guardian angel awakened him in the morning, and together they would join in prayer and praise to God. Padre Pio wrote to Father Agostino:

> Again at night when I close my eyes, the veil is lifted and I see Paradise open up before me; and gladdened by this vision I sleep with a smile of sweet beatitude on my lips and a perfectly tranquil countenance, waiting for the little companion of my childhood to come to waken me, so that we may sing together the morning praises to the Beloved of our hearts. *(Letters 1)*

When Padre Pio was a newly ordained priest, Father Agostino visited him periodically in Pietrelcina and also corresponded with him through letters. Padre Pio benefitted greatly from Father Agostino's wise counsel. It became obvious that the demons, who often tormented Padre Pio, were not pleased with the spiritual help that he was receiving from Father Agostino. They made many efforts to interfere. Often, Padre Pio would develop a violent headache when he started to answer one of Father Agostino's letters. The headache would be accompanied by a severe pain in his right arm which would make it impossible for him to hold a pen in his hand and write. In addition, some of the letters exchanged between Father Agostino and Padre Pio were obviously tampered with. Some were mysteriously marred with ink stains.

Padre Pio told Father Agostino about the trouble the demons were causing. He also explained the situation to the parish priest of Pietrelcina, Father Salvatore Pannullo. Father Pannullo asked Padre Pio to summon him the next time he received a letter from Father Agostino as he wanted to be present when the letter was opened. Padre Pio did as instructed.

The next time Padre Pio received a letter from Father Agostino, Father Pannullo was standing right beside him. Upon opening the letter, Padre Pio and Father Pannullo discovered that it was completely covered with ink. Father Pannullo then placed a crucifix on the letter which made it a little easier to read. Father Pannullo left a written testimony regarding the letter and said:

I, the undersigned, archpriest of Pietrelina, under holy oath, attest that the present letter, opened in my presence, arrived blotted out as it is, and was completely illegible. I put a crucifix on it, blessed it with holy water and recited holy exorcisms; I was able to read it as it is now. In fact, I called my niece, Grace Pannullo, a teacher. She read it in the presence of Padre Pio and myself, ignorant of what had happened before I called her.

On another occasion, a letter arrived for Padre Pio from Father Agostino which consisted of nothing more than a blank sheet of paper. Padre Pio did not need to ask Father Agostino if he had forgotten to compose a letter. He was perfectly aware that the devil had tampered with it.

In order to confound the devil, Father Agostino got in the habit of writing to Padre Pio in French. Padre Pio had never studied French but he was able to read the letters with ease. From time to time he would reply to Father Agostino in French. Father Agostino also wrote to him in Greek and once again, he had no difficulty understanding.

Father Pannullo was perplexed about the letters that Padre Pio was receiving from Father Agostino. He asked him how it was possible for him to read the letters. "You know, my guardian angel explains everything to me," Padre Pio replied. On rare occasions, Padre Pio was also heard conversing in languages he had never studied.

On September 20, 1912, Padre Pio wrote to Father Agostino and said:

> The heavenly beings continue to visit me and to give me a fore-taste of the rapture of the blessed. And while the mission of our guardian angels is a great one, my own angel's mission is certainly greater, since he has the additional task of teaching me other languages. *(Letters I)*

On one occasion, Father Agostino asked Padre Pio if Jesus often appeared to him. Padre Pio replied that Jesus frequently appeared to him and spoke to him. Sometimes he appeared with the visible marks of the crucifixion on his body. Padre Pio told Father Agostino that the Blessed Virgin Mary as well as his guardian angel also appeared to him.

In 1911, Padre Pio was sent to the Capuchin monastery of Venafro in the province of Isernia. Father Agostino was present in Venafro when Padre Pio went into a state of ecstasy. It was the first time that Father Agostino had ever seen him in a state of ecstatic prayer. He listened closely to the words Padre Pio spoke and realized that he was conversing with his guardian angel. While Father Agostino could see nothing, it was obvious to him that Padre Pio was able to see and communicate with angelic beings.

Padre Pio encouraged his spiritual daughter, Annita Rodote of Foggia, to have great devotion to her guardian angel. He wrote to her from Pietrelcina on July 15, 1915 and said:

> May your good guardian angel always watch over you; may he be your guide on the rugged path of life. May he always keep you in the grace of Jesus and sustain you with his hands so that you may not stumble on a stone. May he protect you under his wings from all the snares of the world, the devil and the flesh.
>
> Have great devotion, Annita, to this good angel; how consoling it is to know that near us is a spirit who, from the cradle to the tomb, does not leave us even for an instant, not even when we dare to sin. And this heavenly spirit guides and protects us like a friend, a brother. *(Letters III)*

On one occasion, when a man was making his confession to Padre Pio, it became apparent to him that Padre Pio was aware of his needs, even before he had a chance to verbalize them. "The angel told me about your problems," Padre Pio explained. "I suffered greatly to hear of them. I understand your moments of sadness and moral suffering. Always remember that you are in my heart just as I am in yours."

Padre Pio had a lifelong devotion to St. Michael the Archangel. He prayed to the Archangel daily. He had experienced the protection of St. Michael many times throughout his life. Every year, he would fast in order to prepare himself for St. Michael's feast day on September 29. When hearing confessions, Padre Pio frequently asked individuals to recite prayers in honor of St. Michael as their penance. He often urged people to visit Monte Sant' Angelo, the ancient shrine dedicated to St. Michael. It is one of the few sanctuaries in the world that is dedicated to an angel.

Among the many pilgrims that have traveled to the shrine of St. Michael the Archangel, there have been eight popes as well as many canonized saints including St. Francis of Assisi, St. Bernard of Clairvaux, St. Gerard Majella, St. Bridget of Sweden, St. Thomas Aquinas and more. Emperors, kings, and princes through the centuries have also knelt in prayer at the holy grotto. It is indeed providential that the shrine of St. Michael is located on Mount Gargano, just a short distance from San Giovanni Rotondo.

In the summer of 1917, as a young priest, Padre Pio went on pilgrimage to St. Michael's shrine accompanied by a number of Capuchin students. A cart and horse were provided by the father of one of the students. Padre Pio walked for part of the journey and also rode in the cart. The Capuchins prayed the Rosary and sang hymns to the Blessed Mother on the way. Upon arriving at the shrine, Padre Pio remained for a long time in prayer, kneeling at the foot of St. Michael's altar.

Raffaelina Cerase, a spiritual daughter of Padre Pio, once learned an important lesson regarding Padre Pio's trust in the holy angels. Raffaelina was a Third Order Franciscan who lived in the town of Foggia. When she wrote to Padre Pio, she sometimes included Mass offerings. Because she wanted to make sure that the letters arrived safely, she sent them by registered mail. Padre Pio felt that sending the letters in such a fashion showed a lack of trust and a lack of faith. He said to Raffaelina, "I think it best that you do not send your letters by registered mail. They have been put in very good hands." The "hands" he was speaking of were the hands of his guardian angel.

Father Alessio Parente was assigned to be the sacristan at Our Lady of Grace monastery from 1959 -1961. From 1965 -1968, he served as Padre Pio's personal assistant. Padre Pio was very appreciative of all that Father Alessio did to help him. He told one of his spiritual children that Father Alessio took care of him with great solicitude, like a "faithful puppy dog." Father Alessio was filled with joy when he learned what Padre Pio had said about him and treasured the words for the rest of his life.

One morning at the conclusion of the Mass, Father Alessio had a very unusual experience. He had just distributed Holy Communion at the altar rail and had taken the empty ciborium back to the altar to purify it. Father Alessio poured water in the ciborium to wash it and then dried it with a purificator. He was just about to put the lid on the ciborium when, out of the corner of his eye, he became aware of something moving. From his right side, he saw a host float down from mid-air into the ciborium. He instinctively looked around to see if someone was there beside him, but no one was. He was shocked by what he had witnessed and told Padre Pio about the incident. Padre Pio advised him to be more attentive and not to rush when he was distributing Holy Communion. Padre Pio added that an angel had put the consecrated host in Father Alessio's ciborium so as to keep it from falling on the floor.

Father Alessio used to assist Padre Pio when it was time for him to get into bed for the night. Afterward, he would wait in Padre Pio's cell for Father Pellegrino to come in for the night duty. Laying in bed, Padre Pio would always recite the Rosary. Frequently, Father Alessio heard Padre Pio interrupt the Rosary by saying such things as, "Tell her that I will ask Jesus." "Tell her that I will pray deeply about it." "Tell him that I will remember him at my Mass." It was only later that Father Alessio realized that Padre Pio was carrying on a conversation with the guardian angels of some of his spiritual children.

One afternoon, Padre Pio was sitting alone on the veranda, just outside his cell. He was praying the Rosary. Father Alessio felt it would be a good opportunity to go over some of the mail with Padre Pio. Many people wrote to Father Alessio and asked him to relay their individual messages to Padre Pio, seeking his counsel and advice. Father Alessio would always discuss the items with Padre Pio and then write back with Padre Pio's recommendations.

Father Alessio told Padre Pio about a woman who had just written with a question about her job. She had an opportunity to make a job change and she was hoping that Padre Pio might be able to advise her about it. When Father Alessio put the question to Padre Pio, he was surprised at his response. "I am very busy right now," Padre Pio replied. "I cannot answer your question at this time."

Father Alessio was confused. It was obvious to him that Padre Pio was not busy. He was sitting alone with his Rosary in his hand. He always had his Rosary in hand. Father Alessio remained silent but he continued to think about the irony of Padre Pio's remark. "There have been many guardian angels here today," Padre Pio explained to Father Alessio. "They were bringing me messages from my spiritual children. Did you see them?" Father Alessio told

Padre Pio that he had never seen a guardian angel in his life. He finally under-stood why Padre Pio had said that he was busy. He was busy communicating with that celestial world which very few mortals were privileged to glimpse.

Father Alessio knew that he was truly blessed to be able to assist Padre Pio on a daily basis. He was also on call through the night, because Padre Pio was often sick and needed help in the night hours. Father Alessio was not able to get sufficient sleep and frequently felt the physical and mental strain of the exhausting schedule.

Each morning, Father Alessio helped Padre Pio get ready for Mass. He would also help him up the altar steps and then remove his gloves before the Mass began. Afterward, he would rush to his room in order to catch a short nap. He was always so tired that he would usually fall asleep instantly. He had his alarm set so that he would be back in the church by the end of the Mass in order to help Padre Pio down the stairs of the altar. He would lead Padre Pio through the sacristy and then take him back to his cell.

Many times, Father Alessio was sleeping so deeply that he would not hear his alarm go off. At that point, he would hear someone knocking loudly at his door. When he answered the door, there was no one there. Mysteriously, the entire corridor would be empty. He would then realize that he had over-slept and rush down to the church. Padre Pio would be invariably giving the final blessing. Father Alessio would be just in time to assist Padre Pio down the altar steps. This same scenario happened every time that Father Alessio's alarm clock failed to wake him up.

Every day, when it was time for Padre Pio to hear confessions, Father Alessio would take Padre Pio's arm and walk with him to the confessional. Once Padre Pio was situated in the confessional, Father Alessio would rush back to his cell to take a quick nap. Each time his alarm clock failed to wake him up, he would have a most unusual experience. He would hear a dis-tinct voice saying to him, "Alessio, it is time to go to the church!" He would instantly wake up and hurry down to help Padre Pio out of the confessional. Sometimes he was a little late, but Padre Pio would always be there waiting for him. He would never attempt to walk through the crowded corridors by himself. Father Alessio was always there to protect him and to fend off the overly zealous devotees. Some carried scissors with them, and would like nothing more than to cut off a piece of Padre Pio's habit or cut a bit of his hair for a relic.

One day, Father Alessio was sitting by Padre Pio's side, thinking about his problem with oversleeping. He felt ashamed of himself for being so unreliable. He told Padre Pio that he could not understand why his alarm clock failed to wake him up. "You must buy yourself another alarm clock," Padre Pio said. "I am not going to continue to send my guardian angel to you each day to wake you up!" It was then that Father Alessio realized for the first time who had been knocking on his door and calling to him in his sleep.

On one occasion, Father Alessio heard heavenly music in the monastery of Our Lady of Grace. It sounded like a choir of beautiful voices singing together in perfect harmony. Some of the other Capuchins also heard it. They couldn't understand where the music was coming from and when they asked Padre Pio for an explanation, he told them that it was the voices of angels, taking souls from purgatory to Paradise. Evidently the Capuchins must have looked incredulous when they heard Padre Pio's explanation, for he then added, "Why should the music of angels surprise you?" When asked on another occasion if angels were present at the Mass, Padre Pio answered that the whole celestial court was present at every Mass.

Once, at the end of a very busy day, Padre Pio was assisted by Father Gabriel and Father Giambattista, who lent their arm to him and escorted him out of the chapel. Father Gabriel told Padre Pio that he should get more rest as he looked exhausted. "When you go to bed for the night, you should ask your guardian angel to minister to you," Father Gabriel said. "But I cannot ask that of him," Padre Pio replied. "As you may know, he has to travel." Father Gabriel, thinking that he had a good suggestion, then said, "Since your guardian angel has to travel about so much, could Father Giambattista and I lend you our guardian angels?" "No, never!" Padre Pio replied. "It does not work that way. A person can only be assisted by his own angel, not another's."

Father Dominic Meyer was serving at St. Felix Friary in Indiana when he was summoned to San Giovanni Rotondo. He served at Our Lady of Grace monastery from 1947 to 1953. He translated for the German and English visitors when they were speaking to Padre Pio. He also helped with the large volume of mail that came into the monastery and answered many of the letters of the German and English pilgrims.

One day, Father Dominic opened a letter from a woman who lived in the United States. She wanted to know if Padre Pio was able to see her guardian angel when she sent him with a message or was he only able to hear his voice. Father Dominic thought the woman's question was ridiculous. His voice was dripping with sarcasm when he read the letter regarding the guardian angel to Padre Pio. Padre Pio made Father Dominic understand in no uncertain terms that he was not pleased with his attitude. "Father Domenico," Padre Pio said firmly, "When that woman sends her guardian angel to me, I see the angel just like I see you!"

Although Father Dominic was initially skeptical about guardian angels, little by little Padre Pio taught him about the reality of the angelic realm. On one occasion, Father Dominic noticed that Padre Pio looked extremely tired. Padre Pio had an explanation for his fatigue. He told Father Dominic that the guardian angels had kept him up almost all night. Through contact with Padre Pio, Father Dominic eventually grew to have a strong belief in angels.

When Padre Pio died on September 23, 1968, several pilgrims who were in San Giovanni Rotondo reported to the Capuchins that they saw angels in the night sky. At the time of the sun's rising, the angels disappeared just as mysteriously as they had come. Knowing Padre Pio's lifelong devotion to the angels, one can hardly be surprised.

———

Father Agostino made a trip to Naples during the summer of 1912. On the return trip home, he reached the town of Benevento just after midnight. He continued on to Pietrelcina and arrived there about three o'clock in the morning. He decided to stop at Padre Pio's house. Upon arriving, he was surprised to find that the door was open. When he walked inside, he discovered that Padre Pio was in bed but he was not asleep. Father Agostino asked him why he had not locked the door for the night. "Aren't you afraid to leave the door unlocked?" he said. "No, not at all," Padre Pio replied. "I have the guardian angels of the house keeping watch through the night. There is no reason to fear."

———

Rosina Pannullo was a relative of the parish priest of Pietrelcina, Father Salvatore Pannullo. Rosina had heard that Padre Pio possessed remarkable powers of intuition and she wanted to see for herself if it was true. She told Padre Pio that she was going to go to his room and take one of his personal possessions. Understandably, Padre Pio was not at all pleased with Rosina's remark. "You will not be able to take anything from me," Padre Pio said. "There is an angel who stands guard at the door of my home. He will not let you pass."

Padre Pio told Father Pannullo about the incident with Rosina. "Rosina did not tell me what she planned to take from my room," Padre Pio said. "However, I know that she was going to try to take my breviary." When Father Pannullo questioned Rosina about it, she admitted that it was true. After speaking to Padre Pio, she decided not to carry out her plan.

Rosina's father, Alfonso, also hoped to verify for himself whether Padre Pio truly had the remarkable intuition that people often spoke about. He decided to test Padre Pio's abilities. On one occasion, Alfonso, had the audacity to say to Padre Pio, "I am going to enter your home and take something out of it." "That would not be a good idea!" Padre Pio replied. "Perhaps something would happen to you and you would not be able to carry out your plan." Alfonso paid no attention to the warning.

One day, Alfonso started to walk up the steps to Padre Pio's house, when he suddenly began to feel very strange. He was not able to walk any farther than the first step. His legs became completely immobile. He feared that he might be having a stroke. When he turned to go down the stairs, he had no trouble walking. The next time he saw Padre Pio, he told him about the sudden paralysis and asked him for an explanation. "Well, I have a very good guardian angel on watch at my door," Padre Pio said. "I am well protected!"

———————

Margharita, who lived in the town of Bari, visited San Giovanni Rotondo for the first time in 1948. She was very depressed because of the recent death of her father. Attending Padre Pio's Mass and making her confession to him lifted her out of her sadness. She decided to move to San Giovanni Rotondo permanently. She told Padre Pio about her decision but he made no reply.

Margharita had a very difficult time finding a place to live and finally had to settle for a tiny one room hut in the countryside. It was an isolated dwelling and had neither electricity nor running water. There was not a single neighbor nearby. Even though it was a far cry from what she had hoped for, she was grateful at least to have a roof over her head.

To Margharita's way of thinking, most of the people who moved to San Giovanni Rotondo seemed to have a much easier time than she did of finding accommodations and making ends meet. As far as Margharita was concerned, it was not fair. One day, without warning, Padre Pio suddenly said to her, "Well, did you come here for the good of your soul or to set yourself up in a comfortable life?" Margharita knew then that she needed to correct her attitude.

Margharita rose at 4:00 a.m. each morning in order to walk to the church of Our Lady of Grace to attend the morning Mass. In the winter time, the harsh winds and cold temperatures made the walking very difficult. In addition, making her way alone in the pitch darkness filled her with fear.

One morning on her way to Mass, Margharita heard a distinct voice which said, "One, two, one, two." The voice almost seemed to be measuring her footsteps. When she stopped, the voice would stop. When she walked, the voice would resume. In the confessional she spoke to Padre Pio about the unusual experience. "I am afraid for my sanity," Margharita said. "All the way to Mass I heard a voice which said - One, two, one, two. It makes no sense." "It is nothing to be worried about," Padre Pio replied. "It was the voice of your guardian angel. He was counting your footsteps to keep you company. He is letting you know that he is watching over you so that you will not be afraid anymore."

Margharita still had many challenges to face. Due to her uneasiness at living in such an isolated place, it was usually hard for her to get to sleep at night. One night she prayed to Padre Pio to take away her fear. The next morning when she woke up, she found a beautiful German Shepherd dog sitting on her front porch. When she started out for Mass that morning, the dog walked on the path just in front of her, as if leading the way. To her great surprise, when Mass was over, he walked home with her. That night he slept on her doorstep. He seemed to have made himself perfectly at home and his presence took away Margharita's anxieties. She could sleep soundly from then on, with no fear at all.

Assunta Lops grew up in San Giovanni Rotondo. When she was fifteen years old she joined several other ladies who had a small store in town and with them, she began to sew the woolen half-gloves that Padre Pio wore to cover his stigmata.

On a number of occasions, Assunta went in person to deliver the gloves to Padre Pio. Sometimes she kissed the stigmata on his hands when his hands were uncovered. Once, when she took some new pairs of gloves to Padre Pio, he said to her, "Don't touch my wounds. They are very painful today."

One day, Assunta went to the church and found Padre Pio there by himself. She heard talking but no one was there. She asked Padre Pio about it. "Who was talking to you, Padre Pio?" Assunta asked. "It was the angels," Padre Pio replied. "They keep me company and they sing."

In 1955, Cecil Humphrey-Smith of England, who was working as a chemist for the Heinz Company, was sent to the Po Valley in northern Italy where he did quality control work with the tomato crops in the area. Because Cecil had to work very long hours, he did not get sufficient sleep. One night, on the way home from work, he fell asleep at the wheel and had a terrible car accident. He was taken to the Municipal Hospital in Piacenza with a fractured skull, a broken vertebrae in his neck, and other broken bones.

The next day, Cecil's good friend, the Marquis Bernardo Patrizi, came to visit him in the hospital. Bernardo, who was a good friend of Padre Pio, sent his guardian angel to Padre Pio to tell him that Cecil was involved in a very serious car accident and needed prayer. Evidently, Bernardo did the right thing because the next time Bernardo went to San Giovanni Rotondo, Padre Pio confirmed that he had received the message.

Cecil soon returned to his wife and family in England but his health steadily declined. He had several bad falls which caused him further problems. He suffered from dizziness, fainting spells, and debilitating and agonizing headaches which made him ill and barely able to function. The headaches were like "red hot claws of steel" that moved from the top of his spine to his head with a terrible intensity. In order to bring Cecil relief, the doctor prescribed heavy pain killers which he soon became dependant on.

Seven years after Cecil's car accident, Bernardo traveled to Canterbury, England to pay him a visit. When he saw the pitiful condition Cecil was in, Bernardo invited him to accompany him to Italy so that he could be examined by several doctors there. Cecil accepted Bernardo's invitation. He saw several excellent doctors in Italy but to no avail.

While in Italy, Bernardo took Cecil to San Giovanni Rotondo to meet Padre Pio. On the day they arrived in San Giovanni Rotondo, Cecil was weak and ill. In the sacristy of the church of Our Lady of Grace, along with a number of other men, they waited for Padre Pio. When Padre Pio came into the sacristy, Bernardo told Cecil to kneel down and to kiss Padre Pio's hand. Bernardo introduced Padre Pio to Cecil by saying, "This is my good friend, Cecil. He is an Englishman. He was just ignorant enough to crash his car into a wall!" Padre Pio looked at Cecil and then tapped him on his head three times. He struck his head forcefully, right on the spot where the agonizing pain was localized. At Padre Pio's touch, the pain vanished. From that moment onward, Cecil never suffered from another pain in his head. Seven years of intense suffering, was gone in an instant.

When Bernardo telephoned Cecil's wife Alice in Canterbury and explained to her that Cecil had been healed, she was incredulous. She could hardly believe it. Bernardo spoke to Padre Pio and said, "From the time you touched Cecil on the head and blessed him, he has been relieved of his terrible headaches. Cecil's wife Alice cannot really grasp the fact that he has been healed. If you would be willing to send her a telegram, I think she would believe that Cecil is fine now." Padre Pio agreed to send a telegram.

Bernardo was one of the trustees of the funds for the Home for the Relief of Suffering. It was Bernardo who brought Barbara Ward to San Giovanni Rotondo to meet Padre Pio (see Chapter 5). Through Barbara's efforts, the hospital received the financial help it needed so that the construction work could be completed.

Bernardo and other collaborators of the hospital often gathered together with Padre Pio in the evenings to discuss important matters regarding the Home for the Relief of Suffering. Bernardo started taking Cecil with him to the informal gatherings. Cecil noticed that during the discussions regarding the hospital, while Padre Pio listened with attention to whatever was being said, he also prayed. It was the same when he was having a conversation with someone. Cecil became aware of the fact that Padre Pio prayed constantly. No matter what else he might be doing, he was able to keep his mind recollected in prayer.

Cecil began to travel once or twice a year to San Giovanni Rotondo in order to see Padre Pio. Once, when Cecil and Bernardo were talking to Padre Pio in his cell, Padre Pio took Cecil's hand in his own and held it all through the conversation. Padre Pio seemed to love their visits.

On one occasion, Padre Pio asked Cecil if he loved his mother. "Of course I love my dear mother," Cecil answered. "Doesn't everybody?" Cecil thought it was an odd question to be asked. Padre Pio asked him the same question on many occasions. Finally, it dawned on Cecil that Padre Pio was speaking, not of his earthly mother, but of his heavenly mother, the Madonna.

Through his friendship with Padre Pio, Cecil learned a lot about the angels. Once when Cecil was getting ready to leave the monastery, as he said goodbye to Padre Pio, he told him that he would write to him soon. "Son," Padre Pio said, "I have more letters than I can read. I am not able to keep up with my mail. Send your guardian angel to me instead." From that time forward, whenever Cecil needed Padre Pio's counsel, he sent his guardian angel to him with the message.

———

Once, a married couple had a young daughter who was very ill. She had a persistent high fever, and although measures were taken to reduce it, the fever would not break. The mother decided to send her guardian angel to Padre Pio, asking for his prayerful intercession. Almost immediately, there was a reduction in the fever. Right after that, the girl drifted off into a deep and peaceful sleep. When the woman told her husband what had happened, he told her that he too had been praying to his guardian angel, asking his angel to deliver a message to Padre Pio requesting prayer for their daughter.

The father decided to go to the monastery of Our Lady of Grace and thank Padre Pio personally for the recovery of their child. "Did you know that I sent my guardian angel to you?" the man asked Padre Pio. "Yes," Padre Pio answered. "I received the message. First, your guardian angel came to me and about three minutes later, your wife's angel came."

———

One evening, Capuchin Brother Bill Martin was standing with Padre Pio at his cell window. Many people had gathered below Padre Pio's window and were waving goodnight to him. Padre Pio gave his priestly blessing to the crowd just like he did every evening. After the blessing, Brother Bill noticed that Padre Pio became very still. He seemed to be staring intently at something in his cell. Brother Bill looked in the direction that Padre Pio was staring, but there was nothing there. Padre Pio also appeared to be listening with attention to something that was being said to him. Brother Bill could hear nothing. Finally, Padre Pio said to Brother Bill, "Where is Martha Gemsch tonight?" Martha Gemsch was one of Padre Pio's spiritual daughters who always joined the other pilgrims each evening in bidding Padre Pio goodnight. Bill did not know the whereabouts of Martha.

The next time Brother Bill saw Martha, he told her that Padre Pio had asked about her. Martha explained to Bill that she had taken a trip to Rome. While in Rome, she thought about Padre Pio and the blessing that he gave each night at his window. Since she could not be there, she sent her guardian angel in her place. Martha confirmed what Brother Bill had suspected all along. Padre Pio had been talking to Martha's guardian angel.

———

Carmela Marocchino, who was Mary Pyle's housekeeper, spent many years living happily in Mary's large home. Carmela was very close to Padre Pio. Sometimes when the weather was bad, Carmela would hesitate to walk to the monastery church. "Do not be afraid," Padre Pio would say to Carmela, "The angel of the Lord will be at your side."

On one occasion, Carmela felt deeply concerned about a particular problem in her life. She wanted to send her guardian angel to Padre Pio with a request for assistance but it was quite late at night. She didn't want to bother Padre Pio at such a late hour so she decided against it. The next time she saw

Padre Pio she explained why she had not sent her angel. Padre Pio told her that she could indeed send her angel to him at any time of the day or night. He was always happy to receive the message.

That God whom we desire to see and hold before us, is always ready to come to our assistance. Always faithful to his promises and seeing us fighting valiantly, he will send us his angels to sustain us in the trial.

- St. Pio of Pietrelcina

The angel of the Lord encamps around those who fear him, and he delivers them.

- *Psalm 34:7*

CHAPTER 9

Nicola Pazienza

Nicola Pazienza was a deeply religious man who was admired for his strong faith and outstanding moral character. He loved to pray the Rosary and took care to have his Rosary with him at all times. His friend, Antonio Di Maggio, was very much aware of Nicola's deep piety. One day he suggested to Nicola that he make a trip to San Giovanni Rotondo. "There is a holy priest who has recently been transferred to the monastery of Our Lady of Grace," Antonio said. "His name is Padre Pio. Many people believe that he is a saint. Since you are so religious, I think you should go and see him."

Although Nicola had not heard of Padre Pio, he was familiar with Our Lady of Grace monastery. Regularly, the lay brothers from the monastery made their rounds in the small surrounding towns and villages, seeking any offerings of food or supplies that could be donated to the Capuchin community. They often knocked on Nicola's door. The lay brothers from St. Matthew of the Crucifix monastery did the same. Nicola always welcomed the lay brothers and did what he could to help them.

Nicola told his wife Theresa what Antonio had shared with him about Padre Pio. With all her heart, Theresa wanted her husband to visit San Giovanni Rotondo in order to meet Padre Pio. Nicola too, was very impressed by what Antonio had told him. He wanted to visit the saintly priest but at the time he could not make any plans. He had his wheat harvest to tend to and it happened to be the time when the wheat needed to be winnowed.

Nicola was very proficient in all aspects of farm work. After the wheat was harvested, he would winnow it by throwing it upward into the breeze. The heavy wheat would fall back to the ground and the chaff would then be blown away by the wind. For many days he had waited, but unfortunately there had been no wind.

Just as Nicola finished speaking to Theresa about Padre Pio, a gentle breeze began to blow. He was then able to winnow the wheat and afterward, he stored it in his loft. When the task was completed, he mounted his mule, and with his Rosary in his hand, he headed for San Giovanni Rotondo.

When Nicola arrived in San Giovanni Rotondo, he learned that in order to see Padre Pio, he would have to present either a letter of introduction or a special permit issued by the local police. Nicola had no idea that such paperwork was necessary. He had neither a letter of introduction nor a permit. He didn't think that he would have time to go to the police station and request a permit. His visit to Padre Pio's monastery had to be a short one because his family was waiting for him to return home that very day. He decided to take a chance and try to enter the monastery without a permit.

Nicola noticed that there was a guard who was standing watch in front of Our Lady of Grace monastery. He monitored all of the visitors who approached. When the guard saw that Nicola did not have a permit or a letter, he told him that he would not be able to see Padre Pio. Nicola was very disappointed. He had been looking forward with great anticipation to meeting him. As Nicola was speaking to the guard, one of the Capuchins came out of the church and motioned to Nicola. "Padre Pio would like to see you," the Capuchin said to Nicola. Nicola was truly surprised. How could Padre Pio have possibly known that Nicola was standing outside, hoping to enter the monastery? They had never even met.

Nicola followed the Capuchin into the monastery and was soon standing in front of Padre Pio. "Oh, I see that you have arrived," Padre Pio said. "Who did you come with and how long did it take you to get here?" Padre Pio asked. Once again, Nicola was caught by surprise. It certainly seemed as though Padre Pio had been expecting him. "It took me three hours to get here on my mule," Nicola replied. "I came by myself." "You got here in half the time it would take an ordinary person to make the trip," Padre Pio said. "The reason why you made such good time is because you were accompanied by Jesus and Mary." Nicola was becoming more astonished by the minute. At the end of their conversation, he received a blessing from Padre Pio and was able to kiss his hand.

When Nicola returned to his home in the countryside, he told his wife Theresa all that had transpired. She was so amazed by her husband's words that she began to cry. For Nicola, the graces from the short visit to Padre Pio would long endure. As time went by, Nicola became concerned about the attitude of several of his neighbors. For a reason that Nicola could not understand, they seemed to harbor feelings of jealousy and resentment toward him and his family. One day, when Brother Bernardino, a Capuchin lay brother from Our Lady of Grace, visited his home, Nicola told him about his concerns. He asked Brother Bernardino to take a message to Padre Pio for him. "Please tell Padre Pio that I am very worried because of the hostility of some of my neighbors. I am afraid that they might try to harm my family." Brother Bernardino agreed to relay the message to Padre Pio.

The next time Brother Bernardino visited Nicola, he told him that he had spoken to Padre Pio about the situation. After he explained Nicola's problem to Padre Pio, Padre Pio replied, "Tell Nicola to carry on just as he always has and not to worry. The neighbors will do him no harm because the Virgin Mary and the Guardian Angel are always with him."

In Padre Pio's presence, one felt that nothing on this earth was of any importance, except one thing - to be in the grace of God.

- Kathleen Thornton

CHAPTER 10

Padre Pio - A Remarkable Confessor

*P*adre Pio, in his lifetime, reconciled innumerable souls back to God through the confessional. He was always in great demand as a confessor. People were willing to wait many days and brave any inconvenience in order to make their confession to him. In the early days, before there were accommodations for the pilgrims, the men who waited to make their confession to Padre Pio would sometimes sleep at night in the fields near the monastery. Some would even pitch tents in the open areas. When the sun rose, they would resume their place in the confessional line.

For years, Padre Pio spent the greater part of each day in the confessional. It was for this reason that he was often spoken of as a "martyr of the confessional." Pope Pius XII referred to Padre Pio as the "confessor of Europe." Once, Archbishop Andrea Cesarano of Manfredonia and Pope Pius XII were talking together about Padre Pio. "What does Padre Pio do?" the pope asked. "Your Holiness," Archbishop Cesarano replied, "He takes away the sins of the world."

The Lord endowed Padre Pio with extraordinary spiritual charisms for his ministry in the confessional. He was given the gift of reading hearts and of infused knowledge. These gifts were present even in the early days of his priesthood. In 1921, Padre Pio wrote a letter to Father Agostino and explained that the knowledge he possessed "came down from above," indicating that it was given to him by God. To Cleonice Morcaldi, the daughter of the mayor of San Giovanni Rotondo, Padre Pio said, "I see you inside and out, just like you see yourself in a mirror."

Father Nello Castello of Padua, Italy, went to confession to Padre Pio on numerous occasions. Father Castello described confession to Padre Pio as both "jolting and enlightening." He said, "Padre Pio gave me counsel that reflected the whole range of my existence, past and future. At times he would surprise me with suggestions unconnected with the sins I confessed. But later, events made it clear that his counsels had been prophetic. Padre Pio knew my problems better than I did."

One woman who made her confession to Padre Pio was plagued with a multitude of problems. Padre Pio said to her, "You must not be anxious or worried about anything because I am here with you." To another who was undergoing severe trials he said, "Unite yourself to my prayers." To the penitents, Padre Pio was a confidant, a friend, a counselor and above all a father. People could feel his concern and his loving care. He said to Monsignor Giancarlo Setti, whom he asked to oversee the Padre Pio prayer groups worldwide, "Monsignor, you look after the prayer groups and I will look after your soul."

Many people testified that their encounter with Padre Pio in the confessional brought a profound sense of peace and healing to their minds and hearts. To a woman who felt intense sorrow because of the death of her child, Padre Pio said, "I want you to know that your child has gone to a place where there is no more pain, no more suffering. That should be a great consolation to you." And indeed, his words were truly a great consolation to the woman.

Father Vincenzo of Casacalenda wrote:

> Padre Pio was always at our disposal. Even when we could not get near him because of the crowds, it was enough for us to turn our thoughts to him. We felt him standing by us, not only protectively but so many times also tangibly, through the prodigious perfume of sanctity which we were conscious of.

He always stood by us both materially and spiritually. He accepted all our requests, met all our anxieties, listened to all our sins. He took upon himself all our miseries as if they were his own, to such an extent that he sometimes lamented, "I can't go on any more." This humble confession of the heaviness of his cross, moves and comforts us at the same time. His was an endless love.

Father Vincenzo also made mention of Padre Pio's gift of reading hearts. He said:

> I was afraid of Padre Pio's gaze - a gaze which searched you. And yet, it was not a hard gaze; no, it was a sweet one. When he looked at you, he stripped you. If Padre Pio looked at you and smiled, you felt you had received a blessing. If he did not look at you, you were afraid.

In the confessional, people frequently asked Padre Pio for his counsel regarding family situations, vocational choices, business concerns, health issues, and even advice on farming matters. He was glad if he could help people on any level, but above all else, his desire was to help people on a spiritual level. He wanted people to realize their need for God. Professor Michael Melillo, one of Padre Pio's spiritual sons, once said to Padre Pio, "Father, please give me some spiritual advice that I can use for my whole life." Padre Pio answered him and said, "You have been born to know, to love and to serve God, and to be happy with him eternally in heaven."

Antonio Monari had a remarkable experience the first time he entered Padre Pio's confessional. Antonio stated:

> I was expecting to see a saint but I never imagined I would experience what I did. I told Padre Pio the many troubles of my family and myself and he listened paternally. I asked him for a grace for which I had waited many years for in vain. "Men can do nothing my son," Padre Pio said and he pointed upward. "Only God who is above can help us. I will pray for you," he added. He then gave me his blessing. I cannot describe to you the feeling of profound emotion I felt, so much so that when I got up, I lost my balance. He touched me affectionately

on the right side of my head. My right ear, in which I was completely deaf, suddenly opened and I have been able to hear perfectly ever since.

As a confessor, Padre Pio wanted people to understand the seriousness of sin. "We have a greater fear of mortal sin than of fire," Padre Pio once said. On another occasion he said, "Beware of sin as of a poisonous viper." When penitents put questions to him regarding moral issues, his answers left no doubt as to the difference between right and wrong and the proper course to follow. One man said, "Padre Pio's words were firm, candid and pure." A man once confessed to him that he had thoughts against chastity. "How many times have you had those thoughts?" Padre Pio asked. "Six or seven times," the man replied. "But seven is not the same as six because it means one more deadly sin," Padre Pio answered.

Padre Pio had a great fear of offending God and was ready to go to any length to avoid doing so. He had no illusions about human nature. He said, "As long as there remains a drop of blood in our bodies, there will always be a struggle between right and wrong. Looking back on his life, he once said, "Temptations that concern my secular life are those that most upset me . . . They bring on a cold sweat and make me tremble . . . In those moments, all I can do is cry."

In 1915, Padre Pio wrote to Father Agostino:

> The thought of going astray and . . . offending God fills me with terror. It paralyzes my limbs, and both body and soul feel as if they are being squeezed in a powerful vise. My bones feel as if they are being dislocated . . . crushed and ground up.

The general opinion was that making one's confession to Padre Pio was of profound spiritual benefit. Nevertheless, to confess to Padre Pio was not an easy task for most. As one person described it, "To go to confession to Padre Pio was to allow him to look right inside your soul." As a confessor, he was strict and demanding. He had great moral strength in directing souls and he did not hesitate to tell the penitents what they needed to do in order to change their lives. He often told people what they did not want to hear. He had a strong character and was afraid of no one. Many people wanted to make their confession to him but were held back by their fear. One man stated, "It is less frightening to take a difficult examination at the university than to make one's confession to Padre Pio."

Mr. Livio Dimatteo met Padre Pio in 1959. On one occasion, Livio had been undergoing a strong temptation which he was convinced was, "from the devil." Because of it, he was afraid to make his confession to Padre Pio. When he finally gathered up the courage and entered Padre Pio's confessional, Padre Pio placed his hand, much harder than usual, on Livio's head. Livio was certain that Padre Pio knew all about the temptation and would assist him through his prayers.

In the confessional, Padre Pio did not want people to make excuses for their sins and omissions. A woman from Gioia del Colle, Italy visited Padre Pio on one occasion. During her confession, she said that she missed Mass the previous Sunday because of the rain. "Yes, but when you left to come to San Giovanni Rotondo, it was raining too," Padre Pio replied. "You must never miss Mass again on Sunday unless illness prevents you from attending," he added.

As time passed, Padre Pio's fame as a confessor drew immense crowds to the monastery of Our Lady of Grace. As the crowds grew larger, Padre Pio, by necessity, became more inaccessible to the pilgrims. Outside of the confessional, it was almost impossible for a person to be able to have a conversation with him. Once, one of his spiritual daughters complained to him about the lack of time he had to give her in the confessional. He said to her, "I have spoken to you for many years. Now I ask you to put into practice those things that I have told you to do."

An atheist was once introduced to Padre Pio and the visit resulted in the man's conversion. He said, "I went to see Padre Pio when I had a thousand reasons for not believing in God. With great delicacy, little by little, he led me back to the faith and gave me the moral stability I lacked."

Padre Pio attached enormous importance to the frequent reception of the sacrament of confession. He used to say, "Even if a room is sealed off completely, dust will still accumulate in it." Padre Pio practiced what he advocated to others. He went to confession frequently. Before making his confession, he prayed deeply and sought the intercession of the Virgin Mary. He always felt a great remorse for his sins and often cried when making his confession. To Father Benedetto, who was his spiritual director for twelve years, Padre Pio wrote, "I am seeking the amendment of my life, my spiritual resurrection, true and substantial love, the sincere conversion of my whole self to Him."

Padre Pio knew that being a minister of the sacrament of reconciliation was a great responsibility. The responsibility often weighed heavily on him. He once said to Capuchin Father Domenico Laballarte, "In the confessional we dispense the blood of Christ. Be careful not to pour out such precious blood too easily or too lightly."

One man who had initially been denied absolution by Padre Pio stated that Padre Pio was the only person who had been able to help him break away from his destructive lifestyle. "Thanks to Padre Pio, I was able to understand the gravity of my sins," the man said. Previously, the man had always justified his immoral conduct and had no desire to change. People tried to show him the error of his ways but nothing that anyone said made a difference to him. The shock of being denied absolution by Padre Pio caused the man to reflect on his life. He made a good examination of conscience and later made a sincere confession and received absolution.

When twelve-year-old Mariella Lotti of Cosenza approached Padre Pio's confessional, his words startled her. "If I heard your confession right now, we would get nowhere. You are not prepared to make your confession at this time," Padre Pio said. Mariella, as well as her parents, felt offended, but when Padre Pio gave a further explanation for his actions, they not only understood, they agreed with him. It proved to be a turning point in young Mariella's life. Another young woman wanted to make her confession to Padre Pio but she was not willing to make the needed changes in her life. Padre Pio spoke of her and said, "She is just like coal. When exposed, it stains. When lit, it burns."

Padre Pio had a true understanding of human weakness and was willing to go to great lengths to help a person. However, if a person was not sorry for his sins, Padre Pio did not feel that he could do much for that individual. Padre Pio recommended to some individuals that they go to one of the other Capuchins to make their confession, rather than to him, without explaining the reason why. When he sent people out of the confessional because they were not adequately prepared to make their confession, it weighed on him. "If you could only understand how I suffer when I have to refuse absolution,"

Padre Pio said. "But it is better to be criticized by a man in this life than by God in the next life." He never advocated that other priests adopt his unconventional methods. "What I do, you cannot do," he once said to a fellow priest.

Padre Pio prayed continually for the salvation of all people. To a woman who was in great need he said, "Rest assured that I will pray for you. Even after my death I will remember you in my prayers." To another he said, "You must understand the responsibility I have assumed before Jesus for you. If something bad should happen to you which is to your spiritual detriment, Jesus will ask me to account for it directly." To a woman who asked him how often she could write to him, he responded, "Write to me whenever you have the desire or the need. In me, you will always find a father."

Angelo Battisti, an administrator at the Home for the Relief of Suffering, knew that Padre Pio spent long hours praying for the intentions of his spiritual children. Angelo once offered a suggestion to Padre Pio. "It is far too time-consuming for you to pray for people on an individual basis," Angelo said. "There are just too many people who are requesting your prayers. Why don't you pray for the people in general rather than individually? It would save you a lot of time." "I cannot do that," Padre Pio replied. "I must present their needs to God, one at a time."

Father Ruggero observed that many of the pilgrims who greeted Padre Pio handed him personal letters which contained their prayer requests. It seemed that it would be impossible for Padre Pio to read all the letters that he received. Like Angelo Battisti, Father Ruggero wondered how Padre Pio could find the time to pray for so many people. He asked Padre Pio how he could keep up with the task. Padre Pio touched his hand to his heart and said, "This is where they all pass. They are all here in my heart."

Padre Pio insisted that people dress modestly whenever entering the church to attend Mass or to make their confession. To many, his standards of modesty were considered to be extreme. As time passed, Padre Pio became even stricter regarding church attire. One priest who knew of Padre Pio's rigid standards, told him that he could not insist on such a strict dress code in his parish because he feared that the members of his congregation would become angry and quit. "An empty church is better than a profaned one," Padre Pio replied.

Padre Pio's fidelity to his priestly ministry as a confessor was revealed to Dr. Filippo Pancaro on one occasion. Dr. Pancaro, who was on staff at the Home for the Relief of Suffering, once gave Padre Pio a thorough physical examination. Besides having a high fever, Padre Pio also complained of dizziness, weakness, and a disturbing ringing in his ears. His exhaustion at the time was so great that he could hardly stand on his feet. Dr. Pancaro told Padre Pio that he needed to rest more in order to regain his strength. He advised him to discontinue hearing the evening confessions for a while.

Padre Pio was very disappointed at the doctor's words. "If that is an order, I will do it," Padre Pio said. "But only if it is an order. I do not want to cut back on hearing confessions." Padre Pio then asked the doctor for his prayers. "I ask you to pray for me to the Virgin Mary," Padre Pio said. "Pray that my health will be restored." Dr. Pancaro assured him that he would do so. Padre Pio told the doctor that if he had a choice between losing his sight or his hearing, he would prefer to lose his sight. "As long as I have my hearing, I will always be able to continue to hear confessions," he said. He once told Father Agostino that he would prefer to be taken to the confessional in a wheelchair rather than to stop hearing confessions.

Several hours before he died, Padre Pio asked the priest who was assisting him, Father Pellegrino Funicelli, to hear his confession. After making his confession, he said to Father Pellegrino, "Ask all my brothers to forgive me for all of the trouble I have caused them. If the Lord should call me tonight, please ask all of my spiritual children to say a prayer for my soul."

―――――――――

Biagio Fusco saw Padre Pio for the first time in 1919. Some of his relatives had urged him to make the trip to San Giovanni Rotondo and he also felt motivated by a certain sense of curiosity regarding Padre Pio. He happened to arrive at the monastery just as Padre Pio had begun to say Mass. Biagio began to think about how far he had drifted from his faith. His moral and spiritual life had been on the downhill slide for a long time. He was so moved by Padre Pio's Mass that he felt suddenly inspired to change his life and to return to the sacraments. Biagio was also able to make his confession to Padre Pio.

The church and the confessional were very crowded that day. The Italian state police (the Carabenieri) were present to maintain order in the church.

After Biagio returned to his home, he continued to think about Padre Pio. Before his visit to Padre Pio, nothing could motivate him to change his life. He was attached to his sins and did not have the will or the desire to change. But the short visit to Padre Pio produced a radical transformation in his life. Sometimes Biagio noticed the unexplainable scent of violets, roses, and incense in the air. He felt it was a sign that Padre Pio was trying to encourage him to sustain his faith in its first steps.

Several years later, Biagio returned to the monastery of Our Lady of Grace and was able once again to make his confession to Padre Pio. When Biagio confessed a particular sin, Padre Pio interrupted him and said, "You confessed that sin two years ago. You are a backslider." Biagio knew that Padre Pio heard confessions day in and day out, for many hours a day. He was astonished that Padre Pio was able to remember what he had confessed to him in the past.

The next time Biagio visited San Giovanni Rotondo, he had a very important matter to discuss with Padre Pio. In the confessional, he explained to Padre Pio that he would soon be taking an examination for a teaching position. He had been trying for four years to obtain a job as a teacher, to no avail. Biagio asked Padre Pio to pray that he would pass the test and also to pray that he would secure a teaching job. Biagio had a wife and six children to support and he constantly worried about his precarious financial situation. As Biagio was telling Padre Pio about the upcoming test, Padre Pio raised his eyes upward. His face became serene and beautiful. As Biagio gazed at him, he was convinced that all would be well.

Shortly after that, Biagio received a letter in the mail which offered him a teaching position in a nearby town. The letter was dated July 27, 1923, the same date that he had made his confession to Padre Pio and had requested his prayers. With great joy and thanksgiving in his heart, Biagio accepted the teaching position.

Biagio went to the school board in order to negotiate for the school that he wanted to work at. The board member who met with him told him how fortunate he was. "Jobs these days are extremely scarce," he said. "You are indeed very lucky to have been hired. It is almost like a miracle!" At his words, the air became filled with a strong perfume. Biagio knew at that moment that Padre Pio was present and was interceding for him. Biagio was assigned to work at the school of his choice and after a short time the job became permanent.

German-born Friedrich Abresch lived in Bologna, Italy where he worked as a professional photographer. He converted to Catholicism in order to please his fiancé, Amalia, who was a Catholic. Friedrich was a Catholic in name only. He did not have faith in the teachings of the Church. He rarely went to Mass and as time passed he began to feel a great antipathy for anything that had to do with Catholicism. Later, he took up the study of spiritualism, occultism, and magic.

When Friedrich learned about Padre Pio, his curiosity was aroused. He was fascinated by the stories of the miracles and healings associated with Padre Pio. He wanted to make a trip to San Giovanni Rotondo to meet Padre Pio. In Friedrich's mind, the only negative factor was that Padre Pio was a Catholic. Could these obvious manifestations of God's power really be coming from a Catholic priest? Friedrich wondered how it could be possible.

Friedrich was finally able to make the trip to see Padre Pio in 1925. He was twenty-eight years old. When he arrived at the monastery of Our Lady of Grace, Padre Pio greeted him, but was by no means cordial. He only made a few rather cold remarks. Friedrich had traveled a long distance from Bologna to the little town of San Giovanni Rotondo and was somehow expecting a friendlier reception.

Later, when Friedrich made his confession to Padre Pio, Padre Pio told him that in his previous confessions, he had withheld serious sins from his confessor. His words, which were true, shocked Friedrich. He wondered how Padre Pio could have known. Padre Pio then asked Friedrich if his previous confessions had been made in good faith. He answered that they had not. Friedrich told Padre Pio that he did not believe in the sacrament of confession. Although he felt that it was a useful psychological and social tool, he did not believe that it could impart grace. However, Friedrich had been deeply moved by his few moments with Padre Pio and by the fact that Padre Pio could see into the secret depth of his soul. "I did not believe in the sacrament of confession before," Friedrich said to Padre Pio. "But now suddenly, by talking with you, I believe in it," he added.

As though in great pain, Padre Pio told Friedrich that his beliefs were all heresies. He added that all of his past communions had been sacrilegious. "Make a good examination of conscience," Padre Pio said. "Try to remember when you last made a sincere confession. You must make a general confession." He told Friedrich that he would hear his confession later in the day. "Jesus has been more merciful to you than he was to Judas!" Padre Pio said. He then left Friedrich in the sacristy and went to hear the women's confessions.

Friedrich felt shaken to his roots by his contact with Padre Pio. He also felt dazed and confused. He tried to gather his thoughts together but he could not seem to concentrate. He made a supreme effort to recall the last time he made a sincere confession. Try as he might, he could not remember. He tried to focus his mind and make an examination of conscience so that he would be prepared to make a general confession.

Friedrich decided that he would tell Padre Pio that he had been a Lutheran before converting to Catholicism. He would explain that he had been conditionally baptized into the Catholic Church. At that time, all of his sins were forgiven. He would begin his confession by talking about his childhood.

When Friedrich knelt before Padre Pio once again in the confessional, before he could finish his first sentence, Padre Pio interrupted him. "When did you make your last good confession?" Padre Pio asked. Friedrich was not sure if he had ever made a good confession. He told Padre Pio that he could not remember. Padre Pio then reminded him of the time, adding some of the particulars of that confession. It took place shortly after Friedrich was married. That confession had long slipped from his memory but he realized that Padre Pio was right. "Begin your confession from the time I have just mentioned," Padre Pio said. Friedrich was astonished that Padre Pio had such detailed knowledge of the events of his past life. He realized that he had come in contact with the supernatural.

Padre Pio then enumerated all of Friedrich's mortal sins by asking him questions about those very sins. He was even able to state the number of times he had neglected to go to Mass. Everything was laid bare before Friedrich's eyes. He made Friedrich understand the gravity of the state of his soul. "You have launched a hymn to Satan, whereas Jesus, in his tremendous love, has broken himself for you," Padre Pio said. He then gave Friedrich a penance. When Padre Pio pronounced the words of absolution, Friedrich found it hard to breathe. He felt like he was suffocating. But after he left the confessional, his joy was so great that he could hardly contain himself.

From that day forward, Friedrich attended Mass every day. Friedrich later prepared a written testimony stating that he believed, not only in all of the dogmas and precepts of the Catholic Church, but also in all of the Church's traditions and ceremonies, even down to the smallest. He stated that his faith was so strong that no one would ever be able to shake it. He would prefer to lose his life rather than his faith.

Friedrich had a great desire to be near Padre Pio. He and Amalia decided to move from their home in Bologna to San Giovanni Rotondo. There, they became active members of the Third Order of St. Francis. They were very happy living close to Padre Pio and participating in the spiritual life of the church of Our Lady of Grace.

One day, while in the church of Our Lady of Grace, Friedrich took some photographs of Padre Pio during the celebration of the Mass. He had not asked permission to do so. Much to Friedrich's surprise, the photos all turned out blank. The next time he wanted to take a photograph of Padre Pio, he asked for his permission. Padre Pio was strongly opposed to the idea and would not agree to it. But Friedrich was persistent. He asked the Capuchin superior for permission and he gave his consent. Padre Pio submitted out of obedience to his superior but he still resisted the idea. When Padre Pio was told that the photos were a consolation to many people, he finally became more accepting. Friedrich became Padre Pio's official photographer and left a number of exceptional photographs of him to posterity.

In honor of their spiritual father, when Amalia and Friedrich welcomed their newborn son into the world, they named him Pio. Both Friedrich and his son Pio, served Padre Pio's Mass on many occasions. Padre Pio predicted that Pio Abresch would one day become a priest and would have a high position in the Church. His prophecy came true. Pio Abresch was ordained to the priesthood in 1956. Monsignor Pio Abresch was sent to Rome and was assigned to work at the Congregation for Bishops at the Vatican. Friedrich Abresch died in August 1969, almost one year after the death of Padre Pio.

———————

Very Reverend Father Donatus von Welle was elected the Minister General of the Capuchin Order in1938. He held Padre Pio in the highest esteem and had visited him in San Giovanni Rotondo on several occasions. On one visit, as Father Donatus was preparing to attend Padre Pio's early morning Mass, he was informed that Padre Pio was very ill. Father Donatus went to Padre Pio's cell and saw that he was in great pain. The doctor was called in to examine him. He tried to ease his suffering and make him more comfortable but all of his efforts proved to be unsuccessful.

Father Donatus celebrated the Mass that morning in Padre Pio's place. After the Mass, some men approached Father Donatus and told him that they wanted to go to confession to Padre Pio. They had traveled all night in order reach San Giovanni Rotondo. Father Donatus explained that Padre Pio was very ill. He added that if Padre Pio was feeling better on the following day, he would be able to hear their confessions at that time. The men explained that they could not wait till the following day. They were all factory workers and had to leave San Giovanni Rotondo that very afternoon in order to get back to work. They asked Father Donatus if he would hear their confessions and he was very happy to do so.

In hearing their confessions, Father Donatus discovered that the men had not been to confession in many years. He felt certain that there was a connection between Padre Pio's sudden illness and the graces the factory workers received that day. Father Donatus was convinced that Padre Pio was offering his sufferings for their conversion.

———————

There was once a man who lived in Rome who had fallen upon hard times. He had searched for work for months with no success. Because he was not able to support his wife and children, he felt like a total failure. Each day, his situation became more desperate. There would be an endless search for work. He would come home to his family with empty pockets and with no hope of finding employment. When he woke up each morning, he dreaded the new day.

One morning, the man's depression was so great that he could not think in a rational manner. He decided that it would be better to end his life. While his wife and two children were sleeping peacefully in another part of the house, he turned on the gas in the kitchen. He told himself that his problems would soon be over. Suddenly he heard his son calling his name and it caused him to come to his senses. He quickly turned off the gas and rushed to see what his little boy wanted. After he put his son back to bed, his eyes fell on the crucifix that was hanging on the wall. His wife had put it there. He felt that his wife was fortunate because she had a strong faith in God. He however, had no faith.

One day when the man was on a bus, he struck up a conversation with the person who was sitting next to him. That person happened to be the famous actor, Carlo Campanini. The man told Carlo about his many difficulties. Carlo asked him if he had ever heard of Padre Pio and the man replied that he had not. Carlo shared some facts about Padre Pio's life. He explained that Padre Pio was a very holy Capuchin priest and a great intercessor with the Lord. Carlo felt that Padre Pio would be able to help the man. He suggested that they go together to San Giovanni Rotondo to see Padre Pio and the man agreed to go.

On the way to San Giovanni Rotondo, the man wondered to himself why he had agreed to make the trip. He was not a person of faith. He had no interest in things of a religious nature. He couldn't imagine that he would enjoy spending time at a monastery. He also thought that it was very odd that Carlo Campanini would have such a strong religious inclination. Carlo had fame, fortune, friends, and the respect and admiration of millions. What would motivate him to have so much devotion to a Catholic priest?

The next morning the man went with Carlo to Padre Pio's Mass. It was the very first time he had ever attended Mass. He tried to follow along as best he could but he was not able to understand the formal prayers or the scripture readings. It was all new to him. He could not grasp it. When the others in the congregation knelt down, he followed suit. When they stood up, he stood up. He tried to say the name Jesus. For the duration of the Mass he kept repeating the name Jesus. It was his only prayer.

After Mass, the man went into the sacristy with a number of others in order to receive Padre Pio's blessing. Padre Pio was walking toward the fountain in the sacristy to wash his hands when he noticed the man. Padre Pio looked at him with a penetrating gaze and then smiled at him. The man felt an instant connection. He could not explain it, but for some strange reason, it seemed as though Padre Pio had been expecting him.

Later on in the afternoon, the man saw Padre Pio again and was able to speak to him. "I do not believe in God," the man said to Padre Pio. "That is not true," Padre Pio replied. "There was a time when you did not believe in God. But that was in the past. As for now, you do believe." Padre Pio then took the man to his cell and heard his confession. The man told Padre Pio that he did not know how to pray and Padre Pio gave him simple instructions in prayer. The man still felt a sense of guilt and shame over the sins of his past and he told Padre Pio so. "Do you think that St. Peter will want to know about this when you go to heaven?" Padre Pio asked. "Of course he will not!" Padre Pio added. He then gave the man a fatherly embrace. The darkness and the pain that had been in his heart for years, suddenly vanished. Unashamedly, he began to cry. When he left the monastery, he had one last coin in his pocket. He gave it to a beggar who was standing nearby. He was now completely penniless but ironically, he felt freer than he had in years.

When the man returned to Rome, he was faithful to attend Mass every Sunday with his wife and children. He asked for instruction and was taught how to use the Missal in order to follow the prayers and readings of the Mass. He still had many difficulties to face in his life, but he no longer felt hopeless. His new found faith gave him the light he needed to see each day to its completion and to give thanks to God for blessings received.

———

When Dr. Remo Vincenti and his son visited San Giovanni Rotondo, his son obtained a ticket from the booking office so that he could make his confession to Padre Pio. When his son's ticket number was close to being called, Remo suddenly realized that there was a problem. Just a few days before, his son had gone to confession and Padre Pio did not hear confessions if it was less than ten days since a person's last confession. Remo advised his son to stay in the line anyway and to take his chances. Perhaps Padre Pio would make an exception to the rule. In the meantime, Remo prayed with great intensity, "Padre Pio, please hear my son's confession. Do it out of love for the Blessed Virgin. Don't send him away. Please!"

Remo was very happy that his son was able to make his confession to Padre Pio. Everything had worked out so well. Before Remo and his son left the monastery to return to their home in Terni, Italy, they went to say good-bye to Padre Pio. When Padre Pio caught sight of Remo, his face brightened. Before Remo had a chance to utter a single word, Padre Pio said to him, "I would have done it out of love for you!" Remo then understood that Padre Pio had heard his heartfelt prayer.

———————

Dr. Ezio Saltamerenda was the director of the Biotherapeutic Institute in Genoa, Italy. Ezio had been an atheist from the time he was a teenager. As the years passed, he felt an ever greater hostility toward religion and looked with disdain on people who believed in God. Ezio felt that it was his duty to convince people that religion was for the weak and feeble minded.

On one occasion, Ezio was introduced to an industrialist from Genoa, Mario Cavaliere. Mario happened to be a spiritual son of Padre Pio. In Mario's office, Ezio noticed a photograph of Padre Pio on the desk. As he glanced at the photograph, he felt a strange tightness in his throat. Mario noticed Ezio staring at the photo and told him some brief facts about Padre Pio's life.

Even though priests and clergymen were not people that Dr. Ezio admired or respected, the words that Mario spoke about Padre Pio made a deep impression on him. The next morning, he felt an overwhelming urge to meet Padre Pio. He could not understand where the desire was coming from but he felt powerless to resist it. He left for San Giovanni Rotondo that very evening.

When he arrived at the monastery of Our Lady of Grace, he was told to wait for Padre Pio in the sacristy. When Padre Pio walked into the sacristy, Ezio felt the same tightness in his throat that he had felt when he saw Padre Pio's picture for the first time. Suddenly, without having any idea why, Ezio felt like crying.

Ezio was informed that the only way he could speak to Padre Pio was if he made his confession to him. He decided to wait in the confessional line.

When it was his turn, he explained to Padre Pio that he wanted to ask him for a blessing for a relative who was sick. He did not want to make his confession. Padre Pio had a severe expression on his face and said to him, "Do you ever think of the state of your soul?" "Yes, I do think of the state of my soul," Ezio replied. Padre Pio then asked him what he believed the purpose of life was. "The purpose of life is the preservation of the species," Ezio replied. Padre Pio told Ezio that his soul was in a dreadful state and then he asked him to leave the confessional. Ezio tried to stand up but for some strange reason he felt riveted to the ground. He was completely confused. Finally, he managed to leave the confessional.

Even though Ezio's first encounter with Padre Pio had not gone well, he wanted to see him again. He wondered what the second encounter would be like. Fighting the fear in his heart, he gathered up his courage and returned the next day. He tried to be as inconspicuous as possible as he stood in the corridor among a group of men who were waiting for Padre Pio. When Padre Pio saw Ezio, he said to him, "Man from Genoa, you live near the seaside but you do not know how to wash. You have a dirty face!" Then he added, "You are a strong boat without a captain." Once again, he asked him to leave.

All of the men who were waiting in line had heard Padre Pio's words. Ezio felt the embarrassment of being humiliated in public. In his heart, he felt a great anguish. He went for a walk in an open field near the monastery. He tried to clear his mind and to think about what he should do next. He was hurt by Padre Pio's coldness, but it only made him long with a greater intensity to be near him. He told one of the other Capuchins all that had happened. The Capuchin was very kind to Ezio and tried to encourage him. He took him to Padre Pio's cell. As they entered the cell, Ezio became aware of the beautiful fragrance of violets. When Padre Pio saw Ezio, he told him to go downstairs and wait for him. He would come down soon to hear his confession.

Ezio made a sincere confession and he cried unashamedly throughout. Later he was to say that making his confession to Padre Pio was the most beautiful moment of his life. His previous encounters with Padre Pio had been painful, no doubt, but that was all in the past. After he received absolution, he spoke to Padre Pio from his heart and said, "I hope that the sorrow that I have felt for my sins and also my conversion to the faith has been of some consolation to you." "My son," Padre Pio replied lovingly, "Indeed, it has been a great consolation to me. God bless you always." Later he told Ezio that he would always be with him in spirit.

Ezio had not been mistaken. Padre Pio had called him "my son." Ezio's heart was bursting with joy. When Dr. Ezio Saltamerenda returned to his home in Genoa, he was a changed man. It was the beginning of a completely different life for him, and he shared his new found faith with everyone.

———

There was once a lady from Germany who made her confession to Padre Pio. She was fluent in Italian and was planning to make her confession in Italian. Before she could say even one word, Padre Pio began speaking to her in German. She noticed that his accent was perfect. Some time later, she saw Padre Pio again. She spoke to him in German but he made no reply. She spoke to him a second time in German. He said nothing. Finally, she spoke to him in Italian and said, "Padre Pio, you spoke so well with me in German in the confessional. Why is it that you will not do so now?" "Oh," he replied. "Confession is a completely different matter."

———

Gina Deiana was engaged to be married and was looking forward to the day of her wedding with great anticipation. Two months before the wedding, her fiancé broke up with her. He did not have the courtesy to speak to Gina in person about his decision or even to call her on the telephone. He simply left her a short note indicating that their relationship was over. Gina was devastated by his actions and sunk into a deep depression. Her sadness became so overwhelming that she lost all joy in living.

Soon after the break up, Gina happened to read an article about Padre Pio in a magazine. She had a strong desire to visit Padre Pio and so she invited her aunt to make the trip with her to San Giovanni Rotondo. They left from their home in Genova, and arrived at Padre Pio's monastery two days later. The year was 1952. They felt fortunate to book a room in the one and only hotel in the town.

The following morning, Gina and her aunt attended Padre Pio's early Mass. Later that day, a woman whom Gina had never seen before, approached her and said, "You are the girl whose fiancé broke up with her. Am I right about that?" "But how did you know?" Gina asked. "Padre Pio told me about you," the woman answered. "He wants you to stay here in San Giovanni Rotondo longer than you had intended to. Also, he would like to speak to you." "But our funds are very limited. We cannot afford to stay any longer than planned," Gina said. "Don't give it another thought. I will be happy to lend you the money," the woman replied. The woman's name was Angelina Serritelli. She was one of Padre Pio's spiritual daughters and she went to great lengths to assist him in any way that she could.

Gina was amazed by her conversation with Angelina Serritelli. She and her aunt were strangers in the little town of San Giovanni Rotondo. No one but Gina's mother knew about their trip. But Padre Pio obviously knew that Gina was there. He had sent Angelina to greet her. Gina called her mother in Genova and told her that she and her aunt would be staying longer than they had anticipated.

While in San Giovanni Rotondo, Gina was able to make her confession to Padre Pio. During the confession, she told Padre Pio that her fiancé had abandoned her and that she was very depressed. Although she had made an effort to get over the traumatic incident, she had not succeeded. She told Padre Pio that she had stopped receiving Holy Communion because she had been so upset.

In a fatherly way, Padre Pio counseled Gina. "Be calm," he said. "You must try to stop thinking about your fiancé and how he betrayed you. He was not worthy of you." Gina felt at peace for the first time in a very long time. Padre Pio spoke to her with great tenderness, almost making light of the sins that she confessed. He then gave her a picture of Jesus. On the back of the picture, he had written the words, "Let Jesus be the center of all your aspirations." After making her confession to Padre Pio, Gina was able to put the past behind her and move forward in life.

––––––––––

Giuseppe Minto of Milan, Italy was a Camilian friar of the Institute of St. Camillo of Alberoni. The members of his religious congregation cared for the sick and infirm. One of the sick patients that Giuseppe was assisting, spoke to him about Padre Pio and encouraged him to visit San Giovanni Rotondo.

Giuseppe was finally able to make the trip in March 1959. When he met Padre Pio and kissed his hand, he perceived a beautiful fragrance which he described as a mixture of roses, incense, and carbolic acid. He also had the opportunity to assist as altar server at Padre Pio's Mass on several occasions. During the Mass, just before the Eucharistic prayer, as Giuseppe poured water over Padre Pio's wounded hands, he felt immensely blessed.

After the Mass, Padre Pio made his thanksgiving behind a curtain. Giuseppe happened to look past the curtain and he was able to see Padre Pio clearly. In his hand, he had a large stack of letters from people requesting his prayers. Padre Pio's lips were moving and he was gesturing as though he was talking to someone, but there was no one there. Giuseppe understood then that Padre Pio was speaking to God.

Giuseppe waited in the sacristy to make his confession to Padre Pio. He sat on a bench with many other men. Near him was an engineer, who was so frightened at the prospect of making his confession to Padre Pio that he was trembling. Giuseppe felt sorry for him and tried to say a word to console him. When the engineer's turn came, he started to walk toward the confessional but was so overcome by emotion and fear that he fell to the floor. Padre Pio was very loving. He encouraged the man to step forward and he pointed him to the kneeler.

Once, when Giuseppe was making his confession to Padre Pio, he began speaking about something that was totally unrelated to the matter at hand. Padre Pio stopped him short. "There is no time to lose, my son," Padre Pio said. He did not want to waste a minute. Before Giuseppe left San Giovanni Rotondo to return to Milan, he asked Padre Pio to give him a word to take back to the other priests and brothers in his religious congregation. "Say this to your brothers," Padre Pio replied. "Let us sanctify ourselves and treat the sick well. Let us live well and we will bring upon ourselves the blessings of the Lord."

––––––––––

Romana Bianchi had been suffering from arthritis of the spine for several years. She was in constant pain and no medicine that the doctor prescribed brought her any relief. She spent most of her time in bed, hardly able to move. Romana had a husband and three children to care for but it became increasingly difficult for her to see to the needs of her family. She decided to make a trip to San Giovanni Rotondo to visit Padre Pio and to ask him to pray that her health would be restored. She also had another special intention. Romana's father-in-law lived in her household and their relationship was very strained. Romana hoped that they could resolve their problems so that peace would return to the home. It was a situation that needed prayer.

Romana traveled from her home in Gemona del Friuli in northeastern Italy to San Giovanni Rotondo. The year was 1963. In the confessional, Padre Pio asked Romana if she went to Mass on Sundays. She told him that she did not. Next, he asked her if she had gone to Mass on Easter Sunday. Again, she said no. Padre Pio became upset and raised his voice in disapproval.

Romana was not put off by Padre Pio's strong words, nor was she intimidated by his sternness. She did what very few people had the courage to do. She spoke up to him. "Listen, I am desperate," Romana said to Padre Pio. "If I was not desperate, I would never have traveled such a long distance from one end of Italy to the other in order to see you. I am here because I need help. My heart feels like ice. For a long time, I have been on the point of giving up completely. I have been so sick that I cannot even pray."

Romana's words caused Padre Pio's attitude to soften. She continued with her confession. When she was finished, Padre Pio gave her absolution. When he said, "Go in peace," a great peace filled Romana's heart. She went back to Gemona del Friuli, healed in body and also in spirit. The chronic pain left her and never returned. She felt like her old self again. Not only that, her relationship with her father-in-law improved dramatically. Peace was restored to their relationship and she grew to have a deep affection for him. In the last years of his life, when he became bedridden, Romana cared for him lovingly and considered it a privilege.

————

Probo Vaccarini traveled from his home in Rimini to San Giovanni Rotondo in order to make his confession to Padre Pio. Eight of Probo's friends asked him to speak to Padre Pio on their behalf. Probo decided that the best way to present his friends' prayer petitions to Padre Pio was to write them out on a single piece of paper.

While making his confession to Padre Pio, Probo kept thinking about the note in his pocket with the petitions on it. He wondered when would be the appropriate time for him to talk to Padre Pio about his friends' needs. Padre Pio noticed Probo's restlessness. After Padre Pio gave him absolution, he said to him, "I want you to leave now!" "But wait," Probo said. "Eight of my friends would like you to pray for their intentions. I have their names and their petitions which they have asked me to relay to you." "You should not be thinking about your friends while you are in the confessional," Padre Pio replied. "If you do not leave at once, I will."

Padre Pio stood up and made a motion to leave. A strange feeling suddenly came over Probo. He felt rooted to his place. He could not move. He could not have left the confessional if he had wanted to. Padre Pio seemed to be aware of how uncomfortable Probo felt. He once again took his seat. "Go ahead and ask me what you want to regarding your friends," Padre Pio said. Probo took the paper with the petitions on it out of his pocket. It was completely blank. "You must hurry," Padre Pio said. "There are many other people who are waiting in line to make their confession. We do not have any time to lose." "I don't understand what happened," Probo replied. "The paper that I wrote the petitions on is now blank!" He noticed that Padre Pio had a broad grin on his face.

Padre Pio then proceeded to make seven statements. Each statement was an accurate reference to the petitions of Probo's seven friends. Probo wondered why Padre Pio had only addressed the needs of seven of his friends when it was actually eight who made the request. As it turned out, the person that Padre Pio omitted, had the opportunity to go to San Giovanni Rotondo and speak for himself.

———

On one occasion, Padre Pio was in the choir loft of the church, making his thanksgiving after Mass. Brother Costantino approached him and told him that there was a man downstairs in the church who wanted to make his confession. He asked Padre Pio if it would be all right if he brought the man up to the choir loft so that he could make his confession. Padre Pio made no reply. Brother Costantino waited for a time and finally went back downstairs.

A few moments later Brother Costantino returned to the choir loft. "Padre Pio," Brother Costantino said, "The man who wants to make his confession to you is still downstairs. He cannot wait any longer. He is a chauffeur and there are people calling for him to drive them to their destinations." "That man has made the Lord wait for twenty-five years," Padre Pio said. "He can wait five minutes for me to finish my prayers!"

Brother Costantino was not sure what Padre Pio was talking about. He went downstairs for the second time. The man was still standing in the corridor. "I have to leave now," the man said impatiently. "I cannot wait a minute longer. Besides that, I am afraid to make my confession to Padre Pio." "Why are you afraid?" Brother Costantino asked. "I am afraid because it has been twenty-five years since my last confession."

Umberto Iorio once traveled from Morcone to San Giovanni Rotondo in order to make his confession to Padre Pio. He was twenty-five years old. "Do you go to Mass?" Padre Pio asked. "I attend Mass once in awhile," Umberto replied. "Why do you live in the desert?" Padre Pio asked him, referring to the way he was neglecting his spiritual life. "You must start going to Mass and then you can come back and I will hear your confession," Padre Pio said.

Umberto got up casually from the kneeler. With a nonchalant attitude, he walked out of the confessional. From all appearances, he seemed to be completely indifferent to what Padre Pio had said to him. As soon as he left the church and walked out into the open air, he began to sob. As though a light had been turned on inside his mind, he suddenly understood the error of his ways. He felt a deep remorse. After that brief encounter with Padre Pio, Umberto never missed Mass again.

A woman once made her confession to Padre Pio and when she was finished, Padre Pio said to her, "I am not going to give you a penance because you have already done your penance. Your sins are forgiven." The woman was confused by Padre Pio's words and asked him for an explanation. "For twenty-three years you have lovingly cared for your husband," Padre Pio said. "It has been a long and a hard road for you and for your family. Your compassion and your loyalty to your husband will be rewarded. I want you to know that when your time comes to pass from this life to the next, you will have a peaceful and a beautiful death."

What Padre Pio had said to the woman was true. The woman's husband was confined to a wheelchair and for years she had taken care of him with great solicitude. Some time later, the woman had a heart attack. The family felt blessed because a priest came to her bedside and was able to give her the Last Rites before she passed away. Her five children were with her as she was dying and witnessed her peaceful passage into eternity.

———————

Cornelia Zolezzi of Chiavari, Italy had a pressing problem in her life and took a trip to San Giovanni Rotondo in hopes of speaking to Padre Pio about it. Cornelia owned an apartment in Chiavari and when she made a temporary move to Florence, she sublet her apartment to a woman whom she thought would be an ideal tenant. Later, when Cornelia was returning to Chiavari to take up residence, she gave the woman advanced notice to vacate the apartment. However, the woman refused to leave. Cornelia had no choice but to move back into her apartment while her tenant was still occupying it. It soon became an intolerable situation. Cornelia had no privacy and as time passed, she grew more and more unhappy about the situation.

At the time of Cornelia's visit, people were not allowed to make their confession to Padre Pio if it had been less than a week since their last confession. There was sound logic behind the rule. Considering the ever-growing number of people who flocked to Padre Pio's confessional, the long lines and the long wait became unmanageable.

Cornelia knew that she was breaking the rules when she stood in the women's line for Padre Pio's confessional. She had been to confession just a few days previously. However, she was so distraught about her living situation that she was willing to take her chances in order to speak to Padre Pio.

Cornelia walked into Padre Pio's confessional and knelt down. "You are in the grace of God," he said to her, indicating that she had recently made her confession and that all was well. He would not hear her confession. Cornelia was disappointed but there was nothing she could do.

When Cornelia returned to Chiavari, she was very surprised to find that her tenant had moved out of the apartment. One of the neighbors told Cornelia that a moving van had arrived in front of the apartment in the morning. After all of the woman's furniture and personal belongings were loaded into the moving van, the driver and the woman left together. When Cornelia inquired as to the time that the woman left, her neighbor told her that she left at about 8:30 a.m. That was the same time that Cornelia had knelt before Padre Pio in the confessional.

———————

Guido Biondi visited San Giovanni Rotondo and made his confession to Padre Pio for the first time in 1956. In the confessional, Padre Pio asked Guido if he attended Mass on Sundays. Guido replied that he went to Mass once in awhile. "Then you must leave," Padre Pio told him. "Come back in one month and I will hear your confession at that time," Padre Pio added. Guido was angry when he rose from his kneeling position. He could hardly wait to get out of the confessional. He felt indignant and humiliated that Padre Pio had dismissed him in such a rough way. When he walked out of the church, he immediately went to the bus stop in order to catch the first bus that was leaving for Foggia.

On the bus trip to Foggia, Guido's anger began to subside. As he thought about what had transpired in the confessional, he became more objective. He was able to understand why Padre Pio had spoken to him the way he had. Guido took stock of his life, and for the first time, he felt guilty about many of the actions of his past. He had turned his back on God and in doing so, he had lost his way. He suddenly felt the crushing burden of his many sins.

After Guido returned to his home, he went over every detail of his brief encounter with Padre Pio. He wanted with his whole heart to speak to Padre Pio again but he felt too embarrassed to do so. Padre Pio had rejected him and he did not feel that he could ever face him again.

Guido had a very good job in the automobile industry where he was supervisor to more than one hundred employees. Back at work, he found it difficult to concentrate. He began to lose weight and his health deteriorated.

He neglected his responsibilities at work. One day, he had great difficulty breathing. His body was wracked with pain. He prayed to Padre Pio and at once his painful symptoms disappeared. The answered prayer from Padre Pio gave him the courage to make a return trip to San Giovanni Rotondo.

At the monastery of Our Lady of Grace, Guido noticed a Capuchin who greeted five men that were standing nearby. The Capuchin motioned for the men to follow him. What seemed to be a force outside himself impelled Guido to join the group of five men. They followed the Capuchin up some stairs and then down a long and narrow corridor. Suddenly, they were standing in front of Padre Pio's cell. They knocked on the door and heard a loud voice inviting them to come in. Guido was the last one to enter Padre Pio's cell.

Padre Pio greeted the men and asked them for an update regarding someone who was ill. Guido understood then that the five men he had followed into Padre Pio's cell were all doctors. They worked at the Home for the Relief of Suffering. One of the doctors spoke to Padre Pio at length about the individual who was ill. After the doctors conversed with Padre Pio for a while, one by one, they kissed his hand and then left. Guido was suddenly standing all alone with Padre Pio. Fear gripped his heart. Padre Pio smiled at him and offered him his hand. Very moved, Guido kissed Padre Pio's hand and then left.

Those few moments with Padre Pio had made a remarkable impression on Guido. He knew that it was no accident that he had followed the five doctors to Padre Pio's cell. He was certain that it had been arranged by Divine Providence. That very evening, Guido had an opportunity to make his confession to Padre Pio. He no longer felt afraid. He was able to make a sincere confession. Padre Pio was very kind to him. He blessed him and gave him absolution. When Guido rose to his feet, he felt purified and immensely happy.

Guido's friend had been waiting for him in the little square just outside. When Guido left the confessional, he could hardly contain himself. He ran out of the church and with great joy, he began to shout to his friend, "He has absolved me, he has absolved me!"

———

There was a man once who entered Padre Pio's confessional and found it to be a very disheartening experience. The year was 1963. Padre Pio did not even permit the man to kneel down, but instead asked him to leave at once. The man felt insulted. He went to one of the other Capuchins and told him what had happened and how upset he was. "Padre Pio treated you that way because he cares about you," the Capuchin told him. "He wants you to change your life and to save your soul." The Capuchin then heard the man's confession and gave him absolution. He counseled the man and told him that it was very important for him to get his life back on the spiritual track. He noticed that in many ways, the man's ideas about religion were very shallow. He knew very little about his Catholic faith.

Unfortunately, the man did not heed the Capuchin's advice and continued to live a sinful life. He betrayed his family's trust and on many occasions was dishonest in his business practices. However, after meeting Padre Pio, something slowly started to change within him. He visited San Giovanni Rotondo on seven more occasions but always made sure that he kept a good distance from Padre Pio's confessional. Once had been enough.

Through his visits to the monastery, the man learned of Padre Pio's daily schedule. He knew that Padre Pio passed through the St. Francis hall each day after hearing the women's confessions. One day, he had a great desire to see Padre Pio. He did not want to speak to him. He simply wanted to see him.

The man went to the St. Francis hall and stood in a corner so that he would not be noticed. He did not want to attract any attention to himself. Padre Pio soon came out of the elevator and entered the St. Francis hall. Although many people surrounded him, he kept his arms folded across his chest so that no one could kiss his hands.

The man was surprised to see that Padre Pio had spotted him standing in the corner and was staring at him. Padre Pio then walked directly over to him and stretched out his hand. The man was very happy for the opportunity to kiss Padre Pio's hand. Padre Pio then blessed him. The man could not believe his good fortune.

One day, the man gathered enough courage to return to Padre Pio's confessional. He spoke to Padre Pio from his heart. He told Padre Pio that he had been trying to overcome the sins in his life but had not been able to completely free himself from them. "But is that not repentance?" Padre Pio said to him lovingly. Padre Pio's encouraging words filled the man with hope. He made a good confession and felt truly blessed to receive absolution from Padre Pio.

Monsignor John Gannon had a great devotion to Padre Pio and visited him in San Giovanni Rotondo on a number of occasions. Padre Pio always referred to him as the "American Monsignor." Monsignor Gannon spoke to Padre Pio's assistant, Father Eusebio Notte and said, "There must be many American priests whom Padre Pio refers to as the "American Monsignor." "No, you are the only one he refers to in that way," Father Eusebio replied.

Once, Monsignor Gannon was speaking with some friends at the monastery of Our Lady of Grace. Suddenly, a man approached the group with a ticket for Padre Pio's confessional in his hand. "I am not going to be able to use this ticket," the man said. "Would any of you like to have it?" "You should give it to Monsignor Gannon," a man in the group replied. Monsignor Gannon now had a ticket for Padre Pio's confessional, but he had a problem. He could not speak Italian and Padre Pio did not hear confessions in English. One of Monsignor's friends who spoke Italian offered to help him. He told him to write out his confession and he would translate it into the Italian dialect that Padre Pio spoke. Monsignor Gannon was very grateful for the help.

Monsignor Gannon practiced making his confession in Italian until he felt confident that Padre Pio would be able to understand him. In the confessional, Monsignor began to read from the paper that his friend had transcribed for him. When he got half way through his confession, Padre Pio suddenly interrupted him. He repeated what was on the rest of the paper, word for word. Monsignor Gannon knew that it was impossible for Padre Pio to see what was written on the paper that he had in his hand. He could hardly believe what had happened.

Monsignor Gannon remained close to Padre Pio through the years. In 1962, he received a letter from Father Eusebio Notte. In the letter, Father Eusebio told Monsignor Gannon that Padre Pio faithfully remembered him before the Lord, especially during Mass. "Padre Pio said that you are his spiritual child," Father Eusebio wrote. "You belong to him and he has some rights on you. He does not forget you in his prayers and he does not want you to forget him."

———————

Italian-born Dino Segre was a well known and highly esteemed author. He took the name Pitigrilli as his signature name for all of his published works. Dino was talented and successful and had more money than he could spend. Although he was not religious, as time passed, Dino began to think more and more about the deeper meaning of life. In the process, his interest in spirituality gradually began to grow.

At the advice of a friend, Dino decided to make a trip to San Giovanni Rotondo in order to see Padre Pio. Dino was famous throughout Italy but while he was visiting the monastery of Our Lady of Grace, he wanted to remain completely anonymous. He hoped that no one would recognize him. On the morning that he attended Padre Pio's Mass, he sat in the very back of the church and tried to remain as inconspicuous as possible.

During the Mass, when Padre Pio prayed for the living and the deceased, he spoke to the congregation and said, "Pray, brethren. Pray with your whole hearts for someone who is here with us today, someone who is in great need of our prayers. One day he will receive Holy Communion at the Lord's table. He will be instrumental in bringing others with him back to the Church, others who have lived without God, just like he has."

Dino was thunderstruck by Padre Pio's words. He was certain that Padre Pio was speaking about him. There was not a doubt in his mind. Dino felt as though his heart was breaking. He began to cry. Try as he might, it was impossible for him to stop the flood of tears.

After the Mass, Dino had an opportunity to make his confession to Padre Pio. The moment he knelt down in the confessional, Padre Pio quoted from scripture and said to him, "What does it profit a man to gain the whole world and lose his soul?" Of course, Dino knew the answer to the question. It profited a man nothing. Padre Pio was obviously speaking about the worldly life that Dino had been leading for many years. Padre Pio then said to him, "The Lord has been very good to you."

The encounter with Padre Pio marked a turning point in the life of Dino Segre. After he left San Giovanni Rotondo, he went to his publisher and insisted that certain books he had written be permanently taken off the market. He was aware that his decision would cause him to incur a great financial loss, but he didn't care. He knew that Padre Pio set a very high moral and spiritual standard. With all his heart, he wanted his literary works to reflect that standard. For the rest of his life, he wrote only books that had a Christian theme, books that would help encourage others in the practice of their faith.

Eighteen-year-old Andre Mandato attended Mass every Sunday without fail. Even so, he only went to confession once in a great while. To Andre, it did not seem necessary. He never had any serious sins to confess or any pressing problems that he needed to discuss with a priest. But more important, he lacked faith in the value of confession. He knew very well that the Church taught that the sacrament of reconciliation imparted sanctifying grace to the penitent. However, in his heart, Andre was not convinced that it was true. Andre's attitude underwent a complete change when he made his confession to Padre Pio for the first time.

Andre was very surprised in the confessional when Padre Pio began to name his sins. "You use bad language; you swear," Padre Pio said to Andre. "It is true," Andre replied. There was no denying the fact. "You know in your heart that it is wrong," Padre Pio said. "You swear and then you ask God for forgiveness. But simply asking God for forgiveness is not enough."

Padre Pio's words shocked Andre. He had always believed that asking God for forgiveness was enough. But as he reflected on it, he was able to grasp what Padre Pio was trying to convey to him. If a person asked forgiveness of God for a sin that was committed, that person should make a supreme effort never to commit the sin again. Unfortunately, that was not always the case. In Andre's life, it was not the case. Andre was suddenly able to understand the true malice of sin, and the seriousness of offending God.

When Andre left the confessional, he felt crushed. He began to cry and was unable to stop. The confession to Padre Pio marked a true turning point in his life and brought about a great spiritual change within him.

When disturbed by passions and misfortunes, may the sweet hope of his inexhaustible mercy sustain us. Let us hasten confidently to the tribunal of penance where he awaits us at every instant with the anxiety of a father, and even though we are aware of our inability to repay him, let us have no doubts about the solemn pardon pronounced over our errors. Let us place a tombstone over them, just as the Lord has done.

- *St. Pio of Pietrelcina*

Jesus will assist you and give you the grace to lead a heavenly life and nothing whatever will be able to separate you from his love.

- *St. Pio of Pietrelcina*

CHAPTER 11

Karl Klugkist

The Russian prince, Karl Klugkist, was born in Kiev on March 25, 1871. After being exiled at the beginning of World War I, he moved to Italy. Karl, who was intelligent and well educated, was also a deeply spiritual man who was seeking a closer walk with the Lord.

In 1919, Karl learned of Padre Pio for the first time. A priest that Karl met in Foggia, Italy told him a few details of Padre Pio's life. The priest had known Padre Pio when Padre Pio was a fifteen-year-old student in the Capuchin novitiate in Morcone. The priest told Karl that all of the young aspirants in the novitiate loved Padre Pio. The priests and instructors at Morcone felt the same. They admired him for his goodness and for his humility. According to the priest who spoke to Karl, "There was not a trace of evil in Brother Pio." Karl then read some articles in the newspaper about Padre Pio which further sparked his interest. He had a number of spiritual problems at the time and decided that it would be beneficial to go to San Giovanni Rotondo and speak to Padre Pio, asking for his counsel.

Karl had to wait two days to get a seat on the bus that traveled from Foggia to San Giovanni Rotondo. San Giovanni Rotondo was a popular destination at the time as many people wanted to make their confession to Padre Pio and to attend his Mass. Karl was finally able to board the bus but it was anything but a comfortable journey. It took two hours for the rickety old bus to maneuver along the worst kind of roads enroute to the monastery of Our Lady of Grace. On the journey, Karl enjoyed looking out the window at the wide expanse of sky. He also enjoyed the fresh mountain air which he found invigorating. However, the closer that he got to San Giovanni Rotondo, the more oppressive the landscape became. The bleakness of the area made Karl feel depressed.

Karl was happy that he had been able to obtain a letter of introduction from the archbishop of Gaeta. The letter included a request that Karl be allowed to speak to Padre Pio. When he arrived at the monastery of Our Lady of Grace, he handed his letter to the first Capuchin he saw. The Capuchin instructed Karl to go through the monastery courtyard and then enter the church through the small door that was just beyond.

When Karl walked into the church, the first thing he noticed was a Capuchin priest who was hearing a man's confession in an open confessional. The priest was sitting in a chair and was leaning his arms on the back of a chair that was in front of him. The penitent who knelt beside the priest looked to be a local farmer. Slowly, the priest who was hearing the man's confession raised his head and looked up at Karl. Karl recognized the priest immediately. It was Padre Pio. For some reason, he had not expected to see him so soon after arriving at the monastery. Karl felt both surprised and afraid at the same time.

The corridor was packed with men waiting in line to make their confession to Padre Pio. At the other end of the corridor, there was another door. There were a number of men trying to force their way through the door so that they too could get in the confessional line. They were dressed in work clothes and they all appeared to be farmers from the local area. The noise and commotion that the men were making struck Karl as very irreverent. He quickly summed up the situation and realized that in order to talk to Padre Pio about what was on his mind, he would need to get in the confessional line.

Karl took his place in the line and began to prepare himself for his encounter with Padre Pio. From where he was standing in line, he could easily observe Padre Pio. Karl noticed that Padre Pio remained immobile, with his arms either crossed or resting on the chair in front of him while he heard confessions. He kept his head lowered. As Karl looked at Padre Pio, he was awed by the beauty of his face. It was the most beautiful face that he had ever seen. Karl got caught up in gazing at Padre Pio, and forgot all about making his preparation for confession.

Karl continued to stare at Padre Pio. Just before he gave absolution to the man who was in the confessional, Padre Pio recited a prayer in a low voice. Karl was close enough to hear the prayer. It sounded as though Padre Pio was speaking in another language. It reminded Karl of an Asian language. Karl, who was fluent in a number of languages, could not identify the words.

Karl was still trying to focus his mind and prepare himself for confession. He let six men go in front of him in the line. All of a sudden, a man, thinking to do Karl favor, pushed him forward. Karl could postpone the encounter no longer. As he knelt before Padre Pio, he realized how truly unprepared he was to speak to him.

Padre Pio asked Karl when he had made his last confession. Karl told him that it had been the day before. "What sins have you committed since yesterday morning?" Padre Pio asked. Karl could not think of a single sin to confess. "I did not realize that I was going to have the opportunity to make my confession to you today," Karl explained. "I am not really prepared to do so. I came here hoping that I might be able to have a chat with you." The moment the words were out of his mouth, Karl regretted them. "That is impossible," Padre Pio answered. "There are too many people waiting in line. I cannot allow people to have a chat with me. If you have something to tell me, you must tell it to me during confession."

Karl had written out the items that he wanted to discuss with Padre Pio on a piece of paper. He wished that he had the paper with him but unfortunately he had left it in his suitcase. He knew that he had to speak quickly. There was not a minute to waste. Karl then began to talk about himself, jumping from one period of his life to another in no particular order.

As Karl spoke, he continued to study Padre Pio. He felt the full impact of his holiness. He was convinced that he was in the presence of a true saint. Padre Pio was different from anyone that Karl had ever met. Spiritually, he seemed to be in a class all by himself. To Karl, he appeared like a bright light, shining in the midst of the world's darkness. He was direct and confident and there was no trace of false sweetness or sentimentality in his manner. At one point, Padre Pio blew on his hands several times, as if they were burning. He showed absolutely no self-consciousness in doing so.

Padre Pio listened with the greatest attention as Karl spoke, but he did not make eye contact with him. Because of it, Karl felt as though there was no personal relationship or personal connection between he and Padre Pio. Although Karl could have talked much longer, he finally stopped himself after about ten minutes, knowing that many others were waiting in line for the same opportunity.

When Karl finished speaking, Padre Pio said to him, "You are seeking the way but you have already found the way." He did not admonish or scold Karl. He did not tell him what course to take in his life. He did not try to influence his will. He left him completely free to make his own decision. Then he spoke in the mysterious language that Karl had heard before but could not understand. Before leaving the confessional, Karl kissed Padre Pio's hand. To his great surprise, he noticed a beautiful perfume coming from his hand.

During his visit to the monastery of Our Lady of Grace, Karl felt blessed to be able to attend Padre Pio's Mass. When Padre Pio came out of the sacristy, a great silence fell upon the congregation. At the Mass, Karl was seated close enough to the altar to see Padre Pio's hands very clearly. Padre Pio had removed his gloves and Karl saw a red circular mark about the size of a small coin in the middle of each of his hands. Karl noticed blood flowing from the wounds in his hands during the Consecration. Karl could not contain his emotions. Upon receiving Holy Communion from Padre Pio, he began to weep.

After the Mass, two men approached Padre Pio and wanted to make their confession. Karl was standing nearby and noticed that Padre Pio would not agree to it. "Those men did not come here to make their confession," Padre Pio said.

During the days of his visit to Our Lady of Grace monastery, Karl occasionally walked to town. Whenever he did so, it always felt as though he had stepped back into civilization. Life at the monastery seemed to be far removed from the secular concerns of the modern world. Padre Pio reminded him more of a prophet from the Middle Ages than a man of the twentieth century.

On one of his visits to town, Karl met the local state commissioner. The commissioner told Karl that he had first-hand knowledge regarding Padre Pio's gift of reading hearts. One day, the commissioner went to the monastery to say goodbye to Padre Pio. He was going to be leaving his job in San Giovanni Rotondo in just a few days and another individual would soon be taking his place. Padre Pio smiled at the commissioner and said, "You are mistaken. You will not be leaving. You will stay in San Giovanni Rotondo for many months." The commissioner was surprised at Padre Pio's words. He did not want to disagree with him openly but he knew that Padre Pio was wrong. He had already received his transfer orders. However, a change was made at the last minute and the commissioner was asked to continue on with his job in San Giovanni Rotondo.

Karl enjoyed talking to the local citizens of San Giovanni Rotondo. They often told him interesting stories regarding Padre Pio. Karl learned that a blind woman had come to San Giovanni Rotondo from a long distance, hoping that her sight might be restored through contact with Padre Pio. When she finally had the opportunity to speak to Padre Pio, he said to her, "I cannot obtain the grace that you are asking for. But do not become discouraged, because you will soon be able to see." The woman went away in great distress. She told the priest who had accompanied her on her journey that she had given up all hope of ever being able to see again. She kept thinking of Padre Pio's words, "I cannot obtain the grace you are asking for." She believed that Padre Pio had simply tried to pacify her when he told her that she would soon be able to see. But less than two hours later, while on the trip home, the woman suddenly began to see.

When Karl returned to his home in Rome, he spent many hours in church, praying to the Lord for enlightenment. He was trying to discern the path that God might be calling him to follow. He was very happy that he had been able to speak to Padre Pio before leaving San Giovanni Rotondo. Padre Pio told him that he would remember him in his prayers. One day, when Karl was praying in front of the Blessed Sacrament, he saw two hands coming out of the tabernacle. The hands were holding a white habit with a red and blue cross on it. To his great surprise, the habit was coming toward him. He thought that his mind might be playing tricks on him. He closed his eyes and then opened them again. He rubbed his eyes to make sure that he was actually seeing what he thought he was seeing. It was true. It was not his imagination. He saw the white habit clearly. Finally, it disappeared.

Karl shared the unusual experience with his confessor. His confessor told him that there was a religious order called the Trinitarians who wore a white habit with a red and blue cross. His confessor then introduced him to the superior of the Trinitarians. Karl noticed that the habit the superior was wearing was identical to the one he had seen in the vision.

Karl realized that God had answered his prayers and had given him a clear sign of the vocation that he was to follow. He asked for admittance and was accepted into the Trinitarian Religious Order in Rome. He made simple vows and took the name, Brother Pio. He was sent to Canada where he made his solemn vows in 1924. Upon his ordination to the priesthood, he took the name Father Pio of the Most Holy Trinity. He felt Padre Pio's loving presence helping him and guiding him in his priestly ministry. He always attributed the good that he was able to accomplish to Padre Pio's intercession. Karl Klugkist (Father Pio of the Most Holy Trinity) died in Halifax, Nova Scotia in 1948 after a long and fruitful ministry in the Lord's service.

Let the Holy Spirit act within you. Give yourself up to all his transports and have no fear. He is so wise and gentle and discreet that he never brings about anything but good. How good this Holy Spirit, this Comforter, is to all, but how supremely good he is to those who seek him.

- *St. Pio of Pietrelcina*

CHAPTER 12

Padre Pio's Prophetic Spirit

O n January 20, 1936, Dr. Guglielmo Sanguinetti and several other men were visiting Padre Pio in his cell. As they were talking, Padre Pio suddenly interrupted the conversation and asked the men to kneel down with him and to pray. "We must pray for a soul who will soon appear before the judgment seat of God," Padre Pio said. When they were finished praying, Padre Pio asked his friends if they knew who they had been praying for. They replied that they did not know. Padre Pio told them that they had been praying for George V, the King of England. Dr. Sanguinetti told Padre Pio that he had just read in the paper that the King's health was not a cause for alarm. He had a head cold and no more. He was not in any danger. "What I am telling you is the truth," Padre Pio answered.

About midnight, Father Aurelio heard a knock at his cell door. When he opened the door, there stood Padre Pio. "Let us pray for a soul who at this very moment has passed away and is now appearing before the tribunal of God. I am talking about the King of England," Padre Pio said. The two priests prayed together for a while. The next day, the newspapers announced that the King had died. His death occurred at the same time that Padre Pio and Father Aurelio were praying together for him.

It was generally not Padre Pio's habit to make statements about political or world leaders. However, at the time of King George V's death, Padre Pio spoke of him and asked his friends to pray for his soul. It is not known whether Padre Pio had spoken of him at any other time. And what do we know of the King? We know that he was a man of faith and that he made it his practice to read from the Holy Scriptures every day. As a Protestant, he treated the Catholic Church with admirable respect. When George V became the King of England, he made a decision in favor of the Catholic Church. He refused to abide by the tradition in his country that considered the Catholic Mass to be "of a superstitious and idolatrous origin." History tells us that as the King of England, George was diligent and committed, and he influenced his country for good.

———————

Giovanna Boschi, had attended Padre Pio's Mass in San Giovanni Rotondo for more than forty years. She also felt blessed that in those many years, she had been able to go to confession to Padre Pio on a regular basis. On one occasion, Giovanna decided to visit her good friend Margherita Hamilton in Rome (see Chapter 21). During the visit, she noticed a magnificent red rose on the terrace of Margherita's house. She picked it and put it in a vase. Setting it on a table next to a little framed picture of Padre Pio, Giovanna said to Margherita, "This rose is so beautiful that I am going to take it to Padre Pio."

Soon another friend came over to Margherita's house to visit. The three ladies admired the rose sitting next to Padre Pio's photograph. That afternoon they had a wonderful time conversing together. After a time, Margherita happened to glance at the little table beside them. "Look," Margherita said to her companions, "The rose is not in the vase. It has disappeared!" The women lifted up the table and looked on the floor. They looked to the left, to the right, in front and behind. They looked everywhere in the general area, but the rose was nowhere to be seen. "This is impossible," Margherita said. "The three of us never left the house. We have been sitting here all afternoon. The rose was here and now it is gone. Things cannot just vanish into thin air!" There was absolutely no explanation for the occurrence.

About three weeks later, Margherita and Giovanna decided to go to the monastery of Our Lady of Grace to visit Padre Pio. When they arrived at the monastery, they found Padre Pio in a small sitting room. To their great surprise, he was holding a beautiful rose in his hand. It was the rose that Giovanna had intended to give him, the one that had vanished into thin air. "Thank you very much for the rose, Giovanna," Padre Pio said. "I appreciate your kindness."

Needless to say, Giovanna and Margherita were shocked. Right before their eyes, they saw the miraculous rose. Giovanna said to Padre Pio, "Father, do you think I might be able to have that rose back?" "Of course you can," Padre Pio replied. She took it home and put it in a frame. The rose would always remain one of Giovanna's most treasured possessions.

———

Once, a young woman was preparing to make a trip to the monastery of Our Lady of Grace in order to make her confession to Padre Pio. She also wanted to discuss some very important personal matters with him. Before leaving for the monastery, the girl's mother spoke at length to her about Padre Pio. Her mother then kissed the palm of her hand three times and made a request. "Just as I have kissed the palm of your hand, I ask you to kiss Padre Pio's hand for me," her mother said.

The young woman was irritated by her mother's words, which did not seem to be of much importance. She explained to her mother that her time would be very limited in the confessional. She was certain that it would be impossible for her to kiss Padre Pio's hand three times. She would be lucky if she had the chance to kiss Padre Pio's hand even once. But to kiss the palm of his hand? That did not seem likely. Most people kissed the back of his hand, if they had the opportunity to do so at all. "I have some very important things to discuss with Padre Pio," the young woman said to her mother. "In my mind, I am reviewing everything I want to say to him so that I will not forget. I cannot promise you that I can do anything other than that."

As the girl was making her confession to Padre Pio, he gently brought the palm of his hand to her lips. The girl kissed his hand and then continued her confession. Two more times, he put the palm of his hand against her lips. She had no idea why he did so. After the confession was over, she walked out into the courtyard in front of the church. She told several people who were standing nearby about her confession to Padre Pio. She explained how he had pressed his hand to her lips. She asked them if they knew why he might have done so. None of the people had an answer to her question. It was not until the next day that the girl finally realized what had happened. Padre Pio was granting her mother's wish.

———

There was a woman who had received a great grace through the intercession of Padre Pio. She wanted to visit Padre Pio at the monastery of Our Lady of Grace and she asked her husband to take her there. Her husband was a devout Catholic, but he was skeptical about Padre Pio. He doubted all the claims he had heard about his sanctity. He finally told his wife that he was willing to take her to San Giovanni Rotondo but he did not care to speak to Padre Pio.

During their days at the monastery, his wife tried to reason with him. "You have the opportunity to receive a blessing from Padre Pio and to have our son receive a blessing too. I am hoping and praying that you will take advantage of that opportunity," his wife said. Finally, he gave in to his wife's pleadings. The last day of the trip, he took his son to the place where the men waited for Padre Pio each day to receive his blessing. He stood off in the distance and hid himself in the shadows. After a time, Padre Pio came in. To some, he gave his blessing, to others he spoke a word of encouragement, and to others, he reached out and took the letters they handed him. When Padre Pio saw the man and his son, he turned to the son and said, "I know your name. Your name is Francesco Pio, just like mine." Then he looked at the father and exclaimed, "I said that to your son in order that you would believe." From that day forward, he believed.

———

Luciano Livellara, who lived in Venice, Italy, was very concerned about his mother's health. He traveled to San Giovanni Rotondo in order to speak to Padre Pio about his mother. After he made his confession to Padre Pio, he asked him to remember his dear mother in his prayers. As Luciano started to rise from the kneeler to leave, Padre Pio stopped him. "Now, about that other matter," Padre Pio said. "Break it off immediately! Do you understand?" Luciano understood at once what Padre Pio was talking about.

Luciano was deeply in love with a girl that he had been dating for a year. She had just recently told him that she was married. He had tried to end the relationship, but because of his love for her, he had not been able to do so. "I want to break up with her," Luciano said to Padre Pio. "I have prayed about it and I have tried to end the relationship, but I have not been successful." "Break it off immediately. Do it now!" Padre Pio repeated. Luciano got the message loud and clear. He went home to Venice, determined to do what Padre Pio had asked him to do. He never saw the girl again.

———————

Dr. Sciubba was one of Padre Pio's spiritual sons. One day, he spoke to Padre Pio about one of his relatives who had decided to divorce her husband. The husband had mistreated her and was the cause of much unhappiness in the family. The marriage had become an "absolute disaster." Dr. Sciubba believed that his relative was doing the right thing by seeking a divorce. Padre Pio did not agree with him. Each case was different, but in regard to this couple, Padre Pio did not feel that a divorce was the right solution. He told Dr. Sciubba quite frankly that the marriage should not be dissolved.

Dr. Sciubba went back to his relative and told her that Padre Pio was not in favor of her divorcing her husband. She thought deeply about it and decided to change her course of action. She wrote Padre Pio a long letter, sharing some of her heartaches regarding her marriage. The next morning, she decided to go to the post office and mail the letter. Before she left the house for the post office, there was a knock on her door. To her great amazement, her husband was standing at the door.

As it turned out, her husband had been to see Padre Pio to seek his counsel. He told Padre Pio that after many years of separation, he now wanted to reconcile with his wife. "Go to your wife and make up with her," Padre Pio advised. "But I do not have the courage to do so," the man replied. "I treated her badly and I am ashamed of my behavior. I do not feel like I can face her." "Then tell her that I have sent you to reconcile with her," Padre Pio said. "I am sure she would not believe me if I told her that," the man answered. "Then tell her that I have already read the letter that she wrote to me," Padre Pio said. Padre Pio then told the man some of the particulars in the letter, the letter that had not been sent yet.

As the man stood on the front porch and faced his wife, he was able to ask her for forgiveness. "I want our marriage to work out," he said. "I have been to see Padre Pio because I wanted to speak to him about our relationship and our future. He too wants our marriage to work out. He told me that you wrote him a letter in which you poured out your heart to him." His wife listened to her husband's words with amazement. She was the only person who knew anything about the letter. And yet, Padre Pio obviously knew the contents. He had told her husband about it. The woman could feel her husband's sincerity as he asked for forgiveness. She was able to let go of the painful events of the past. The couple reconciled with each other and felt the happiness once again of a loving marriage.

———————

A mother of five children traveled from Bologna to San Giovanni Rotondo on one occasion to see Padre Pio. She asked Padre Pio to accept her as one of his spiritual children and he agreed to do so. When she returned to Bologna she invoked Padre Pio's presence every day and prayed, "Padre Pio, please watch over my five children; protect them and bless them."

Being a busy mother of five children and living a long distance from San Giovanni Rotondo, more than five years passed before she was able to return to see Padre Pio. When she finally saw Padre Pio again, she made her confession to him. At the conclusion she said, "Padre Pio, watch over my five children; protect and bless them." Padre Pio said, "How many times are you going to ask me that?" "What do you mean?" the woman asked. "This is the first time I have mentioned it." "No, you have asked me that every day for the last five years!"

Father Agostino of Campolieto was visiting Padre Pio in San Giovanni Rotondo on one occasion. When it was time to say goodbye, he asked Padre Pio for his blessing and told him that he would soon be going back to Algeria. Padre Pio did not want him to do so and told him that there was danger awaiting him there. Father Agostino thought about Padre Pio's warning but did not feel that he could cancel his trip.

When Father Agostino returned to Algeria there was a conflict that arose between the French people who lived in the country and some of the other ethnic groups. Because Father Agostino spoke French, he was considered a suspect. One night, at 11:30 p.m. the police came to his door and arrested him. At that moment, Father Agostino remembered Padre Pio's words. He was taken to the police station and questioned. He was finally released at 5:00 a.m. the next morning. The Capuchins in San Giovanni Rotondo noted that Padre Pio became suddenly ill at 11:00 p.m. the same night that Father Agostino was arrested. He remained ill until five o'clock the next morning.

Mario Amendola was one of Padre Pio's spiritual sons. Mario had a cousin who had fallen upon hard times. He was out of work and penniless. He spoke to Padre Pio about his desperate situation. Padre Pio advised him to move to the city of Falconara. "I do not think that is a good idea," the man said. "I have friends in Rome who can help me but I do not know anyone in Falconara." Padre Pio advised him once again to go to Falconara.

The man decided to follow Padre Pio's advice. He moved to Falconara with his wife and children. One morning, a stranger approached him and said, "I work for the manager of a union. He told me that he would like to see you at his office." The man went to the manager's office and was offered an excellent job. The wages were more than he had ever hoped for. It was like a dream come true. How happy he was to have followed Padre Pio's advice!

Monsignor Gannon had an unusual experience on one of his visits to Padre Pio. After attending the afternoon holy hour at the monastery, he happened to see Father Pierino Galeone. For some strange reason, he had the irresistible urge to give Father Galeone some of his possessions. He took off his watch and gave it to Father Galeone. He also handed him his fountain pen as well as all of the money he had in his wallet. He could not explain his actions. He only knew that he had to do it.

Father Galeone had his hands cupped to receive the items and he was laughing all the while. Monsignor Gannon asked him why he was laughing. "This morning when I saw Padre Pio, he told me that I would be receiving a number of gifts today," explained Father Galeone. "But it is neither Christmas nor Easter. Why would I be receiving gifts?" Father Galeone asked. Padre Pio simply repeated again, "You will be receiving many gifts today." Although the incident was indeed mysterious, Monsignor Gannon was happy that Padre Pio had used him to play a part in it.

———————

Angelo Tomasini was the father of eight children. When one of his sons became ill, Angelo prayed to Padre Pio and asked for his intercession. To Angelo's great joy, his son was healed of his illness. Angelo was convinced that Padre Pio had answered his prayers. He decided to make a trip to the monastery of Our Lady of Grace in order to thank Padre Pio personally for his son's recovery. He was able to take two of his sons with him on the trip.

After taking a train to Foggia, Angelo and his two sons boarded a bus to San Giovanni Rotondo. Once they arrived in the little town, Angelo observed that there were only a few rooming houses available for visitors to the area. Unfortunately, they were all in very poor condition. Nevertheless, Angelo felt grateful that he was able to find lodging.

The next morning, Angelo and his sons went the short distance to the monastery church of Our Lady of Grace. Angelo then stood in line to make his confession to Padre Pio. When Angelo's turn came, as he began his confession, he noticed the unpleasant odor of sulfur in the air. He wondered if it had something to do with the sins that he was confessing at that very moment. He did not know. He had heard that people often perceived the heavenly fragrance of roses or lilies when they were near Padre Pio. But he was not so fortunate.

As Angelo made his confession, Padre Pio stared intently at a spot on the wall, directly above Angelo's head. He then started flicking at the invisible object with his forefinger and thumb. He seemed to be trying to drive away something that he saw there. Was it a spirit? Was it a demon? Angelo wondered but he did not know the answer. However, the unpleasant odor of sulfur still pervaded the air. Angelo knew that it was not a positive sign by any stretch of the imagination.

In the confessional, Angelo told Padre Pio about his son's remarkable healing. "I traveled the long distance to San Giovanni Rotondo because I wanted to thank you for your prayers. It is because of your intercession that my son has been healed," Angelo said. "But it is not me you should thank," Padre Pio replied. "It is the Lord you must thank because it is he who healed your son. I did nothing. Also, I would advise you to lead a better life if you claim to be a Christian."

After Angelo made his confession, he asked Padre Pio if he would accept him and his two sons as his spiritual children. Padre Pio replied that he would accept them. Angelo explained to Padre Pio that he had a wife and six other children who were not able to make the trip with him. He wanted Padre Pio to accept them also as his spiritual children. "Yes, I will accept them too," Padre Pio replied. "I hope that you can come back to San Giovanni Rotondo again sometime. You can then bring all the members of your family with you," Padre Pio added. Angelo thought of his family at home and was very happy to know that they would all be under Padre Pio's protection.

That afternoon, Angelo and his two sons attended the Benediction service in the monastery church. The next morning, they got up very early in order to attend Mass. During the Mass, Angelo knelt on the altar steps, right next to Padre Pio. Angelo noticed that while Padre Pio was saying Mass, his face, which was normally rather pale, was flushed with a red glow. Angelo began to doubt what he was seeing. His mind became flooded with negative thoughts. "This cannot be real," Angelo said to himself. "My eyes are deceiving me. Padre Pio is a counterfeit." Angelo knew that he was being tested. He had proof of Padre Pio's holiness. There was no reason for him to doubt it. He had already experienced Padre Pio's gift of reading of hearts, of miraculous healing, and more. Angelo talked back to the dark thoughts in his mind and before long they subsided.

Before Angelo left San Giovanni Rotondo to return to his home, he spoke to Padre Pio about his anxieties regarding a legal matter. There was a trial that was coming up in the near future and Angelo was very concerned about it. He explained to Padre Pio that he had committed no wrong. Padre Pio told him that he did not need to worry about the trial. "Be calm," Padre Pio said. "Everything has been filed away."

Shortly after Angelo returned home, he received notice from his employer that his job assignment was changing and that he was being transferred to a town not far from Rome. Angelo did not want to relocate to Rome. He was very happy where he was and he was afraid that the change would not be good for his family. However, Angelo had no choice in the matter.

The first day on his new job, Angelo spoke to the authorities regarding the upcoming trial. He was told that he did not need to concern himself about it because everything has been filed away. Angelo couldn't believe it. The very same words that Padre Pio had used were now repeated. The next time Angelo went to San Giovanni Rotondo, he told Padre Pio that he had been transferred and was now living and working near Rome. Padre Pio assured him that the move was going to be beneficial to every member of his family.

————

Nino Salveneschi made a trip to San Giovanni Rotondo in order to make his confession to Padre Pio. He also wanted to ask him for his counsel. In the confessional, Nino said to Padre Pio, "I came here to make my confession to you more than thirty years ago. I cannot remember whether it was 1923 or 1924." "It was 1924," Padre Pio replied. "It was in the summertime." Nino was shocked that Padre Pio remembered him as well as the time of his visit. It seemed impossible. Later, Nino had confirmation from his wife of the exact year and the season of the year. It had actually been thirty-one years previously, in the summer of 1924. Even though San Giovanni Rotondo was just a small village then, Nino had to wait two days to make his confession. Nino remembered clearly that he stood in line behind Prince Radziwill of Poland.

Everyone had to wait their turn in line and no one was given special privileges, no matter what their status or social rank.

In the confessional thirty-one years later, Padre Pio advised Nino, who was a writer by profession, to always take great care to write books that would be uplifting and beneficial for people. Nino told Padre Pio of the cross he was bearing. He had lost his eyesight while living in Belgium, and wanted to know how he could best cope with the loss. Padre Pio advised him to try to accept the trial without bitterness or complaint. Nino thought of the words of Job in the Old Testament - *The Lord gave and the Lord has taken away. Blessed be the name of the Lord* (Job 1:21). At the conclusion of Nino's confession, Padre Pio told him to go in peace and that he would remember him in his prayers.

Even though his encounter with Padre Pio was short, Nino felt a great sense of peace. That peace remained with him in the difficult years that were to follow. In his many trials, he was able to feel Padre Pio's presence. He later said that he felt that he owed his faith in God to Padre Pio.

I ask you to love the Calvary of God, crucified in the darkness; stay near to Him and rest assured that Jesus is within your hearts more than you are able to believe or imagine.

- St. Pio of Pietrelcina

Take care of your spirit, flee idleness and all immoral conversation . . . always remembering the words of the Apostle that our virtue is preserved in very fragile vessels.

- St. Pio of Pietrelcina

CHAPTER 13

Carlo Campanini

C arlo Campanini, the famous comedian and actor, met Padre Pio for the first time in 1939. Carlo had learned a little about Padre Pio from his friend, Mario. They were both working for a theater company at the time.

When Carlo and Mario knocked on the monastery door at Our Lady of Grace, they were greeted by Brother Gerardo. When they told the Brother that they were interested in speaking to Padre Pio, he told them that since it was Holy Week, it would be impossible. He explained that Padre Pio always suffered from the wounds of the stigmata, but his sufferings intensified during Holy Week. No one was allowed to visit him at that time.

Carlo tried to convince Brother Gerardo to make an exception to the rule. He said that he and Mario had been looking forward to meeting Padre Pio with great anticipation. They had used their time off from work to make the trip from Bari. However, Brother Gerardo would not change his mind.

Instead of leaving, Carlo and Mario decided to stay at the monastery for a while. They walked around the grounds and made a visit to the little church that was connected to the monastery. They hoped that if they waited long enough, they might run into Padre Pio. In order to pass the time, Carlo and

Mario were cracking jokes and laughing as was their habit. It did not occur to them that it was disrespectful for them to be talking so loudly in a sacred place. Suddenly, one of the Capuchins came out of the church and complained about the noise they were making. The Capuchin happened to be Padre Pio. At once, Carlo noticed the strong odor of carbolic acid in the air. It was so strong that it caused his throat to constrict.

Many people noticed the fragrance of flowers or perfume around Padre Pio but when a strong odor of carbolic acid or sulfur or disinfectant was present when Padre Pio greeted someone, it usually indicated that the person in question needed to change his life. That happened to be true in Carlo's case. At the time of his first visit to San Giovanni Rotondo, he was living a life that was very far from God.

Padre Pio asked Carlo and his companion to state their business. "We are two poor stage actors," Carlo said. "We are all poor," Padre Pio replied. "But why have you come to the monastery?" "We have come here to make our confession," Carlo answered. Padre Pio told them both to prepare themselves and he would hear their confession after Mass the following day. As Carlo looked at Padre Pio, a certain fear gripped his heart and he began to tremble. He felt that his whole life was laid bare to Padre Pio.

The next morning, Carlo and Mario attended Padre Pio's Mass. It was the longest Mass that Carlo had ever attended in his life. He was out of practice, for one thing. Kneeling on the hard stone floor of the church caused him to feel severe pain in his knees. It was almost more than he could bear. He felt a great sense of relief when the Mass was finally over.

At the time of Carlo's visit to Padre Pio, his greatest anxiety was that his work caused him to be separated from his children. He and his wife were always on the road, traveling from one city to another. Their children were living with one of their relatives. Carlo wanted to ask Padre Pio to pray that he could find work that would enable his family to be reunited. If it meant that he had to leave his acting career, he was prepared to do so. However, when he made his confession to Padre Pio, he could not bring himself to ask Padre Pio for anything. At the end of the confession, Padre Pio gave Carlo absolution, but before he did so, he made him promise to change his life. Carlo gave his word that he would make the necessary changes.

After visiting Padre Pio, Carlo returned to Bari and then moved to Rome. He found steady work in Rome that made it possible for his family to be reunited. It was a dream come true. He knew that Padre Pio had answered the secret prayer of his heart, the prayer that he had not been able to verbalize.

Nevertheless, Carlo continued to be preoccupied with worldly pursuits. He felt guilty about his immoral lifestyle but did not have the will to make the necessary changes. Padre Pio had asked Carlo to change his life, but he had not done so. For that reason, he did not want to return to San Giovanni Rotondo to see Padre Pio.

When Carlo won a leading role in a very successful film, his acting career began to soar. His photograph could be seen on the cover of numerous magazines and his name frequently appeared in the newspapers. People recognized him when he went out in public. He was offered starring roles in one movie after another and was making more money than he had ever dreamed of. But fame and fortune did not bring him happiness. Spiritually, Carlo was in a dark place. He was depressed most of the time and was haunted by a feeling of emptiness. His life had lost its meaning and its joy. He longed for peace of mind and peace of soul and prayed to God for assistance.

One day, Carlo's wife told him that the parish priest had spoken to her and suggested that their home be consecrated to the Sacred Heart of Jesus. They had even set the date. The priest wanted them all to receive Holy Communion on the day that their home was consecrated. That posed a big problem for Carlo. He would have to go to confession before he could receive Holy Communion. He dreaded the thought of it because he had many serious sins on his conscience. The embarrassment regarding what he would have to reveal in the confessional was very hard to think about. He did not know if he had the courage to go through with it. Carlo had not been to Mass or confession in a long time.

Carlo knew that it was important to his wife to have their home consecrated. He also knew that if he made a sincere confession, he would be obliged to change his life. He did not feel that he was ready to do that. He kept postponing the confession. Several times he went to church and stood in the confessional line but then lost his courage and left just before his turn came. He began to make one excuse after another to his wife. He finally told her that he was sorry but he would not be able to be there on the day the priest was coming to consecrate their home.

One day, Carlo made a visit to the parish of St. Anthony. He looked at the confessional line and knew that he would never have the time to wait in such a long line. "Please come to the front and take my place in line," a stranger said to him. Carlo was surprised but he took the man's place in line. Finally, he made a sincere and heartfelt confession and felt blessed to receive the grace of absolution.

Carlo and his family were all together when their home was consecrated to the Sacred Heart of Jesus on January 8, 1950. With great joy in his heart, Carlo was able to receive Holy Communion on that day with all the members of his family. He wanted to tell Padre Pio about the wonderful changes in his life and decided to make a trip to San Giovanni Rotondo to see him. He had nothing to fear now. He had already confessed the sins of his past. He would never have to do so again.

In San Giovanni Rotondo, Carlo waited in line to make his confession to Padre Pio. In the confessional, Padre Pio told Carlo to kneel down and to begin his confession from the year 1946 forward. Carlo's heart sank. He explained to Padre Pio that he had been to confession just two days before and had already confessed the serious sins of past years. But for some reason, it did not seem to matter to Padre Pio. He told Carlo for a second time, "Begin your confession from 1946. I know that you feel ashamed for the things that you have done in the past. You would rather that I did not know about them. But whether I know of them or not is of no importance. What matters most is that you have offended God by your sins. For some reason, that thought does not bother you."

Carlo began his confession as instructed, but he kept his head lowered. Padre Pio called him a coward and said, "I want you to look at me as you confess your sins." Carlo did so. After Carlo finished his confession, Padre Pio told him that he wanted him to once again make a promise to change his life. Carlo gave him his word that he would do so. This time he truly meant it. Finally, Padre Pio pronounced the words of absolution. Padre Pio gave him a Rosary and told him to pray it as often as he could. He promised Carlo that he would always be near to assist him in any difficulty. Before Carlo left the confessional, Padre Pio embraced him.

From that moment forward, Carlo's life underwent a complete transformation. There was a great peace in his heart as well as a desire to lead a good Christian life. The next morning, Carlo was able to attend Padre Pio's Mass. When he received Holy Communion from Padre Pio, it felt like a hot ember had been placed on his tongue. He felt the burning sensation in his mouth for several hours.

Before Carlo left San Giovanni Rotondo, he asked Padre Pio for his continued prayers. Carlo was aware that in some sense, his spiritual life would always be an uphill climb. He told Padre Pio that he was afraid of the temptations that he knew he would encounter once he returned home. Padre Pio said that it was good to be afraid of temptations, and that one should always have a certain fear of them. He advised Carlo to stay away from all the dark forces and satanic influences of the world. Padre Pio assured him of his spiritual support.

It was very evident that Padre Pio's spiritual support was with Carlo through the ensuing years. Carlo attended Mass and received Holy Communion every day upon Padre Pio's recommendation. With his work schedule, it was very difficult to do, but he always found a way to do it. He also turned down many starring roles in films. He was acting upon Padre Pio's advice to never take a part in a movie that had immoral content. Padre Pio had explained to Carlo that the people who made such movies would have to answer to God for their actions. That included everyone from the producers to the actors to the carpenters who built the sets to the people who sold the tickets.

Padre Pio also warned Carlo never to tell off-color jokes or use bad language. If a movie script had even one vulgar word in it, Carlo would not consider being a part of the project. Movie directors and producers could not understand why Carlo was passing up such lucrative job opportunities. When they asked him for an explanation, he simply told them that he was a spiritual son of Padre Pio and that Padre Pio set a very high standard.

Whatever gains I had, these I have come to consider a loss because of Christ. More than that, I even consider everything as a loss because of the supreme good of knowing Christ Jesus my Lord. For his sake I have forfeited all things and I consider them so much rubbish, that I may gain Christ and be found in him, not having any righteousness of my own based on the law but that which comes through faith in Christ.

- Philippians 3:7-9

Never let us put aside the thought of our ultimate aim. And what is this ultimate aim? To know God, principally, is why he conceived our days, our years. Therefore, let us try never to forget this ultimate aim, for everything depends on it. And for what reason? To serve him with faith, with love, and with constancy. Let us try to excel in all of this, then. Since God created us for love, he takes care of us for love, and for love he has promised us the prize.

- St. Pio of Pietrelcina

CHAPTER 14

John McCaffery

John McCaffery was a man of many talents and accomplishments. In different periods of his life he had worked as a writer, a university professor, a journalist, and a business man. In Donegal, Ireland, he tried his hand at farming, which he enjoyed very much.

During World War II, John lived in Switzerland where he was the head of an underground resistance operation against the Nazis. It was in Switzerland that he first heard about Padre Pio. One day John's confessor, Father Rizzi, gave him a book about Padre Pio. He told John that Padre Pio had the stigmata as well as many other extraordinary spiritual gifts. John accepted the book but knew that he would not read it. For one thing, John had always been skeptical about so-called mystics and from what Father Rizzi told him, Padre Pio definitely seemed to be in that category. John's intellectual mind set made him suspicious of any kind of supernatural phenomenon. John prided himself on his rational approach to life. As far as he was concerned, mysticism was something to be avoided. The book on Padre Pio would remain on his shelf, but he knew he would not open it.

The next conversation that John had regarding Padre Pio happened when World War II was coming to a close. John's confessor at that time was a Capuchin priest in Milan, Italy named Father Gian Antonio. Father Gian Antonio told John that he had visited Padre Pio in San Giovanni Rotondo on one occasion. Because Father Gian Antonio was a priest, the Capuchins invited him to stay overnight at the monastery.

During his visit, Father Gian Antonio noticed the great respect which every one of the Capuchins demonstrated toward Padre Pio. He told John that it was very impressive. He reasoned that the Capuchins who lived with Padre Pio on a daily basis knew him like no one else. Since their esteem for him was so obvious and so sincere, it was a good indication that Padre Pio was a holy priest. When Father Gian Antonio made his confession to Padre Pio, he experienced a deep and profound sense of peace.

After sharing his story, Father Gian Antonio gave John two photographs of Padre Pio. Still, John's heart was unmoved. As time passed, other people spoke to John about Padre Pio. A friend invited him to go to San Giovanni Rotondo to attend Padre Pio's Mass. John was not enthusiastic about the idea. Why should he travel such a long distance to attend the Mass of Padre Pio? There were many Catholic churches where John lived in Milan and Mass was said every day. He reasoned that Jesus was present at every Mass in every part of the world. That was where the Christian found his strength, not in chasing after so-called saints. Although he was reluctant to accept the invitation, John finally agreed to accompany his friend to San Giovanni Rotondo. He had been hearing about Padre Pio from various friends and associates for at least ten years.

All of John's doubts about Padre Pio disappeared when he attended his Mass. Padre Pio radiated an aura of sanctity. The way in which he pronounced the sacred invocations had a powerful effect on John. Every word was spoken slowly and solemnly. The congregation was made up for the most part by poor people - farmers, laborers, and those of the working-class. John observed that all who were present seemed to be aware of the sacredness of the Mass.

After the Mass, the men in the congregation followed Padre Pio into the sacristy. They stood in complete silence while Padre Pio took off his priestly vestments and then made his thanksgiving. Others stood in an orderly line in the corridor, waiting for Padre Pio to come out of the sacristy.

On his first visit to San Giovanni Rotondo, John and several others were invited to visit Padre Pio in his cell. They were able to converse with Padre Pio for over an hour. When it was time to say goodbye, John was reluctant to leave. Meeting Padre Pio and attending his Mass had been a far greater experience than he had ever imagined.

Three times a year, John traveled from Ireland to Milan, Italy where he had business interests. He would stay in Milan for six weeks at a time before returning to his family in Ireland. After his first visit to Padre Pio, whenever he could break free from his work, he would travel by train from Milan to San Giovanni Rotondo.

John soon became a familiar face at the monastery. Through his visits, he became acquainted with many of the Capuchins who lived with Padre Pio. Giovanni Vignolini, Padre Pio's infirmarian, was one of them. Giovanni had access to Padre Pio's cell at all times. He cared for Padre Pio whenever he was ill, which was often. He also assisted Padre Pio in taking care of the wounds of his stigmata. Giovanni frequently allowed John to accompany him to Padre Pio's cell. Whenever John was with Giovanni, he was able to walk right past the monastery porter without being stopped and turned around.

As time passed, and through many visits, John and Padre Pio became very close. Often, when John's friends learned that he was making a trip to San Giovanni Rotondo, they asked him to relay their prayer requests to Padre Pio. John knew that Padre Pio's time was very limited. John came up with a good plan of action. Before he spoke to Padre Pio, he spent some time in silence in the church of Our Lady of Grace. One by one, he would recall each one of his friends to mind as well as their prayer requests. Then, when he saw Padre Pio, he would simply say, "I have these prayer intentions in my heart, not only my own, but also those of my friends, and I would like to ask for your prayers."

On one occasion, John realized that he had made a mistake when he asked Padre Pio to pray for the intentions of his friends. As he was mentally going over the list, he had accidentally forgotten two individuals who had asked to be remembered in prayer. When John realized his error, he decided to tell

Padre Pio. Before he could say a word, Padre Pio said to him, "Oh yes, don't worry. I am going to pray for those two as well."

John soon learned that nothing could be hidden from Padre Pio. He frequently read John's mind by telling him exactly what he had been thinking. From time to time, Padre Pio would relate to John what John had been discussing with the other Capuchins. Even though Padre Pio had not been present during the discussions, he somehow knew all the details and could repeat the conversations almost verbatim. Without ever seeing John's business calendar, Padre Pio at times, would remind him of the appointments he had scheduled for the upcoming week. In addition, when John was struggling with a difficult personal problem, Padre Pio always seemed to be aware of it. John never had to explain anything to him. Sometimes Padre Pio gave John advice that did not seem quite up to the mark. But John soon learned that if he followed the advice and took the recommended course, things would always work out to his best advantage.

On one occasion, Padre Pio said to John, "You have spent your life traveling from one country to another. Since the time of your childhood, I bet that you have never spent more than seven years in any one given place." Later, John thought about what Padre Pio had said. When he did some calculations, he realized that Padre Pio had been right. Throughout his life, John had spent almost seven years exactly, living in one particular area before relocating to the next.

Those who were close to Padre Pio were well aware of his remarkable intuitive knowledge. Even though Padre Pio did not listen to the radio, read the newspaper, or watch television, he always seemed to have a complete grasp on world affairs. He could discuss international politics with remarkable insight. At times, he knew the contents of letters he had received, that is, before opening them. On one occasion, when Padre Pio was sick in bed, one of the Capuchins brought a number of letters and packages to him to be blessed. He blessed all but one item, which was an envelope. "I am not going to be able to bless that," Padre Pio said as he pointed to the envelope. It aroused the curiosity of the Capuchins who were present in his cell. They later discovered that the envelope in question contained a betting ticket for the football game. Whoever had slipped it in with the other letters, obviously did not realize that Padre Pio refused to bless gambling ventures.

When John was a professor at the Genoa University in Italy, one of his students had a brother who decided to test Padre Pio's powers of discernment. In the confessional, he told Padre Pio that he was there, not to confess his sins, but to ask for prayers for one of his sick relatives. It was not true. The young man did not have any sick relatives. The moment the words escaped his lips, Padre Pio became angry and ordered him out of the confessional. The young man soon realized the error of his ways. Not long after, he returned to Padre Pio's confessional and apologized. He then made a sincere confession.

At the time of John's visits, Mass was still said in the small church of Our Lady of Grace. On seven occasions, John had the blessing to be the altar server at Padre Pio's Mass. One time, one of John's friends hired a professional photographer to take pictures, not only of the Mass, but also of John assisting Padre Pio as altar server. He knew that John would treasure the photos. Padre Pio noticed the photographer in the church before the Mass started and spoke to him. He gave him permission to take no more than two photos. The photographer happily agreed. But the temptation to take more than two photographs evidently won out. During the Mass, he used two rolls of film. When he went to develop them, every picture came out blank.

Even though John would have loved to have had a photograph taken while he was serving Padre Pio's Mass, he possessed something which he cherished even more - a precious relic of Padre Pio. It was a piece of bloodstained bandage that had covered his stigmata. It had originally belonged to one of the Capuchins in San Giovanni Rotondo. How the Capuchin came to possess the relic is a story in itself.

One day, the Capuchin asked Padre Pio if he would like him to carry some water to his cell. Padre Pio was happy for him to do so. However, the Capuchin had ulterior motives. He was hoping to find a relic in Padre Pio's cell. He took the water to his cell, and once inside, he spotted some of the bandages that Padre Pio had used to cover his stigmata. He quickly pocketed them and was relieved that Padre Pio had not seen what he had done. Obtaining a relic was much easier than he had ever imagined. He decided to try his luck for a second time. The next evening, the Capuchin spoke to Padre Pio and offered once again to carry water to his cell. "Absolutely not!" Padre Pio replied. "I have a great distaste for thieves!"

Once, John arrived at the church of Our Lady of Grace before dawn, in order to be one of the first to enter when the doors opened. That would assure him of a seat close to the altar for Padre Pio's Mass. John noticed that another priest, Father Vincenzo, was preparing to say Mass in one of the side chapels of the church. Father Vincenzo did not have an altar server that day. John thought hard about what he should do. He had a great desire to attend Padre Pio's Mass that morning and he had found an excellent seat right in the front. John decided to make the sacrifice; he offered to be the altar server for Father Vincenzo's Mass. Evidently, it was the right decision, for at the moment of the Consecration, John perceived a strong and beautiful fragrance of perfume. John knew that it was Padre Pio's way of thanking him for helping Father Vincenzo.

Another memorable time when John experienced the charismatic perfume of Padre Pio was when he was engaged in a conversation with one of his business associates. At the time, his business associate was having more than his share of personal problems. While they were talking, John was wondering to himself whether he should say something about Padre Pio. The man was not a Catholic and John was certain that he knew nothing about Padre Pio. While John was turning the idea over in his mind, he suddenly perceived a beautiful fragrance of perfume. He understood at once that the fragrance was Padre Pio's way of saying, "Yes, you should say something." The man was very receptive and seemed genuinely interested in what John shared with him about Padre Pio.

John's wife also experienced the extraordinary perfume of Padre Pio. On one occasion, while John was in Milan, Mrs. McCaffery wrote to him from Ireland, telling him of a problem concerning one of the family members. Shortly after she sent the letter, she became aware of a beautiful perfume that pervaded her home. She immediately thought to herself, "This is Padre Pio. He must be aware of the letter that I just sent."

Shortly after that, John and his friend Piero Pellizzari, were visiting Padre Pio one day at the monastery. Piero said to Padre Pio, "John's wife had a wonderful experience. She became aware of your presence by the sign of perfume. It happened at her home in Ireland." Padre Pio then looked at John and said to him very gently, "Even beyond the sea." He was referring to the fact that there were no barriers that prevented him from being with his spiritual children, wherever they might be.

Once, John met an American priest at the monastery. He told John that his short encounter with Padre Pio had been very disappointing. He had been offended by Padre Pio's brusque manner. He told John that he would never again return to the monastery of Our Lady of Grace. Padre Pio had been rude to him in front of a number of people and what was worse, had declined to hear his confession. The priest was angry as well as hurt. John told the priest that in the past, he too had occasionally experienced Padre Pio's apparent coldness. Of course it was not a pleasant experience, but John had reflected on it and had been able to draw some conclusions. John realized that when Padre Pio treated him in a cold manner, the problem was with him and not with Padre Pio. It happened when there were sins in John's life. John was very much aware of those sins and he knew by experience that they could not be hidden from Padre Pio. John told the young priest, "In my own case, I feel that if Padre Pio wanted to walk all over me, I would lay down on the ground and invite him to start walking."

The priest listened with attention to what John told him and seemed very satisfied with the explanation. The next day, he was able to visit Padre Pio in his cell and make his confession. It turned out to be a grace-filled experience. Padre Pio accepted the priest as his spiritual son and a strong and lasting bond of friendship developed between the two.

John met another man in San Giovanni Rotondo who, like the American priest, found his first meeting with Padre Pio to be more than a little upsetting. The man was an industrialist from northern Italy. Thirty years before, he had come across a book on Padre Pio almost by accident. He found the book in a hotel where he was staying, and having nothing better to do, he read it. After he finished the book, he never gave it a second thought.

Later, the man became involved in spiritualism and took it upon himself to share his knowledge about the subject with his family. One of his sons took great interest in spiritualism and eventually became a proficient and successful spiritual medium. But tragedy struck the family when his son had a nervous breakdown. He finally had to be committed to a mental institution. His father was distraught, and while trying to think of a way to help his son, he remembered the book on Padre Pio that he had read some thirty years before.

He decided to travel to San Giovanni Rotondo and speak to Padre Pio about his son.

At the monastery of Our Lady of Grace, he was able to see Padre Pio. But before he could explain the tragic situation, Padre Pio said to him sternly, "You jeopardize the life of your son and then you have the nerve to come to this monastery! How could you do that?" The man was shocked and angered. He left San Giovanni Rotondo and vowed to himself that he would never return. But later, having no other ideas regarding how to help his son, the man decided to visit Padre Pio again. The second visit to the monastery was no better than the first. There were no words of consolation from Padre Pio, no offer of assistance, no sign of hope. His son's condition showed no improvement. The man returned a third time to see Padre Pio. On his third visit, Padre Pio spoke to him and told him that his son would indeed get his mental faculties back. The words proved to be prophetic for his son's condition began to improve. He made a complete recovery and was able to live a normal life, free from any mental impairment.

The man continued to visit San Giovanni Rotondo whenever he was able to. One day he was standing in the church, near the area where Padre Pio was hearing the women's confessions. Several times, Padre Pio looked up from the confessional and stared at him. Each time he did so, the man lowered his eyes. Finally, the man reasoned to himself, "Why am I lowering my eyes each time that Padre Pio looks at me? It makes no sense. If he looks my way again, I am going to look right back at him." Padre Pio looked at him once again, and true to his word, the man stared right back at him. As he did so, it was as though two flames shot out of Padre Pio's eyes, as if to consume him. He lowered his eyes immediately.

Once, on the eve of the feast of St. John the Baptist, John and several others were engaged in a conversation with Padre Pio. They were standing together in the hallway right outside Padre Pio's cell. "Well, John," Padre Pio said, "since you share the same name as St. John, tomorrow is your feast day too. I will be praying for you as well as for your wife and children tomorrow at the Mass." Padre Pio bid goodbye to the other men he had been talking with and invited John to come inside his cell to visit. However, on that particular night, John noticed that Padre Pio looked very ill. He was deathly pale and seemed completely drained of strength. Just as John entered the cell, Padre

Pio started to faint. Luckily, John caught him before he hit the ground and was able to help him to a chair.

As Padre Pio rested in the chair, John noticed that his ankles and feet were very swollen. One of the Capuchins once described Padre Pio's feet as looking like "two watermelons," because of the swelling. Padre Pio's personal attendant said that he was in a panic whenever he had to help Padre Pio put on his shoes. The slightest touch to his instep always caused Padre Pio great pain.

John told Padre Pio how sorry he was to see that he was sick. He told him that he should try to get some rest as the hot temperatures of the summer months were upon them. The recent days had been particularly hot and uncomfortable. "It is not the days so much as the nights that cause me suffering," Padre Pio said to John. Padre Pio held up his hands covered with the woolen half-gloves and confided to John, "The pain in these hands becomes so intense at night that it is hard for me to sleep."

The next day, John visited Padre Pio in his cell once again. He seemed to be feeling much better. "On this feast day of St. John the Baptist," John said, "I wonder if I could ask you for a favor?" "What favor would you like to ask of me?" Padre Pio asked. "I would like you to sign a holy card for me," John replied. Padre Pio was happy to do so. John noticed that it was very difficult for him to hold a pen. The wound in his hand made it hard for him to wrap his fingers around it. It was also difficult for him to write legibly. John noticed by the expression on Padre Pio's face that it was painful for him to write. Although John treasured the holy card, after seeing what it cost Padre Pio to write the personal message, he regretted that he had asked him for the favor.

During one of his visits to the monastery of Our Lady of Grace, John met a man named Giovanni and soon they became fast friends. Giovanni was known simply as Giovanni da Prato, since he was originally from Prato, Italy. He had a deep conversion experience through his contact with Padre Pio. Giovanni had received the gift of faith and was able to completely reform his life.

Giovanni da Prato drove a taxi for a living and in times past, he had a serious drinking problem. When he drank too much, he would often become violent. Once, after an evening of excessive drinking, he struck his wife and then collapsed in a drunken stupor across the bed. Suddenly, he felt the bed moving. He looked up to see a Capuchin, holding onto the bed rail and shaking the bed. The Capuchin, who had a very angry look on his face, was staring directly at Giovanni. "You have gone too far this time!" the dark-robed figure said to Giovanni and then he simply disappeared.

Giovanni told his wife about the mysterious Capuchin who had stood beside his bed. "I have been praying to a priest named Padre Pio," his wife said. "I have been invoking his presence so that he will protect me against your drunken rages." Later, she admitted that she had sewn a picture of Padre Pio inside Giovanni's pillow case. His wife's words aroused his curiosity. He got in his taxi and made the long journey from Tuscany to San Giovanni Rotondo. He had to find out if Padre Pio was the same man that he had seen in his bedroom.

When Giovanni arrived at the little church of Our Lady of Grace, he noticed many people standing both inside and outside the church with rosaries in their hands. The sight of it was disgusting to him. He assumed that they were all religious fanatics. Giovanni had very little respect for people who claimed to have faith. He had always considered religion to be a matter of superstition.

Giovanni was standing in the sacristy of the church when he saw Padre Pio for the first time. He immediately recognized him as the man who had stood beside his bed. "So, the mangy old sheep has arrived!" Padre Pio said when he saw Giovanni. It was definitely not a warm welcome. Giovanni wanted to speak to Padre Pio privately. Ever since he had the strange experience of seeing Padre Pio in his home, he had begun to think about the meaning of life. If faith was important and if God really existed, Giovanni wanted to discuss the matter with Padre Pio. He was told that the only way to do so was to go to confession to him. He decided to take the plunge.

In the confessional, Giovanni was shocked to hear Padre Pio say to him, "You must leave at once. I cannot hear your confession. You must find another priest. I do not want to go to hell for you!" After hearing the harsh words, Giovanni had no peace of mind. He was angry at Padre Pio for speaking to him in such a cutting manner, but after a short time, his anger subsided. As an active member of the Communist party, Giovanni had spent years persecuting people who professed religious faith. But now he needed some answers and he felt that Padre Pio was the one person who could supply them.

Giovanni felt at a total loss as to what to do next. He could not bring himself to make his confession to another priest. He had heard that Padre Pio's parents, Grazio and Giuseppa Forgione were buried in the local cemetery. He walked to the cemetery and was able to find their graves. He wanted to say a prayer to them but he did not know how to pray. He had never said a prayer in his life. Instead he lit two candles, one for Grazio and one for Giuseppa. He spoke to them from his heart, "You are Padre Pio's parents. Please tell your son to accept me as one of his spiritual children. I want to change my life and I also long to hear a kind word from him."

One morning, after Giovanni and his wife attended Padre Pio's Mass, Padre Pio spoke to him briefly. He tapped Giovanni on the head and said to him, "It is not true what you were thinking in the church today, ignoramus! I want you to learn how to pray the Rosary!" Obediently, Giovanni went and bought a little devotional book with instructions on how to pray the Rosary.

Not long after, Padre Pio heard Giovanni's confession. For the sins that Giovanni had forgotten, Padre Pio named them for him. During his confession, Giovanni broke down and cried. Padre Pio cried as well. Giovanni handed his Communist party membership card to Padre Pio and asked him to throw it away. Padre Pio said, "Yes, that is good. I will indeed destroy it." Giovanni invited many of his former Communist friends to visit the monastery. He introduced them to Padre Pio and many were converted.

Padre Pio explained to Giovanni that he had hurt a lot of people and needed to make amends for his past sins. He told Giovanni that he must go to the last Mass each Sunday until further notice. At that time, the fasting rules of the church were such that one had to fast from midnight until the time one received Holy Communion the following day. That meant that every Sunday, Giovanni would have to fast from the previous night until the end of the next day.

Everyone without exception went to Sunday Mass in the morning, in part because of the strict fasting rules. People were generally quite hungry after fasting from midnight the night before. They usually went directly home after Mass in order to have breakfast. No one received Holy Communion at midday or at the end of the day. For Giovanni, not only was the penance difficult, it was also humiliating. As he walked down the isle to the communion rail all by himself and knelt there alone, he felt embarrassed. He had to endure the rude remarks of the people in the church who whispered together about him and stared at him curiously.

Giovanni's penance lasted for almost one year. He never asked that the length of time be shortened and he completed it without a complaint. At the end of the year, he spoke to Padre Pio and told him how happy he was that his penance was finally over. Padre Pio said to him, "Giovanni, I too suffered during that year. I was stretched out on the cross and I shed my blood for you."

Giovanni wanted to live his new found faith to the fullest. He knew that Padre Pio was interceding for him and helping him to turn away from sin. Most of his destructive behaviors fell away easily. He stopped using profanities in his speech and he made many other positive changes in his life. There were a few bad habits, however, that he found difficult to break. He spoke to Padre Pio about it. Padre Pio said to him, "Giovanni, you put in your good will and I will take care of the rest of it."

Giovanni visited the monastery as often as he could. Sometimes he would reflect on his life and say to himself, "Why am I so captivated by this elderly priest? Why have I left everything for him?" Giovanni knew in his heart that he would never return to his former way of living. On several occasions, while sitting in the little church of Our Lady of Grace, he had seen Padre Pio's face shining with an unearthly beauty. He asked one of the pilgrims if he had seen the radiance on Padre Pio's face. "Indeed I have seen the same thing," the man replied. Giovanni spoke to Padre Pio about it. "Father, your face is so very beautiful." "Why would you say something like that to me?" was Padre Pio's only reply.

One day at the monastery, Giovanni was present when Padre Pio and some of his fellow Capuchins were talking together. The subject of Padre Pio's stigmata came up. "Tell us how you received the stigmata," one of the Capuchins said to Padre Pio, but he made no reply. Several of the Capuchins gave their opinion on the matter. Each one had a different idea. "It was the crucifix in the choir loft of the church that imprinted the wounds of Christ on Padre Pio's body," one of the Capuchins stated. "And what do you think happened, Giovanni?" Padre Pio asked. "I have a different thought about it than the others," Giovanni replied. "I think that Jesus came down from heaven and embraced you. At his embrace, you received the stigmata." "You are closer than all of the others in your explanation," Padre Pio replied. But he would make no other comment.

John McCaffery had an adventure with Giovanni da Prato on one occasion that he would never forget. One day, he happened to see Giovanni at the monastery. Giovanni told John that he had a great desire to see Padre Pio. "Oh, but it is impossible," John replied. "Padre Pio is sick and confined to his cell. No one is allowed to visit him today." "I will tell you a secret if you promise not to tell anyone," Giovanni said. "I happen to have a key that leads to the monks' cells." "How on earth did you manage to get a key?" John asked. But Giovanni would not answer the question. "Don't worry about how I got the key. Let's just try our luck!" Giovanni said.

Giovanni's bold and daring spirit gave John the courage he needed to do something that was very much against the rules. The two men walked past the "no visitors allowed" sign in the monastery and unlocked the door that led to the cloister. They walked down the hall very quietly so as not to arouse attention and then opened the door to Padre Pio's cell. Once inside, they saw that Padre Pio was all alone. They spent just a few moments with him. Padre Pio gave them both a blessing. Giovanni had received his heart's desire. When he left Padre Pio's cell, he was very happy and very satisfied.

Just like Giovanni da Prato, John on one occasion, had an overwhelming desire to see Padre Pio. It was on the feast of Corpus Christi. John decided to take the train to San Giovanni Rotondo, even though he knew he would have to catch a train and return to Milan that very evening. He felt that if he could see Padre Pio that day, it would be well worth the long hours of travel time.

The feast of Corpus Christi was indeed a magnificent celebration in San Giovanni Rotondo. A full band ensemble provided the music while young girls in beautiful white dresses led the large outdoor procession, strewing flowers along the processional path. The Blessed Sacrament followed behind under its traditional canopy.

John had arrived in San Giovanni Rotondo in ample time and was in the church well before the festivities began. Unfortunately, he had not been able to see Padre Pio like he had hoped to. An announcement was made in the church that instructed everyone, both clergy and laity to exit the church and assemble outside. The Corpus Christi procession was about to begin. Directly after the procession, John would have to catch the train to return home.

John knew that Padre Pio would not be able to participate in the Corpus Christi celebration that day. It would be impossible for him to walk in the procession. John was certain that Padre Pio would remain inside the monastery. His desire to see Padre Pio was so great that, instead of following the line of people who were exiting the church, he stayed behind. Quietly, and with great care so as not to draw attention to himself, John walked up the stairs that led to the choir loft. He waited there until he was certain that everyone had gone outside. When John was convinced that he was completely alone in the church, he left the choir and made his way to the corridor near Padre Pio's cell. By positioning himself in the corridor, John would be sure to see Padre Pio if he left his cell for any reason.

As John waited, the thought occurred to him that Padre Pio might be angry with him. He had purposely disobeyed the instructions that had come over the church's loudspeaker. Instead of exiting the church like all the other people, he had hidden in the choir loft. John knew that Padre Pio had a great respect for rules and made it a point to observe them to the letter. John had seen Padre Pio's anger on previous occasions. It could be a shattering experience to be the object of his anger. The more John though about it, the more nervous he became.

John decided that he better have an explanation ready, a line of defense, just in case he saw Padre Pio and found that he was upset with him. He would tell Padre Pio the truth. He would explain to Padre Pio that he came to the monastery that day because he had a great desire, a great need to see him. If it was simply a matter of attending the Gesu Sacramentato procession, he could have just as easily stayed in Milan. John turned the phrase over in his mind, "Gesu Sacramentato." He was very pleased with himself for thinking of it. He had never heard it used before.

Suddenly John heard footsteps and then he turned to see Padre Pio coming toward him. John greeted Padre Pio and said, "I was hoping that I could see you today. I hope you are not upset with me for staying behind in the church." "No, I am not upset with you," Padre Pio said. "Let's go to the sitting room and have a visit." John breathed a great sigh of relief.

John asked Padre Pio how he was feeling and he replied in his customary manner, "Let us thank God." He did not like to speak about his health problems. By simply saying "Let us thank God," to any inquiries about his health, he showed that he left all such concerns in God's hands.

John and Padre Pio had a long conversation together and when it was finally time to part, Padre Pio said to him, "May the angel of the Lord accompany you always." With a look of merriment in his eyes, he added, "Before you catch the train to go back to your home, you will have time to participate in the Benediction ceremony outside. The Gesu Sacramentato is just now approaching from the street." That phrase, "Gesu Sacramentato" that John had been turning over in his mind and to which he felt a certain ownership, evidently had not been hidden from Padre Pio.

John's visit with Padre Pio on the feast of Corpus Christi had indeed been wonderful. But there had been another occasion, a chance meeting with Padre Pio that had not gone so well. Later, John and Dr. Sanguinetti would recall the incident and see the humor in it, but at the time it happened, it was no laughing matter.

On that particular afternoon, John, Dr. Sanguinetti and one other gentleman, happened to see each other at the monastery. Dr. Sanguinetti suggested that they go to the small room adjoining the choir loft and discuss some of the upcoming plans for the Home for the Relief of Suffering. At the time, Dr. Sanguinetti was heavily burdened with many difficult decisions that he had to make regarding the hospital. He was trying to raise funds, publish an informational newspaper regarding the hospital, and oversee the construction plans.

The informal business meeting that Dr. Sanguinetti suggested would cause the men to miss the sermon that was about to begin in the church. However, they would be finished with their discussion by the time Padre Pio was ready to give Benediction. "You know, the sermons of the visiting Capuchin are boring," Dr. Sanguinetti said. "I am not able to stay awake when he is preaching. We will just talk together quietly while the sermon is going on. When we hear Mary Pyle and her choir start to sing, it will be our cue to go in the church for Benediction."

The plan sounded like a good one, but the men would soon regret it. When Padre Pio rounded the corner and saw the three men discussing business together, he became angry. John and his two companions instantly regretted their decision, but it was too late. "How could you do it?" Padre Pio said. "How could you have a discussion while the Capuchin is preaching a sermon? You must go downstairs at once to the church!" To the men, it seemed like Padre Pio had overreacted. Nevertheless, they followed his advice and went into the church.

Through the years, John observed that Dr. Sanguinetti always seemed to feel totally at ease whenever he was with Padre Pio. That was rare. Because almost everyone had a certain awe of Padre Pio, it was very difficult for most people to feel completely comfortable in his presence. Not Dr. Sanguinetti. He was able to be truly natural, truly "himself." Knowing that, Padre Pio could let his guard down and could relax in his company. It was something that he was not able to do with many people.

Once, John and Dr. Sanguinetti were saying goodbye to Padre Pio after visiting him. Padre Pio suddenly became serious. For some time, he stared intently at John and at Dr. Sanguinetti, and finally said to them, "Who knows when and where we will meet again." John wondered what Padre Pio meant by the mysterious comment. Shortly after that and quite unexpectedly, Dr. Sanguinetti died of a heart attack. His death came as a terrible blow to Padre Pio. It left a great void in his heart. It seemed that no one was able to console Padre Pio over the loss of his dear friend.

Several months later, John returned to San Giovanni Rotondo for a visit. When Padre Pio saw John, he began to cry. They went into a private room in the monastery so that they could talk together. "You probably did not think that you would ever see me in a state such as this," Padre Pio said to John. The tears flowed freely from his eyes. "We lost our good friend," Padre Pio added. "Unlike you or me, God saw that Dr. Sanguinetti was ready to be with him in eternal life." John tried to comfort Padre Pio in his sorrow but no words could console him.

In addition to Dr. Sanguinetti, another one of Padre Pio's spiritual children that John felt fortunate to meet was a woman named Elena Bandini. Elena, a Third Order Franciscan, had dedicated herself totally to her faith and to many charitable and apostolic works. She began writing to Padre Pio and seeking his spiritual direction in 1921. In 1937, she moved from her home in Mugello to live permanently in San Giovanni Rotondo. She served Padre Pio's apostolate in innumerable ways.

When Elena was diagnosed with stomach cancer, her strength of character and her heroic attitude became apparent to all. The suffering that Elena endured was almost unbearable. However, she did not pray for a healing. She

offered all of her sufferings to God and united them to Padre Pio's sufferings, for his intentions. John visited Elena right before she died. His heart was
moved with pity to see her in so much pain. Her resignation to her illness was
beautiful and her profound spirituality was evident, even on her death bed.
Finally, her sufferings became so intense that she prayed to Padre Pio that
her end would come. "It will just be a little longer. Just a little more straw
to burn," Padre Pio said. Elena finally passed away on October 5, 1955. John
spoke to Padre Pio about her death. "Elena was such a saintly person," John
said. "She lived a holy life and she died a holy death. I believe that she went
straight to heaven." Two large tears rolled down Padre Pio's cheeks. "Oh yes,
that is true," Padre Pio replied. "Elena went to heaven with no stop at all!"

On one occasion, John told Padre Pio about a brand-new book that had
just been published in Ireland. "What is the book about?" Padre Pio asked. "It
is a book about you," John replied. At John's words, Padre Pio became distraught. With tears in his eyes he said, "You are the ones who are good. Not
me. I know that God has given me many graces. But it frightens me to think
about it because I do not think that I have made good use of the gifts that I have
been given. I think that anyone else would have made better use of them than
I have." John tried to convince him otherwise but he was not able to change
Padre Pio's mind.

During John's visits to the monastery of Our Lady of Grace, he met a
number of interesting people who shared their stories with him. Many had
received miracles through the hands of Padre Pio. John witnessed some of the
miraculous cures with his own eyes, including the complete healing of a man
who had throat cancer. The pain of the man's illness was intense and he was
only able to speak in a hoarse whisper. As his disease progressed, his speech
became completely inaudible. It even became difficult for him to breathe.

The man and his wife had moved from Milan to San Giovanni Rotondo in
order to be close to Padre Pio. Every day, he stood in the sacristy, waiting for
Padre Pio as he passed through the sacristy to the church. When Padre Pio came
into view, the man would simply look at him and in silence, he would pray to
him for healing. But the man's faith was put to the test. He had been suffering
from the disease for over a year, and his condition was growing steadily worse.

One evening, when the man was in bed and trying to sleep, the pain of
his disease became intolerable. He had the sensation that he was suffocating.

Try as he might, he could not seem to get enough air. He became so desperate that he got out of bed and went to the monastery. The monastery door was locked, so he rang the bell. When one of the Capuchins came to the door, the man pleaded with him and said, "I have to see Padre Pio. I am very sick and I need his help!" "But the church is closed for the night," the Capuchin replied. "Padre Pio is in the choir praying his night Office. No one can speak to him at this late hour. You must come back tomorrow."

The man's pleadings finally touched the heart of the Capuchin and he led him to the choir loft where Pio was praying with the rest of his religious community. At once, Padre Pio saw the pitiful condition the man was in and got up from his prayers and walked toward him. Weeping, the man threw himself on his knees before Padre Pio. Padre Pio then placed his hand on the man's head in a blessing. At Padre Pio's touch, all of his pain disappeared. He felt an intense joy coursing through his body. The feeling was so overwhelming that he did not think that he could endure it. He wrenched himself away from Padre Pio and stood up. Padre Pio evidently was aware of the blessing that the man had received for he smiled at him and said, "That surely was beautiful, wasn't it! But now you must go back to your home and go to bed because it is late."

Padre Pio later advised the man to have surgery in the city of Bologna and gave him the name of a highly-skilled doctor who could help him. The man followed Padre Pio's advice and had the operation. The next time he returned to the monastery, his voice was strong and he had regained his former vitality. He said that the doctor had given him a clean bill of health. John was amazed to see the complete transformation in the man.

John was a witness to another miracle, which concerned a man from Lecco, Italy who was blind. The man visited Padre Pio and begged him for his intercessory prayers. The man knelt down and implored Padre Pio saying, "Even if sight returns to only one eye, I would be so grateful and so satisfied." He kept repeating the words. Padre Pio answered him and said, "Do you want healing in one eye only?" Then Padre Pio promised the man that he would pray for him. The man's eyes had a sunken appearance and John described his eyes as looking like two "dried and shriveled peas." The man received a miracle, for the next time he returned to the monastery of Our Lady of Grace, both of his eyes were completely normal in appearance. With tears of gratitude, he thanked Padre Pio for his prayers. An interesting fact of the story is that the man's vision was restored in one eye only. Padre Pio spoke to him later and said, "Remember, do not put limitations on God. Ask him for all that you need. Always ask for the big grace!"

As John witnessed the healings around him, he reflected on his own poor health. He had a heart condition which caused him to experience heart palpitations and made him so uncomfortable that at night he had to sleep sitting up in a chair. He was frequently tormented by severe and recurring headaches. One night he lost consciousness and was rushed to the hospital. He had suffered a partial stroke. He often feared that he would die an untimely death and he worried about his wife and children. Who would provide for them if he should pass away?

One day at Padre Pio's Mass, John prayed silently and with great intensity, begging Padre Pio to intercede and to heal him of his heart condition. That afternoon, John saw Padre Pio in the monastery. Padre Pio spoke to John very tenderly and said, "I want you to know that my prayer for you is that you go to heaven. I want you to be satisfied with that. I ask you to pray for me as well, that I might go to heaven. Do you understand what I am saying?" "Yes, I understand," John replied. He was disappointed at Padre Pio's words but he tried his best not to show it. Padre Pio had obviously been aware of John's prayers at the Mass that morning. His comment indicated to John that he was praying for his salvation, not necessarily for his health. Evidently, John was not going to receive a healing for his failing heart.

After speaking to John, Padre Pio continued to converse with the others who were present. John was preoccupied with thinking about the remark that Padre Pio had made to him. He was trying to hide his feelings of sadness. Several times that afternoon, John noticed that Padre Pio was staring at him with a very penetrating gaze. When it was time to say goodbye to Padre Pio, all the men who were gathered knelt down to receive his blessing. Once again, Padre Pio scrutinized John with great intensity. He blessed all of the men and then embraced John in such a way that John's head rested on Padre Pio's chest, near the wound in his heart. Padre Pio held John's head against his heart wound for some time. It was the third time that day that Padre Pio had embraced John in such a way.

After Padre Pio departed, the others who were present told John how lucky he was. He had obviously been singled out for a special blessing that day.

Some time later, Padre Pio placed the palm of his right hand against John's heart. After that, John never again had any signs or symptoms of a heart condition. The next time he went in for a checkup, the doctor informed him that his heart was in perfectly good condition.

After Padre Pio's death on September 23, 1968, John McCaffery never went back to San Giovanni Rotondo. He had visited Padre Pio countless times over a period of many years. With Padre Pio gone, John could not bring himself to return. He knew that it would not be the same. John had made many good friends in San Giovanni Rotondo. He was not to see any of them again. He went back to his home in Donegal, Ireland where he stayed for the rest of his life. His friends remained in his heart, just like Padre Pio. He would treasure his precious memories of Padre Pio for the rest of his life.

We are hard pressed on every side yet not crushed; we are perplexed but not in despair; persecuted but not forsaken; struck down but not destroyed.

- *2 Corinthians 4:8-9*

CHAPTER 15

Desmond Montague

C anadian born Desmond Montague served the Allied cause during World War II as an airman and navigator. He was assigned to the Royal Air Force Squadron Number 142 which specialized in long range bombing missions. Along with the others in his squadron, Desmond was stationed in Foggia, Italy. They all lived in tents on the military base. Desmond had heard many positive statements about the mild climate in southern Italy but during the time that he was in Foggia, he found it ironic that it rained incessantly.

One day, Edward Wiseman, the pilot of the aircraft that Desmond was assigned to, asked him if he knew the meaning of the word, "stigmata." Desmond told Edward that he was familiar with the term. Desmond was a devout Catholic. He kept a Rosary in his pocket at all times and had always been a person of faith. His own brother was a Catholic priest. Edward Wiseman told Desmond that he had heard that there was a priest living at the monastery of Our Lady of Grace in the nearby town of San Giovanni Rotondo who had the stigmata. Desmond was interested in what Edward shared about the priest but he was also very skeptical. He was almost sure that it was not true.

The next day, Desmond and his good friend Lyell Bachelder, a fellow air force officer, decided to find out for themselves if Edward's information about the priest who reportedly had the stigmata was correct. The two men walked from the airfield where they were stationed to the monastery of Our Lady of Grace in San Giovanni Rotondo. Due to the heavy wartime bombing that had taken place in and around Foggia, there were no longer any roads to travel on. They walked over hills and embankments through the dry and desolate terrain.

When Desmond and Lyell finally arrived in San Giovanni Rotondo, the first person they met was a friendly American woman named Mary Pyle. Mary confirmed that what Edward Wiseman had told them about the priest was true. Mary told them that the priest's name was Padre Pio and that he had the five wounds of Christ, the stigmata. "Would you like me to take you over to the church so that you could meet him?" Mary asked. Desmond and Lyell said that they would be very happy to be introduced to him.

Mary took the two army officers over to the church and gave them specific instructions. She said that it was important that all visits with Padre Pio be conducted in a dignified and respectful manner. She added that they should let Padre Pio handle the visit his way.

Desmond and Lyell followed Mary upstairs to the choir loft of the church. Mary directed them to a pew where she told them to kneel. It was in that very choir loft that Padre Pio had received the stigmata on September 20, 1918. "Padre Pio will soon come into the church and kneel in the pew right behind you," Mary told the two men. "When he comes in, do not turn around and stare at him." She explained that Padre Pio was a very humble person and did not want to be the object of anyone's curiosity. He did not like to feel that he was "on display."

Soon Desmond and Lyell heard Padre Pio come into the church. Just like Mary Pyle had told them, Padre Pio knelt down in the pew behind them. They could hear his soft voice and the sound of his beads as he prayed the Rosary quietly. After a time, Padre Pio touched them on the shoulder and they stood up to greet him. Padre Pio seemed happy to meet the two officers. He had magnificent dark eyes and a beautiful smile. Trying to be discreet, the two men could not help but glance at Padre Pio's hands. Mary Pyle had already confirmed to them that Padre Pio had the stigmata. They noticed that Padre Pio wore brown woolen half gloves which covered the wounds completely.

Padre Pio was very friendly to the officers. He gave both of them a small crucifix as a gift. He also gave them his priestly blessing. Before he said good-bye, he patted both of the men on their heads. The simple and loving gesture reminded them of the way a father might affectionately pat the heads of his own sons. Padre Pio made Desmond and Lyell understand that he would watch over both of them.

A short time later, the two men made a second trip to Padre Pio's monastery. They were able to attend Padre Pio's Mass but were not able to speak with him. They brought jam, sugar and tea for Mary Pyle and for the Capuchins. On their previous visit, they had noticed that those items were in short supply due to wartime food rationing.

The next day, Lyell woke up feeling very ill. A visit to the doctor revealed that he had contracted malaria. His condition was so serious that he had to be hospitalized. Desmond and the other members of the crew were departing on a bombing mission to Budapest, Hungary that very evening. Lyell's position as bombardier had to be filled by another airman.

The crew left on the evening of April 16, 1944 with the railway yards of Budapest as their central target. They all considered it to be a routine bombing raid, no different from many others they had already participated in. The aircraft used for the bombing mission was a Wellington Mark II - a twin-engine night bomber. At that time, flights were accomplished by celestial navigation. Noting the position of the stars as well as consulting air almanacs and tables, and using instruments that measured horizon and altitude, the navigator could plot a very accurate course to the designated target area.

After successfully completing their bombing mission in Budapest, Desmond and the other crew members set course to return to their military base in Foggia. They kept on a constant lookout for dangerous German night fighter planes. That particular night, the stars were magnificent, shining like jewels against a dark canopy of endless sky.

They were not far from Belgrade, Yugoslavia when suddenly and without any warning, their aircraft was fired upon. In seconds, the plane went violently out of control. The pilot quickly gave his order over the intercom, "Emergency! All jump!"

The men always wore their parachute harnesses during flight, with the parachute pack right beside them for immediate access. Hearing the pilot's order, Desmond quickly tried to clip his pack to the parachute harness so that he could jump out of the plane. However, the simple task proved to be impossible. The sudden change in altitude and the strong gravitational forces that were present prevented Desmond from moving his arms. Completely immobilized, he was pressed against the wall of the plane. As the plane made a nose dive to the ground, Desmond was certain that he was going to die. He said a very quick prayer, "Jesus, Mary, and Joseph, help me!" and then he lost consciousness.

When Desmond regained consciousness, he was shocked to find that he was wrapped up in his parachute. How could it be? He had not been able to clip his parachute pack on after the plane had been hit. The plane had gone down in a mountainous region of Yugoslavia. He estimated that it had been approximately two hours since the plane had crashed. Desmond had received only minor injuries. There was a deep cut on his leg and on his face. Also, some of his teeth had been broken off. Other than that, he was in good condition. It seemed like a miracle to him that he had survived. All of the other members of the crew had died in the crash.

Desmond quickly buried his parachute. He did not want the Germans to suspect that there were any survivors in the plane crash. He then walked toward an isolated farmhouse which he saw in the distance. As he drew closer, he noticed that there was debris from his fallen plane in the yard of the farmhouse. Desmond knocked on the door. The farmer and his wife who greeted Desmond were very kind. The wife cleaned and dressed the wounds on his leg and face. The man handed him a glass of an unidentifiable liquid which he was very happy to accept. As he drank it, he felt an intense burning sensation in his throat and stomach. It turned out to be straight vodka.

Desmond could sense the fear of the farmer and his wife. Under the circumstances, their fear was understandable. In German-occupied Yugoslavia, it was very dangerous for anyone to assist a member of the Allied troops. By allowing Desmond to come inside their house and by helping him, the couple were putting their own lives in danger.

Desmond was hoping that the farmer would help him to escape by directing him to the Yugoslavian partisans who, at that time, were resisting the German occupation. The farmer put Desmond in his wife's care and left the house momentarily. He soon returned with several well-armed German soldiers. They arrested Desmond on the spot. He would spend the next thirteen months in Prisoner of War camps in different parts of Germany.

As the war drew to a close, the Prisoner of War camp south of Lubeck, Germany where Desmond was held captive was liberated by General Montgomery's troops. World War II, which caused more casualties than any other war in history, finally ended on May 8, 1945. Desmond was flown back to England on the eve of V-E Day and a short time after that, returned to his home in St. John, New Brunswick. When he saw his mother, she said to him, "Desmond, I am certain that it was the priest in Italy who saved your life!" After his first trip to the monastery of Our Lady of Grace, Desmond had written to his parents and told them all of the details of his visit. He also sent them a photograph of Padre Pio. Desmond had a wonderful reunion with his entire family. He felt strong, both physically and mentally, and was profoundly grateful to be alive.

Desmond then traveled to Montreal, Quebec to be reunited with his good friend, Lyell Bachelder. Desmond learned that Lyell had made a complete recovery from the malaria that had prevented him from participating in the doomed bombing mission to Budapest. After Lyell recovered, he was assigned to a Canadian Bomber Squadron. He flew on sixty bombing raids in enemy territory. At that time, the mortality rate for airmen sent on bombing missions was as high as 50 percent. Lyle safely and successfully completed all of his assigned missions.

When Lyell greeted Desmond, he had the crucifix that Padre Pio had given him in his hand. Lyell repeated the words of Desmond's mother and said, "Des, it is because of Padre Pio's protection that we are both alive!"

Desmond's brother, Father Robert Montague, was deeply grateful that Desmond had survived the grave dangers of the war. He hoped that someday he would be able to go to San Giovanni Rotondo so that he could thank Padre Pio personally for saving his brother's life. In 1963, he was finally able to make the trip.

Father Robert did not speak Italian and he knew that Padre Pio did not speak English. He was concerned about the language barrier and wanted to make sure that he would be able to communicate with Padre Pio. At the monastery of Our Lady of Grace, he met a man who was fluent in both Italian and English. He asked the man if he would relay his message to Padre Pio and he happily agreed. One day, when Father Robert and his new found friend were at the monastery, the unexpected happened. Padre Pio approached the man and before the man could utter a single word, Padre Pio said to him, "Tell the young priest from Canada that I am aware that he has come here to offer thanks on behalf of his entire family for my intercession in saving his brother's life during the war."

You reached down from on high and took hold of me. You drew me out of deep waters. You delivered me from my strong enemy, from those who hated me.

- 2 Samuel 22:17-18

CHAPTER 16

Luigi Pulcinelli

*L*uigi Pulcinelli was a student officer in the 12th Regiment of the Italian Army during World War II. His unit was stationed in a remote area between Foggia and Manfredonia, in southern Italy. September 8, 1943 was the day that the Italian Armistice, or surrender of Italy to the Allied forces, was announced. Word that the bloody war was ended between the Allies and Italy did not reach Luigi Pulcinelli and the other members of his company until the following day, September 9. The news was received with great joy by the members of the 12th Regiment. Soon they would all be going home to be reunited with their families. However, the joy for Luigi and the other members of his company was short-lived.

That same day, German soldiers arrived in armored vehicles and surrounded the headquarters where Luigi was stationed. Since Italy had been one of the Axis powers (with Germany and Japan), the Germans immediately viewed the Italians as traitors. Luigi and the others in his unit happened to be a short distance away at the time that the German soldiers arrived. When they discovered that the German soldiers were nearby, they fled toward the mountains. For greater safety, they broke up into small groups. After crossing a river, the groups all scattered in different directions.

Luigi and the others in his group moved quickly, knowing full well the danger they were in. Soon they came to a rock quarry. A miner who was at the quarry told Luigi and the other soldiers that the Germans were searching everywhere for them. The Germans were hoping to capture every man in their disbanded regiment. Considering the miner's warning, the soldiers decided that it would be safer to split up into even smaller groups. By now, they had run out of ammunition. They knew that it would be easier to travel by leaving their heavy weapons behind. They placed their guns at the bottom of a well and quickly continued on their way.

Luigi, along with five other soldiers, continued to walk at a fast pace through the dry and desert-like Gargano region. They forced themselves to push forward for as long as they could. When they were overcome with exhaustion and could go no further, they spread out hay on the hard ground and spent the night in a field. They woke up the next morning as the sun was rising. Together, they tried to carefully consider their next move. They saw a shepherd tending his animals nearby and told him their plight. They asked him if he might know of a safe place where they could go in order to escape their captors.

The shepherd told the soldiers that there was a monastery called Our Lady of Grace in the nearby town of San Giovanni Rotondo. The Capuchins who lived there were very kind and very holy. It would be a safe place for the soldiers to hide. The shepherd gave them the direction to travel in. After the soldiers had reached the small town of San Giovanni Rotondo, they headed up the one and only path that led to the monastery. It was a poor and narrow dirt road, a mule track.

Mass was already in progress when Luigi and his five companions walked into the monastery church of Our Lady of Grace. They all felt nervous as they entered the darkened church. They hoped that the shepherd was correct in saying that the monastery would be a safe haven for them. In order not to draw attention to themselves, they sat on the very back benches. They were relieved that no one seemed to notice their presence.

At once, Luigi was struck by the Capuchin priest who was at the altar celebrating Mass. He seemed different from any priest that Luigi had ever come in contact with. He was deeply recollected, deeply prayerful during the solemn Mass. A profound peace pervaded the little church. Just before the priest gave his final blessing, he made an announcement to the congregation. "There are some disbanded soldiers who have just arrived at the church," the priest said. "More will soon be arriving. They are in need of civilian clothing. I would like anyone who is able, to bring the needed clothing to the church right away." Luigi and his companions were stunned at the priest's words. After that, the priest gave his final blessing and the Mass was ended.

There was a little square right outside of the church with a few benches and a large shade tree. After the Mass, Luigi and the other soldiers sat down on the bench and discussed what had just happened in the church. How did the priest know that they were disbanded soldiers? They had come into the church after the Mass had started and had taken their seats in the very back. No one had noticed their presence. How could the priest possibly have seen them in the darkened church?

As they were discussing the matter, a man walked over to them and introduced himself. "It is a mark of good fortune that you have made your way to the monastery of Our Lady of Grace today," the man said to the soldiers. Luigi told the man how surprised they had all been to hear the priest's announcement at the end of Mass, asking the congregation for civilian clothing. "How could that priest have possibly known our situation?" Luigi asked. "That priest has the gift of reading hearts," the man explained. "His name is Padre Pio and he is a saint. He has the holy stigmata, the five wounds of Christ." Neither Luigi nor the other soldiers had ever heard of Padre Pio.

The man told Luigi and his companions that he would like to take them back inside the church and introduce them to Padre Pio. The soldiers all felt nervous at the thought. However, they were also glad for the opportunity to meet the saintly priest. They followed the man back inside the church and into the sacristy where they found Padre Pio. Padre Pio was friendly to the soldiers and spoke to them briefly. He gave them all a blessing. As they were leaving the church, they saw a large pile of civilian clothing at the doorway, brought by the local people at Padre Pio's request.

Some of the women in the town prepared a large and sumptuous lunch for the soldiers. Luigi described it as a meal "fit for a king." After their long march from Manfredonia, the men were all famished. They fully enjoyed the magnificent lunch. Mary Pyle, Padre Pio's long time assistant, was one of the women who provided the food. Each day, a fine breakfast, lunch and dinner was prepared for them. Many of the families who lived in San Giovanni Rotondo offered the soldiers lodging. At the Mass, Padre Pio had asked the local people to assist the six soldiers. They were certainly answering his call with great generosity. While in San Giovanni Rotondo, the soldiers wanted for nothing.

Luigi and his companions attended Padre Pio's Mass every morning. Afterward, they went directly to the sacristy to spend a few moments with Padre Pio. Every day, Padre Pio repeated the same words to them, "Do not be in a hurry to leave. You must stay here a little longer. Don't worry. I will tell you when it is safe for you to go."

One day after the Mass, Padre Pio said to the soldiers, "It is now safe for you to leave. As you depart for your homes, put all of your trust in the Virgin Mary." After spending five days in San Giovanni Rotondo and attending Padre Pio's beautiful Mass each day, the men found it hard to say goodbye. In that short period of time, they had come to have full confidence in Padre Pio. They trusted his words completely when he told them that it was the right time for their departure. The soldiers kissed Padre Pio's hand and left that very day with his blessing.

Their destination was the train station in the town of Apricena. Traveling on foot through the rugged terrain of the Gargano region was difficult and exhausting. When they finally arrived in Apricena, they were disappointed to learn that no trains were scheduled to leave the station. They were then informed that the Germans were still imprisoning and deporting many people. They walked for five more days until they arrived in Campobasso. There, they were relieved to find that the trains were running.

After a two day train journey, Luigi arrived in his hometown of Castiglione del Lago. How happy he was to finally be reunited with his mother, father, brother, and friends. He felt that he had truly been protected on his journey back to his home. From the time he had left San Giovanni Rotondo, he had not crossed the path of a single German soldier.

Two of the soldiers who had initially gone with Luigi to the monastery of Our Lady of Grace had not been as fortunate. When Padre Pio advised the six men to stay in San Giovanni Rotondo until he told them when it was safe to leave, the two soldiers disregarded his words. Feeling a great desire to get back to their families, they did not have the patience to wait any longer. Against Padre Pio's advice, they left. One died on the way to his home and the other was captured by the Germans, imprisoned and then deported.

In 1948, five years after his first visit, Luigi Pulcinelli returned once again to the monastery of Our Lady of Grace in San Giovanni Rotondo. But this time he came under much happier circumstances. It was his honeymoon, and he had come to the monastery to introduce Padre Pio to his new bride. He returned many more times to the monastery of Our Lady of Grace. Luigi cherished his memories of the saintly priest. He often repeated that the most beautiful experience of his life was the time he spent with Padre Pio at the end of World War II. Those five days of attending Padre Pio's Mass and receiving his blessing left an indelible mark on Luigi's soul.

I am ready for anything, as long as Jesus is content to save the souls of my brothers, especially those he has entrusted to my care.

- St. Pio of Pietrelcina

CHAPTER 17

Stories from the War Years

The efficacy of Padre Pio's prayers for the deceased was revealed on one occasion in a startling way. During the first World War, the main door of the monastery of Our Lady of Grace was locked every evening after the ringing of the Angelus bell. An iron bar secured the door and kept the monastery safe from intruders. One evening, the superior of the monastery, Father Raffaele, heard voices shouting, "Viva Padre Pio! Viva Padre Pio!" (Long live Padre Pio!) He immediately notified the porter, Brother Gerardo. "Strangers have somehow managed to enter the monastery, even though the door is locked," Father Raffaele said. "They are downstairs in the hallway shouting in unison. You must go down there immediately and make them leave!"

Brother Gerardo left at once to take care of the matter. He returned a short time later and said to Father Raffaele, "The door is locked and secured and there are no intruders downstairs." Father Raffaele was perplexed. He knew what he had heard and he could not doubt it. He was also well aware that unusual incidents happened from time to time at the monastery of Our Lady of Grace. Those unusual events almost always involved Padre Pio. Father Raffaele had lived with Padre Pio long enough to know that he was living in a supernatural reality. As one of the Capuchins described it, "Padre Pio was living with one foot on earth and one foot in heaven."

Father Raffaele decided to ask Padre Pio about the mysterious voices he had heard in the hallway. The next morning he said to Padre Pio, "Something very strange happened last night. Even though the doors were locked, I was certain that intruders had broken into the monastery. I distinctly heard them shouting your name in the corridor and saying, "Viva Padre Pio!" I have no doubt about what I heard. When Brother Gerardo went downstairs to escort the people out, there was no one there. Do you know anything about this?" "Those were the souls of deceased soldiers who had walked up the hill to thank me for my prayers," Padre Pio replied. "There are more souls of the dead than of the living who climb the hill to the monastery to request my prayers."

Teseo Isani was a military officer who was stationed in Verona, Italy during World War II. During that time, a friend confided to Teseo that for many days he had been hiding an American soldier in his home. He was aware of the danger of the situation. If he was caught by the Gestapo, it would be his death sentence. He asked Teseo if he would be willing to take the American soldier and he agreed to do so.

For a temporary solution, Teseo hid the American in his truck under a large load of wood. Unfortunately, soon after Teseo did so, the Gestapo became suspicious. Teseo's truck was searched and the American was found. Teseo was immediately arrested and placed in custody. He was condemned to death for his crime of harboring an enemy.

In the detention facility, Teseo waited for his execution day. There was nothing he could do to save himself. One day, Teseo suddenly heard a very distinct voice which said to him with great insistence, "Escape! Escape!" Teseo did not know where the voice had come from. He was not sure of the meaning of the message either. He did not have the means to escape. He knew that if he tried to walk out of the detention facility, he would be instantly shot. There were armed guards stationed at every check point who were not afraid to use their weapons at a moment's notice. However, Teseo reasoned to himself that he was going die anyway. "What does it matter if I die today or tomorrow?" he said to himself.

Teseo opened the door of his cell and looked down the hall. Armed guards were standing at various posts all along the corridor. He decided to take the plunge. He stepped out into the corridor and started walking and to his utter amazement, the guards did not seem to notice him. Suddenly, one of the guards became aware of Teseo and reached for his gun. He pointed it at Teseo and pulled the trigger but it failed to go off. Teseo then broke into a run and managed to flee unharmed.

The Nazis posted Teseo's picture throughout the city of Verona. A large sum of 100,000 lire was offered to anyone who could find the fugitive. But Teseo was safe. He had already made his way into Switzerland.

Three years later, Teseo listened with great interest as someone told him about a holy priest named Padre Pio who lived in the southern part of Italy. He decided to make a trip to Padre Pio's monastery in hopes of meeting him. At the monastery of Our Lady of Grace, Teseo was able to make his confession to Padre Pio. That evening when he returned to his hotel, he had a very unusual experience. As soon as he opened the door to his room, he heard a voice which said to him, "Escape! Escape!" It was the very same voice he had heard during the Second World War. Since he had just spoken to Padre Pio, he now recognized the voice as belonging to Padre Pio. He made his way immediately back to the monastery. When Teseo stood in the presence of Padre Pio once again, he was overcome with emotion and burst into tears. Padre Pio understood. Referring all of the credit to God, Padre Pio said simply, "Let us thank the Lord."

————

Francesco Cavicchi and his wife visited Padre Pio's monastery for the first time in June 1967. Francesco's wife had a great desire to meet Padre Pio. She spoke to Francesco about it and insisted that he accompany her. He did not share his wife's enthusiasm regarding the trip to the monastery but in order to please her, he finally agreed to go.

Francesco had learned that Padre Pio would not hear a person's confession if it had been less than ten days since their last confession. Francesco had been to confession just three days before. But since he had made a special trip to San Giovanni Rotondo, he did not want to miss the opportunity. He decided to take a chance and go to confession anyway and he hoped that he would not be found out.

Padre Pio was hearing the men's confessions in the sacristy of the old church. As Francesco waited in the confessional line, he grew more and more uneasy. He wondered to himself how he had the nerve to disregard the "ten-day rule." Padre Pio looked out at the men waiting in the line, and his eyes fell on Francesco. "Come forward, my son," Padre Pio said to Francesco. "I have been waiting for you for a long time." Francesco could not grasp the meaning of his words. How could Padre Pio have been waiting for him for a long time? They had never even met.

Francesco knelt down in the dim light of the sacristy. As he made a move to kiss Padre Pio's hand, Padre Pio withdrew it from him. It was not a good sign and Francesco knew it. Next, Padre Pio asked Francesco the question that he did not want to hear. "How long has it been since your last confession?" There was a silence while Francesco pretended to be thinking about the answer to the question. He told Padre Pio that he could not remember when he made his last confession.

Padre Pio then asked him some other questions, and Francesco breathed a sigh of relief. He had not been sent out of the confessional like he feared. He was grateful that he was still kneeling beside Padre Pio. Once again Padre Pio asked him, "Now tell me, how many days has it been since your last confession?" Before Francesco could answer, Padre Pio changed the subject and began talking about the Prayer Groups. Finally, he said once again, "How long has it been since your last confession?"

Francesco did not know what to say. He was sure that Padre Pio could read his heart and his mind. It seemed obvious that Francesco was trying to avoid the question. Francesco had kept head down and his eyes lowered from the time he had entered the confessional. He did not have the courage to look at Padre Pio full in the face. But now, for the first time, Francesco lifted his gaze and looked directly at him.

Padre Pio was looking at Francesco with an expression of great tenderness and love. "I do not remember how long it has been since my last confession," Francesco repeated. Padre Pio then became serious. "You have a short

memory, don't you. But let me ask you this. Do you remember the bombardment in Rimini many years back? Do you remember the air raid shelter? Do
you remember the trolley bus? But why am I asking you to go back in time?
You cannot even remember what you did less than one week ago!"

Padre Pio was speaking to Francesco about an incident that had happened
back in 1943, during the Second World War. Francesco remembered the incident well. He would never be able to forget it for as long as he lived. He was
twenty-eight years old at the time and worked for the State Railway in the
city of Rimini.

On that particular November day in 1943, Francesco happened to be riding the trolley bus back to his home for his lunch break. There were about ten
other people on the bus that day. Included in the number was a middle-aged
Capuchin monk. Suddenly, the sirens in the city gave warning of an air raid.
Bombs then began to fall all around. The bus driver accelerated to a frantic
speed in an effort to escape the danger. When fragments from falling bombs
cut the electric power lines, the driver was forced to stop the bus. The passengers were filled with panic. Francesco was certain that he was going to die.

In the midst of great fear and confusion, everyone then exited the bus and
ran toward an air raid shelter that was nearby. Due to an obstacle in his path,
Francesco had great difficulty getting off of the bus. He was the last person
to enter the air raid shelter. Inside the shelter, the Capuchin monk who had
been on the bus, had already begun to recite the Rosary. It had a calming
effect on all who were gathered there. Soon everyone was praying with the
Capuchin. Meanwhile, bombs continued to explode all around. The air raid
shelter shook on its foundation and Francesco knew that it could collapse at
any moment. However, amid all the noise and destruction, there was no panic
or screaming inside the shelter. The Capuchin monk seemed to inspire confidence in everyone. Thirty minutes passed. The small group had just finished
reciting the Rosary when the sirens in the city gave the "all clear" signal.

The Capuchin was the first to leave the shelter. Everyone then followed
out behind him. "Were you the monk who was on the bus with me?" Francesco asked Padre Pio. "Well, who did you think it was?" Padre Pio answered.
"I have already explained to you that Jesus and the Blessed Mother can inter-
vene in our lives, even if we are not aware of it." Francesco had always known
how lucky he had been to escape death that frightful November day. He was

convinced that Divine Providence had assisted everyone who was in the air raid shelter with him. At the time, he had not even heard of Padre Pio.

When Padre Pio saw Francesco in the confessional line, he told him that he had been waiting for him for a long time. The wartime incident that Padre Pio brought to Francesco's attention had happened twenty-four years before. Had he actually been waiting for Francesco to return after all those years? Francesco was convinced that he had.

––––––––––

Corporal Joe Asterita was an American serviceman who was stationed in Cerignola, Italy during World War II. Along with other soldiers in his squadron, Joe used to visit Padre Pio in San Giovanni Rotondo when he had the opportunity. Joe was fluent in Italian with the added benefit of being able to understand the dialect of those who lived in San Giovanni Rotondo. He often translated for the other GI's who wanted to speak to Padre Pio.

On one occasion, Padre Pio told Joe that five people who had visited the monastery needed a ride back to their homes in Foggia. He asked Joe to drive them back. Joe told Padre Pio that it was against United States Army regulations to use military vehicles to provide transportation for civilians. Padre Pio was very firm and insisted that Joe do him the favor. Joe carefully considered the matter but finally decided against it. The risk of getting caught was too great. "Army regulations forbid me to transport those who are non-military. I am sorry but I cannot break the rule," Joe said.

Speaking with authority, Padre Pio then said to Joe, "Remember this. Anytime I ask you to do something for me, it will work out. You need have no fear." Joe was finally convinced. He then allowed the two men, two women and a little boy to get into his military jeep. Shortly after they were on the road, Joe saw two Military Police Officers coming in their direction. The Military Police Officers looked in the jeep but passed right on by without stopping Joe. At that moment, the air became filled with a delightful perfume. As they continued on the road to Foggia, they encountered one Military Police Officer after another, but they were never pulled over. The fragrant perfume stayed in the air until the five Italian citizens were dropped off safely in Foggia.

Padre Pio often reminded people of the importance of praying for the souls of the departed. He used to say, "We must empty purgatory with our prayers." When Padre Pio celebrated Mass, during the time of the prayers for the living and the deceased, he would pause for an extended period of silence. At times, the Lord enlightened him regarding the state of those who had already passed away. He once said to Father Alessio Parente, "You are going to be amazed to find souls in heaven who you would never have expected to find there."

In the monastery of Our Lady of Grace, there was a wooden box mounted to the wall with a notice above it reminding the Capuchins to pray for the deceased. A categorical list was posted, which included souls of deceased priests, souls close to heaven, forgotten souls, etc. Small disks were inside the wooden box with numbers on them referring to the category of souls to pray for. Regularly, Padre Pio would take a disk from the box and pause in silence as he devoutly recited the prayer for the deceased - *Eternal rest grant unto them, O Lord, and let perpetual light shine upon them. May they rest in peace. Amen.*

There was a woman (name withheld) who lived in Italy whose husband had died in the Second World War. After the death of her husband, her in-laws treated her and her two children very badly. The woman was in great financial need but her in-laws were not willing to help in any way. To make matters worse, they took possession of the home that had belonged to her and her husband.

The woman and her children moved from the city into the country, thinking that it would be less expensive. When her eldest son was about to make his first Holy Communion, the woman had a dilemma. She could not afford to buy the proper clothing for him for that very special day. She decided to alter one of her husband's suits to fit him. In that way, her son would be able to be dressed appropriately, just like all the other children. Her relatives refused to return her husband's suit to her. They also confiscated most of the household possessions. Finally, they sold her husband's home and kept all of the profits for themselves. The woman tried to confront them about the injustice of their actions, but they refused to speak to her.

The woman needed advice about her many problems, especially her desperate financial situation. She wanted to talk to Padre Pio but she could not afford to make the trip to San Giovanni Rotondo. Her faith in Padre Pio was indeed great. She knew in her heart that nothing was impossible and she never lost hope that one day she would be able to visit him at the monastery of Our Lady of Grace.

As it turned out, the woman won 25,000 lire in the Italian lottery. The unexpected money enabled her to make the trip. Everything seemed to work out in her favor. Once she arrived in San Giovanni Rotondo, she began to look for lodging. Finding a room was harder than she had ever imagined. Although she had to settle for sleeping in the corridor of a local establishment, she was grateful that at least she had a roof over her head.

The woman attended Padre Pio's Mass and was very inspired. She had the unmistakable impression that Padre Pio was in "direct contact with God." She felt carried away into a place of great peace. The Mass had such an impact on her that she felt totally transformed. She began to have the desire to change her life. She had been living with a man whom she loved very much. She decided that when she returned home, she would end the illicit relationship. She wanted to talk to Padre Pio about her decision.

The woman was very nervous when she stepped into Padre Pio's confessional. "I want to make a full confession," she said to Padre Pio. "I want my life to change. When I go back to my home, I want to feel like I have felt during these days that I have spent here in San Giovanni Rotondo." "Are you truly sorry for your past sins?" Padre Pio asked her. "Yes, I am truly sorry for all of them," the woman replied. "Go in peace," Padre Pio said. He gave her absolution and placed his wounded hand on her head. He let his hand rest on her head for quite a long time. "When I return to my home, what can I do so that I will be able to live as I have lived these days near the monastery?" the woman asked. "When you go back to your town, you will meet someone who will help you," Padre Pio answered.

About a week after returning to her home, the woman happened to make the acquaintance of a kind lady who helped her in incalculable ways. She remembered that Padre Pio had told her that she would meet such a person. Back at the factory where she worked, she made a public statement. She apologized to all of her co-workers and told them that she was sorry that she had used bad language in the past. "I apologize for the off-color jokes I once told you all. I promise you that you will never hear me tell them again." She let go of the resentment and anger that she had held in her heart for her relatives. She knew that her desire for revenge was wrong and through prayer she was able to overcome her feelings of bitterness.

The woman decided not to marry again. Eventually, she was able to receive her deceased husband's war pension which was a great financial help to her. She continued to pray to Padre Pio faithfully. Through Padre Pio's intercession, one of her sons received a physical healing. As the years passed, the woman's situation continued to improve and she received many graces for which she felt a profound gratitude.

Jerry Berrigan wrote to us at Padre Pio Devotions regarding his experience with Padre Pio during World War II. This is Jerry's story:

I met Padre Pio when I served in the U.S. Army Air Corps during World War II. I had enlisted in January 1942 and was eventually sent to the U.S. military base in Cerignola, Italy. As a Staff Sargeant, I was assigned to the ground crew and worked in the technical supply department for the U.S. fighter planes. I was also the assistant to our chaplain, Father Stanley Kusman, S.M., a Marianist priest.

One day, Father Kusman asked me an unusual question. "Jerry, how would you like to visit a saint today?" He went on to tell me a little bit about Padre Pio and invited me to go with him to Padre Pio's monastery. I had never heard of Padre Pio but I was happy to accept his invitation. Two other GI's from my squadron went along with us.

Father Kusman drove us to the monastery of Our Lady of Grace in a military jeep. The church of Our Lady of Grace was a poor little country church. It was very plain and very simple. As soon as we walked through the door, I realized that I had forgotten something and I went back out to the jeep to get it. When I walked back into the church, I was overwhelmed by an intense fragrance of fresh flowers. The wonderful scent of carnations, lilies, and roses filled the air. I looked around but there were no flowers anywhere inside.

Father Kusman was in the sacristy, conversing in Italian with a Capuchin who wore a brown habit with a cord at his waist. As I drew closer, I realized that he was talking to Padre Pio. As I looked at Padre Pio, I felt wonderstruck. I knew immediately that he was an extraordinary human being. Father Kusman then introduced me to him. I did not speak Italian but even if I did, I would not have been able to say even one word. I felt overwhelmed by his presence. Father Kusman asked Padre Pio if we could attend his Mass on our next visit and if I could be his altar server. "Si, si," he replied. There were a few children in the church making noise and Padre Pio let them know in no uncertain terms that they were to be quiet. That was my first brief meeting with Padre Pio.

After we left to return to the base, I told Father Kusman and the other GI's about the beautiful fragrance of flowers in the church. None of them had experienced it. Father Kusman then explained to me that it was a sign of blessing from Padre Pio. Father Kusman also shared more about Padre Pio's life with us. He told us that Padre Pio had a spiritual connection with the German mystic, Therese Neumann. Therese Neumann was a simple and devout lay woman who lived in a small farming village in Konnersreuth, Germany. Her deep spirituality touched many souls. She had many of the charismatic gifts that Padre Pio possessed, including the gift of reading hearts, miracles, healing, and more. Like Padre Pio, she bore the five wounds of Christ. Many of the American GI's went to Germany to visit Therese at the end of World War II. Padre Pio had a great deal of knowledge about Therese Neumann. Father Kusman had been told that Padre Pio had visited her through bilocation.

The next time Father Kusman took us to the monastery, I was apprehensive. Thinking about being Padre Pio's altar server was more than a little unsettling. I hoped that I would be able to perform all the duties of the altar server well and that I would not forget any of the Latin responses.

It turned out to be a very long Mass. As I knelt on the stone floor of the dimly lit church, my knees began to ache. It was very cold inside the church. Since it was wartime, the congregation consisted mainly of women and children. Most of the men in the village had no doubt been called up to serve in the Italian army. During the Mass, everyone stared at Padre Pio's hands. I saw that the wounds in the center of his hands were bleeding at the time of the Consecration. All of the American soldiers who were there that day were deeply impressed.

Meeting Padre Pio and assisting at his Mass served to strengthen my faith. It also gave me a sense of confidence that I would be protected. As soldiers in the Second World War, our lives were in constant danger. I felt a peace within and I knew that I had met a living saint.

After the war, I attended Holy Cross College in Massachusetts. I eventually got a PhD in English and I enjoyed being a college professor for more than 25 years. I turned 90 years old in 2010. The experience of meeting Padre Pio has stayed with me for my whole life.

Let us always keep before our eyes the fact that here on earth we are on a battlefield and that in paradise we shall receive the crown of victory; that this is a testing-ground and the prize will be awarded up above; that we are now in a land of exile while our true homeland is heaven to which we must continually aspire.

- St. Pio of Pietrelcina

You think you know my love for you, but you don't know that it is much greater than you can imagine. I follow you with my prayers, with my suffering, and with my tears.

- St. Pio of Pietrelcina

CHAPTER 18

Elide Bellomo

---

*E*lide Bellomo was a dressmaker by trade and lived in Sestri Levante, a resort town not far from Genoa, Italy. When Elide's aunt became terminally ill, Elide tried to show her as much love and support as she could. Elide's aunt wanted to be well prepared spiritually when her final moment came. She had always had a fear of death. She showed Elide a holy card of Padre Pio and spoke to her often of him. "Please pray to Padre Pio so that I might have a happy death," she would frequently say. Because her aunt spoke so much about Padre Pio, Elide decided to make a trip to San Giovanni Rotondo. She would ask Padre Pio in person to pray for her aunt. Elide knew how pleased her aunt would be to hear of her plan.

In February 1947, Elide set out for San Giovanni Rotondo. She took a train from Sestri Levante to Foggia and did not arrive in Foggia until the following evening. When the train pulled into the station, she learned that she had just missed the last bus that was going to San Giovanni Rotondo. She would have to wait until the following day for the next bus. She was so disappointed at the news that she began to cry. Elide was exhausted from the thirty-hour journey. The train had been so crowded that she had to stand for most of the trip. In addition, not anticipating the winter weather, she had not dressed properly. She had been cold and uncomfortable since the time she had left her home.

The station master noticed Elide's tears and asked her why she was crying. When she explained her frustrations to him, he took pity on her and led her to a small private room in the station. "You can sleep in here for the night," the station master said. "The chair will be more comfortable to sleep in that the bench in the lobby. The stove will keep you warm. I will close the door so that no one will bother you. We will be sure to wake you up early in the morning so that you can catch the bus for San Giovanni Rotondo."

The next morning, Elide was in better spirits. She boarded the bus and was happy to be on her way. The weather grew colder as the bus approached San Giovanni Rotondo. When the bus dropped her off, it was a two-mile walk through the snow in order to reach the monastery. Elide regretted that she had brought only a light jacket to wear. She also regretted that she was wearing sandals and had no other change of shoes.

The following day, Elide went to Padre Pio's Mass. After Mass, she waited in line to make her confession. When she heard Padre Pio's stern voice speaking to a penitent in the confessional, she lost her courage and decided to leave the line. Just as she was preparing to leave, the woman behind her gave her a strong push forward. Soon she was kneeling before Padre Pio. Fear clutched at her heart. Padre Pio's voice was very gentle as he talked to her. It reminded her exactly of the way her own dear father used to talk to her when she was a little girl. As a matter of fact, Padre Pio used many of the same phrases that her father had used in days gone by.

Elide told Padre Pio that she had traveled to San Giovanni Rotondo in order to ask for prayers for her aunt. "First make your confession, and then tell me about your aunt," Padre Pio said. Elide started to make her confession but she could not find her words. Padre Pio helped her through the confession by asking her questions.

After the confession, Elide asked Padre Pio if he would accept her as his spiritual daughter. It was not something that she had planned to say. "Yes, I will accept you," he answered. Then he asked Elide to tell him about her aunt. Elide told him of her aunt's fear of death and of her desire to be well prepared at the time of her passing. Padre Pio listened carefully to all that Elide had to say. When she was finished talking, Padre Pio paused for a few moments of silence. "All will go well for your aunt," Padre Pio said. He told Elide that she could be assured of his prayers.

Elide left the confessional greatly uplifted. All the inconveniences and hardships of the journey to San Giovanni Rotondo now seemed like trifles. The next day she left to go back to her home in Sestri Levante. A short time later, her aunt passed away. She had just received Holy Communion and was making her thanksgiving when she slipped peacefully into eternal life. It was truly a beautiful death. Elide knew that Padre Pio's prayers had assisted her aunt.

Meeting Padre Pio had made a great impression on Elide and she looked forward with great anticipation to the time when she could make a return visit. Several months later she was able to make another trip to San Giovanni Rotondo. "You are going to move here permanently," Padre Pio said to Elide. "When the Home for the Relief of Suffering is completed, you will work there." "Oh no," Elide replied emphatically, "It would be impossible. I am a dressmaker by profession. I have no skills that would enable me to work in a hospital. Besides, my mother needs me. I would never be able to leave her." Very gently Padre Pio said to her, "I will take care of your mother myself." "But if my mother was to get sick, she would want me nearby." "I will take care of that too," Padre Pio replied. "You do not have to worry about anything. The hospital is now being built. You will come here and work. It is God's will for you," Padre Pio said firmly.

Elide knew that she would never move to San Giovanni Rotondo. It was a small backwater town that had nothing to offer her. Sestri Levante, on the other hand, where Elide made her home, was a lovely seaside resort city on the Mediterranean coast. The weather was mild and agreeable and the coastline was beautiful. Surrounded by her family and friends, Elide was very happy there. She had no intention of moving to San Giovanni Rotondo. She was convinced that only an act of God would cause her to leave her hometown.

When Elide returned to Sestri Levante, she began organizing pilgrimages to San Giovanni Rotondo. She wanted others to experience the same blessings that she had experienced while visiting Padre Pio's monastery. Elide's pilgrimages became very popular. She took small groups as well as large groups and had no trouble filling the seats.

On one occasion, when Elide was in San Giovanni Rotondo, she got word that her mother was ill. She returned home immediately. Fortunately, her mother's condition had improved by the time she arrived home. Her mother had always said that she wanted Elide to be with her at the time of her death. She said to Elide, "I am at peace now. Even if I were to die soon, I feel prepared. I think Padre Pio is calling you to live near him. He needs you to help him with his work. I want you to move to San Giovanni Rotondo and assist him." Not long after that, Elide's mother had a beautiful dream. In her dream, Padre Pio was standing at the foot of her bed and he gave her a blessing. She died the very next day.

Elide was deeply saddened by the loss of her mother. She returned to San Giovanni Rotondo and wept as she told Padre Pio about her mother's death. "What am I going to do now?" Elide said to Padre Pio. "My mother, whom I loved so much, is gone. How will I continue?" "I am now your entire family - mother, father, and brother," Padre Pio replied. "Your mother is in heaven. We must do our very best so that we too can arrive there someday. Let us concentrate on that." His words brought her great comfort and great peace.

Elide moved to San Giovanni Rotondo in 1954. Two years later, the Home for the Relief of Suffering opened its doors. Padre Pio told Elide for the second time that she was going to work in the new hospital. "But I can't," Elide said. "I don't have the experience." Very quietly Padre Pio said to Elide, "Just do what you are told."

The first day that Elide reported for work at the Home for the Relief of Suffering, she was greeted by a doctor and was given a white coat to put on, just like the one that he had on. The doctor gave her instructions on how to admit the patients and how to fill out the necessary forms and paperwork. Elide was able to learn the job quite easily. After about an hour of instruction, the doctor left her on her own. She found the work very enjoyable.

At the time, Elide was renting a single room, which was located very close to the hospital. A very nice little house became available for rent and Padre Pio told Elide that she should take it. Elide explained to Padre Pio that her salary at the hospital was not enough to cover the monthly rent. "Take the house," Padre Pio said. "You will always have enough money for your needs with extra left over." Elide rented the house. As it turned out, Padre Pio had been right. Elide was able to pay the rent each month with money left over.

Elide loved her job as admitting clerk at the Home for the Relief of Suffering. She was happy to be serving Padre Pio's work. When she was asked to do the washing and ironing for the Capuchins who were in residence at Our Lady of Grace monastery, she gladly accepted the task.

One day, as Elide was doing the laundry for the Capuchins, she had the idea to keep one of Padre Pio's undershirts. She knew that there were very strict rules in place regarding Padre Pio's personal items. He was not allowed to give any of his possessions away. Elide knew that she could get into a lot of trouble for disobeying the rules. But the temptation to keep an article of Padre Pio's clothing was so great that Elide gave in to her strong desire. One day, she sent the freshly laundered clothing and habits back to the monastery minus one of Padre Pio's shirts.

The next time Elide went to confession to Padre Pio, she was very nervous. She hoped that he would not guess what she had done and at the same time she knew that it was practically impossible to keep a secret from him. In the confessional, Padre Pio's first words to Elide were the words that she did not want to hear. "Have you stolen something that belonged to someone else?" he asked. "It is true," Elide answered. "What is it that you stole?" Padre Pio asked. "I stole a shirt," Elide replied. "You stole a shirt? Well, who did it belong to?" Padre Pio inquired. "It belonged to you." At that point, Elide could not contain her emotions any longer and she began to cry. "Well, did you need this shirt that you stole?" Padre Pio asked. "Oh yes, I did need it. I truly needed it," Elide answered. "Very well then," Padre Pio said and then he changed the subject. "Now tell me what else you have been doing," he exclaimed. He never mentioned the "stolen property" to her again. Elide was elated. She was able to keep the prized relic and all thanks were due to Padre Pio.

One morning, Elide was standing outside the church waiting for the doors to open for Mass. Two women who were standing nearby were having a lively discussion and Elide could not help but overhear what they were talking about. "I am going to send my guardian angel to Padre Pio," one of the women said. "I will ask my angel to take a special message to him." Elide thought that the talk about guardian angels was ridiculous. The women were obviously superstitious. When the Mass was concluded, Elide made her confession to Padre Pio. "Will you always assist me?" Elide asked him. "Yes, I will," Padre

Pio replied. "I will always be near you and I will send you my guardian angel to help you." Elide realized that Padre Pio was trying to show her the error in her thinking. She was sorry she had judged the women in such a harsh way.

Padre Pio's spiritual children who resided in San Giovanni Rotondo were fortunate to be able to receive Padre Pio's daily blessing. Often before doing the simplest tasks, like going to an appointment or making a trip to town, they would ask Padre Pio for his blessing. In the late afternoons when Padre Pio took his recreation in the monastery garden, Elide would sometimes stand outside the garden wall and call to him, "Padre Pio, I am right outside the garden gate here. May I have your blessing?" Padre Pio would then open the gate, make the sign of the cross in blessing over Elide and then close the gate. Very satisfied, Elide would take her leave, usually to go back to her job at the hospital.

Receiving an individual blessing from Padre Pio was curtailed in 1960 with the visitation of Monsignor Carlo Maccari. Monsignor Maccari was sent to San Giovanni Rotondo from the Holy Office in Rome to investigate complaints that had been made against Padre Pio. There had been accusations in reference to possible financial irregularities at the Home for the Relief of Suffering. There were complaints regarding the unruly behavior in the church on the part of some of the pilgrims. There were complaints about Padre Pio himself. Numerous rumors about him had been circulating for years. Elide was working at the Home for the Relief of Suffering when Monsignor Maccari made his visitation.

Monsignor Maccari stayed at the Home for the Relief of Suffering during the time of his visit. Much to the dismay of the Capuchin superior at Our Lady of Grace monastery, he took it upon himself to intercept Padre Pio's personal mail and read it. Even confidential letters were opened and scrutinized. It seemed as though Monsignor Maccari had brought with him certain preconceived ideas and even prejudices against Padre Pio. Before he returned to Rome, he set forth a number of directives that were to be strictly enforced. People would no longer be allowed to speak to Padre Pio as he was entering or exiting the confessional. The sacristy and the monastery garden became off limits to all members of the laity. A railing was to be built around the women's confessional to make it more difficult for people to see and to speak to Padre Pio.

Padre Pio never contested the decisions of high church officials in reference to his ministry in San Giovanni Rotondo. He was very much aware that
there was open hostility toward him. He would not speak to anyone about
Monsignor Maccari's visit and just as he had done in the past, he followed all
of the directives to the letter.

Elide felt very sad about the restrictions that had been put in place as
a consequence of the visit of Monsignor Maccari. Like many others, Elide
depended on Padre Pio's daily blessing. Elide came up with a solution to the
problem and she spoke to Padre Pio about it. She told him that when he went
to the garden in the afternoon for his recreation period, she would be standing on the other side of the wall. Of course, he would not be able to see her
but she would be able to look through the keyhole of the gate and see him. "I
would like you to pause as you pass by the garden gate and give me a blessing,"
Elide said to Padre Pio. "I will be waiting there." Padre Pio was happy to agree
to Elide's request. Elide continued to receive his daily blessing, "through the
garden wall" and Padre Pio did not break a single rule in doing so.

On January 30, 1964, Pope Paul VI announced that Padre Pio was
restored to full freedom in his priestly ministry. Like many times in the past,
it had been a waiting game. The accusations and complaints against him were
eventually all shown to be false.

Padre Pio continued to direct his spiritual children step by step on the
path toward holiness. Once, Elide's brother surprised her by giving her a television set as a gift. She was delighted to receive it. When she told Padre Pio
the good news about her new gift, he was not at all pleased. "I am sorry that
you have invited the devil into your home!" Padre Pio said adamantly. Elide
was shocked at his words. However, she could see that he meant what he said.
Elide got the message loud and clear and decided to return the television to
her brother.

Elide became very proficient as the hospital receptionist and admitting
clerk at the Home for the Relief of Suffering. She enjoyed the work very
much. One day without warning, Padre Pio told her that her job was going
to be changed. She would become the hospital's switchboard operator. The
hospital had grown and expanded so much that a central switchboard had
to be installed. Elide panicked at the thought of being in charge of a busy
switchboard. "But I can't do that," Elide said to Padre Pio. "I have no experi-

ence. I don't think I would be up to the task. I am afraid that it would be too difficult." "I want you to do what I am asking of you," Padre Pio said. Elide complied with Padre Pio's wishes. A technician trained her in the work. She was able to learn the job so easily that she was convinced that Padre Pio had assisted her.

After Padre Pio's death in 1968, Elide continued to live on in the little house in San Giovanni Rotondo, the one that Padre Pio had urged her to rent. The house had a lovely garden in the back which she enjoyed very much. She was very contented there. She eventually retired from her job at the Home for the Relief of Suffering. Padre Pio had assured Elide that her needs would always be supplied. Time proved the truth of his words. Elide never lacked for anything. She felt blessed that she was able to give the extra money that she had at the end of each month to those who were less fortunate. She was convinced that Padre Pio was watching over her from heaven.

I don't know how to thank the Heavenly Father for his mercy when he introduces souls to me to whom I can be helpful in some way.

- St. Pio of Pietrelcina

CHAPTER 19

Dreams of Padre Pio

---

*L*ina Fiorellini met Padre Pio in 1919. At that time, Lina was employed by the Pontremoli family. She thought very highly of the family and felt blessed that she could work for them. Lina spoke to Padre Pio and asked him to always keep the Pontremoli family in his prayers. "They are good people," Padre Pio replied. "I will remember them before the Lord and pray to Jesus for their salvation." Lina often shared her Catholic faith with Lucia Pontremoli and her son, Aldo. Although they were not Christians, they listened to Lina with great interest and respect. Lina also told them many stories about Padre Pio.

Aldo, who was a professor at the University of Milan, was preparing to go on an expedition to the North Pole. The whole world was following the upcoming expedition with great anticipation. It was scheduled for the spring of 1928. Shortly before Aldo and the crew left for the North Pole, they were granted an audience with Pope Pius XI. Aldo was so inspired by meeting the Pope that he sought out a Catholic priest and asked for baptism. Several days later, he left on the expedition. Tragically, Aldo lost his life, as did the other crew members, when the airship they were traveling in collided into ice.

A few months after Aldo's death, Lina had a vivid dream. In her dream, Aldo spoke to her and said, "I owe my salvation to you and to Padre Pio." He then kissed her on the forehead. The next time Lina went to San Giovanni Rotondo, she told Padre Pio about the dream. "Was Aldo speaking the truth to me in my dream?" Lina asked. "Yes, your dream was true," Padre Pio replied. "Aldo went from the North Pole to Paradise!"

Lina continued to pray for Aldo's mother, Lucia Pontremoli. Padre Pio encouraged Lina to offer up all of her sufferings for the conversion of souls, including Lucia's. On Holy Thursday, 1946, Lucia asked for baptism. Padre Pio was filled with joy when Lina told him the good news. Lina and Padre Pio had both been praying for Lucia for more than twenty-five years.

————

Pope Pius XII (Eugenio Pacelli) was admired for his profound and lifelong devotion to the Blessed Virgin Mary. He was ordained as a bishop on May 13, 1917, the day of the first appearance of Our Lady of Fatima to Jacinta, Francisco, and Lucia, the three shepherd children of Fatima, Portugal. When Eugenio was elected pope in 1939, and took the name Pope Pius XII, he placed his pontificate under the special protection of the Virgin Mary. Pope Pius XII has often been spoken of as the most Marian pope in Church history. He consecrated the world to the Immaculate Heart of Mary in 1942. In 1954, he introduced a new Marian feast to the Church, the Queenship of Mary. He was the first pope to call for a Marian year, a practice which was continued by Pope John Paul II in 1998. Many of the saints canonized by Pius XII had great devotion to the Virgin Mary such as Louis de Montfort, Pope Pius X, Catherine Labouré, Anthony Mary Claret, and Gemma Galgani.

Maria Guerriero of Rome, among others, was involved in a very extensive writing and research project which, when finished, would be given over to Pope Pius XII. The information that was being compiled was in reference to the Assumption of the Blessed Virgin Mary.

In August 1940, Maria's two sisters, Laura and Antonietta, were preparing to make a trip to San Giovanni Rotondo. Maria asked her sisters to tell Padre Pio about the material on the Assumption which she was preparing for Pope Pius XII. When Maria's sisters relayed the message to Padre Pio, he was very pleased. He told Laura and Antoinetta that if the Blessed Virgin had chosen Maria for such an important task, she must persevere in it, even if it was tedious and even if the results were not immediate. He assured them that he would keep Maria in his prayers.

Maria devoted herself to the project in all of her free time. She often worked late into the night, after her daily duties were done. She had never been strong physically and after a time she began to suffer from exhaustion. Finally, her health broke. She was tormented by severe and prolonged headaches. The headaches were so painful that they proved to be debilitating and eventually, she had to spend her days in a darkened room with her eyes closed. Maria's family was very worried about her health. They wrote to Padre Pio and asked him for his continued prayers.

One night, during the time of her illness, Maria had a dream. She dreamed that she was knocking at the door of the monastery of Our Lady of Grace. In her dream, Brother Gerardo, who, in reality, was the doorkeeper of the monastery, answered the door. She told him that she was in great need and that it was urgent that she speak to Padre Pio. "It is impossible," Father Gerardo said. "Women cannot enter the monastic enclosure. You can only speak to Padre Pio if you make your confession to him." With tears in her eyes, Maria asked Brother Gerardo to tell Padre Pio that she was ill. He did what Maria asked him to do. After a short time, Brother Gerardo returned. He led Maria into a small room in the monastery. In her dream, Padre Pio came into the room. Two trickles of blood were flowing from his left temple down his cheek. "How selfish I am," Maria thought to herself. "Here I am complaining about my headaches and now before my very eyes, I see what Padre Pio suffers day in and day out." Maria felt like apologizing to Padre Pio. He tapped her on the head three times and then said to her, "Maria, you are cured now."

When Maria woke up, she was completely free of pain. She felt strong enough to get out of bed and she was able to set about her work as though she had never been ill. That very day she wrote Padre Pio a letter, thanking him for the healing. She was able to continue with her research and writing regarding the Assumption of the Virgin Mary and on January 31, 1941 her work was finally completed and put on the desk of Pope Pius XII.

During the summer of 1941, Maria traveled with her sisters to San Giovanni Rotondo. While there, she made her confession to Padre Pio. In the confessional, Padre Pio smiled at Maria and to her great surprise, he tapped her on her head three times, exactly like he had done in her dream. "Am I still your spiritual daughter?" Maria asked. "Yes, you are," Padre Pio answered. "Remember that a father is always a father. Children can stray, but you will never stray. Let us thank the Blessed Virgin who has protected you. You have been working for her for a long time. Don't be discouraged if your work does not have immediate results. Satan has always tried to attack Our Lady but he will never succeed. She will always be able to overcome him."

On November 1, 1950, in the Apostolic Constitution, *Munificentissimus Deus*, Pope Pius XII proclaimed the Assumption of the Blessed Virgin Mary as a dogma of the Catholic Church. Pope Pius XII passed away on October 9, 1958. Just as in his life, after his death, signs of his love for the Virgin Mary were evident. His remains were buried in Rome in the crypt of St. Peter's Basilica on the feast day of Our Lady of Fatima, October 13, 1958. The Congregation for the Cause of Saints at the Vatican issued a decree which was approved by Pope Benedict XVI in 2009. The decree gave its stamp of approval to the heroic virtues in the life of Pope Pius XII and the title of "Venerable" was then added to his name.

Giuseppe Di Sessa's dear wife, Anna Maria, died in October 1940. Two months later, he went to see Padre Pio and told him about his wife's death. He explained to Padre Pio that he prayed for his wife every day and offered many sacrifices on behalf of her soul. Padre Pio told Giuseppe that for the sake of his family, he should consider remarrying. Giuseppe explained to Padre Pio that he had decided not to marry again. For a second time, Padre Pio made the suggestion to him that he should remarry. As Giuseppe was leaving, Padre Pio said to him, "I hope that you come back to San Giovanni Rotondo again. As far as the question of a remarriage is concerned, you will see that I am right."

Six years later, Giuseppe met a woman named Maria Grazia. Maria told Giuseppe about a dream she once had that was very meaningful to her. In her dream, Padre Pio told her that she should marry. She explained to Padre Pio that she had decided not to marry and told him that she felt called to another mission. "Marriage too is a mission," Padre Pio said to her. "If marriage is a mission, then make it work out for me," Maria replied. Then she woke up.

Giuseppe and Maria fell in love and when Giuseppe proposed marriage to her, Maria happily accepted. After the wedding, Giuseppe and his new bride made a trip to San Giovanni Rotondo to see Padre Pio and to tell him the good news.

———

Mrs. Bertolotti first learned about Padre Pio in 1946. She longed to make a trip to San Giovanni Rotondo but the years passed and she was never able to do so. One night, she dreamed that she was at the monastery of Our Lady of Grace. She saw a man who walked toward the booking office where tickets could be obtained for Padre Pio's confessional. The man had a letter in his hand that was addressed to Mrs. Bertolotti. He handed her the letter and with that she woke up.

Mrs. Bertolotti thought about the meaning of the dream. It almost seemed to her that she was being called to visit Padre Pio. The dream made such an impression on her that she made preparations to travel to Padre Pio's monastery. It was a cold and rainy afternoon when she got ready to board the train. Due to the many difficulties in her life, there was a sadness in her heart that day. The dismal weather did nothing to lift her spirits.

As soon as Mrs. Bertolotti arrived at the monastery, she went to the booking office and obtained a ticket for Padre Pio's confessional. She had to wait ten days before her number was called. She was able to attend Padre Pio's Mass every day while she waited. Spending time in prayer in the church of Our Lady of Grace and attending Padre Pio's Mass each day made her feel like she was "in heaven." The days passed quickly and her heart was filled with a wonderful peace.

Finally, Mrs. Bertolotti's number was called. After making her confession, she asked Padre Pio to accept her as his spiritual daughter and he agreed to do so. Before she left the confessional, she kissed his hand. When she returned to her home, she felt as though she had been completely transformed. The years ahead brought their share of problems, but Mrs. Bertolotti was no longer overwhelmed by them as she had been in the past. Her visit to

Padre Pio had supplied her with the strength she needed to face all of the trials in her life.

————

Maria Colabianchi visited San Giovanni Rotondo for the first time in 1952. She attended Padre Pio's Mass every day for ten days as she waited to make her confession to him. Maria felt that Padre Pio was truly her spiritual father. She frequently prayed to him, asking for his intercession. She hoped that someday all of the other members of her family would be able to travel to San Giovanni Rotondo and attend his Mass.

On one occasion, Maria's sister-in-law told her about an unusual dream that she had. She dreamed that she and her husband (Maria's brother) were in a church that she had never seen before. A Capuchin priest whom they did not know turned to her husband and said, "I see that you have arrived." With that, the dream ended.

At the time of the dream, Maria's sister-in-law was expecting her first child. Shortly after the dream, her sister-in-law began to have strong abdominal pains. When she was examined by her doctor, it was found that she had a tumor in her womb. Her doctor advised her to have an operation and informed her that there was a 90 percent chance that she would lose the baby during the surgery. She refused to consent to the surgery. There were many days of anguish and great fear and she was plagued by intense and constant pain. The doctor told her that even if she did not have the operation, in all likelihood she would lose the baby.

Maria advised her sister-in-law to pray to Padre Pio for his intercession. She did what Maria suggested and sent up her heartfelt prayers to Padre Pio. She and her husband then traveled to Rome to have a consultation with a well-know physician and specialist. The doctor in Rome advised against the surgery. Instead, he recommended a series of twelve injections.

Maria asked a friend who lived in San Giovanni Rotondo to go to Padre Pio in person and inform him about her sister-in-law's precarious state. Her friend agreed to do so. When Padre Pio heard the news, he sent a message back to the family. "The woman must place herself under the doctor's care," Padre Pio advised. He also told the family to be assured of his prayers.

In November 1961, Maria's brother made a trip to San Giovanni Rotondo. For months, he had been filled with anxiety about his wife and their unborn child. He arrived at the monastery in the late afternoon and was able to participate in the evening devotions that were held in the church. He was told to go directly to the sacristy after the devotions and to wait for Padre Pio if he wanted to receive his blessing.

That evening, the sacristy was very crowded, with lines of men on either side. As Padre Pio was passing through the sacristy, he seemed to single Maria's brother out. Padre Pio looked directly at him and said, "I see that you have arrived." The words Padre Pio had spoken to him were the very words that he had spoken in his wife's dream. From that time forward, his wife's condition improved. She soon gave birth to a beautiful baby girl who was healthy in every way.

———

One of Padre Pio's spiritual daughters was hired to work in the sewing room at the Home for the Relief of Suffering. Among many other projects that she worked on, she made the very first curtains for the hospital. She was able to have the curtains ready well before inauguration day on May 6, 1956. The woman also made the nurses uniforms as well as the operating room gowns for the doctors.

The woman had a great devotion to Padre Pio. She made several of his brown habits and whenever any of his habits needed alteration, she was called upon to do the work. She always counted it a great privilege. She also used to make the small cushions that Padre Pio rested his wounded hands on when he prayed for extended periods of time in the choir loft of the church. She chose green velvet for the material because it was a color that was restful to the eyes.

Once, when she was making her confession to Padre Pio, she told him about a dream she had. In her dream, Padre Pio was a newborn baby. He was a beautiful baby but already the marks of the stigmata were on his body. Especially vivid in the dream, were the wounds on his hands. The woman asked Padre Pio what the dream might mean. Padre Pio's face became sad and he said to her, "It means that Our Lord, Christ Crucified, has allowed you to see his wounds."

———————

There was once a Capuchin Brother at Our Lady of Grace monastery in San Giovanni Rotondo who was assigned to help Padre Pio with many of his daily tasks. The Brother had a great devotion to Padre Pio and performed his work in an exemplary way. Every morning between 4:00 a.m. and 4:30 a.m. he would go to Padre Pio's cell to assist him. The routine was always the same. Padre Pio would be sitting in his chair either reading his breviary or praying the Rosary. The Brother would then kiss his hand and proceed to straighten the covers on his bed and do other simple tasks in his cell.

One night, the Brother had a terrible dream. In truth, it was a nightmare. In his dream, Padre Pio was very elderly and very ill. He was withdrawn and hardly able to move or speak, and it seemed as though he was about to die. In the dream, there was also another Padre Pio. He was floating in the air high above and was smiling, suffused with a beautiful light. But the Padre Pio that was predominant was the suffering one. When the Brother woke up, he was so upset that he burst into tears. He thought that the dream might have been a premonition of the future. Perhaps as Padre Pio grew older, his sufferings would increase more and more.

The Brother's dream occurred in 1957. Padre Pio's hospital, the Home for the Relief of Suffering had just recently opened. Padre Pio was busy, not only with the many concerns of the hospital but also with the expansion of the Prayer Groups that he had founded. In addition, there was a steady flow of pilgrims who constantly poured into San Giovanni Rotondo in order to attend Padre Pio's Mass and make their confession to him. While his health was not the best, he was still able to accomplish a great deal of work each day. He seemed to have the necessary energy to do so.

The Brother could not get the disturbing dream out of his mind. He went to the little monastery chapel of Our Lady of Grace and with tears in his eyes, he prayed before the tabernacle. "Jesus, I beg you," the Brother prayed. "Please do not let anything bad happen to our Padre Pio. He has already suffered so much. I know that he belongs to you but he belongs to us too and we love him. Do not let his sufferings increase. Give them to me instead. I don't want Padre Pio to have to endure any more pain." After praying at length in the chapel, the Brother made a great effort to put the dream out of his mind. He decided not to tell anyone about it.

The next morning, the Brother was at Padre Pio's door at the usual time of 4:30 a.m. Like always, he found Padre Pio sitting in his chair, reading his breviary and preparing for the early morning Mass. The Brother greeted him and kissed his hand. Much to his great surprise, Padre Pio slowly rose from his chair to a standing position. Padre Pio then embraced him and said, "I want to thank you my son, for what you did for me last night!" Padre Pio had felt the prayers that the good Brother had offered up for him and he was very grateful.

There was a woman (name withheld) who was married to a very successful businessman. Soon after their marriage, her husband became cold and indifferent. When he got home from work in the evenings, he hardly spoke to her. Whenever he could find the chance to get away, he would leave the house and not return until very late in the evening. Feeling neglected and alone, the woman became very depressed. She prayed for a solution to the problem.

The woman possessed a holy card of Padre Pio. On one particular day, feeling the painful reality of her situation, she took the holy card in her hand and prayed, "Padre Pio, I am very sad about the state of my marriage. Please wake my husband up and help him to change. Come to him in a dream or do whatever is necessary, in order to shake him out of his indifference toward me. Show him the error of his ways. Please save our marriage!" Even though the woman knew practically nothing about Padre Pio, she was glad that she had prayed to him and asked for his help.

That evening her husband returned home very late as usual and during the night he had a strange dream. In his dream, he was in a beautiful building. It looked like a brand-new hospital and it had a lovely marble staircase.

As he walked down the staircase, he saw five monks who were coming up the staircase toward him. Each one was wearing a brown habit. Following behind them was a sixth monk. The five monks walked past him but the sixth one stopped in front of him. The monk looked at him sternly and then raised his hand in a warning gesture. At once, the man thought of his wife and how badly he had been treating her. He recognized the monk who had looked at him in such a severe manner. It was Padre Pio.

The man felt shaken by the dream. He suddenly felt remorseful for his conduct toward his wife. The dream had seemed so real that it woke him up out of a sound sleep. He could hardly wait till morning so that he could tell his wife.

The next morning, the man knelt down at his wife's bedside. He gently touched her hair in a caress in order to waken her. He spoke to her with great tenderness and asked for forgiveness for his coldness and for his neglect. She could hardly believe it. He had not spoken to her with such affection since they were first married. Moreover, she had never known her husband to apologize for anything. To see him kneeling at her bedside was perhaps the greatest surprise of all. Because of his pride, he was definitely not the kind of man to get down on his knees for any reason whatsoever.

Later, the woman made a trip to San Giovanni Rotondo and was able to visit the Home for the Relief of Suffering. The hospital was beautiful in every way. She noticed the wide and attractive marble staircase near the entrance. She remembered that her husband had told her that in his dream, he had been in a beautiful hospital that had a marble staircase. Because of the dream of Padre Pio, her husband made a great effort to change. Their marriage was blessed with happiness from that time forward.

———

Andre Mandato was one of Padre Pio's spiritual sons. In order to provide a better life for his family, Andre decided to move with his wife and children from Bologna, Italy to the United States. He sent in his application and all of the necessary paperwork, requesting a permanent visa to the United States. One night, Andre dreamed that Padre Pio spoke to him and said that his application had been rejected. "Andre, if you turn in another application and choose a new sponsor, you will be accepted," Padre Pio said in the dream. When Andre woke up, he could not stop thinking about Padre Pio's words. Could it be true? That very afternoon, he learned that his application had been rejected. He followed Padre Pio's advice by selecting a new sponsor. He also submitted another application and soon received a permanent visa for the entire family.

––––––

One of Padre Pio's spiritual daughters met Padre Pio when she was just eighteen years old. She was suffering from poor health at the time. Padre Pio put his hand on her head and said to her, "Do not worry about anything." His hand felt like a very heavy weight pressing on her head and she was healed instantly at his touch. Later, when she married and had a family, there were many trials to face. She found out that her husband was unfaithful to her. To add to her heartache, one of her children became addicted to drugs. During this difficult time in her life, she had a vivid dream of Padre Pio. In her dream, she was in a country setting and in the distance she saw Padre Pio who was running toward her.

As she pondered the meaning of the dream, she was convinced that it meant that Padre Pio knew all about her problems and was interceding for her. She recalled that the first time she made her confession to him, he told her not to worry about anything. She placed herself under Padre Pio's protection and had faith that he was praying for her.

––––––

After Bernadette Palo had long-discarded her Catholic faith, she became interested in spiritualism and in the occult. One night she dreamed that she saw Padre Pio standing in front of a church. She told Padre Pio that something was bothering her. Padre Pio smiled at her and said, "Give it up! Give it up!" Bernadette understood that Padre Pio meant that she should give up her study of the occult. "But if I do that, how can I make progress on the spiritual path? How can I be good?" Bernadette asked. "God thinks you are good enough already," Padre Pio replied. After the dream, Bernadette had a desire to go to confession. She prayed for the courage to do so. She finally made her confession and returned to the sacraments after an absence of twelve years.

————

Aure Caviggioli was an antique dealer who lived in Monte Carlo, Italy. Absorbed in his work and in other interests, he had put his spiritual life on the back burner. On one occasion, he visited San Giovanni Rotondo and attended Padre Pio's Mass. He felt so uplifted by the experience that he returned to the monastery several more times. Because he felt a certain uneasiness when he was in Padre Pio's presence, he was hesitant to make his confession to him.

Aure possessed a beautiful antique painting of the Virgin and Child that dated back to the 16th century. When an acquaintance asked Aure about the value of the artwork, Aure told him that it was worth millions. That very night, Aure had a dream. In his dream, Padre Pio was looking directly at him and he had a very severe expression on his face. "You paid 25,000 lira for that painting," Padre Pio said. "It is not worth millions and you know it!"

When Aure woke up the next morning, he reflected on the dream. What Padre Pio had said to him in the dream was indeed true. The painting had cost him 25,000 lira. After much thought, Aure decided to give the painting to Padre Pio. He traveled to the monastery of Our Lady of Grace and presented it to him. Padre Pio smiled at Aure and accepted the painting. He seemed to be genuinely happy to receive the gift.

————

Professor G. Felice Checcacci, a native of Genoa, Italy, had spent many years living in Asia. He had left his Christian faith far behind him, believing it to be a break off from several other world religions. When Felice returned to Italy, he read a book about Padre Pio which made a great impression on him. It caused him to reexamine all of his beliefs. One night he had a dream of Padre Pio. In his dream, Padre Pio spoke to him and said, "Come and see me." Felice did not pay too much attention to the dream. About three months later, he had another dream. In his dream, Padre Pio said, "I waited for you but you have not come." And finally, he had a third experience in which Padre Pio said to him, "If you won't come to see me, at least write to me!"

The very next day, Felice wrote a letter to Padre Pio, recommending himself to his prayers. In the letter, he told Padre Pio that he was searching for peace of mind and peace of heart. In the late afternoon, just two days after sending the letter, Felice had a very strong desire to go to church. He had not done so in more than thirty years. As he sat alone in the quiet church, he was startled to hear a voice within his heart saying, "Faith is not up for discussion; you either believe it or you do not believe it. You either accept it or you reject it; there is no middle ground. You must choose one way or the other." Felice was certain that it was Padre Pio who was speaking to his heart.

Felice knew that for a long time, he had been drawing his own conclusions about Christianity. He was using his reason and his intellect to try to understand transcendental truths. It wasn't possible. From that moment on, his life underwent a complete change. He felt a great sense of peace in his heart and he returned to the practice of his Christian faith.

––––––––––

Settimo Manelli once had a dream in which she saw Padre Pio in the glory of heaven. His face was transfigured with a great beauty. Everything around Padre Pio shone with a marvelous light. Especially beautiful was the intense and vivid color of the blue sky.

The next morning Settimo went to Padre Pio's Mass and afterward she told him about her dream. "Your face had such splendor in my dream," Settimo said. "I don't want to hurt your feelings, but as I look at you now, you do not look attractive. Your face has no signs of that glory which I saw in my dream." Padre Pio smiled and said to her, "I do not look attractive?" About a year later, Settimo saw Padre Pio again. She was standing in the corridor of the monastery when he greeted her. He looked at her and said, "It certainly was beautiful, wasn't it!"

––––––––––

Ginesta and her family lived in San Giovanni Rotondo where Ginesta worked with her father at his grocery store. As a child, she had a number of serious health problems but her condition improved as she grew older. Genesta's father loved her very much and could not help but worry about her. Hoping for the best for his daughter, he was often preoccupied with thoughts about her future. One night Ginesta had a dream. In her dream, Padre Pio visited her at her father's grocery store. "Ginesta," Padre Pio said, "You must tell your father that it is my responsibility to look after you. That includes not only the present but also the future. It also includes your future wedding. You must tell your father not to worry about you because I will see to everything you need." The next morning, Ginesta relayed the message to her father.

———

Antonio Ciannamea, who had traveled to San Giovanni Rotondo to see Padre Pio on many occasions, once had an unusual dream. In his dream, Padre Pio was sitting in his customary chair in his cell and Antonio was kneeing beside him. Through Antonio's parted lips, Padre Pio placed a tube and breathed into it three times. Padre Pio's cheeks swelled as he blew the air into the tube. When Antonio felt Padre Pio's breath, he experienced a great sense of well-being. Padre Pio then said to him, "Go with God's grace." With that, Antonio woke up.

For the most part, Antonio did not believe in the symbolism of dreams. But because the dream of Padre Pio had seemed so real, Antonio felt that it held a message. Exactly what that message was, he did not know. When he told his wife about the dream, she became worried. She told him to be careful when he was at work, because to her, the dream seemed to be a kind of warning.

That day, Antonio visited a number of the different departments in the factory where he worked. About six tons of molten lead were about to be turned into the framework for the batteries of electricity accumulators. Some of the employees were busy cleaning filaments from the frameworks while the conveyer belt was bringing lead bars forward for collection and loading.

The head factory technician had a piece of tube that he was placing into the lead. Suddenly, a shower of boiling lead flashed through the air. It reminded

Antonio of a burst of violent machine gun fire. The solidified lead landed on Antonio's hair, clothing and shoes. Antonio was filled with terror, but to his great relief not a drop had touched his skin. Miraculously, he was unhurt. The employees who were nearby and who had witnessed the near catastrophe told Antonio how lucky he was to have escaped injury.

That night, Antonio had another dream about Padre Pio. In his dream, Padre Pio was standing at the altar in his priestly vestments. Antonio knelt before him. Padre Pio turned to Antonio, blessed him and said, "Let us give thanks to God!" When Antonio woke up, he then understood. Padre Pio had foreseen the accident and had protected him through his intercessory prayers.

———

There was a man from Italy (name withheld) who was brought up in a good Catholic family but when he grew older he abandoned his faith. When asked what he believed in, he said simply, "nothing." He became a self-declared atheist. The man married and had a family but secretly he was living a double life. He was unfaithful to his wife and had no desire to change.

One night, when the man was at a hotel with his girlfriend, he surprised himself and those around him by suddenly stating that he was leaving. He told his friends that he was going to drive to San Giovanni Rotondo to visit Padre Pio. All of the people who were with him thought that he was joking. Everyone knew that he was not the kind of person who would be interested in visiting a priest. The odd thing was, the man knew almost nothing about Padre Pio. Perhaps he had heard a few facts about Padre Pio's life somewhere along the way, but there was nothing concrete that he could remember. Why he would suddenly have the overpowering urge to visit Padre Pio was a complete mystery.

It was about 2:30 a.m. when the man left the hotel. As he walked through the lobby toward the exit door, the hotel doorman asked him where he was going at such an hour. "I am driving to San Giovanni Rotondo to see Padre Pio," the man exclaimed. The doorman was well aware of the man's worldly lifestyle. "But why would you want to go to a monastery in the middle of the night? What is the attraction?" the doorman asked. But the man could offer no explanation. He did not have an answer.

The man arrived at the monastery of Our Lady of Grace before sunrise. He waited patiently in the darkness for the church to open. When Padre Pio began his Mass, the man became completely absorbed in it. All through the Mass, he experienced a wonderful feeling, something that he could not explain because he had never experienced it before. After the Mass, one of the Capuchins came up to him and asked him if he wanted to go to confession to Padre Pio. The thought had not even entered his mind, but since the Capuchin had suggested it to him, he decided that it was a good idea.

In the confessional, Padre Pio said to him, "It has been a long time since your last confession, hasn't it. How long has it been?" "It has been fourteen or fifteen years," the man replied. "Oh no, it has been a lot longer than that!" Padre Pio said. "What you want from me, I cannot give you. You must go to another who will give it to you." The man had no idea what Padre Pio was talking about.

The man left without making his confession. He had not even received a blessing from Padre Pio and yet he felt very happy and very satisfied. He was grateful that he had been able to see Padre Pio for those few moments. Attending Padre Pio's Mass had been a beautiful experience, more than he had ever imagined. He left San Giovanni Rotondo greatly uplifted. He knew that he wanted to return again.

Shortly after that, the man had a dream. In his dream, he saw Padre Pio walking down a staircase toward him. He was accompanied by another person who was dressed in white. Padre Pio took a folded paper from the pocket of his habit and handed it to the man. The words, "St. Alphonsus Liguori" were written on the paper. Then he woke up. He frequently thought about the dream and wondered about its meaning.

A short time later, a nun who lived in the same town as the man, asked him for a favor. She needed a ride to Foggia and wondered if he might be able to take her there. He was happy to assist her. On the way to Foggia, he told her about his dream and asked her what she thought it meant. "Perhaps it means that Padre Pio would like you to carry a picture of St. Alphonsus Liguori with you," the nun said. Not long after, the nun brought him a picture of St. Alphonsus Liguori. The man was astonished to find that the picture was inside of a folded paper that was identical to the size and shape of the paper that Padre Pio had given to him in his dream. He carried the little picture with him at all times.

The nun told the man that St. Alphonsus had lived in the town of Pagani at the Redemptorist House. Many of his relics were still preserved and venerated there. She thought it would be meaningful for him to visit the Redemptorist House and she encouraged him to do so. He decided to follow the nun's advice and shortly after that he made a trip to the small town of Pagani.

At the Redemptorist House, the man asked to see a priest. Soon the resident priest came out and greeted him kindly. He showed him the chapel and the various relics of St. Alphonsus. He also showed him the room that St. Alphonsus had lived in. As the man stood in St. Alphonsus' room, he suddenly felt a strong desire to go to confession. Almost as if reading the man's mind, the priest said to him, "Would you like to make your confession?" "I would like very much to do so," the man replied. At that moment, he remembered the words that Padre Pio had spoken to him, "What you want from me, I can't give you. You must go to another who will give it to you." The man was convinced that the priest who was standing before him was the one whom Padre Pio was referring to when he said, "You must go to another."

The man knelt down and made a sincere confession. Unashamedly, the man cried throughout the lengthy confession. The priest cried along with him. After the confession, the priest took him to the chapel where he gave him Holy Communion.

The man realized that Padre Pio had been leading him back to God, one step at a time. On his first visit to the monastery of Our Lady of Grace, he had been totally unprepared to approach the sacraments. But now, he was a completely changed person. He had a great desire to see Padre Pio again. When the man returned to the monastery of Our Lady of Grace, Padre Pio greeted him with love and called him "his son." He made his confession to Padre Pio and received absolution. He returned on many more occasions to the monastery of Our Lady of Grace.

———

When Nancy Sinisi developed a kidney disease, the doctor explained to the family that her condition was life-threatening. She was placed on dialysis three times a week and became a candidate for a kidney transplant. Nancy's mother had recently learned about Padre Pio. She decided to write a letter to him, asking him for his prayers for her daughter's recovery. The year was 1967. One day when Mrs. Sinisi was telling her family some of the details of Padre Pio's life, the room became filled with a beautiful perfume.

It wasn't long before Mrs. Sinisi received a letter in reply from San Giovanni Rotondo. The letter said that Padre Pio was praying for Nancy. The letter also stated that prayer must always be made according to the will of God.

While Nancy was waiting for the kidney transplant, Mary Ann, Nancy's sister, became so concerned that she sent Padre Pio a telegram and requested his prayers. That night Mrs. Sinisi had a dream. In the dream, Padre Pio said to her, "It was not necessary for a telegram to be sent to me. I was already praying for Nancy!" The surgery went very well and the Sinisi family was confident that Padre Pio had assisted Nancy with his intercessory prayers.

––––––––––

Vincenzo Mazzone's six-month-old son, Raffaele, became seriously ill in 1967. He suffered from a continuous high fever. He was seen by a number of doctors who could not come to an agreement regarding a diagnosis. He was given varying treatments and medicines, but his health did not improve. On the contrary, his condition was becoming worse with each passing day.

During this time of uncertainty and anxiety regarding little Raffaele, Vincenzo's wife had a dream. In her dream, Padre Pio was standing at a window, opening the curtains. He told her that little Raffaele should be in a place where the air was fresh. Then the dream was over. After she told her husband about the dream, they decided to make a trip from their home in Cerignola to San Giovanni Rotondo. Although it was difficult, they managed to get an immediate appointment with the pediatrician at the Home for the Relief of Suffering.

When the pediatrician examined Raffaele, he could find nothing wrong with him. His temperature was normal and he appeared to be in perfect health. Vincenzo and his wife were elated. The next night, after the evening devotions at Our Lady of Grace church, Vincenzo went to the sacristy in order to thank Padre Pio for his intercession. As Padre Pio passed by, Vincenzo knelt down. He had little Raffaele in his arms and he held him up to Padre Pio. With a slight smile, Padre Pio stopped and gave little Raffaele a blessing.

————

Father Placido of San Marco in Lamis was very close to Padre Pio. After Padre Pio's death on September 23, 1968, Father Placido wondered if perhaps his own time on earth might be drawing to a close. He spoke about it to Father Alberto D'Apolito. Father Alberto assured Father Placido that he was indeed healthy and would surely live for many more years. But Father Placido could not be convinced.

Not long after that, Father Placido told Father Alberto that he had a dream of Padre Pio. In the dream, Padre Pio said, "Father Placido, you must prepare yourself. You will be joining me very soon." "Will I be joining you in a few more years?" Father Placido asked. "No," Padre Pio replied. "You will be joining me in just a little while. You will not see the end of this year." Father Placido died on December 25, 1968. He did not see the end of the year.

————

Lilia Glorioso was the leader of a prayer group in Castelbuono, Italy. In 1972, she and her husband were celebrating their twenty-fifth wedding anniversary. They were happy that all five of their children could be present for the joyful occasion. The anniversary celebration turned out to be a wonderful success. One of their daughters, Marianna, was returning to her home in Palermo right after the celebration. Marianna's fiancé and two other friends were traveling with her. On the trip home, Marianna's fiancé fell asleep at the wheel and their car crashed into a wall. Tragically, Marianna died in the accident. The other three passengers were not hurt.

Concetta De Garbo was a friend and a neighbor of the Glorioso family. On the very night that Marianna died, Concetta had a dream. She dreamed that she was walking on the main street of Castelbuono when a car stopped in front of her. The driver spoke to Concetta and told her that Padre Pio was inside the car. Padre Pio then spoke to Concetta and asked her where she was going. She told him that she was going to visit her sister who was very ill. "I will go with you," Padre Pio said to Concetta and he invited her to get in the car.

In Concetta's dream, she and Padre Pio soon arrived at her sister's house. Padre Pio prayed for Concetta's sister and blessed her by placing his wounded hand on her. He then went over to the window which looked out onto the house of the Glorioso family. "Be sure to tell her to hurry because I will not be able to wait for her!" Padre Pio said to Concetta. She did not understand what he was talking about.

In her dream, Concetta then went over to the window and stood next to Padre Pio. As she looked out the window, she saw a woman across the street who seemed to be in great distress. She was dressed in black and her eyes were red from crying. "Oh, it is Lilia, the mother," Padre Pio said. "I feel so sorry for her. She is suffering so much!" With that, Concetta woke up. Upon waking, Concetta heard loud voices as well as crying that seemed to be coming from the street. She went to the window and discovered that the noise was coming from the home of the Glorioso family. She got dressed and hurried over to their house. She then learned that Marianna had died.

That same day, Concetta visited her sister who had been gravely ill. Concetta was surprised to see that her sister looked well. Her sister told her that all of her pain was gone and that she had never slept so well or so peacefully as she had on the previous night. In addition, her bodily strength had returned. Concetta remembered that in her dream, Padre Pio had prayed for her sister. Her sister made steady progress and soon gained weight and was able to go back to work. When Concetta took her for a medical examination, the doctor gave her a clean bill of health.

———

Note: I learned about the Gervais family (see dream entry below) through an email I was sent by a woman named Ann Douglass. Ann told me that in the late 1970's she read an article in the Church World, which was the Catholic diocesan newspaper of Maine at that time. The article was about the Gervais family and their devotion to Padre Pio. The family had been deeply touched by an experience that Mrs. Gervais had with Padre Pio.

Because of it, they decided to start a Padre Pio prayer group in Maine. Ann had never met the Gervais family but suggested that if I wanted to find out further information about them, I might try to contact one of the parishes in Maine in order to find their whereabouts. How happy I was that I was able to find Michael Gervais and that he shared his story with me.

Michael Gervais and his parents once attended a series of inspirational talks given by the Oblates of Mary Immaculate in Augusta, Maine. One evening, one of the priests, Father Valliere, spoke about Padre Pio during his presentation. The Gervais family had never heard of Padre Pio. Mr. Gervais was so interested in what Father Valliere had said that he went to the Bangor Library and put in a request for several books on Padre Pio. They were evidently popular books because it took more than a month for them to arrive. The books had obviously been rebound because the covers were plain and devoid of pictures. Mr. Gervais placed them on the washing machine across from the kitchen window in his home and looked forward to reading them.

The next morning, Michael's mother told the family that she had a very unusual dream the night before. The dream made such an impact that it woke her up out of a sound sleep. In her dream, Mrs. Gervais was awakened by a loud noise coming from the kitchen. When she went to investigate, she saw a bearded man with piercing dark eyes who was rattling the kitchen window, trying to get in the house. He looked like he was about thirty-five years old. Her husband let the man in the house. Mrs. Gervais then noticed a car parked in front of the house. As she stared at the car, she noticed that words suddenly began to appear in a scroll-like manner on the side of the car. The words said, "You and me and the Divinity and your children." The dream then ended.

The next evening, Mrs. Gervais finally got a chance to look at the library books that were still sitting on the washing machine near the kitchen window. Inside one of the books was a picture of Padre Pio. She recognized him instantly as the man she had seen in her dream. He appeared to be about the same age and had the same dark and piercing eyes. In the photograph, he was celebrating Mass. Underneath the picture were the words, "Oh God, grant that through the mystery of this water and wine, we may be partakers of his Divinity, who had deigned to become partakers of our humanity, Jesus Christ thy Son, our Lord."

———————

There was once a woman (name withheld) who, due to deeply-rooted psychological problems, had not been out of her house for twenty-five years. In all of those years, she had not seen her brother. Finally, her brother contacted one of the relatives and found his sister's address. It was then that he learned the particulars of her problems. One night, the woman had a dream about a saintly looking priest who smiled at her. Also, one afternoon she noticed the fragrance of roses in her home. One day, the homebound woman summoned up the necessary courage and was able to leave the house and go to Mass. Not long after that, she found a magazine about Padre Pio and purchased it. She recognized him as the priest she had seen in her dream. Finally, her dear brother visited her. He told her that he had been praying to Padre Pio so that she would regain her confidence.

———————

Tom Dunne had a motorcycle accident and his left hand was damaged as a result. From that time forward, he always had pain in his hand. Tom began to pray the novena to Padre Pio every day. One night, before Tom went to bed, he was reading a book on Padre Pio. The book told a story of a woman who asked Padre Pio if she could suffer some of the pain that he was suffering. Padre Pio said to her, "If you had even a part of the pain that I have, you would die." Tom then said a prayer to Padre Pio with all the sincerity of his heart. "Padre Pio," Tom prayed, "I have chronic pain in my hand. My hands are important to me, but nevertheless, I would never ask you to suffer my pain." At that time, Tom had been enduring the pain in his hand for ten years. Not long after, Tom had a dream in which he saw Jesus and Padre Pio smiling at him. When he woke up, the pain in his left hand was gone, never to return.

———————

There was a woman (name withheld) who worked diligently to make a success of the family business. Her brother ran the ice cream manufacturing side of the business. He put in very long hours and was accustomed to working seven days a week. Nevertheless, the business failed to turn a profit. When her brother passed away, some of the other family members took on his part of the work. Unfortunately, the business went from bad to worse. Finally, the woman decided to sell it and pay off the bank loan and the debts that had accumulated. Otherwise, she would be facing bankruptcy. About that time, the woman had a beautiful dream. In her dream, she saw Padre Pio who looked very happy. Padre Pio and her brother were together. "Everything is all right now," Padre Pio said to her in the dream.

From that day forward, the business prospered. There was a steady increase in customers to the extent that the woman had to buy more equipment and additional refrigerators. More employees had to be hired as well. Truly, Padre Pio had been watching over his spiritual children.

———

Janet Desnoyers, of Longmeadow, Massachusetts, had a dream in which she was standing with Padre Pio outside his cell. The two shared a close friendship and as they talked together, Padre Pio told Janet that he had something that he wanted to give her, something he knew that she would like. He went inside his cell for a moment and then came back with a picture which he gave to Janet. It was a picture of the Visitation monastery in Tyringham, MA. The picture showed one of the rooms of the monastery with several of the Sisters present. On the wall behind the Sisters was a picture of Our Lady of Guadalupe. In her dream, Janet hugged Padre Pio and told him that she would always treasure the gift. Since it was indeed Our Lady who imprinted her image on Juan Diego's cloak, Janet thought to herself that she must try to get closer to Our Lady of Guadalupe. Padre Pio then said to Janet, "Mary will sanctify you." At that, the dream ended.

———

Note: We met Janet Desnoyers (whose dream entry is above) at the Visitation monastery in Tyringham, Massachusetts. The monastery is home to 17 cloistered, contemplative nuns and is located on 133 beautiful wooded acres in the Berkshire mountains. We learned that the community of nuns there has a devotion to Padre Pio so we made arrangements to visit them.

Janet attended the same morning Mass at the monastery in Tyringham that we attended. Afterwards, we struck up a conversation. We were so happy that she shared her dream about Padre Pio with us. She told us that she thought it was odd that in her dream, Padre Pio handed her a picture of Our Lady of Guadalupe. Janet had never been particularly attracted to such icons of the Blessed Mother but after having the dream, she began to contemplate Mary as Our Lady of Guadalupe. She also told us that she had never seen a picture of Our Lady of Guadalupe at the Tyringham monastery.

Later, I wrote to one of the Visitation Sisters, Sister Miriam Rose, and asked if there was a picture of Our Lady of Guadalupe in the monastery. Sister Miriam Rose wrote back and told me that a picture of Our Lady of Guadalupe hangs on the wall in the private quarters of the cloister, just outside the nuns' refectory. And an additional interesting fact - the Order of the Visitation Sisters was founded by St. Jane Frances de Chantal and St. Francis de Sales in 1610. In the United States, St. Jane Frances de Chantal's feast day had previously been celebrated on December 12. It was transferred to August 12 in order to celebrate the feast of Our Lady of Guadalupe on December 12.

Imagine Jesus crucified in your arms and on your chest, and say a hundred times as you kiss his chest, "This is my hope, the living source of my happiness; this is the heart of my soul; nothing will ever separate me from his love."

- *St. Pio of Pietrelcina*

CHAPTER 20

Brother Modestino Fucci

*M*odestino Fucci was born in Pietrelcina, Italy on April 17, 1917. The people of Pietrelcina were proud that their town was the birthplace of its most famous citizen, Padre Pio (Francesco Forgione). Modestino's mother, Anna Fucci, loved to share her memories of growing up in Pietrelcina and having Francesco Forgione and his family for neighbors. Anna's family home was very close to the Forgiones' home. Also, in the countryside of Piana Romana, the two families owned land next to each other. Anna told and retold her stories of Francesco to Modestino and he never tired of hearing them. Modestino's father also shared his own memories of Francesco on many occasions.

Modestino's mother, Anna, recalled that as a child, Francesco was quiet and also very devout. Anna described young Francesco as having an "exceptional reserve and a deep spirit of prayer." She used to observe him as he walked passed her house and she noticed that he always carried a Rosary in his hand. He also spent a lot of time in church, either with his parents or with his grandmother. Anna often visited the Forgione family in their home. From time to time, she invited Francesco to play with her and the other children in the neighborhood, but he usually declined the invitation.

By the time Anna got married and started raising a family, Francesco Forgione had been ordained to the priesthood and was known to everyone as Padre Pio. In Pietrelcina, Padre Pio was regarded by all as a holy priest. Sometimes when he passed by Anna's house, she would ask him to take care of her little son Antonio and play with him while she took food out to the field workers on her land. Padre Pio would sit on a stone by the front door of Anna's house and hold Antonio while she went about her duties. When Antonio grew up, his relatives told him how Padre Pio used to tend to him when he was a baby. Antonio's esteem for Padre Pio was so great that he preserved the stone that Padre Pio used to sit on and he guarded it as a relic.

When Anna's daughter, Incoronata, was born, Anna decided to postpone her baptism. She would set the baptismal date when her husband returned from military duty. Padre Pio was not happy about her decision. He would say, "Anna, we must make Incoronata a Christian! I want to baptize her." Whenever Padre Pio saw Anna, he would bring the subject up to her. The dialogue went on for months. "We must wait until my husband returns from his military duty," was Anna's reply. One day Padre Pio said to Anna, "Let's baptize Incoronata tomorrow. Your husband will be returning tonight."

Anna was very doubtful about Padre Pio's words, but to her great surprise, at midnight her husband returned home. The next day Padre Pio blessed and baptized the baby, offering his heartfelt prayers on her behalf. As it turned out, Incoronata's life was filled with many graces. Later, when Anna heard the news that Padre Pio had received the stigmata, she said that she was not surprised. She explained that she had always known that Padre Pio was a saint. She had known it from the time that she and Padre Pio were children.

The stories that Modestino heard from his mother and father through the years regarding their memories of Padre Pio, made a profound impression on him. His own vocation to religious life came about as a result. Angelo Caccavo, Modestino's school teacher in Pietrelcina, also shared many interesting anecdotes about his "most famous" student, Padre Pio. After hearing so much about Padre Pio, Modestino had a great desire to meet him.

Modestino was twenty-two years old when he met Padre Pio for the first time. The year was 1940. He traveled to San Giovanni Rotondo to ask Padre Pio for his blessing and his prayers as he had just been called up to serve in the Italian army. His mother, Anna, accompanied him to the monastery.

Modestino and his mother were able to attend Padre Pio's Mass. With deep emotion, Modestino watched the devout way Padre Pio celebrated Mass. It was the first time he had ever seen a priest shed tears during the Holy Sacrifice of the Mass. Modestino and his mother were also able to make their confession to Padre Pio. Making his confession to Padre Pio, marked a turning point in Modestino's life and his love for prayer began to intensify. As time passed, he began to have a great desire to dedicate his life totally to God.

For his military service, Modestino was assigned to the Ministry of War in Rome as a postman. His thoughts were constantly on Padre Pio. He often spoke of Padre Pio to the other enlisted men. One day, two officers told Modestino that they would like to meet Padre Pio. Modestino agreed to take both of the officers to San Giovanni Rotondo. One of the men worked at the Ministry of Agriculture and the other was a captain in the army.

Modestino and the two officers were dressed in civilian clothing when they arrived at the monastery of Our Lady of Grace. They soon saw Padre Pio. Before Modestino could introduce his two friends, Padre Pio looked at the two men and said jokingly, "Oh, the poor army. Oh, the poor agriculture department!" They were amazed that he knew their military standing since they had never met him before. Modestino and his two companions fell to their knees and asked Padre Pio for a blessing. Padre Pio blessed the men and assured them of his protection.

Afterward, the three men departed to return to Rome. Shortly before their arrival in Rome, the train that they were traveling in was bombarded. Every part of the train was destroyed except for the compartment that Modestino and the two officers occupied. They thought of Padre Pio and how he had said that he would protect them.

During the time of his military service, Modestino spent his free time praying in the church of St. Francesca Romana in Rome. After much prayer and reflection, he felt that he had a calling to the religious life and he spoke about it to a priest, Father Placido Lugano. Father Lugano assured him that the Benedictines in Rome would be very happy to welcome him into their Order. Modestino wanted to join the Benedictines, but before he made his final decision, he wanted to talk about it with Padre Pio.

While on leave from military service, Modestino went to Pietrelcina to see his family. After being with his family, he made plans to visit Padre Pio.

He did not have the money for transportation to San Giovanni Rotondo so he decided to walk the twenty-five mile distance. There were five other men from Pietrelcina who accompanied him on the journey. They were glad for the opportunity to visit Padre Pio. Along the way they experienced hunger, thirst, and great fatigue. They offered up all of the discomforts of their journey as a sacrifice to God.

During the days of their visit, Padre Pio often spoke to Modestino and his friends in a small sitting room adjoining the little church of Our Lady of Grace. He spoke with great love about Jesus, the Blessed Virgin Mary, and the guardian angels. Modestino and his friends shared news with Padre Pio regarding their mutual acquaintances in Pietrelcina. During the visit, Modestino had intended to speak to Padre Pio about the calling he felt to join the Benedictines, but the right moment never presented itself.

After a two week stay in San Giovanni Rotondo, when it was time for Modestino and his friends to make the journey back to Pietrelcina, they found it hard to say goodbye to Padre Pio. They also felt a certain dread, thinking of the hardships of the long walk home. Padre Pio noticed their hesitancy to leave and told them not worry about the return journey. "Divine Providence will come to your assistance," Padre Pio said. That very day, Modestino and his friends learned that a car would soon be arriving from Pietrelcina. It was bringing the belongings of Padre Pio's brother, Michael Forgione, who was moving to San Giovanni Rotondo. Arrangements were made so that the driver could take Modestino and his companions back to Pietrelcina the next day.

That evening at the monastery, Tonino, the driver, developed a high fever. Modestino was with Padre Pio when the thought came into his mind that the return trip to Pietrelcina would be cancelled. The moment that Modestino had the thought, Padre Pio turned to him and said, "You will definitely be going back to Pietrelcina tomorrow!" Padre Pio then asked Father Bernardo to take Tonino's temperature for a second time. Father Bernardo did so and found that he still had a high fever. A short time later, Padre Pio shook the thermometer and took Tonino's temperature himself. His fever had gone down significantly. Those who were present were amazed at the rapid improvement in Tonino's condition. The next day, Tonino felt well enough to drive Modestino and the others back to Pietrelcina.

In the summer of 1945, Modestino had the opportunity to spend one year living and working in San Giovanni Rotondo. He found board and room with a local family in exchange for his services to them. Every day, using a horse and carriage, he would transport the family members to their jobs and would pick them up again in the evening. During the day, he was free assist at Padre Pio's Mass in the morning and to spend time with him each afternoon.

Brother Modestino encountered many difficulties on his new job. Some of the members of the family that he worked for, tried his patience to the limit. One day he became so upset that he told the family he was quitting. He spoke to Padre Pio about it and asked him for advice. Padre Pio said to him, "Son, you know that I care about you. What you want from me, you will have!" Then he embraced Modestino in a loving and fatherly way. For a moment, Modestino rested his head on Padre Pio's chest. Suddenly, all the bitterness and resentment that was in his heart vanished.

Brother Modestino finally found the right moment to talk to Padre Pio about his desire to join the Benedictine congregation in Rome. However, Padre Pio was not pleased with the news. The reason for his disapproval was not entirely clear to Modestino. They discussed the matter together every day. Padre Pio left Modestino free to make his own choice. "If you want to join the Benedictines in Rome, then join," Padre Pio said. "I will not try to stop you. But I will not give you my blessing. Remember this, if you decide to go there, a great disaster awaits you." Modestino did not know what Padre Pio meant by the mysterious statement, but the words frightened him. He decided to reconsider his plan. He finally made the decision to become a Capuchin lay brother. When he went to the monastery and told Padre Pio the news, Padre Pio was deeply moved. In their great joy, they both wept.

A few years later, Modestino learned the sad news that there was indeed a "great disaster" that occurred at the Benedictine monastery of Saint Francesca Romana in Rome. Robbers broke into the monastery and tragically, several of the friars were killed.

After completing the required studies in the Capuchin novitiate, Modestino (now Brother Modestino) was assigned to the monastery in Pietrelcina as a lay brother. There were a number of challenges to be faced at his first assignment and he shared his concerns with Padre Pio. Padre Pio embraced him and said, "My son, you must act in obedience to your superiors. I will always be with you and St. Francis will watch over you."

Brother Modestino kept very busy with his assigned duties in Pietrelcina. One day, he visited his father who had just returned to Pietrelcina from San Giovanni Rotondo. His father, who was ill at the time, told Brother Modestino that before he left the monastery, he asked Padre Pio when he would see him again. Padre Pio told him that they would meet again in the next world. The remark was mysterious, to be sure. Brother Modestino wondered what Padre Pio's words meant but he did not have to wait long to find out. The very next morning, his father had a stroke and passed away.

The next time Brother Modestino traveled to San Giovanni Rotondo, he asked Padre Pio about his father. "Is my father in heaven?" he asked. "Your father did not live a blameless life. He has to expiate for his sins," Padre Pio replied. Modestino understood then that his father was in purgatory and he began to offer many prayers and sacrifices for his father's soul. Several months later, Padre Pio sent a message to Brother Modestino through one of the Capuchins and said, "Tell Brother Modestino that his father is saved. Brother Modestino's prayers saved him. He is now in heaven."

On one occasion, Brother Modestino accompanied a group of children from the city of Agnone to San Giovanni Rotondo to see Padre Pio. It was in the summer time and it happened to be a very hot day. The children were all wearing shorts. When they arrived at the monastery, Brother Modestino was told that Padre Pio was in the garden visiting with friends. Brother Modestino took the children into the garden and asked Padre Pio to give them a blessing. "But the children are not properly dressed," Padre Pio replied. "First, let them dress themselves properly. Even though they are young, they have to learn to keep their dignity." Another time, Brother Modestino was present when a man came to the confessional in a short-sleeved shirt. Padre Pio would not receive him. He told him to put on a long-sleeved shirt and then return and he would hear his confession.

Brother Modestino made his confession to Padre Pio on many occasions. He always made a thorough examination of conscience before entering the confessional. He had a tendency to be overly scrupulous and often worried that he might have forgotten some of his sins that needed to be confessed. The thought of it caused him a great deal of torment. Brother Modestino decided to jot his sins down on a piece of paper. That way, when he was making his confession, if he forgot anything, he would simply look at his paper and it would be an instant reminder.

Padre Pio was aware of Brother Modestino's tendency toward scrupulosity and he wanted him to overcome it. In the confessional, when Brother Modestino reached in his pocket and pulled out the paper with his list of sins on it, Padre Pio became stern. "This is not a deed executed in front of a notary," Padre Pio said. "Put that paper away now!" Brother Modestino did as he was told.

On one occasion, Brother Modestino informed Padre Pio of the date he would be coming to see him again. "But you cannot come on that date under any circumstances!" Padre Pio replied. "Don't you know what day that is? It is the feast of Our Lady!" Padre Pio's love for Mary was truly profound. He looked forward to her feast days with great anticipation and prepared for them spiritually through prayer and fasting. He would not consider having visitors on those days.

Brother Modestino visited Padre Pio in his cell on many occasions. Padre Pio's cell was a reflection of true "Franciscan simplicity." It contained just the bare essentials. He had an iron bed with a thin mattress. A small table in the room held his books and religious articles. A painting of Our Lady of Purity hung on the wall near his bed. Padre Pio's cell had what Brother Modestino referred to as a "mystical silence." Brother Modestino felt the presence of God whenever he entered Padre Pio's cell.

Once, Brother Modestino visited Padre Pio in his cell and found him stretched out on his bed in great pain. He told Brother Modestino that he was suffering from a kidney problem. On another occasion, Padre Pio complained to Brother Modestino of a terrible pain in his stomach. "Even though I have eaten so little today, nevertheless, I have this stomach pain," Padre Pio said. That particular evening, it happened to be snowing. It was cold inside of Padre Pio's cell, but even so, Brother Modestino noticed that Padre Pio was perspiring. "I am burning up," he said to Brother Modestino. "I do not wish this on anyone. If you only knew how much I suffer!" On another occasion, with tears in his eyes, Padre Pio said to Brother Modestino, "Son, my life is one continuous martyrdom."

Not only was Padre Pio's fragile health a source of continual suffering, his environment too often tested him to the limit. Once, Padre Pio confided to

Brother Modestino how oppressive it was to have crowds of people pursuing him all the time. "Even someone who is in prison is given some time each day to have a few moments of privacy and freedom," Padre Pio said. "But I am watched and followed all the time. I don't have even a moment to myself!" Brother Modestino felt very sorry for him but there was nothing he could do.

Brother Modestino's esteem for Padre Pio continually increased with the passing of the years. Making his confession to Padre Pio and receiving spiritual direction from him was always a grace-filled experience. But it was by attending Padre Pio's Mass that Brother Modestino came to realize the true greatness of Padre Pio and the power of his prayers.

Padre Pio seemed to be restless when he entered the sacristy each morning. As he put on his priestly vestments in preparation for the Mass, he became completely unaware of what was going on around him. He did not want to talk. If anyone asked him a question or spoke to him for any reason, he would not respond.

Padre Pio's face was pale and sorrowful when he left the sacristy. When he got to the top of the steps and kissed the altar, the color came back into his cheeks. At the *Confiteor* of the Mass, when, in unison with the congregation, he asked for forgiveness for his sins, his eyes filled with tears.

Brother Modestino knew that Padre Pio suffered, not only from the five wounds of the stigmata, but also from the crowning of thorns, the scourging, and the shoulder wound. In January 1945, Brother Modestino was the altar server at Padre Pio's Mass. He was standing very close to Padre Pio at the altar when he noticed that little boils had appeared on his forehead, similar to thorn pricks. He saw Padre Pio touch his fingers to his forehead as though trying to remove something that was bothering him. Brother Modestino also saw a small cross in the center of Padre Pio's forehead.

Padre Pio died on September 23, 1968. As one devotee said, "God called Padre Pio at the end of an intense life and at the end of a hard day." After Padre Pio's death, the Capuchins felt that it was important to preserve his personal belongings for posterity. Brother Modestino was given the job of transferring Padre Pio's priestly vestments, the sacred vessels he used at Mass, his clothing, and his personal possessions into special protective storage containers. Everything had to be identified, catalogued, numbered and dated. A declaration of authenticity was attached to each of the items.

As Brother Modestino carried out the task, he saw with his own eyes, the marks of Christ's Passion on many of the articles of Padre Pio's clothing. He saw large bloodstains on Padre Pio's white cotton socks. Five handkerchiefs that had belonged to Padre Pio were stained with tears and blood. Three of the handkerchiefs had been used by Padre Pio to wipe the perspiration from his brow. There were also numerous pieces of bloodstained linen cloth that Padre Pio had used to cover his heart wound.

Brother Modestino discovered blood on Padre Pio's woolen undershirt on the right shoulder area. He remembered that on one occasion when he and Padre Pio were talking, Padre Pio had confided to him how painful it was for him to change his clothes. Padre Pellegrino Funicelli once told Brother Modestino that on several occasions when he had helped Padre Pio change his woolen undershirt, he had seen a round bruise on his shoulder, sometimes on the left shoulder and sometimes on the right.

It made Brother Modestino very sad to sort and inventory Padre Pio's personal items. He often cried as he transferred Padre Pio's clothing into the storage containers. One shirt in particular stood out among all the others for the large amount of blood. The shirt was made of linen and had long sleeves. It had been worn by Padre Pio on Good Friday in 1921. It was just three years earlier that Padre Pio had received the stigmata. It happened on the morning of September 20, 1918. The feast of the stigmatization of St. Francis had been celebrated a few days before, on September 17. Padre Pio was all alone in the church of Our Lady of Grace on Friday, September 20. The superior, Padre Paolino of Casacalenda was out of town. Brother Nicola was also away that morning. All of the students of the Seraphic Boarding School were outside in the monastery courtyard for their period of recreation.

As was his habit, Padre Pio had gone up to the choir loft to make his thanksgiving after Mass. In plain sight was the crucifix that was a permanent fixture in the church. It had been carved from cypress wood by an unknown 17th century sculptor. In a profound way, the sculptor had been able to capture the agony of the dying Christ. On that Friday morning, as Padre Pio prayed in the quiet church, he received the wounds of Christ.

The next day, September 21, Padre Pio's spiritual daughter, Nina Campanile spoke to Padre Pio in the sacristy of the church. She asked him to say a Mass for her sister, Vittoria, who was gravely ill. As she handed the Mass offering to him, she noticed what looked like a burn mark on the back of his hand. When she commented on it, he quickly hid his hand under his sleeve. The next day, Nina went to Father Paolino, the superior of the monastery, and told him that Padre Pio had received the stigmata. She explained to him that she had seen the marks on Padre Pio's hand. Father Paolino was certain that Nina was mistaken. But some days later, he decided to find out for himself.

One day, unannounced, Father Paolino visited Padre Pio in his cell. He took a close look at his hands and saw the wounds that Nina had described to him. Father Paolino did not question Padre Pio about it. Instead, he immediately notified the provincial, Father Benedetto, and asked him to come at once to the monastery.

Father Benedetto instructed Father Paolino not to speak to anyone else about the marks of the stigmata that he had seen on Padre Pio's hands. He did not want the information to be made public. Even Father Agostino Daniele, who had been close to Padre Pio for years, was not told about the matter. Father Paolino then spoke to Nina Campanile and stressed to her the importance of keeping the matter a strict secret. But Nina felt the need to tell her mother and sisters about the extraordinary incidence. Over the next several months, more people learned about it. People also noticed the open wounds on Padre Pio's hands when he celebrated Mass. Gradually the news spread to the surrounding towns. Eventually the news spread to the whole world.

Father Benedetto wrote a letter to Padre Pio, telling him to send back a full account of what had happened on September 20. Padre Pio was compelled to write the details in obedience to Father Benedetto. He wrote back to Father Benedetto on October 22 and explained for the first time, what had happened:

> I yielded to a drowsiness similar to a sweet sleep. All the internal and external senses and even the very faculties of my soul were immersed in indescribable stillness. Absolute silence surrounded and invaded me. I was suddenly filled with great peace and abandonment which effaced everything else . . . All of this happened in a flash.

Padre Pio went on to say in the letter that he suddenly saw a mysterious "Exalted Being" whose appearance was similar to the personage who had pierced his side with a lance one month before, on August 5. The difference was that on September 20, the hands, feet, and side of the "Exalted Being" were dripping with blood. Looking at the mysterious person filled Padre Pio with terror and he believed that he was going to die. He felt sure that he would have died if the Lord had not come to his aide and strengthened him. The vision vanished and Padre Pio discovered that his own hands, feet, and side were dripping with blood.

Later, Padre Pio's long time friend from Pietrelcina, Father Giuseppe (Peppino) Orlando, questioned him about the stigmatization. Padre Pio's eyes filled with tears and his lips trembled when he spoke to Father Orlando about it. He said that on the morning of September 20, as he was praying in the choir loft, he saw a brilliant light. In the middle of the light appeared the wounded Christ. The wounded Christ was the same "mysterious Exalted Being" that he referred to in his letter to Father Benedetto. Christ did not speak to him. When the vision was over, Padre Pio found himself on the floor. His hands, feet, and side were bleeding. He was in so much pain that he did not have the strength to get up. Finally, and with great effort, he made his way slowly back to his cell. Once in his cell, he cleaned the blood from his wounds, changed his habit, and then, in his weakened state, laid down on his bed.

Years later, another one of Padre Pio's close friends, Father Raffaele of Sant' Elia a Pianisi, had a conversation with him about the stigmata. Padre Pio told Father Raffaele that on September 20, the wooden crucifix that was in the monastery church was suddenly transformed into the living Christ. Rays of light and flames of fire then issued forth from the wounds in Christ's body and pierced Padre Pio's hands and feet. Because Padre Pio rarely ever spoke about the subject, the information he shared with Father Orlando and the additional details he told Father Raffaele are very valuable.

The marks of the stigmata would remain imprinted on Padre Pio's body for fifty years. During those years, the wounds kept their symmetry, never changing in size or depth. They never became infected. They never widened. They never healed. Dr. Giorgio Festa, who was sent from Rome to examine the wounds in 1919, stated that the blood had the fragrance of perfume. He also observed "a luminous radiation" (rays of light) along the border of the wounds. The supernatural characteristic of Padre Pio's stigmata could not be explained. As had been stated, "Padre Pio's wounds and their emission of blood came to be regarded as a prolonged miracle."

Some people had almost a romanticized idea of Padre Pio's stigmata, but the Capuchins who took care of him, knew the truth about it. They said that the wounds were frightening, even terrible to look at. Father Alessio described Padre Pio's hands as being corroded and torn. They reminded him of a leper's hands. Father Alessio said, "I had always wished to see Padre Pio's hands, but once I saw them I prayed, "God, don't ever let me see his hands again." Father Eusebio Notte had a similar experience. "I assure you that the sight of Padre Pio's stigmatized hands will never be erased from my memory," Father Eusebio said. "Likewise, I will never be able to forget his gashed chest."

Toward the end of Padre Pio's life, the stigmata began to slowly disappear. On September 22, during Padre Pio's last Mass, it was observed that the wound on his right hand had disappeared completely. However, there were still visible scabs on his left hand. Not only were his hands seen by the people who attended his Mass that morning, they were also captured on film. Dr. Francesco Lotti, the head pediatrician at the Home for the Relief of Suffering, had received permission to film Padre Pio's Mass on September 22. He felt especially happy to receive the permission because his sons happened to be the altar servers for that Mass. No one suspected that it was to be Padre Pio's last Mass. In the film, which is truly a gift to posterity, Padre Pio's hands are clearly visible. Before the Mass was over, several of the scabs had fallen from his left hand.

Dr. Giuseppe Sala, who was Padre Pio's personal physician, was present at the time of Padre Pio's death. There was still one scab on the palm of his left hand. Ten minutes after he died, there were no longer any signs of the stigmata. The skin on his hands, feet, and side, where the wounds had been, was now smooth and regenerated, uniform in color, and soft to the touch. There was no scarring whatsoever.

We will never be able to truly comprehend all of the profound mystical aspects of Padre Pio's life, and even his death. Capuchin Father Aldo Broccato wrote:

The mystery of Christ's death and resurrection is the central mystery of the Catholic faith. It is the mystery to which we always have to look so that we will not forget the meaning of our life. Padre Pio for more than fifty years was marked with the signs of the stigmata that identified him with Christ and made him an image of the Crucifix. In reality, our world needs saints who will witness with their lives, the mystery of Christ's resurrection. If we honor St. Pio of Pietrelcina, it is because he confirms that the resurrection follows the painful moments of the Cross. This is the path toward holiness.

Pray a great deal for me as I am living constantly on the Cross of the Lord, in the midst of those whom he has confided to me.

- St. Pio of Pietrelcina

Modern man needs Padre Pio, this humble and simple friar, who lived in our time, who witnessed the changes which are taking place at such a speed in this modern world yet did not allow himself to be swept away in the whirlwind of human realities or to become subjected to purely human ideals. He knew how to raise everything to the level of the heavenly spirit.

- Archbishop Giuseppe Carata

CHAPTER 21

Clarice Bruno

C larice Bruno, was born in Chicago, Illinois into a devout Italian Catholic family. She attended Catholic schools throughout her youth and graduated from the fine Catholic institution, Rosemont College, in Villanova, Pennsylvania. Clarice, for the most part, took her Catholic faith for granted. She doubted many of the teachings of the Church. There was an indifference, an apathy in her heart regarding matters of religion. Although she attended Mass on Sundays, she did not consider herself to be a good Catholic.

Clarice made preparations for a trip to Chiavari, Italy in order to visit her friends and relatives. It was supposed to be a brief visit but it stretched out to be much longer. She enjoyed her trip to Chiavari so much that she decided to move there permanently.

After moving to Chiavari, Clarice felt a new lease on life. She enjoyed being reunited with her relatives and was happy to be making new friends. One night she had a vivid dream. In her dream, she was on her way to the church of Our Lady of Grace in Chiavari when the road suddenly became covered with large rocks. She tried to climb over them, but it proved to be impossible. Suddenly a large hand came from behind the rocks and helped her. At once, she found herself standing in front of the church. The large obstacle had been surmounted.

In front of the church, Clarice saw a Calvary composed of three wooden crosses. She was never able to lift her eyes from the base of the crosses because of the scene just beyond on the horizon. There, she saw a sea that was shimmering with an unearthly beauty. Sunlight danced upon the water and sparkled like diamonds. Clarice could not take her eyes from the beatific scene. Her heart felt an intense joy. When she woke up, she pondered the meaning of the dream. The beauty of the dream was beyond anything in her experience. She wondered if it could be a sign of something important that was soon to come into her life. She did not know.

At that time, Clarice was struggling with a heavy cross, a sorrow in her life. Her cross was waiting for her when she awoke in the morning and stayed with her until she fell asleep at night. She became very discouraged. Finally, she confided some of her anguish to a kind woman she had met a short time before. The woman advised her to seek the intercession of Padre Pio. She shared some of the facts surrounding Padre Pio's life with Clarice.

Clarice felt skeptical about the woman's words regarding Padre Pio. However, when the woman told her of some of the graces she had received through the intercession of Padre Pio, Clarice became more interested. "I think you should write a letter to Padre Pio," the woman said. "In the letter, you can explain all that is troubling you. You can ask Padre Pio to pray for you." Clarice became convinced that it was a good idea and quickly penned a letter and sent it. Clarice assumed that Padre Pio would soon write back to her. She imagined that it would be a long letter filled with spiritual insights and wise counsel. What she did not know was that all of Padre Pio's correspondence was handled by his secretaries.

One night as Clarice was getting ready for bed, she noticed a very strong scent of roses in her room. She could find no explanation for the beautiful fragrance. She knew that there were no flowers in the house. There were certainly no flowers in her bedroom. She looked under her bed just to make sure that no one had hidden roses there, but just as she had suspected, she found nothing.

The next morning, Clarice greeted her uncle, her father, and several other friends who were sitting around the dining table downstairs. Clarice's uncle, who lived at the house with her and her family, told her that he had a very strange experience the night before. As he was getting ready for bed, his room became filled with the fragrance of sweet-smelling flowers. It was a fresh and delightful fragrance and it lingered in the room for a long time. The fragrance of gardenias, then carnations, and finally violets followed. It happened between 12:30 a.m. and 1:00 a.m. He thought that it might be a premonition of the death of a friend or relative. Clarice told her uncle that she too had the same experience the night before, when the beautiful scent of roses filled her room at about 12:30 a.m.

The next time Clarice saw the woman who had shared the story of Padre Pio's life with her, she told her what she and her uncle had experienced in their home. The woman then explained to Clarice that Padre Pio often let people know that he was interceding for them by allowing them to experience a wonderful fragrance. Clarice had never heard of such a gift. She thought about the letter that she had written to Padre Pio. She had sent it to him just three days before. She was convinced that he had received her letter and was letting her know by the scent of roses that his spirit was with her. Clarice felt a great hope rise up in her heart. She had faith that Padre Pio was going to help her in her difficulties.

Clarice wrote a second letter to Padre Pio. She thanked him for the fragrance of roses that she had experienced. She included a donation in the letter. She told him that she had faith in him and that she was waiting for a reply. A few days after she wrote the second letter, she noticed the fragrance of lilies all around her. The wonderful fragrance came suddenly and with great intensity and then vanished just as suddenly as it had come.

Clarice decided to write a third letter to Padre Pio. Again she thanked him for the fragrances of roses and lilies. She wrote that she was waiting to hear his words of wisdom and again she enclosed a donation in the letter. After she sent the letter, the delightful perfumes ceased altogether. There were no more tangible signs of Padre Pio's nearness.

Every day, Clarice went to the post office to see if a letter from Padre Pio was waiting for her, but no letter ever came. She often thought about her dream and the hand that lifted her over the barrier of rocks and placed her right at the entrance to Our Lady of Grace church. There was a barrier in her own life, a cross that she carried daily. More than anything else, she wanted to be freed from it. She clung to the hope that Padre Pio would be able to help her.

One night, Clarice's darkened bedroom became illuminated with a soft light, similar to moonlight. As unbelievable as it was, she saw Padre Pio standing at the foot of her bed. He was wearing a brown Capuchin robe. Around his waist was his Capuchin cord and he rested one of his hands on it. He was wearing gloves that only covered part of his hands. There was fear in Clarice's heart and at the same time there was no fear. Padre Pio said three words to her but she did not understand the meaning of the words. She tried to turn on the light next to her bed, but for some reason the light would not turn on.

A second time, Padre Pio repeated the three words, the words that she did not understand. Again she pushed the switch to turn on the light, but it would not turn on. For a third time, Padre Pio said the mysterious words. Then he vanished. The soft glow that reminded her of moonlight vanished right along with him. Clarice touched the light switch and this time it turned on easily. Just as the light came on, she saw her bedroom door swing open as if somebody was leaving the room.

Seeing Padre Pio at her bedside was something that Clarice would never have believed possible. She had waited a long time for a letter from him but she had never received one. She was not concerned about that anymore. She had received something much greater than a letter. Padre Pio had come to her in person. Clarice was certain now that Padre Pio was aware of her needs and that he would lead her on the right path.

Several months later, Clarice traveled to Rome to visit her good friend, Margherita Hamilton. Clarice shared with Margherita what she had recently learned about Padre Pio. Margherita told Clarice that she ought to consider visiting Padre Pio in San Giovanni Rotondo. After discussing all the particulars, they decided to make the trip together. From Rome, they boarded a train to Foggia and then took a bus to San Giovanni Rotondo.

When Clarice and Margherita arrived in San Giovanni Rotondo, they felt as though they had stepped back in time. San Giovanni Rotondo in the post World War II years was a primitive village. Both men and women rode mules and horse-drawn carts through the town. Electricity and running water seemed to be in short supply and in some parts of the town, nonexistent. The local women carried urns as they walked through the main street of town to the public well. Clarice described San Giovanni Rotondo as a "semi-wilderness."

There were two hotels in the little town and neither were in good condition. Clarice and Margherita felt fortunate to find lodging in the cleaner of the two. In order to get to Padre Pio's early morning Mass, they had to get up in the middle of the night and walk two miles in the darkness. There was not a single light on the road to guide them to the church.

During their first full day in San Giovanni Rotondo, Clarice and Margherita met Mary Pyle. Mary lived in a spacious house that was situated very close to the monastery. Nestled in an almond grove, Mary's pink house was a haven for countless pilgrims who came to see Padre Pio. Clarice and Margherita felt fortunate to be able to rent two rooms in Mary's home for the duration of their visit.

Mary Pyle was well aware that there was a shortage of accommodations in San Giovanni Rotondo and she did what she could to help the situation. She put three cots in the basement of her home in order to offer hospitality to the pilgrims who needed lodging. To provide for more people, Mary added another story to her house.

Although Clarice was very grateful for the hospitality, the room that Mary Pyle offered to her left much to be desired. The room was damp and cold and Clarice could find no way to take the chill off. There was a wood-burning stove in the corner of the room but unfortunately it was broken. The night stand consisted of a piece of wood on top of a stack of bricks. Clarice's bed was very short and very narrow. The mattress was stuffed with dried leaves and corn husks. It was very uncomfortable to say the least. Nevertheless, she preferred the room she had been given to the room in the basement.

One had to admire Mary for her true Franciscan spirit and her detachment from worldly comforts and possessions. Her own bed was even more uncomfortable than the one given to Clarice. It was more like a wooden chest than a bed. No one could understand how Mary was able to sleep on such a hard bed. People often teased her about her bed but she could never be persuaded to exchange it for a more comfortable one.

Mary, who was born into a wealthy family in New York City, visited Padre Pio's monastery for the first time in 1923. She was so impressed by attending his Mass and receiving his priestly blessing that she decided to move to San Giovanni Rotondo permanently. Mary had truly left her wealthy New York City lifestyle far behind her.

Mary was in the process of moving to a very small and modest room near the basement of her house when Clarice and Margherita made her acquaintance. The bedroom that Mary had been occupying was large and comfortable and included a sunny balcony. She decided to move to the lower floor of the house in order to offer her warm and pleasant room to the pilgrims.

During their visit to San Giovanni Rotondo, Clarice and Margherita were impressed by Mary's many works of charity. A number of the people in the town were illiterate. They often knocked on Mary's door, asking her to write letters for them. They would dictate the letters to Mary as she wrote. She was always very glad to be of assistance.

Mary, along with some of her companions, baked the hosts that were used for Holy Communion at the monastery and sewed the priestly vestments of the Capuchins. Her workload was always heavy and she hardly had a moment to spare. Padre Pio was very much aware of Mary's generous heart. He often sent people to her house who had needs of one kind or another, knowing that Mary would help them to the best of her ability.

The children in San Giovanni Rotondo loved to visit Mary in her home. She often played games with them and made sure to keep little prizes on hand for such occasions. One favorite game was "Lotto." Mary always included a Catechism lesson whenever the local children visited her. Due to Mary's continual and dedicated efforts, the children in the area possessed an impressive understanding of their Catholic faith. When the local children were ready to make their first Holy Communion, Mary purchased suits for the boys and white dresses for the girls if their parents could not afford to do so.

Clarice felt very fortunate to be able to spend time with Mary Pyle as well as other devout souls who served Padre Pio's work. Since the time she had arrived, Clarice had been looking forward to going to confession to Padre

Pio. Finally, her opportunity came. When Clarice walked into the confessional and knelt down, she was struck by the fact that Padre Pio's hand was resting on the cord of his Capuchin habit. She remembered that his hand was in the exact same position when he visited her in bilocation at her home in Chiavari. Clarice was also struck by Padre Pio's eyes. They seemed to look right inside her soul. There was also a severity in his gaze.

In the confessional, Padre Pio told Clarice that he would do all the talking. He then began to name her sins one by one, and each time he did so, she confirmed that what he said was true. He counseled her regarding the burden that she had been carrying in her heart for such a long time. He told her that she was enduring a "true calvary." "Even if you are not able to feel joy in carrying your cross, at least try to practice resignation and patience," he said to her.

The confession to Padre Pio was over in less than three minutes. Clarice felt a great sense of peace in her heart. There had been no need for her to explain anything to Padre Pio. It was obvious that he was aware of everything in her life. In a few short words, he was able to counsel her and give her new hope.

Because it was so chilly in Mary Pyle's home, Clarice used to walk briskly up and down the road that fronted her house, in an effort to warm up. One day, as Clarice walked past the church of Our Lady of Grace, she looked inside and noticed that several of the local women were cleaning it. She learned that they followed a regular weekly cleaning schedule. Clarice began to join the women in their work and counted it a great privilege.

The monastery church of Our Lady of Grace had a Franciscan simplicity and beauty that were uplifting to the spirit. Beautiful statues had been placed in the niches and alcoves. A lovely painting of Our Lady of Grace had a permanent place in the sanctuary. Over the altar railing was an arch on which delicate roses and lilies had been painted. It reminded Clarice of her experience in Chiavari when the beautiful fragrance of roses and lilies filled her room.

In the afternoons, the Capuchin priests and brothers would gather in the choir loft of the church for the recitation of their community prayers. At those times, Clarice and the other women who cleaned the church, observed a strict silence, taking care not to disturb the Capuchins in any way. Clarice was able to distinguish Padre Pio's voice from the others during the time of vocal prayers. He never hurried through his prayers but pronounced each word slowly and with great deliberation. Clarice always noticed a sadness in Padre Pio's voice as he prayed with his fellow Capuchins.

Clarice and Margherita were able to attend Padre Pio's Mass each morning and they counted it a great and inestimable gift. At the time of Holy Communion, the people in the congregation walked up to the top of the stairs in the sanctuary. There they knelt before Padre Pio to receive Holy Communion. This saved him from having to walk down to the altar rail to distribute Holy Communion. The painful wounds of the stigmata that pierced his feet, made it very difficult for him to walk.

After Padre Pio's early morning Mass, confessions were heard in the church until 10:00 a.m. When the confessions were over, all activity in the church stopped and did not resume again until the following morning. Each day during their visit, Clarice and Margherita had ample time to explore the town. On occasion, they would walk to the cemetery where Padre Pio's parents were buried and pray at their graveside.

While in San Giovanni Rotondo, Clarice and Margherita made the acquaintance of a kind man named Mario who, along with his wife, owned a restaurant in town. The restaurant had a dirt floor, and oddly enough, there was a well right inside the restaurant. The restaurant looked more like a small cabin than an eating establishment. During the cold weather, the wind would whistle through the cracks in the walls. It was a primitive place, to be sure.

Mario's wife had a great devotion to Padre Pio. On one occasion, when she made her confession to Padre Pio, she told him that she was concerned about her four-year-old son. "I feel worried," she said to Padre Pio. "I have to work in the restaurant all the time with Mario, and I am not able to give my son the time or the attention that he needs." Padre Pio told her not to worry. He told her that he would always watch over her son and that he would protect him from harm. The woman left the confessional greatly consoled.

A few days later, the woman heard the sound of screaming coming from the street. When she rushed out of the restaurant to find out what had happened, she saw her son being pulled out from underneath a large truck. The next time she went to confession to Padre Pio, she told him about the frightening incident. "My son was almost killed by a large truck," the woman said. "Well, did he get hurt?" Padre Pio asked. "No, he did not," the woman answered. "Did he get even a scratch?" Padre Pio asked. "No, not even that," the woman replied. "That's right," Padre Pio said. "I told you that I would protect him."

The days that Clarice and Margherita spent in San Giovanni Rotondo passed quickly. When it was time for them to return to their homes, they knew they had been truly blessed, far beyond their expectations. They made many subsequent trips to San Giovanni Rotondo through the years.

One summer when Clarice was visiting the monastery, she became very ill with a painful intestinal problem. None of the remedies she tried proved to be of any help. She then remembered the blessed water of Padre Pio. There was a well in the courtyard of the monastery and both the well and the water in it had been blessed by Padre Pio. Many of the residents of the town had great faith in its healing powers and took the water home in bottles. Clarice drank some of the blessed water and was immediately healed of her intestinal problem.

Clarice often invited her friends and relatives to join her on her trips to San Giovanni Rotondo. She began organizing pilgrimages as well. She was instrumental in starting a number of Padre Pio prayer groups in her area and she remained dedicated to promoting Padre Pio for the rest of her life. "Try to remain under God's gaze and God will always bear you witness," Padre Pio said to her on one occasion.

When Clarice was diagnosed with an incurable illness, her faith remained strong. She hoped that she would recover but she was completely resigned to the will of God. She said that Divine Providence had always arranged the events in her life for her good. "If it happens that I should die soon, I know that this would be the best possible thing for me," she said to her dear friend Margherita Hamilton. Clarice Bruno died peacefully on August 5, 1970.

I urge you to unite with me and draw near to Jesus with me, to receive his embrace and a kiss that sanctifies and saves us . . . Let us not cease then, to kiss this divine Son in this way, for if these are the kisses we give him now, he himself will come to take us in his arms and give us the kiss of peace in the last sacraments at the hour of death.

- St. Pio of Pietrelcina

In the morning, fill us with your love . . . Give us joy to balance our affliction for the years when we knew misfortune . . . Let the favor of the Lord be upon us.

- *Psalm 90: 14-17*

CHAPTER 22

Padre Pio's Healing Touch

*I*n the early days of his ministry, Padre Pio would sometimes visit the sick in their homes. There was one sick woman that he used to visit who would always ask him to bring her something to eat from his table. One day at the monastery, when Padre Pio was putting his silverware away after his meal, he noticed a very stale biscuit in the back of a drawer in the kitchen. It looked like it had been there for a long time. He thought of the sick woman who always asked him to bring her food. The next time Padre Pio went to visit the woman, he gave her the biscuit. She was very happy to receive it. Later, when he saw her again, she looked surprisingly well. She told him that right after eating the biscuit, she was healed of her illness.

———

Emanuele Brunetto was one of Padre Pio's devoted spiritual sons. On one occasion, he had a very bad infection in his toe. Because of it, he could not walk up the hill to attend Padre Pio's Sunday Mass at Our Lady of Grace monastery. Instead, he had to ride a mule.

One day after the Mass, Emanuele was sitting in the monastery garden. Padre Pio came up to him and asked him what he was doing. "I am waiting for my friend's mule," Emanuele replied. "I have an infection in my toe and I cannot walk today. I will have to use the mule to get down the hill and go home." "Oh, no. You are not going to take a mule down the hill. You will leave here walking!" Padre Pio replied in a commanding voice. "It will be good for you. You will see. Go ahead and start walking now." Emanuele did what Padre Pio insisted that he do. He found that he was able to walk with no problem. By the time he arrived home, he was healed of the painful infection.

———

Giovanni Papini of Florence, was almost blind, having only a very small amount of vision in his right eye. One day he took a bad fall, hitting the side of his head and damaging his one good eye. From that time forward, he was totally blind. His wife was so distraught that she asked her friend Francisco Messina to take a photo of Giovanni to Padre Pio and ask for his prayers. Francisco traveled to Florence to pick up the photograph.

The next time Francisco saw Padre Pio, he showed the photograph to him. "This is my good friend, Giovanni Papini," Francisco said. "Due to a fall, he is now totally blind. He and his wife are requesting your prayers." Padre Pio stared at the photo of Giovanni in silence. "So that is what happened," Padre Pio said. He then put the photo in his pocket. "Tell the family not to worry about Giovanni anymore," Padre Pio said to Francisco. A week later, Giovanni's sight was suddenly restored.

———

In 1923, Peter Pridavok was a seminary student in Austria, preparing for ordination to the priesthood. At that time, he was taking theology classes at the Innsbruck University. While studying at Innsbruck, he became ill and was diagnosed with tuberculosis of the lungs, a deadly disease at the time. Because his condition was contagious, he was removed from his classes and placed in the college infirmary. The local bishop was informed and desired that Peter receive the best medical care that was available. He was sent to San Pancrazio Sanatarium in the town of Arco, in South Tyrol, Italy.

Peter's condition grew worse at San Pancrazio and he felt certain that his days were numbered. He could see the worried expressions on the faces of the doctors and nurses who cared for him. One day, one of the nursing nuns, Sister Salongia, asked Peter if he had ever heard of Padre Pio. He replied that he had not. She told Peter some of the facts of Padre Pio's life. She also said that she spoke of Padre Pio to one of the other patients at San Pancrazio, Professor Brixa from Prague. She asked Professor Brixa if he would like to write to Padre Pio and ask him to pray for his healing. The professor started laughing and explained to Sister Salongia that he was an atheist. Upon further consideration, he decided to write to Padre Pio. In just a matter of days, Professor Brixa was well. He was so amazed by what had happened that he had a complete change of heart and became a deeply religious man.

Peter told Sister Salongia that he would be very glad to write a letter to Padre Pio. Since he only spoke German and Slovak, he asked her if she would transcribe his letter into Italian and she was very happy to do so.

The week that Sister Salongia mailed the letter, Peter had his usual high fever and he continued to have night sweats. On Good Friday, when Peter woke up, he felt much better. He had just taken his temperature when Sister Salongia walked into his room. She had a telegram from Padre Pio in her hand which she read to Peter. The message said, "Padre Pio is praying for you." "I know that he is praying for me," Peter said to the Sister. "How do you know?" she asked. "Because I feel strong and healthy and today I have no fever."

———

Giovanna Russo and her sister Maria grew up in San Giovanni Rotondo. They were both members of the *Young Franciscans*, an organization that was led by Mary Pyle. Mary taught the members about the life of St. Francis of Assisi and formed them in Franciscan spirituality.

When Maria was just a little girl, a large and painful swelling appeared on the left side of her neck and her family became very concerned. This was in the early days, long before the Home for the Relief of Suffering had been established.

Giovanna went to confession to Padre Pio and told him about the boil on her little sister's neck. Padre Pio told Giovanna to take Maria to Mary Pyle's house. Padre Pio trusted that Mary would be able to find someone to help Maria.

When the girls went to Mary's house, there was help available. A doctor from Poland, who often visited Mary, was summoned. He looked at Maria's neck and prescribed poultices to be applied to the painful swelling. He tried his very best to help her. Finally, when the treatment proved ineffective, the doctor said that he was going to have to make an incision and lance the boil.

Giovanna ran back to Padre Pio's confessional and told him the news. She took Maria with her. "Nobody is going to make an incision in your sister's neck!" Padre Pio said to Giovanna. He then touched the painful boil on Maria's neck and prayed for her. The girls went back to Mary Pyle's house because the doctor wanted to see Maria once again. When they arrived at Mary's house, the boil suddenly burst. No incision had to be made.

In 1945, Angelo Salvitti of Chicago, Illinois was hospitalized and was diagnosed with severe colitis. His hospital stay lasted two months. Over the next eight years, he was continually in and out of the hospital for his acute and chronic condition. The colitis caused Angelo to have terrible stomach pains as well as hemorrhaging. It was not unusual for Angelo to hemorrhage ten times a day and often much more.

One Sunday at Angelo's parish, a presentation on Padre Pio was given after Mass in the church hall. Father Charles Carty, who had written a popular biography of Padre Pio was the guest speaker. In addition to his talk on Padre Pio, Father Carty gave a slide show presentation which included many photographs of Padre Pio. Angelo attended the presentation and enjoyed it very much. Learning about Padre Pio gave him a great desire to visit the monastery of Our Lady of Grace in San Giovanni Rotondo. He decided that he would try to save as much money as he could in order to make the trip. At the conclusion of Father Carty's presentation, Angelo said a silent prayer to God, asking him to bless his desire to meet Padre Pio.

When Angelo had saved the necessary money, he began to make preparations for the trip. However, his close friends and associates did not think it was a good idea for him to travel such a long distance. Angelo was sick more often than he was well. For years, he had suffered from chronic pain and fatigue due to the colitis. His friends felt that it would be unwise for Angelo, in his fragile condition, to make the trip. However, nothing they said could discourage him from his plans.

After Angelo and his wife arrived in Italy, they visited some of their family members before traveling on to San Giovanni Rotondo. Angelo ran into a friend from his school years, a woman named Filomena Cipola. As it turned out, Filomena had a great devotion to Padre Pio. She wrote a letter of introduction for Angelo and told him to give it to a man named Nicolino Coccomazzi when he arrived in San Giovanni Rotondo. Nicolino was a friend of Filomena's and he would be able to find a hotel for Angelo and his wife during their visit.

Angelo and his wife arrived in San Giovanni Rotondo in the evening. They found Nicolino easily and gave him the letter of introduction. Angelo did not know it, but Filomena had mentioned to Nicolino in the letter that Angelo was very ill and in great need of Padre Pio's prayers. She could obviously see from Angelo's appearance, that he was not well.

After Nicolino found lodging for Angelo and his wife, he told Angelo that he wanted to take him over to the monastery of Our Lady of Grace and introduce him to Padre Pio. Angelo had never expected that he would have a private audience with Padre Pio. He could hardly believe his good fortune. When Angelo walked into the monastery with Nicolino, he noticed that a wonderful fragrance of perfume was in the air. At that time, he did not know anything about the fragrances associated with Padre Pio.

Nicolino took Angelo to the private quarters of the monastery and knocked on Padre Pio's cell door. Angelo heard Padre Pio's voice bidding them to come in. Suddenly he was face to face with Padre Pio. He had carefully observed his photographs in Father Carty's slide show presentation but seeing him in person was an entirely different experience. Angelo became very nervous. As he gazed at Padre Pio, he felt awe-struck. He was unable to utter a single word.

Nicolino knelt down and kissed Padre Pio's hand. He then introduced Angelo to Padre Pio. Just like Nicolino had done, Angelo knelt and kissed Padre Pio's hand as well. Padre Pio patted him on the head and said, "God bless you, my son." The moment that Padre Pio spoke the words, the burning pain in Angelo's stomach disappeared. Suddenly he was pain-free after suffering the agonizing symptoms of his disease for many years. He was never to have another pain in his stomach again. Likewise, he never had another hemorrhage. From that time forward, he was able to eat all types of food without getting sick.

The next day, Nicolino decided to go back to the monastery and talk to Padre Pio about Angelo. He visited Padre Pio in his cell once again and said, "Padre Pio, Angelo came all the way from the United States in order to meet you. He wanted to speak to you but he became nervous when he was introduced to you. Because of that, he was unable to talk. That is why I have returned. I would like to ask you to remember him in your prayers. He has suffered with a chronic illness for many years." "Yes, I will continue to pray for Angelo," Padre Pio said. "I have already been praying for him for a long time."

––––––––

Paolo traveled from his home in Sicily to San Giovanni Rotondo to see Padre Pio. He was worried because he had a constant pain in his shoulder and he feared that he might have pleurisy. Paolo spoke to Padre Pio about it. "You should not worry," Padre Pio said. "Put your faith in God. I have always had very bad lungs, but as you see, I am still alive." Padre Pio then put his hand on Paolo's shoulder and asked him, "Is your shoulder hurting you right now?" Paolo thought about it and told Padre Pio that he felt no pain in his shoulder. He went back to Sicily completely cured.

––––––––

Mademoiselle Ginette Estebe from Royan, France suffered from paralysis on one side of her body. She was examined by a number of doctors but her condition did not improve. The doctors finally told her that nothing could be done for her. One day, Ginette met a man who told her about Padre Pio. He gave her a biography of Padre Pio's life and a medal that had been blessed by him. Ginette was very impressed by the book and after she finished reading it, she decided to write Padre Pio a letter. Due to her partial paralysis, it took her three days to compose the letter. Right after she sent the letter, she was astonished to discover that she could move her arm and hand. A short time after that, she was completely healed.

Ginette decided to make a trip to San Giovanni Rotondo to thank Padre Pio personally for her healing. Inside the church of Our Lady of Grace, she stood among a very large group of people and waited for Padre Pio. As he passed by the corridor, he noticed Ginette. Among the many people who were gathered, he called her out from the crowd. He asked her to step forward and he gave her a special blessing.

––––––––––

Karol Wojtyla (the future Pope John Paul II) was ordained to the priesthood in Krakow, Poland on November 1, 1946. Shortly afterwards, he was sent to Rome where he studied at the Angelicum University and completed his doctorate in theology. During his Easter vacation in 1947, he took a break from his university studies and made a trip to San Giovanni Rotondo. Twenty-seven-year-old Father Karol attended Padre Pio's early morning Mass, made his confession to Padre Pio, recited the Angelus with him at noon, and attended the Benediction service in the evening.

In 1962, as a newly ordained bishop, Karol Wojtyla returned to Rome once again to take part in the Second Vatican Council. While in Rome, he learned that a friend of his, Dr. Wanda Poltawska, was gravely ill and not expected to live. She had been hospitalized with an intestinal tumor.

Bishop Wojtyla wrote a letter in Latin to Padre Pio and asked him to pray for Dr. Poltawska. He wrote:

> Venerable Father, I ask you to pray for a mother of four children, 40 years old, from Krakow in Poland (during the last war she was in a concentration camp in Germany), whose life and health are in grave danger and possibly may die because of cancer. May God, through

the intercession of the most Blessed Virgin, show his mercy to her and her family.

Yours in Christ,
Karol Wojtyla

The letter from Bishop Wojtyla was given to Angelo Battisti, the administrator of the Home for the Relief of Suffering, who then gave it to Padre Pio. After Padre Pio read it, he said to Angelo, "We cannot refuse this."

When Bishop Wojtyla telephoned Wanda's husband to inquire about the outcome of the surgery, he heard good news. Mr. Poltawska explained that no operation was performed. Instead, Wanda was sent home. "My wife should have been operated on yesterday, but the doctors found that there was nothing more to operate on. The doctors are confronted with a mystery." He went on to explain that Wanda's tumor had completely disappeared.

Just ten days after writing the first letter, Bishop Wojtyla wrote to Padre Pio once again and said:

Venerable Father, the woman from Krakow, Poland, mother of four children, before surgery on November 21, instantly regained her health. Thanks be to God. I render infinite thanks with devotion also to you Father, on behalf of her, her husband and all her family.

Yours in Christ,
Karol Wojtyla

In 1974, as Cardinal Archbishop of Krakow, Poland, Karol Wojtyla's personal devotion to Padre Pio led him to return to San Giovanni Rotondo once again. He celebrated Mass near the tomb of Padre Pio and during the Mass, Cardinal Wojtyla said:

This ancient church is the place where I first met the Servant of God, Padre Pio. And after almost twenty-seven years I have before my eyes his person, his presence, his words, the Mass celebrated by him at a side altar, and then this confessional.

Cardinal Karol Wojtyla was elected pope on October 16, 1978 and took the name Pope John Paul II. On May 25, 1987, Pope John Paul II traveled to San Giovanni Rotondo to celebrate the 100th anniversary of Padre Pio's birth. He was the first pope to visit the area in 700 years. Wanda Poltawska was one of the pilgrims in the huge crowd that attended Mass that day. She was very grateful to be alive and grateful for the prayerful intercession of Padre Pio. On June 16, 2002, in one of the largest liturgies in the Vatican's history, Pope John Paul II canonized Padre Pio before a crowd of more than 300,000 people.

———————

In 1950, Pasquale Zara of Rome, Italy had a serious motorcycle accident. As a result of the accident, his kneecap was broken and had to be kept in a plaster cast for six weeks. After the doctors removed the cast, Pasquale had another unfortunate accident. One day at his office, he slipped and fell. His knee, which was still weak from the previous break, hit the hard floor. Due to the impact, all the stitches burst open and his kneecap broke in many places.

Pasquale had to undergo a second surgery. After the operation, his knee began to suppurate and after several days, blood poisoning set in. He developed a very high fever. His physician, Dr. Matronola treated him with high doses of antibiotics but his condition did not improve.

Dr. Matronola finally told Pasquale the bad news. He was going to have to amputate his leg in order to save his life. It was a terrible moment for twenty-seven-year-old Pasquale Zara. The doctor explained that it was the only option available and advised Pasquale to try to accept it. He told Pasquale to inform all of his family members as soon as possible.

Later that morning, an elderly gentleman visited Pasquale. He explained that he regularly visited the sick who were in the hospital because he knew that many of the patients both needed and appreciated a visit. Pasquale told the man about the sad news he had received that morning from his doctor. The elderly man told Pasquale to have faith and to pray. He said that he had great faith in the power of prayer. He had received a miraculous healing from lung cancer through the intercession of Padre Pio. He asked Pasquale if he had ever heard of Padre Pio and Pasquale told him that he had not. He then shared some of the details of Padre Pio's life.

Before the elderly gentleman left, he and Pasquale prayed together. With all the sincerity of his heart, Pasquale invoked Padre Pio and prayed for healing. While the two were praying, Pasquale noticed a strong fragrance of violets filling his hospital room. It seemed very strange to him. He could not understand where the wonderful fragrance was coming from. He mentioned it to the gentleman who then got a broad smile on his face and said happily, "Son, that is a sign that Padre Pio has heard your prayers. I have no doubt that he will heal you. You will see!"

Padre Pio had indeed heard and answered Pasquale's prayers. The visit from the kind gentleman proved to be a turning point in Pasquale's life. He rededicated his life to the Lord and began to attend Mass regularly. He was healed not only in body, but also in mind, and spirit.

Ida Cuccana, of Modena, Italy suffered from a persistent high fever. She was under a doctor's care, but her condition did not improve. Her fever lingered for forty days. Her family grew more and more concerned as the days went by. Nara, Ida's friend, was praying for her recovery. One day, Nara remembered that when she had visited Padre Pio in San Giovanni Rotondo, she had returned home with a very precious item. It was a piece of chocolate that he had blessed. She gave it to Ida and told her to pray for Padre Pio's intercession. As Ida was eating the chocolate, the fever vanished. She was healed instantaneously.

Giovanni Venuti spent many weeks in the hospital with an illness that the doctors found hard to diagnose. He had very high fevers which were a cause for great concern. The doctors believed that he had a tumor on his liver but later he was diagnosed with kidney trouble. Finally, he was operated on, but after the surgery his condition deteriorated. The doctors told his wife Lucia, that his days were numbered. Many people in the Padre Pio prayer groups in the cities of Manzano, Pordenone, and San Giovanni Rotondo were praying for Giovanni's recovery.

One evening when Giovanni was very ill, Lucia decided to take some of his vests to the monastery of Our Lady of Grace and request that Padre Pio bless them. The Capuchins took the vests from Lucia and said that they would deliver them to Padre Pio. It took some time to get them back, but when they were finally returned, Lucia was very happy to hear that Padre had blessed them all. When Giovanni put on one of the vests, he was instantly cured of his fever. From that time forward, his condition steadily improved.

——————

Mrs. Bassot lived in the south of France. She owned a restaurant that had suffered from a steady decline in business. Although she kept the restaurant, because of the poor state of her health, it was no longer open to the public. Most days, her body was wracked with pain. Just getting out of bed in the morning often took a supreme effort. To add to her unfortunate situation, her husband had left her.

Mrs. Bassot had been working on a painting of the Blessed Virgin Mary for several months. She set up an easel in her now deserted restaurant and tried to paint during her "good days" when the pain in her neck and arms was not quite so intense. She put her heart and soul into the artwork.

One day, when she was putting the finishing touches on the Virgin's face, Mrs. Bassot suddenly had a painful spasm in her arm. The spasm caused her hand to slip, and the paintbrush streaked over the Virgin Mary's eye, marring her beautiful face. Mrs. Bassot was devastated. At that moment, she heard a voice within say, "Don't worry about the painting. I am sending you someone who can help you. Look up and stop crying."

Mrs. Bassot looked upward, and to her great amazement, she saw a priest directly above the painting. He was wearing a brown habit. She gazed at him only for a moment before he vanished. Mrs. Bassot had no idea who he was or why he had visited her in her restaurant. Suddenly, she realized that the chronic and agonizing pain in her neck and arms had disappeared. It was the first time in three years that she was completely pain-free. At once, she felt strong and energized.

Mrs. Bassot told a number of her friends about the apparition that she had seen in her restaurant, describing it in detail to them. She learned that the priest who had appeared to her was Padre Pio. Feeling inspired by the unusual incident, she decided to start a prayer group in her area. Many people admired Mrs. Bassot for her efforts. They began to follow suit and eventually a number of prayer groups sprung up in the surrounding towns.

Mrs. Bassot wanted to honor Padre Pio in a special way. She ordered a very large and beautiful statue of Padre Pio and placed it in her front yard. Everyone who passed by on the street could see it. The statue of Padre Pio reminded her of the day that he had visited her in the restaurant and healed her. Mrs. Bassot's health improved so dramatically that she wanted to go back to work. She reopened the restaurant and her business steadily increased. She kept the painting of the Virgin Mary on display for all to admire. Padre Pio continued to bless her life in countless ways.

————

Antonio Silvis was deported to Germany in 1943, after Italy joined with the Allied forces. Antonio was then placed in a Prisoner of War Camp. There, Antonio met another prisoner, Theodore Grossrubatcher from South Tyrol, Italy. Both men survived the terrible ordeal of the war and eventually made it out of the camp alive. Antonio returned to his home in Foggia, Italy and Theodore returned to South Tyrol.

Antonio was very surprised to get a call from Theodore in 1975. Theodore said that he was going to be passing through Foggia, and he wanted to stop and visit Antonio. Antonio was happy to hear from Theodore. He looked forward to his visit and asked his wife to cook a fine meal for the occasion.

When Theodore arrived at Antonio's home, the two men caught up on all the news. Theodore had a wife and seven children and worked as a garbage collector in South Tyrol. He did his best, but because of his low wages, he was barely able to provide for his family's needs. Antonio noticed that Theodore's clothing was in very bad condition. His pants were too small and literally bursting at the seams. His coat was old and tattered. Even his shoes were in pitiful condition. Antonio wondered how Theodore had ever managed to scrape up enough money to travel the long distance from South Tyrol to Foggia.

During dinner, Antonio noticed that Theodore was drinking heavily and consuming glass after glass of wine. He also drank numerous glasses of liqueur. He smoked cigarettes almost constantly throughout the evening. Even so, Antonio could sense that Theodore had a deep spirituality. With all of his excesses, he still manifested a goodness and a sincerity that was impressive.

Finally, Antonio asked Theodore the question that had been on his mind all evening. "With all of your financial problems, why have you made such a long and costly trip to Foggia?" Antonio asked. "It is because I am going to San Giovanni Rotondo to pray at Padre Pio's tomb," Theodore answered. "I want to pray for Padre Pio's intercession so that I will be freed from my dependence on alcohol and tobacco." Theodore knew that his life was out of control because of his addictions. It was also a hardship on his family because he spent a lot of money on alcohol and cigarettes, money that was greatly needed to put food on the table.

Theodore called Antonio from San Giovanni Rotondo to say that the visit to Padre Pio's tomb had been a truly grace-filled experience. A short time after he had returned to his home, Theodore called Antonio again. He told him that he had received a healing by praying at Padre Pio's tomb and he was completely free of his addictions. Not only that, he had more good news to share. He had secured a much better job with better wages and was now able to provide for all of his family's needs.

Theodore shared the story of Padre Pio's life and spirituality with many of the people in South Tyrol. He began to organize bus pilgrimages to San Giovanni Rotondo so that others could experience the graces that he had experienced. He had to endure many difficulties in leading the pilgrimages. Some of the people who participated complained constantly about the smallest matters. Others joined the trip but failed to come forth with the necessary money to cover their expenses. Still others had eccentricities which tested Theodore to the limit. Nevertheless, he continued to offer the pilgrimages twice a year. Even when his health took a downturn and he became confined to a wheelchair, he still managed to organize the trips and accompany the pilgrims to San Giovanni Rotondo.

In South Tyrol, Theodore also established Padre Pio prayer groups in the towns of Ortisei, Selva Gardena and Santa Cristina and he made sure to be present at every meeting. During the last months of his life, even though he was weak and ill, he continued to attend the Padre Pio prayer group meetings. He wanted to keep the fires of enthusiasm burning in the hearts of everyone. Sadly, after Theodore's death, the attendance waned at the Padre Pio prayer groups. Nevertheless, people would long remember the piety and devotion of Theodore Grossrubatcher and the good that he did for countless souls.

———

There was a man (name withheld) who was an alcoholic who had to be hospitalized due to alcohol poisoning. The doctors who examined him saw the devastating effects of his prolonged use of alcohol. The brain damage was so severe that the doctors said there was no hope at all of recovery. Even with the best medical care and attention, they could not hold out even a ray of hope for the man. The medical staff pronounced him "a vegetable."

One day, someone left a picture of Padre Pio on the table beside his bed. He was never able to find out who left it there but from that moment on, his condition began to improve. He eventually made a complete recovery, with no sign of brain damage. He overcame his addiction to alcohol and was able to return to a normal and productive life.

———

Peter Barrett used to go to the hospital regularly in order to visit the patients and give Holy Communion to the Catholics who requested it. One day, as Peter was making his visits, a nun who worked at the hospital, spoke to him about one particular man who was a patient there. The nun told Peter that she thought the man would appreciate a visit.

Peter went to the man's bedside and introduced himself. The man told Peter that he used to be a Catholic but he had not been to church in many years. The two conversed for a while and before Peter left, he gave the man a prayer leaflet of Padre Pio. The man placed in on the table at his bedside but did not show the slightest interest in it.

Some days later, Peter returned to the hospital to make his rounds. He was told that the man whom he had given the prayer leaflet to, had been asking for him. He was hoping that he could speak to Peter once again. When Peter went to the man's bedside, the man told him that he would like to have one more prayer leaflet of Padre Pio. He had shown the prayer card to his family when they came to visit him and he wanted his wife to have one.

The man told Peter that he had read the back of the leaflet which contained a brief summary of Padre Pio's life. As he read it, it dawned on him that he had totally neglected his own spiritual life. He had worked hard for his employer and had made a great effort to take care of his family's material needs, but he had forgotten God in the process. "I now want to make my confession," the man said. "I was wondering if you could find a priest who would be willing to come to the hospital?" Peter told the man he would be happy to do so. He used the hospital telephone and made arrangements for a priest to come right away. Peter waited at the hospital until the priest arrived. The man made a sincere confession and died peacefully just three days later.

———

Every day Padre Pio prayed the novena to the Sacred Heart of Jesus and he recommended that others pray it as well. There was a woman (name withheld) who once prayed the novena for her husband who was an alcoholic. Their home life was very unhappy because of his alcoholism. One day she went to a showing of a documentary film on the life of Padre Pio. Her husband spent the day drinking. During the film, she prayed with great intensity, asking Padre Pio to help her husband overcome his addiction. The next morning her husband told her that he had decided to stop drinking. Grace was evidently with him because he was given the strength to abstain. Their marriage was blessed with happiness from that time forward.

Father Pio is a giant of sanctity. We wish to thank our Father who is in heaven for having given rise in the Holy Church of God to a man of great faith, of that unshakable faith that moves mountains and creates gigantic good works in this century of struggles, fratricidal wars and egoism. God has given rise in the Italian Church, in this noble region of Puglia, to a giant of sanctity whose heroic virtues recall men of today to their vocation as God's created beings and sons of the Father who is in heaven.

- Cardinal Angelo Sodano

CHAPTER 23

Giuseppe Canaponi

In 1945, thirty-four-year-old Giuseppe Canaponi, a railway worker from Sarteano, Italy was riding to work on his motorcycle when he was hit by a truck. He was hospitalized with a fractured skull as well as numerous broken bones. For a while it was touch and go, and the doctors did not know if Giuseppe would live or die. Gradually, he recovered from all of his injuries except one. His left leg, which had been broken in five places, remained completely rigid and caused him constant pain.

Giuseppe had numerous surgeries on his leg as well as physical therapy, but to no avail. He had to use crutches in order to walk. His left knee too, was a problem. He was not able to bend his knee and was finally diagnosed with "fibrous ankylosis" of the knee. To add to his problems, the incisions made in his leg for the corrective surgeries, did not heal. The open and painful wounds added to his distress.

Giuseppe became very depressed. It had been more than two years since the accident but his condition had not improved. He was declared permanently disabled and forced to retire from his job at the railroad. His health in general was going in a downward spiral and he feared that death was approaching. His wife's strong faith made up for his own lack of faith. She wrote several letters to Padre Pio asking for his prayers for Giuseppe's healing. She told Giuseppe that they should make a trip to San Giovanni Rotondo to see Padre Pio, but he was not interested. He did not think it would be beneficial. Giuseppe's wife continued to talk to him about Padre Pio and he finally agreed to make the trip.

Giuseppe and his wife took a train to Rome and then to Foggia. Giuseppe was in intense pain on the train trip. After they arrived in Foggia, Giuseppe lost his footing and took a very bad fall. He and his wife spent the night in the train station. The next morning, they took a bus to San Giovanni Rotondo. Trying to get situated in a comfortable position on the bus was next to impossible. The bus driver dropped them off almost two miles from the monastery. A single dirt road lay in front of them. They had no choice but to walk the distance.

Giuseppe breathed a sigh of relief when he and his wife finally arrived at the little monastery church of Our Lady of Grace. The trip to San Giovanni Rotondo had been much more difficult that he had ever imagined. He was so exhausted from the journey that he slipped into one of the back pews and laid down. Taking a short rest in the church seemed to revive him.

Inside the church of Our Lady of Grace, there were several Capuchin priests. Giuseppe wondered if one of them might be Padre Pio. One of the Capuchins was hearing confessions in a nearby confessional. The curtain of the confessional was parted slightly and when the priest raised his hand to give the penitent absolution, Giuseppe noticed that he was wearing half-gloves. "That must certainly be Padre Pio!" Giuseppe said to himself. At that very moment, Padre Pio lifted his eyes and looked straight at him. When their eyes met, Giuseppe felt as though he had been hit by a bolt of electricity. His entire body began to tremble.

Giuseppe decided to wait in line to make his confession to Padre Pio. In the confessional, he did not have to worry about remembering all of the sins of his past. Padre Pio remembered them for him, down to the letter. He named them one by one, as Giuseppe listened and affirmed that what he said was true. Padre Pio was very kind and very compassionate. Giuseppe was suddenly able to see his sins for what they were - offenses against God. When Padre Pio gave him absolution, Giuseppe's whole body began to tremble, just like it had when their eyes met for the first time.

When Giuseppe left the confessional, he felt like a new person. His wife saw him walking toward her and noticed that he looked very peaceful. She suddenly realized that Giuseppe was walking without his crutches. "Giuseppe, look. You are not using your crutches and you are walking just fine!" she said. Giuseppe had not noticed it until his wife mentioned it to him. He was just as astonished as she was. Not only was he walking unaided, he was also free of pain. But there was more. His knee had lost its rigidity. He then reflected that he had been able to kneel with ease while making his confession to Padre Pio, something that had previously been impossible for him to do. At the time he was making his confession, it had not occurred to him that he was doing anything unusual.

When Giuseppe returned to his hotel room, he examined his leg closely. He repeatedly knelt down on his "once immobile knee" and had no trouble doing so. In addition, the open and painful sores on his leg, which had bothered him for months, had all healed over. It was true. Giuseppe had received a miraculous healing.

The next day, Giuseppe went to the monastery to thank Padre Pio. "You do not need to thank me because I did not heal you," Padre Pio said. "It was God who healed you. All I did was pray." When Giuseppe went back to the doctor's office for a check up, he was greeted with amazement by his doctor. His doctor was shocked to see the change in his condition. Giuseppe's case was eventually studied in Rome in a special Orthopedic Congress and presented to eight hundred doctors. His instantaneous recovery defied scientific explanation.

As time went by, Giuseppe made many more trips to see Padre Pio. The two became close friends. Giuseppe tried to think of different ways in which he could help the Capuchin community at Our Lady of Grace monastery. Because he had worked as an electrician for the railroad before his accident, he put his skills to good use. He thoroughly examined the wiring system at the monastery and did much repair work to the electrical outlets. Padre Pio was very happy to see the improvements he was making at the monastery.

As time passed, Giuseppe became a part of the inner circle of Padre Pio's closest friends. On one occasion, Giuseppe went to see Padre Pio on a very cold and rainy evening. Even though he was not feeling well, he decided to visit Padre Pio anyway. Due to a sore throat and laryngitis, he was not able to speak above a whisper. He was soaking wet when he walked into Padre Pio's cell. Father Carmelo was visiting with Padre Pio at the time. Padre Pio noticed at once that Giuseppe looked ill. He asked Father Carmelo to see if he could find some warm clothes for Giuseppe to put on. Father Carmelo tried his best but could not find any. Padre Pio began to look around the room and finally found one of his large scarves. He put it around Giuseppe's neck. At once, Giuseppe felt a wonderful warmth coursing through his entire body. "I feel better already," he said to Padre Pio. As he spoke the words, he suddenly realized that his laryngitis was gone. Giuseppe felt such a sense of well-being that he did not want to take the scarf off. He wore it home that night and then kept it on for many days. Finally, Padre Pio told him that he could keep it. Giuseppe was very happy to be in possession of a relic of Padre Pio. Many of Padre Pio's spiritual children had a desire for such a relic, but very few were able to obtain one.

One day, Padre Pio lost his handkerchief and was looking everywhere for it. Giuseppe had a handkerchief with him and offered it to Padre Pio. Padre Pio took it and put it inside his habit, over his heart wound. He always kept a cloth over the wound to absorb the blood. Later, Padre Pio returned Giuseppe's handkerchief to him. Even though it had been washed and ironed, there were still blood stains visible on it.

On one occasion, Giuseppe felt a strong desire to pray for Padre Pio's deceased parents, Grazio and Giuseppa Forgione. He began to pray for them faithfully every day. Later, he became busy with many other concerns, and eventually forgot to include them in his prayers. One day at the monastery, Padre Pio's words surprised Giuseppe. "I want to thank you, Giuseppe," Padre Pio said. "What do you want to thank me for?" Giuseppe asked. "I want to thank you for the prayers you said for my dear parents," Padre Pio replied. Giuseppe had never mentioned to anyone that he had been praying for Grazio and Giuseppa.

From his very first meeting with Padre Pio in the confessional, Giuseppe felt Padre Pio's paternal love and care. He was like a father to Giuseppe. It was true that Padre Pio had a reputation for being stern. That was not Giuseppe's experience. In the years that followed, Giuseppe felt continually supported by Padre Pio's prayers. He once stated that the only time he felt truly happy was when he was with Padre Pio.

Jesus wants to make us saints at any cost. But more than anything, he wants to sanctify you. He gives continuous proof of this to you. It seems that he has nothing in mind except to sanctify your soul.

- St. Pio of Pietrelcina

I attended Padre Pio's Mass shortly after my ordination to the priesthood. It was a great school. It was of more benefit to me than all that I had studied in my years of theology.

- *Father Luigi Pasani*

CHAPTER 24

The Clergy and Padre Pio

F ather Agostino Daniele and Padre Pio met in 1907 at the Capuchin monastery in Serracapriola. At the time, Padre Pio was just beginning his first year of study of sacred theology and Father Agostino was his professor. Father Agostino was one of only two spiritual directors that Padre Pio was to have in his life.

Padre Pio had a great affection for Father Agostino. He used to call him "my consoling angel." Father Agostino in turn felt a paternal love for Padre Pio and used to call him affectionately, "my son." The two Capuchins were to enjoy a deep friendship for more than fifty years. During those fifty years, Father Agostino kept a diary in which he recorded Padre Pio's mystical experiences. He made the first entry in his diary on November 28, 1911 and his last entry was made on November 23, 1961. The diary is filled with valuable information and insights into Padre Pio's life and spirituality.

In 1933, when Father Agostino was getting ready to go to Genoa to the hospital, he stopped to say goodbye to Padre Pio. Padre Pio happened to be ill at the time and was in bed. He wished Father Agostino well and said to him,

"Go in peace Father, because you have someone who is praying and suffering for you."

Father Agostino felt sorry for Padre Pio. He knew what Padre Pio endured on a daily basis and he did not want him to suffer on his behalf. "Let's divide the suffering," Father Agostino said. "Don't give it another thought," Padre Pio answered. Everything went well for Father Agostino at the hospital in Genoa. He also felt constantly protected while he was away from the monastery. He knew that he had Padre Pio to thank for it.

––––––––––

Father Costanzo Perazzini met Padre Pio only once in his life, in 1938. He had traveled to San Giovanni Rotondo from Rimini in order to make his confession to Padre Pio. He was seventeen years old at the time and had recently left the Capuchin novitiate in Cesena. He was at a crossroads in his life and was not sure what the future held for him. Padre Pio told Costanzo that he would someday be a missionary and would work in many different countries. He was surprised by Padre Pio's remarks because had already decided that he was not going to pursue a vocation to the priesthood.

However, Costanzo later had a complete change of heart and on November 13, 1938, he was accepted once again into the Capuchin novitiate of Cesena. He was ordained a priest on May 25, 1945. In 1947, he was sent to India where he worked in the diocese of Lucknow until 1964. After that, he was transferred to Tanzania, and then sent to Ethiopia and for twelve years worked in Dar es Salaam. He felt that Padre Pio followed him during his missionary journeys and protected him in all the critical moments of his life.

––––––––––

Pio Maria Vincentelli entered the Capuchin novitiate on September 4, 1945. He was twenty-three years old. He had previously spoken to Padre Pio at length about his desire to become a Capuchin priest and Padre Pio encouraged him to pursue his vocation. However, his doctor advised him against it because his health was so poor. A well respected doctor in Sienna told Pio Maria in 1940 that he would not live to see the end of the year.

Pio Maria had only been in the Capuchin novitiate for two months when he was diagnosed with nephritis, a disease of the kidneys. His superiors decided that the best course would be to send him back to his home. Pio Maria pleaded with his superiors not to dismiss him. He had to overcome countless obstacles in order to finally be accepted into the novitiate and he could not bear the idea of leaving. He said to his Capuchin novice master, "I would rather die than to go back to the world." Pio Maria remembered that Padre Pio had once told him that none of his health problems would ever be able to stand in the way of his vocation to the priesthood.

Pio Maria recovered from the nephritis with almost no medical intervention. His doctors were astonished at the improvement in his health. He made his solemn profession on January 15, 1950 and on April 3, 1954, he was ordained.

————————

There was once a priest (name withheld) who accompanied a sick man to San Giovanni Rotondo. The priest was very happy for the opportunity to see Padre Pio. His friend too was very glad to be making the trip and was hoping to be cured through the intercession of Padre Pio.

While in San Giovanni Rotondo, the priest had an opportunity to make his confession to Padre Pio. Afterward, the priest thought about what he had experienced in Padre Pio's confessional. He felt that Padre Pio was a good confessor, just like many priests who had heard his confession in the past. However, Padre Pio did not provide the priest with any startling insights into life and he made no prophetic statements. In many ways, making his confession to Padre Pio seemed quite ordinary. During his time at the monastery, the priest did not perceive any of the delightful fragrances or perfumes of Padre Pio that he had heard so much about. Also, the friend whom he accompanied on the trip was not cured.

For the days of his visit, the priest attended Padre Pio's Mass. While assisting at the Mass, he experienced his own human frailty and weakness as a priest. He had already said thousands of Masses in his lifetime but he found that Padre Pio's Mass was different. Padre Pio really spoke to God at every moment and God was present. Like Abraham, Padre Pio even struggled with

God. It was by observing Padre Pio at Mass that the priest came to a true understanding of the greatness of Padre Pio and the depth of his love for God.

———

One day I received a telephone call inviting me to be a guest on Radio Veritas. I was told that Father Vic Robles wanted to talk about Padre Pio on his radio program. My first question was "Who is Father Vic?" and my second question was, "What is Radio Veritas?" Later, when Father Vic traveled from the Philippines to the U.S., I was blessed to be able to meet him and to learn more about his devotion to Padre Pio. This is his testimony:

Father Vicente (Vic) Robles was ordained to the priesthood on November 30, 1987 in the Malolos Cathedral in Malolos City, Bulacan, Philippines. Not long after his ordination, he began to have a great desire to build a shrine dedicated to Divine Mercy in the Philippines. Stepping out on faith, he moved forward with the plans in earnest in 1991. When the Adoration Chapel for the new shrine was blessed, 5,000 people attended the ceremony. The Divine Mercy Shrine in Marilao, Bulacan was given the status of a National Shrine by the Catholic Bishops Conference of the Philippines in 2002. People from all parts of the Philippines and beyond now make pilgrimages there. Father Vic served as the rector of the shrine for fifteen years.

In 2002, when Padre Pio's canonization date was approaching, Father Vic went to a sculptor and commissioned him to create a statue of Padre Pio. Even though Father Vic did not have a sponsor at that time to pay for the statue, he decided to order it anyway. He was going to have the statue blessed on the day of Padre Pio's canonization, June 16, 2002. He also planned to say a special Mass in honor of Padre Pio on that day.

Five days before the canonization, Father Vic turned on the television and learned that a girl in the area had been kidnaped. Father Vic knew the girl's parents, who happened to be benefactors of the Divine Mercy Shrine in Bulacan. The perpetrators of the terrible deed were members of an organized crime ring. Knowing that the family was wealthy, they demanded that a ransom be paid before the girl was returned.

Father Vic wrote a letter to the parents and said that he was going to offer a Mass for their daughter's safe return. He also encouraged the family to pray to Padre Pio and ask for his intercession. The next day, Father Vic went to the studio where his global Catholic radio program on Radio Veritas was being taped. He told the worldwide listeners that he was going to offer his Rosary on the broadcast for the safe return of the girl who was kidnaped. He asked everyone around the world to join in prayer with him for that intention. On that day, one of the kidnappers who was guarding the girl suddenly began to feel guilty about his actions. He happened to be a new recruit in the crime syndicate. Because of his change of heart, the girl was then able to escape and make her way to safety.

The girl's parents were so grateful, that in order to show their appreciation, they gave Father Vic a generous check. As it turned out, it was enough to pay for the statue of Padre Pio. Father Vic always smiles when he explains that in this case, Padre Pio "ransomed himself."

That was Father Vic's first experience of praying for the powerful intercession of Padre Pio. But he would have many, many more similar experiences in the future. On one of Father Vic's trips to the U.S. he was given a number of our *Pray, Hope, and Don't Worry* publications. Back in the Philippines, he distributed them to the people in his parish on the same day that he gave a homily on Padre Pio. One of his parishioners, Blesila (Blessie) Francisco, spoke to him after the Mass. With tears in her eyes, she told him that she loved his sermon about Padre Pio. It was the first time she had heard of him. She also said that the phrase, "Pray, Hope, and Don't Worry" was especially meaningful to her. Blessie had been tormented by worries for many weeks. One of her business clients had failed to pay her what he owed her. Blessie would be plunged into a serious financial crisis if she did not receive the money soon.

Blessie took all the invoices of the unpaid bills of her client and put them inside the *Pray, Hope and Don't Worry* publication that Father Vic had given her. She then began the novena and prayed to Padre Pio for a resolution. A short time later, the manager of the company who owed her the money telephoned her and said that he wanted to make full restitution. He was true to his word and Blessie received all that she was owed.

Blessie felt that she had received a miracle and she wanted to do something for Padre Pio. She learned that Father Vic had a desire to distribute Padre Pio statues to various parishes and religious institutions in the Philippines. Blessie was able to provide the money for the statues to be purchased and distributed.

A Padre Pio statue was then given to San Roque parish in Manila, Emmaus House of Apostolate in Malolos City, Bulacan, the Padre Pio Retreat Center in Pulilan, Bulacan, the convent chapel of the Benedictine Nuns in Mindoro, the Retirement Home of the Holy Spirit Sisters in Quezon City, the Santo Niño de Passion Chapel in Navotas, and St. Joseph's parish in Singapore.

After battling cancer for several years, when Blessie's sister Vicki was hospitalized with only a short time to live, Father Vic suggested that they bring Padre Pio's statue to her bedside and pray with her. It proved to be a great consolation to the whole family. The sadness that the family had been experiencing regarding Vicki's illness gave way to a deep sense of peace. All felt Padre Pio's presence with them in the hospital room. Vicki received many special graces and she was able to accept her death with great resignation. Vicki died on the Solemn Feast of the Epiphany of the Lord.

Father Vic has continued to find many ways to introduce people to the life and spirituality of Padre Pio. He has distributed hundreds of copies of Padre Pio's prayer, *Stay with me, Lord,* to people in the Philippines. When he is called to give the Last Rites to the dying, he brings a picture of Padre Pio to the bedside and also prays the Divine Mercy chaplet. He has been called to assist eleven priests in their final moments. He believes that it is very important to pray with the dying and for the dying. He is aware that many people die alone, with no one to pray for them. Father Vic reminds people that Padre Pio established his Prayer Groups worldwide so that all, both the living and the deceased could benefit from prayer.

In 2006, Father Vic was able to visit San Giovanni Rotondo before traveling on to Poland to attend a Divine Mercy Convention. He invited his parishioners to write out their prayer petitions so that he could place them at the tomb of Padre Pio. What a consolation it is to know that great saints like St. Pio, St. Faustina Kowalska, and many more are ever interceding for us at the throne of God.

———

We met Father Jim Muntz at the Magnificat Catholic Prayer Ministry in Southern California. We were able to speak with him about his visit to the monastery of Our Lady of Grace in San Giovanni Rotondo. This is his testimony:

I was born in Brooklyn, New York and grew up on Long Island, in New York. Somewhere along the way, I heard about Padre Pio and I had a great desire to meet him. I took it upon myself to learn the Italian language so that I could communicate with him. I visited him on four different occasions in San Giovanni Rotondo.

The first time I went to San Giovanni Rotondo and walked into the church of Our Lady of Grace, I could perceive the strong smell of blood. I attended Padre Pio's Mass and I was very impressed by the reverence with which he celebrated the Mass. The Mass lasted a very long time.

After Mass, I waited to make my confession to Padre Pio. The men's confessions were face to face and were held in the sacristy of the church. While waiting in line, I heard Padre Pio shout at the man who was making his confession to him. Padre Pio raised his voice and said, "What was that you said you did?" All of us who were standing in line felt sorry for the man. We all backed up in the line so as to give the man more privacy. For his sake, we wanted to make sure that we did not hear his reply to Padre Pio's question.

I was nervous when I made my confession to Padre Pio for the first time. Padre Pio was very calm as he heard my confession. It only lasted a few minutes. Later, I asked Padre Pio about the desire I had to become a priest. I wanted to know if he thought that I had a vocation to the priesthood. "Yes, you must become a priest," he said. "You must go to the bishop and insist that you be ordained!" I am very shy by nature. I did not feel that I had the courage to insist on anything to a bishop. But because of the advice Padre Pio gave me, I finally spoke to the bishop. After I completed all my theological requirements, I was ordained to the priesthood.

Before the Mass, Padre Pio would always take his gloves off. Sometimes, a scab from the stigmata on his hands would detach itself and fall to the floor when he removed his gloves. People who were nearby watched for this, and if a scab fell to the floor, they would rush to get it.

Padre Pio would rarely allow people in his company if they were living immoral or sinful lives, and had no desire to change. He would often send people away with strong words. He was truly guided by God in his dealings with others. He had the gift of reading hearts, of prophecy, and of discernment of spirits to a remarkable degree. If he counseled a person, he spoke in a direct manner. He did not want to repeat his words.

Each time I went to the monastery of Our Lady of Grace, I was able to make my confession to Padre Pio. While in San Giovanni Rotondo, I visited Mary Pyle. She spoke to me a lot about the Third Order. I was inspired by Mary's words and because of her encouragement, I became a member of the Third Order of St. Francis.

Many people came to Padre Pio asking for healing from their illnesses. Padre Pio often spoke to people about his good friend Pietruccio Cugino. He held him up as a model for others to follow. Pietruccio was blind but he never asked Padre Pio to pray for his healing. Padre Pio wanted people to practice prayer and penance. He felt that too many people were seeking physical healing. He once said, "So many come to San Giovanni Rotondo asking for healing. So few ask for the grace to bear their cross."

I had an undiagnosed illness when I visited Padre Pio in San Giovanni Rotondo. I was not healed of my illness but I received much more that a physical healing. As time went by, I realized the true spiritual greatness of Padre Pio. I have read more than thirty books on his life. I know of no other saint in history that has been given the spiritual gifts that the Lord gave to Padre Pio. I realize how truly blessed I was to meet him.

- *Fr. Jim Muntz*

———

Father Peter Rookey, O.S.M. spoke with us about his trip to visit Padre Pio in the early 1950's. This is his story:

I joined the Order of the Servants of Mary (Servites) and was ordained to the priesthood on May 17, 1941. In 1954, I was appointed as Assistant General of the Servite Order. I was sent to Rome and spent six years at this assignment. Two times I traveled from Rome to San Giovanni Rotondo to visit Padre Pio and make my confession to him. I spoke Italian and I was glad that there would be no language barrier. I also wanted to talk to Padre Pio about the many problems I encountered as Assistant General for the Servites. It was a difficult job in many ways. I felt that Padre Pio could help me with his advice.

Padre Pio did indeed help me. He gave me advice which I have never forgotten, even after these many years. He said to me, "Always, and in all circumstances, be obedient to your superiors."

At the time I visited San Giovanni Rotondo, Padre Pio said Mass at the side altar of St. Francis. When it was time for the Mass to begin, Padre Pio came out of the sacristy with two Capuchins, one on either side. It was apparent to me that they were there to protect him. They reminded me of bodyguards. Padre Pio went into ecstasy several times during the Mass and became completely still.

I had made arrangements with the Capuchins to say my Mass after Padre Pio was finished with his. At the conclusion of his Mass, the same two Capuchins stood one on either side of him and escorted him back into the sacristy. The simple side altar of St. Francis had just the bare essentials - an altar cloth, two candles, water and wine, and a crucifix. As Padre Pio walked toward the sacristy, I approached the simple altar. As I did, I perceived the beautiful fragrance of roses filling the church. It was a heavenly fragrance, not of this earth. I knew that it was a special blessing imparted by Padre Pio for all who were in the church that day.

- *Father Peter Rookey, O.S.M.*

When Father Carl Gismondi, FSSP was assigned to be the pastor at St. Anne's Catholic Church in San Diego, he organized a monthly Padre Pio prayer group. It has been a blessing to the parish. We recently learned that Father Gismondi received a very beautiful grace through Padre Pio. This is his testimony:

Not long ago, I was hearing confessions at St. Anne's parish. It was on a Friday in the middle of the summer and it happened to be a very hot day. We do not have air conditioning at the parish and it can become quite uncomfortable in the summer time. In the confessional, it can be even more stifling.

The confessional is built with maximum insulation in order to be sound proof for the sake of the privacy of the penitent. That means it is also to some degree "air proof." On this particular day, in that very uncomfortable heat, I suddenly felt a very cool breeze coming down from the top of the confessional. I would describe it as "sprinkling down," bringing me a great deal of relief. The cool air flowed only from the top. The sides of the confessional were not affected.

I was startled by the gentle and cool breeze. Before I became a priest, I was an engineer. I wondered, from the perspective of an engineer, how a breeze could possibly be coming from the top of the confessional. I began to analyze the situation but I could come to no conclusion.

After Mass, when I greeted the people who were leaving the church, a woman approached me and said, "Father, I felt so sorry for you while you were hearing confessions. It was so hot in the church that I knew it must be very uncomfortable for you in the confessional. I said a prayer to Padre Pio on your behalf. I prayed, "Padre Pio, please send Father Gismondi a cool breeze to make him more comfortable while he is hearing confessions."

- *Father Carl Gismondi, F.S.S.P.*

We got word that there was a priest in Los Angeles, Father Paul, who was very devoted to Padre Pio. We were able to interview Father Paul and learn about Padre Pio's intercession in his life:

I went through twelve years of Catholic schooling but after I graduated from high school I lost all interest in the Church. I still tried to do good works and to do my part to make the world a better place, but my belief in God and in the value of religion was limited. Many years later, it began to dawn on me that maybe there was more to God after all and I decided to take another look at the faith I was raised in. I reasoned that if God truly existed, the Catholic Church and the Sacraments would be the best way to unite with Him. Returning to the Sacraments would allow me to be available to God's transforming power in the world. I finally made my confession after a thirteen year absence from the Church and began to attend Mass daily.

I used to help my brother who was a parish priest and I assisted him in his various ministries. One day when we were driving, I noticed a picture of a saint that he had placed near the dashboard of his car. I did not know who the saint was, but the moment I looked at the picture, I started to cry. My brother told me that it was a picture of Padre Pio. I had never heard of him as I had been away from the Church for a long time.

It dawned on me at that very moment that I had not made my way back to my Catholic faith on my own like I had assumed. I had a lot of arrogance which was an obstacle in my path but I couldn't see it at the time. When I saw the picture of Padre Pio, I had the deep conviction that it was he who had helped me in my conversion and that he had been praying and interceding for me.

More than fifteen years later I entered the seminary. In 2006, after studying in the seminary for six years, I became a priest for the Archdiocese of Los Angeles and I now serve in the city of Pasadena.

- *Father Paul Griesgraber*

———————

We spoke to Father Dennis Gordon in the rectory of St. Anne's parish in San Diego. This is his story:

Dennis Gordon was brought up in a devout Catholic family in Nogales, Arizona. His parents made a great effort to instill spiritual values in their children. Dennis and his four siblings had the advantage of being able to attend Catholic schools in grammar school and high school. The recitation of the Rosary was a regular part of their family life and good Catholic reading material was always plentiful in the Gordon household.

In order to supplement the religious education that his children received at their school and their parish, Dennis' father took it upon himself to regularly review the Catholic catechism with them. Often on Saturday mornings, he gathered with his children for a study session and even gave them written tests to make sure they understood all of the doctrines of the faith. He brought the teachings of Catholicism to life for them and in the process passed on his enthusiasm and love for the Church to all five of his children.

When Dennis was eight years old, he happened to see a holy card of Padre Pio that belonged to his father and he asked his father about the marks that he saw on Padre Pio's hands. His father explained to him that Padre Pio was so closely united to Jesus that the wounds of Jesus' crucifixion appeared on his body. It made a very deep impression on young Dennis. It also opened his eyes to the meaning of the priesthood and he reflected that a priest must be truly conformed to Christ Crucified. He then read a little booklet about

Padre Pio and learned that his wounds bled more during the celebration of the Mass than at any other time. Dennis' faith was strengthened regarding the real presence of Jesus in the Eucharist as he learned about Padre Pio's great devotion to the Eucharist and to the Holy Mass. Even though Dennis was just a boy, he was able to grasp the lofty spiritual concepts.

During high school, Dennis sometimes wondered if he might have a vocation to the priesthood. He often prayed before a statue of Padre Pio that was in his family's home, asking Padre Pio to lead him on the right path. In addition to his love for Padre Pio, he also had a devotion to St. John Vianney, St. Michael the Archangel, St. Dennis, a Christian martyr of the 3rd century whose name he shares, and St. Peter the Apostle whose name he chose at the time of his confirmation.

During his college years, Dennis was able to take the Padre Pio statue with him when he moved to the East Coast and he continued to invoke the intercession of Padre Pio. After graduating from the United States Coast Guard Academy, as a Coast Guard Officer, Dennis spent many quiet nights on the waters of the Pacific. It was during those times of reflection and silence that Dennis finally felt certain that God was calling him to the priesthood. The question arose as whether to pursue Holy Orders as a diocesan priest or as a religious order priest. In his youth, Dennis and his family had attended the traditional Latin Mass (also called the Tridentine Mass or Mass in the extraordinary form) on several occasions in Tucson, Arizona. Dennis was so inspired by the reverence, solemnity, and beauty of the Mass in the extraordinary form that he never forgot it. It was easy for him to choose where to seek admittance. It would be to the Priestly Fraternity of St. Peter where all of the priests are trained to say the Latin Mass exclusively.

Pope Benedict XVI has described the traditional Latin Mass, as a "precious treasure to be preserved" and in 2007, in his apostolic letter to bishops titled *Summorum Pontificum,* he called for a greater use of it. He said that the Mass in the extraordinary form should be made available in every parish where groups of the faithful desire it. Since the publication of *Summorum Pontificum*, there has been an increase in the number of traditional Latin Masses said in Catholic churches throughout the world.

Following seven years of seminary, Father Dennis Gordon was ordained to the priesthood on May 30, 2008 in Lincoln, Nebraska. Two of Father

Gordon's brothers, Father Terrence Gordon and Father James Gordon are also priests. His other two siblings, a brother and a sister, are deeply committed Catholics who are making great efforts to pass on their faith to their own children.

The years since Father Dennis' ordination have been busy and extraordinarily fruitful. When he initially started hearing confessions, he decided to keep a small framed photograph of Padre Pio with him, as a reminder to him of all that a holy confessor should be. He sees Padre Pio as a model of sanctity for priests and laity alike.

On one occasion, a man at Father Dennis' parish told him how happy he was to be a part of the faith community there and said that he had good reason to believe that he had been divinely guided to the parish. He went on to explain that he had visited a number of the Catholic churches in the area, in an effort to find the one that he felt was right for him. He also held the matter up in prayer. During that time, he had a vivid dream. In his dream, he was standing inside of a Catholic church that he had never seen before. He noticed a monk not far from the altar, sitting in front of a statue of St. Joseph. The monk turned around and looked at him and smiled. He saw then that it was Padre Pio. The Sunday morning that the man visited Father Dennis' parish for the first time, he immediately recognized it as the church he had seen in his dream.

One of the stories that Father Dennis likes to meditate on is the vision that Padre Pio had when he was a young man, shortly before he entered the Capuchin novitiate. Jesus asked Padre Pio to fight an evil being who proved to be a giant. Angelic men stood on one side of Padre Pio and the demons stood on the other side. He was terrified and wanted to run away but Jesus told him that he would always be near to protect him and to help him triumph over the dark forces.

The Old Testament takes up the same theme in the book of Job and says, *Man's life on earth is a warfare* (Job 7:1). In the book of Ephesians we read, *For our struggle is not against flesh and blood, but against the principalities, against the powers, against the world rulers of the darkness of this age, and against the spiritual forces of wickedness in high places* (Ephesians 6:12). Father Dennis believes that Padre Pio's vision holds a lesson of great value for all of us. Since no one is exempt from the temptations and dangers of life, spiritual as well as material, wisdom teaches us to cling to Jesus at all times and to stay ever-alert, while remaining constant and watchful in prayer.

The whole of my person is consecrated to Jesus and I feel myself bound to him by a double tie, as a Christian and as a priest, and exactly for this reason I tremble at the very thought that this double bond could be momentarily loosened.

- St. Pio of Pietrelcina

Today we are the children of mercy and all because of Jesus and Jesus Crucified. Therefore let us cling tightly to Jesus . . . We are now clothed by the mercy of Jesus through his Passion and death, so never let us put aside these garments that will be those in which we will stand before God to hear the invitation of the Heavenly Father: Come O ye blessed ones into possession of my kingdom.

- St. Pio of Pietrelcina

CHAPTER 25

Laurino Costa

*L*aurino Costa was once given a photograph of Padre Pio. It made a remarkable impression on him. Laurino found himself gazing at the photo often. Shortly after receiving photo, he began to have dreams about Padre Pio. Feeling a strong connection to the holy priest, he decided to write him a letter. Laurino had been out of work for many months. Try as he might, he was unable to find a job. He was extremely worried about his financial situation. In the letter, he asked Padre Pio to pray for him so that he would be able to find work. Right away, Laurino received an answer to his letter. Padre Pio wanted Laurino to "come to San Giovanni Rotondo at once."

Laurino wanted to accept the invitation but there were many obstacles in his path. For one thing, he had no money for the train fare from Padua to Padre Pio's monastery in San Giovanni Rotondo. Nevertheless, the desire to visit Padre Pio was growing stronger and stronger each day. One day he decided to hitchhike to the train station in Padua, even though he did not have the money to buy a ticket.

When Laurino arrived at the train station, he happened to run into a friend. "What brings you here, Laurino?" his friend asked. "I am hoping to go to San Giovanni Rotondo to see Padre Pio," Laurino said. "He has invited me to visit him." Laurino then explained that he could not afford to purchase a ticket. It so happened that a man who was standing close by overheard the conversation. "If you would like to come along with me, I am driving to San Giovanni Rotondo," the man said to Laurino. Laurino was amazed at the wonderful way things were working out in his favor. Without his even asking for help, he had been offered free transportation to San Giovanni Rotondo. He happily accepted the man's invitation. The man turned out to be Dr. Giuseppe Gusso, a close friend of Padre Pio's and the medical director of Padre Pio's hospital, the Home for the Relief of Suffering.

At the monastery of Our Lady of Grace, Laurino attended Padre Pio's early morning Mass. Afterward, he followed a large group of men into the sacristy to receive Padre Pio's blessing. Among the many men who were gathered in the sacristy, Padre Pio noticed Laurino and stared at him intently. He motioned to Laurino with his hand to step forward. Laurino became very nervous. "Padre Pio can't be looking at me," he said to himself. "He must be looking at one of the others. This is the first time I have visited his monastery. He doesn't even know me." Then he heard Padre Pio say, "Laurino, come here at once!" Laurino's whole body began to tremble. How on earth did Padre Pio know his name? "Go over to the hospital and prepare the food for my sick," Padre Pio said to Laurino. "I can't do that," Laurino replied. "I don't know how to cook. I have never cooked in my life. I wouldn't even know where to begin." Padre Pio repeated the words a second time, "Laurino, go over to the hospital and prepare food for my sick." Just the thought of it filled Laurino with profound fear. However, Padre Pio was insistent. "If I go to the hospital kitchen and try to cook, will you help me?" Laurino asked. "Yes, I will be there with you and I will assist you," Padre Pio replied.

Laurino walked out of the church and across the plaza to Padre Pio's hospital. The year was 1958. As soon as Laurino entered the hospital, he was introduced to one of the nuns who was employed there. "You must be the new cook for the hospital!" the nun exclaimed. "We have been waiting for you anxiously and are so glad that you have arrived!" Laurino was dumbfounded at her words.

Laurino was even more shocked when he walked into the hospital kitchen. Standing before him were a number of the kitchen employees. They stared at him in silence, obviously waiting for his instructions for the day's meal preparation. He looked around and noticed the massive ovens, stoves, refrigerators, and sinks. The pots and pans looked large enough to feed an army. Just looking at the huge kitchen and the variety of cooking equipment was a frightening experience.

As Laurino continued to look around the kitchen, his fears began to subside. Suddenly, everything seemed somehow familiar to him, as though he had always been a cook. He felt confident that he could do what was required of him. He then proceeded to give the instructions to the kitchen staff. That first day on the job, Laurino cooked for 450 people.

Laurino had only intended to stay a day or two in San Giovanni Rotondo before returning to his family in Padua. But suddenly he had a steady job and an income. He was the head cook of the Home for the Relief of Suffering. It was unbelievable but true. He cooked not only for the patients but also for the doctors, nurses, and all other employees. Padre Pio encouraged Laurino to bring his wife and children to live in San Giovanni Rotondo but Laurino did not want to. He felt sure that his family would not like living in the small southern town. His own first impressions of San Giovanni Rotondo had not been favorable. It was very different from Padua. But Padre Pio was insistent that Laurino bring his family to San Giovanni Rotondo and so he did.

Laurino was very grateful that he had a job. He knew that it was because of Padre Pio's prayers that he had been hired on as the head cook at the hospital. It was a blessing to be working so close to the monastery and to have the opportunity to see Padre Pio regularly.

For a reason that he was not quite sure of, Laurino began to have doubts about Padre Pio. He began to question Padre Pio's sanctity and could not seem to shake the doubts. "Yes, Padre Pio is a good priest," Laurino would say to himself, "but I don't think he is a saint." The uncertainty about Padre Pio plagued Laurino for a period of three years. He never told anyone about it, not even his wife.

One day, when Laurino was about to make his confession to Padre Pio, he was shocked to see that Padre Pio was bleeding. There was a deep cross on Padre Pio's forehead and blood was running down his face from the cross. Laurino began to tremble. He called out to Padre Pio but Padre Pio made no reply. He reached into his pocket for his handkerchief so that he could wipe the blood from Padre Pio's face but his hand seemed to freeze in his pocket. He could not move. Padre Pio stared at Laurino in silence. All that Laurino was able to do was to stare back at him. He felt like he was going to faint.

Finally, after about ten minutes, Padre Pio made a deep and long sigh as though he was coming back to awareness of the world. Padre Pio then asked Laurino how long it had been since his last confession. "It has been nine days," Laurino replied. Padre Pio began to name, one by one, the sins that Laurino had intended to confess to him. As Padre Pio pronounced the words of absolution, the cross on his forehead began to disappear. Suddenly Padre Pio looked completely normal.

The experience with Padre Pio had been so intense, that as Laurino was leaving the confessional, he let out a shriek. Those who were waiting in line to make their confession thought that perhaps he had been reprimanded by Padre Pio. Laurino began to cry. He cried for three days and three nights. Try as he might, he could not get control of his emotions. He prayed the Rosary constantly. He lost his appetite. It was very difficult for him to get to sleep at night. Every time he closed his eyes, he saw Padre Pio bleeding from the cross in the center of his forehead. It was impossible for Laurino to get the image out of his mind.

At the Home for the Relief of Suffering, Laurino's supervisor noticed the change in his behavior and had a heart to heart talk with him. "You must get control of yourself," he said to Laurino. "You have a job to do here. You have a wife and children to think of. It is obvious that you need to calm down and get more rest."

Laurino wanted with all his heart to regain his peace of mind. His world had been turned upside down by his experience in the confessional. He decided to talk to one of the Capuchins about what had happened. He told Father Clemente the full story and asked him what he thought it meant. Father Clemente did not have an answer as to why Padre Pio had revealed himself to

Laurino in such a way. He advised him to speak to Padre Pio directly and to ask for an explanation.

Laurino decided to do what Father Clemente had suggested. One day he walked to the monastery, intending to ask Padre Pio for an explanation as to what had happened in the confessional. He was almost at the monastery door, when he lost his courage and turned back to walk home. A short distance from his home, he decided to make another effort. Once again, he retraced his steps to the monastery.

At the monastery, Laurino went to the area where the Capuchins had their private quarters. He saw Padre Pio standing right outside of his cell, leaning against the door. As soon as Laurino came into view, Padre Pio immediately looked in his direction. Laurino had the feeling that Padre Pio had been expecting him. Laurino suddenly became very nervous. He wanted to talk to Padre Pio about what had happened but at the same time, he knew that he did not have the courage to do so. He turned around to walk away but he suddenly felt frozen to the spot. He was unable to move. "Laurino, what is the matter?" Padre Pio asked. Try as he might, Laurino was not able to utter a single word.

Laurino finally found his voice and said, "Padre Pio, when I made my confession to you, I saw a cross on your forehead. Blood was dripping down your face from the cross. Why did you allow me to see you suffering so much? What did it mean? Is it because of my sins that you suffer like you do?" "No, of course not," Padre Pio replied. "It was a grace that God gave you. It is that simple." From that moment on, peace returned to Laurino's heart. He finally understood. God had given him that experience in order to dispel the doubts he had about Padre Pio's sanctity. After speaking to Padre Pio, the doubts vanished and never returned.

Laurino knew that Padre Pio had a deep affection for him. He always had the strong impression that Padre Pio did not want him to venture away from San Giovanni Rotondo. After Laurino had worked at the Home for the Relief of Suffering for several years, he told Padre Pio that he was going to take some days off in order to visit his mother and father in Padua. "That will be ok," Padre Pio said. "But after you visit your relatives, I want you to come straight back. Please don't be gone too long."

Shortly before Padre Pio died, Laurino told him that he was going to take a brief vacation. "No, do not go," Padre Pio said insistently. But Laurino explained to Padre Pio that he felt the need to take the time off. "How many days do you plan to be away?" Padre Pio asked. "I want to go for seven or eight days," Laurino replied. "Use five days for your vacation but no more," Padre Pio said. Laurino agreed to his request. It wasn't long before Laurino understood why Padre Pio had insisted that he be gone for no more than five days. Laurino was back in San Giovanni Rotondo when Padre Pio passed on to his eternal reward.

What fame he (Padre Pio) had. How many followers from around the world. Why? Was it because he was a philosopher, a scholar, or because he had means at his disposal? No, it was because he said Mass humbly, heard confessions from morning until night and was a marked representative of the stigmata of our Lord. He was truly a man of prayer and suffering.

- Pope Paul VI

CHAPTER 26

Father Denys Auvray

F ather Denys Pierre Auvray, a French priest of the Dominican Order, visited Padre Pio for the first time in 1956. Father Denys was able to talk with Padre Pio during the Capuchins' recreation period, when Padre Pio and the others took a short break from their busy schedules. Since Father Denys did not speak Italian, he spoke to Padre Pio in Latin. Among all the brown-robed Capuchins who were gathered together that day, Father Denys stood out in his long white wool Dominican habit.

Father Denys was very happy that he had been able to talk to Padre Pio but he knew that it would be much better if he could converse with him in Italian rather than Latin. He also had a great desire to make his confession to Padre Pio. He decided to study the Italian language so that he could communicate freely with Padre Pio and receive spiritual direction from him.

Father Denys made many return trips to San Giovanni Rotondo. When he visited, he frequently lodged at the *Villa Pia* hotel, not far from the Capuchin monastery. One afternoon when he returned to his room at the *Villa Pia*, he noticed that it was pervaded by a strong perfume. It had happened on more than one occasion. He spoke to Luigi, one of the employees at the hotel, and voiced a complaint. "Someone is sneaking into my room when I am out and I am very concerned. I always keep my door locked when I am away but I think a woman has been unlocking my door and going inside. I have proof because there is a strong scent of perfume that is still lingering inside the room." In order to prove his point, he invited Luigi to step inside his room. Luigi entered Father Denys' room and noticed the fragrance at once. He did his best to explain the phenomenon to Father Denys. "The fragrance in your room is not because a lady has been coming in while you are away," Luigi said. "The fragrance is from Padre Pio."

Luigi explained to Father Denys that sometimes Padre Pio made his presence known by a wonderful fragrance. As he was talking to Father Denys, the room suddenly became pervaded with the strong fragrance of incense. "You see," said Luigi. "Now we notice the fragrance of incense. It just so happens that Padre Pio is at the church right now presiding at the Benediction service." The penetrating fragrance of Padre Pio's perfume stayed in Father Denys' room for the next fifteen days.

Father Denys was speaking with Padre Pio on one occasion when he made a comment about the weather. "What is it about San Giovanni Rotondo? It certainly rains alot. It rains almost constantly!" Father Denys remarked. "Yes, it does rain a lot here," Padre Pio replied. "But here it also rains the Asian flu." Evidently Padre Pio could sense what was about to happen, because shortly after he spoke the words, Father Denys came down with the Asian flu.

At the monastery of Our Lady of Grace, there were generally always long lines of people waiting to make their confession to Padre Pio. Father Denys was impressed by the fact that Padre Pio met thousands of people in his lifetime, but he saw each person as an individual. He marveled at Padre Pio's gifts of discernment and reading of hearts.

During Father Denys' visits to San Giovanni Rotondo, he met many of the people who collaborated with Padre Pio in his apostolic endeavors. Dr. Sanguinetti was one of the individuals who worked tirelessly for Padre Pio. Emilia Sanguinetti, the doctor's wife, told Father Denys that she made it a practice to go to confession to Padre Pio once each week. On one occasion when she was making her confession, she noticed that Padre Pio's face was swollen. There was also a small cut on his face. She asked him about it and he told her that the injury occurred when he was reciting the exorcism prayers over a woman who was possessed. At that moment, the devil struck out at him. Padre Pio told Emilia that if he had received the blow just a millimeter lower, it would have taken out his eye.

Father Denys heard much talk about Padre Pio's love for the angels. Every day at the monastery, Father Denys observed that Padre Pio prayed to St. Michael the Archangel. One day, he asked Padre Pio, "Are the angels really present to you? Are they with you when you retire for the night and do they ever help you get to sleep?" "Yes, they are with me," Padre Pio replied. "They help me get to sleep unless they are coming to deliver a message from my spiritual children. In that case, they come to wake me up."

On one occasion, Father Denys sent his guardian angel to Padre Pio. It happened when he was preaching a retreat to a religious order of nuns in the seaside town of Biarritz, in the southwest part of France. During the retreat, he suddenly began to feel very ill. Worried that he might not be able to continue with the program, Father Denys prayed with urgency to his guardian angel. "Dear guardian angel," he prayed, "Please take a message to Padre Pio for me. Tell him that I am very sick and I need his prayers so that I can recover. Otherwise, I do not see how I can complete this retreat." To Father Denys' great relief, he soon began to feel better and he managed to finish all the sermons in the retreat.

Later, Father Denys wrote a letter to one of the Capuchins at Our Lady of Grace monastery. He explained that he had sent his guardian angel to Padre Pio and he wanted to know if Padre Pio had received the message. The Capuchin wrote back to Father Denys and told him that he had spoken to Padre Pio about the matter. Padre Pio said that Father Denys' guardian angel had paid him a visit. Padre Pio hoped that Father Denys was feeling better and he had been praying for him ever since he had received the angelic message regarding his illness.

From time to time, Father Denys was troubled by health issues. He told Padre Pio that if the state of his health improved, he wanted to make a pilgrimage to the Holy Land. He had always had a desire to go there. "If I become stronger physically, I would like to go on pilgrimage in thanksgiving to God for the blessing of good health," Father Denys said. "Of course, Divine Providence would have to assist me, because the expenses of such a trip would be enormous, far more than I would be able to afford." Padre Pio listened to Father Denys but made no comment.

One day, in the hotel dining room, Father Denys met a couple from Lebanon, Mr. and Mrs. DeChabert and was happy that he could converse with them in French. They told Father Denys that they had come to San Giovanni Rotondo in order to ask Padre Pio for his prayers. Their son had died tragically in an accident in India just three months previously.

Father Denys felt very sorry for the couple. He knew that it was almost impossible for the pilgrims to speak to Padre Pio privately. There were visitors at the monastery from all parts of the world and the Capuchins did their best to shield Padre Pio from the crowds. Because Father Denys was a priest, he had easier access to Padre Pio. He decided to speak to Padre Pio and see if he could arrange for Mr. and Mrs. DeChabert to meet him.

Father Denys and Mr. and Mrs. DeChabert continued to converse on various subjects. Since the couple lived in Lebanon, Father Denys told them that he had always been interested in the Holy Land. He asked them if they had ever traveled there and they replied that they had. "I am particularly interested in Jerusalem," Father Denys said. "Have you ever been there?" he asked the couple. "Of course we have," Mr. DeChabert replied. "It is only an hour plane ride from where we live in Beirut. And you, have you ever been to the Holy Land?" Mr. DeChabert asked. "No, I have not," Father Denys replied. "I have always wanted to go there but my health is not the best and besides, I would never be able to afford it." "It wouldn't be expensive at all," Mr. DeChabert said. "It would be free. I am going to give you a first-class ticket. I am the Director of Public Transportation in Lebanon." Father Denys was astonished. He thought about his lifelong desire to visit the Holy Land and he remembered the time he had spoken to Padre Pio about it. He had the feeling that Padre Pio had something to do with the unexpected gift.

Father Denys went to the monastery and told Padre Pio about Mr. and Mrs. DeChabert. "The couple's son has recently died," Father Denys said. "They have come here to ask you for your prayers," he added. "All right," Padre Pio answered. "I will be happy to pray for their son." "But they have a great desire to meet you," Father Denys said. "It will not be necessary," Padre

Pio replied. "But it is necessary," Father Denys answered. "They need to see you."

That afternoon, Padre Pio presided at the Benediction service, just like he did every day. After Benediction, Father Denys told Mr. and Mrs. DeChabert to follow him into the sacristy. Padre Pio would be there shortly. When Padre Pio came into the sacristy, Father Denys introduced him to the couple and said, "Padre Pio, this is the couple I was telling you about. Their son died three months ago." Mr. DeChabert had a photograph of his son, and he gave it to Padre Pio. Padre Pio held the photo in his hand and looked at it in silence. Finally, he blessed it. Mr. and Mrs. DeChabert felt greatly consoled.

In 1963, Father Denys traveled to the Holy Land for a three-week stay. Later, he visited Mr. and Mrs. DeChabert in Beirut, Lebanon. Before the trip to the DeChaberts' homeland, Father Denys spoke to Padre Pio about it. "In that country, you will suffer," Padre Pio said. Father Denys was not sure what he meant, but he was soon to find out. The widespread poverty in Lebanon was very painful for Father Denys to witness. To see the privation and the hardship of so many people, caused him great suffering.

To Father Denys, Padre Pio was a model of holiness for all people, both priests and laity. Whenever Padre Pio spoke about God, Father Denys always had the sense that he was speaking about Someone that he had intimate contact with, Someone that he knew very well. When Father Denys looked back on the many times he was able to visit Padre Pio through the years, he knew how truly fortunate he was. To Father Denys, every encounter with Padre Pio had been a time of grace.

In heaven, everything will be spring as far as beauty is concerned, autumn as far as enjoyment is concerned, summer as far as love is concerned. There will be no winter; but here winter is necessary to exercise self-denial and a thousand other little but beautiful virtues which are exercised at times of sterility.

St. Pio of Pietrelcina

CHAPTER 27

Padre Pio - A True Spiritual Father

Yvette Levasseur experienced sadness and hardship from her earliest years. Her parents both died when she was just a child. After her parents' death, her aunt and uncle who lived in Paris, France adopted her. Yvette moved from her home in Great Britain to live with them. Her aunt and uncle owned a small business in the downtown section of Paris where they made shoes for the handicapped. Yvette soon learned the trade and was able to help them in the shoe shop.

When Yvette was sixteen years old, her aunt passed away. Just two years later, her uncle also died. Yvette was on her own and very much alone in the big and bustling city of Paris. She gained strength by attending daily Mass at Our Lady of Victories parish.

After her aunt and uncle died, Yvette continued to make shoes. She lived alone in a tiny room above the shoe shop. It was a struggle to keep the business going and she barely had enough money for necessities. At times, bread and milk were her only staples as she could afford no more.

One day at the bookstore in the parish of Our Lady of Victories, Yvette saw a book on Padre Pio. It looked so interesting that she purchased it. After she read the book, she had a great desire to visit Padre Pio in San Giovanni Rotondo. However, she knew it would be impossible as she did not have the financial means to make such a trip. By a stroke of luck, shortly after reading the book, she met a couple who were going to San Giovanni Rotondo. They invited her to go with them and she happily agreed. The year was 1958. She was able to attend Padre Pio's Mass and to experience what she called the "true greatness" of Padre Pio's presence.

After Yvette returned to Paris, she wrote a letter to Padre Pio asking for his prayers. She received a letter back which said that Padre Pio was praying for her and that he sent her his blessing. Shortly after, Yvette was offered a job. A woman wanted to hire Yvette to accompany her family on a two-month holiday trip to Savoia and tutor her two small children. Yvette thought that it would be to her advantage to accept the job but first she wanted Padre Pio's approval. She wrote to Padre Pio and asked him for advice. Soon a letter came back in the mail. "Do not take the job; remain in Paris," were Padre Pio's words of counsel. Yvette followed his advice.

Meanwhile, business at the shoe shop continued to decline. Yvette decided that it would be better to sell the business and get what money she could out of it rather than continue on a downward spiral and possibly lose everything. She wrote to Padre Pio again and asked for his advice. Once again, the answer from Padre Pio was a definite "no." Yvette trusted Padre Pio completely and did not put the business up for sale.

A third opportunity soon presented itself. A woman wanted to hire Yvette to work as an assistant in her boutique in Luxembourg. To Yvette, it sounded like a good opportunity. It would mean that she would have to leave Paris, but she didn't mind. It was proving to be too difficult for her to make a living there. For the third time, she asked Padre Pio for advice and for the third time, his answer was "no." Yvette decided to obey him blindly.

Shortly after that, Yvette met a very nice man in Paris named Maurice. Before long, they married. Much to Maurice's surprise, shortly before the wedding, he inherited a very profitable business from one of his relatives. Because of the inheritance, Maurice and Yvette were able to live very comfortably. The financial worries that had plagued Yvette for so long, were over for good. Soon their marriage was blessed with a beautiful son. Yvette returned to San Giovanni Rotondo to thank Padre Pio for his prayers and for her many blessings - her loving husband and her new son. To their great joy, Yvette and Maurice were blessed with two more children.

When Yvette thought about her life and all that had happened to her, it became clear to her why Padre Pio had advised her to stay in Paris. It was in Paris that she met her wonderful husband, Maurice. If she had accepted the job opportunities that had presented themselves, she would have had to leave Paris. If she had left Paris, her life would have taken a completely different turn. How happy she was that she followed Padre Pio's advice.

After losing her parents and her aunt and uncle when she was young, Yvette had a great desire for a family of her own. Because she had experienced loneliness and personal loss in her youth, she knew the value and the blessing of family life. A good family was a true gift from God. Yvette would never take her family for granted. She had trusted Padre Pio enough to follow his counsel, even though at the time, his advice seemed hard to understand. In the end, his guidance proved to be perfect.

———

In 1947, Nicola De Vincentis worked as the head station master at the San Severo train station in Italy. One morning upon rising from bed, Nicola's legs gave way from under him and he collapsed on the floor. His entire body felt paralyzed. He was seen and examined by a number of doctors. None, however, were able to determine the cause of his problem. Finally, Nicola's primary doctor urged him to travel to Rome and see the well-known neurologist, Dr. Ugo Cerletti.

Dr. Cerletti examined Nicola and ran a number of tests. He was finally diagnosed as having a tropical virus. The long-term effects of the virus were severe. Dr. Cerletti tried to break the news as gently as he could to Nicola. He told Nicola that he would never be able to recover completely from the virus. He believed that with therapy, Nicola would someday be able to walk again. However, he was certain that Nicola would have to use crutches for the rest of his life. Unfortunately, it would be impossible for him to continue working at the San Severo train station.

Nicola was put on an intense physical therapy program which included galvanic stimulation, leg, thigh, and arm massage, and injections. Very slowly, his condition began to improve as movement returned to his body. He had a problem with his equilibrium which caused him to feel dizzy most of the time. Because he was so unsteady on his feet, he was advised to use a walker for support.

After a five-month stay at the rehabilitation clinic, Nicola was finally released. Shortly after returning to his home, he tripped and broke his right foot. He had to go back to the clinic where he spent another forty days. A short time later, the Foggia Administration of Health gave him a thorough physical examination and officially declared him to be disabled. He was discharged from his job as station master. The ruling was very difficult for Nicola to come to terms with. Thinking about the loss of his job and his uncertain future, filled him with anxiety.

Nicola's friend, Father Placido of San Marco in Lamis who lived at the Capuchin monastery in San Severo, advised him to visit Padre Pio. Nicola had heard of the saintly priest but he knew very little about him. By this time, he had been suffering from the tropical virus for eighteen months. As a last resort, he decided to accept Father Placido's suggestion to see Padre Pio.

Nicola and Father Placido took a bus to San Giovanni Rotondo. The bus driver would not take them up the hill to the monastery of Our Lady of Grace because the road was in such poor condition. Instead, they were dropped off at a crossroads with no choice but to walk the rest of the distance. Holding tightly to Father Placido's arm, as well as using a cane for support, Nicola made a great effort to walk up the hill. However, after taking just a few steps, he lost his balance and fell to the ground. It became clear that he was not going to be able to walk. Father Placido had no resort but to carry Nicola on his back all the way up the hill. Although he was elderly, Father Placido managed to get Nicola up the incline and to the monastery.

When Nicola and Father Placido finally arrived at Our Lady of Grace monastery, they found Padre Pio taking a few moments of leisure in the monastery garden. Upon being introduced to Nicola, Padre Pio embraced him lovingly. He asked Nicola to sit next to him on the garden bench. Nicola then told Padre Pio about his illness and all that he had suffered since he had contracted the tropical virus. The next morning, Nicola and Father Placido attended Padre Pio's Mass. Padre Pio made special arrangements for Nicola to sit in a chair that was placed very close to him at the altar.

Father Placido and Nicola had to return by bus to San Severo after the Mass. Father Placido wanted to make sure that Nicola had a chance to say goodbye to Padre Pio. However, Padre Pio had retired to his cell after the morning Mass and nobody was to disturb him. Father Placido took Nicola to the private quarters of the monastery. He knocked on Padre Pio's cell door and said, "Padre Pio, Nicola and I are leaving now by bus for San Severo. Nicola would like to say goodbye to you." Padre Pio opened the door immediately. He gave Nicola a blessing and said to him, "Trust in the grace of the Lord." He then added, "When you get home, I want you to take a ride on your bicycle. After that, you should make another request for a medical examination from the office of the Administration of Health in Rome."

Nicola thought deeply about Padre Pio's words. Padre Pio's recommendation that he ride a bicycle seemed like very strange advice. For a man in Nicola's condition, riding a bicycle was a dangerous proposition. Even if he wanted to, Nicola was quite certain that he would not be able to manage it. He had not even been able to walk up the hill to Padre Pio's monastery. Father Placido had carried him up. Nicola still had problems with his equilibrium and balance. He had frequent dizzy spells. Padre Pio must have been joking to suggest that he ride a bicycle. But Nicola knew that he wasn't joking. It was obvious that he was perfectly serious.

On the return trip to San Severo, Father Placido and Nicola discussed the matter. Father Placido had full confidence in Padre Pio. He encouraged Nicola to do what Padre Pio had advised him to do. "Padre Pio told you to trust in the grace of the Lord," Father Placido said. "You must follow his advice. Pray about it as well. He has his own reasons for asking you to ride a bicycle. I think you should do what he said." Nicola prayed for guidance. After praying, he seemed to have a great boost of faith and greater confidence in Padre Pio. He decided to follow Padre Pio's unusual advice.

Upon returning home, Nicola got his bicycle out. He waited till the late evening when all of his neighbors had gone indoors. He did not want to make a spectacle of himself. He got on his bicycle and rode it about one hundred yards before taking a fall. He hit the ground so hard that he was almost knocked unconscious. Thinking that he might be dying, he prayed and begged God for help. All of a sudden, he felt someone lift him up from the ground and place him back on the seat of his bicycle. But how was it possible? He was alone. There was no one in sight. Back on the bicycle, he found that he could pedal it with ease. His joints and limbs suddenly felt flexible. The muscle constriction and paralysis had disappeared and he felt strong and energized. His equilibrium had also returned. He knew at that moment that he had been healed.

Like Padre Pio had asked him to do, Nicola went to the Railway Health Administration of Rome and made a request for another medical examination. He marked down on his application that he had received a miraculous healing. A number of doctors and neurologists examined him, under the supervision of Dr. Ugo Cerletti. They were dumbfounded by the change in his condition. After a thorough examination, he was declared fit to resume his job. He returned to his position as head station master at San Severo and worked there until he reached retirement age. He enjoyed excellent health free from any symptoms of the tropical virus. He remained a devoted spiritual son of Padre Pio for the rest of his life.

———————

Francesco Ugliano was making preparations to get his driver's license. He was taking driving lessons and studying for the written examination. He was also trying to decide what type of a car to purchase. Since Francesco was one of Padre Pio's spiritual sons, his wife suggested that he speak to Padre Pio about his plans and ask for his blessing.

Francesco decided to follow his wife's advice. The monastery church of Our Lady of Grace was very crowded on the day of Francesco's visit. He knew that it would be impossible to talk to Padre Pio that day. He asked Enzo Mercurio, who had close contact with Padre Pio, to relay the message and he agreed to do so. When Padre Pio learned of Francesco's desire to get a driver's license, he was strongly against the idea. "Tell Francesco that I do not give my permission for him to drive!" he said to Enzo. "Absolutely not!" he added.

When Francesco heard the news, he discontinued his driving lessons at once and put the whole matter behind him. A year later, Francesco went to the monastery of Our Lady of Grace in order to make his confession to Padre Pio. Afterward, he planned to talk to him about his desire to have a car.

Before he could bring the subject up, Padre Pio said to him, "All right, I give you permission to get a car. But I ask one favor of you. Never speed when you are driving!"

Francesco was elated. When he bought his first car, he wanted to give it a name. He named it simply, "Padre Pio's Car." Many years later, he was returning home from San Giovanni Rotondo with his wife. He knew that he shouldn't be driving. Through negligence, he had let his license expire two years previously. Francesco fell asleep at the wheel and dreamed that he was in a hail storm. The "hail storm" was actually the sound of his back window shattering. His car flipped over and then landed on soft ground in a field that had just been tilled. He and his wife were taken to the Home for the Relief of Suffering. They were examined, declared to be in good condition, and then released.

———

David Fielding had many deep-seated prejudices and false stereotypes in regard to the Catholic Church. David, who was English, was a Protestant, a member of the Anglican Church. When he was eighteen years old, his cynicism reached a high point. He sarcastically referred to the Catholic Church as a mixture of "Italian ornateness and Irish superstition." His hostility toward the Church seemed to intensify as time passed. Later, he began drifting far away from his Christian roots and started to gravitate more toward Eastern philosophies.

One day David wandered into the public library hoping to find something good to read. He glanced at a book on St. Francis of Assisi and also one on Padre Pio and decided to take them home. He suspected that they would be exaggerated tales of miracles and myths for the gullible mind. After David read the books, he had to admit that his preconceived assessment had been totally wrong. He was deeply edified by reading the life of St. Francis of Assisi. The book on Padre Pio too, was also filled with inspiration. The books made such an impression on him that he went to a store and purchased them. Now, they could have a permanent place in his library. He then reread them many times. Even though he felt that St. Francis and Padre Pio were extraordinary saints, he nevertheless felt sorry for them. Unfortunately, they were both Catholics. David's embittered attitude caused him to wish that the two saints had been Anglicans like he was, and English rather than Italian. He was sure they would have soared to even greater spiritual heights if they had been affiliated with the Church of England.

After reading the two books, David's life gradually began to change. Within his heart, he began to feel a deep hunger for God. He visited the Anglican Society of St. Francis and considered joining. He took a simple factory job because it allowed him the time he needed for prayer and quiet reflection. He continued to meditate on the lives of St. Francis and Padre Pio.

David decided to make a thorough investigation of the Catholic Church. Through his reading and study, he realized more than ever before that there were insurmountable barriers that would forever keep him from becoming a Catholic. He truly disagreed with many of the Church's precepts, especially the teachings regarding the papacy as well as devotion to the Virgin Mary. At the time, he also felt that he was in a vocational crisis. He did not know what to do with his life, what career path to follow. After much thought, he believed that there was only one person who might be able to supply him with the answer. That was Padre Pio.

With great care, David wrote Padre Pio a letter asking for his advice about his vocation. He took the letter to a translation agency and had it translated into Italian. At David's request, the Anglican vicar at his church, kindly allowed the letter to lie on top of the church's altar for twenty-four hours. The next day, David mailed the letter.

About a week later, David happened to glance at some of the books in his library that were on Catholic Doctrine. All of a sudden, he felt a tremendous shift in his way of thinking. As David said, it was as though a "mental switch" was turned on inside of him. He was immediately conscious of a great change in his mind. At that moment, he changed from a nonbeliever to a believer in all that the Catholic Church taught and proclaimed. Suddenly, everything seemed so simple and so right.

A week later, David received a reply to his letter. One of Padre Pio's Capuchin secretaries wrote to him on behalf of Padre Pio, sending him Padre Pio's message. A holy card was included in the letter. Padre Pio wanted David to place himself under the guidance of a good priest. He wanted David to know that he was praying for him so that God would lead him on the right path.

David's unexplainable conversion occurred halfway between his writing the letter to Padre Pio and his receiving Padre Pio's reply in the mail. He was convinced that the moment of his conversion occurred when Padre Pio had received his letter and was lifting him up in prayer. He felt that there could be no other explanation for his radical change of mind.

Soon after that, David joined the Catholic Church. Although Padre Pio had not made any specific recommendations in his letter regarding David's vocation, everything began to fall into place. First David taught the Catholic faith in schools and later was able to reach even larger numbers, through the field of publishing. He had received many signs of God's loving hand, guiding and directing his life. He felt a constant flow of blessings. To know that Padre Pio was praying for his intentions was one of the greatest blessings of all.

————

Judy Hayes of Holiday, Florida woke up one morning to find that a large lump had appeared on her neck. She went to the doctor that very morning and was put through a multitude of tests. The results were not good. Judy was diagnosed with Hodgkin Lymphoma in stage four, the final stage. The cancer had already spread to her bones.

Before her first chemotherapy treatment, Judy went to a Catholic Gift Shop. She wanted to get some prayer and novena cards of her favorite saints. She was nervous about receiving chemotherapy and planned to pray throughout the treatment.

In the Catholic Gift Shop, the prayer cards and novenas were on a small rack that could be turned in a circular fashion. Judy turned the rack three times, and three times it stopped at a holy card of Padre Pio. However, her devotion was to St. Jude, St. Anthony, and the Infant of Prague. When she found what she was looking for, she made her purchases. She was just opening the door to walk out of the shop when she stopped and turned back. Judy felt guilty. It truly seemed like the little prayer card of Padre Pio had been calling to her. "O.K. Padre Pio, I will take you home with me," Judy said silently. "I pray that you will be with me and heal me of the cancer."

The chemotherapy and radiation treatments made Judy very ill. Not long after, she came down with pneumonia and had to be admitted to the hospital. She became weaker by the day. She lost the ability to walk. Her condition seemed to go from bad to worse. She developed dangerous blood clots and also had to be treated for congestive heart failure. She was in and out of the intensive care unit. She had to go into surgery to have her gall bladder removed. Finally, after many months in the hospital, she was sent to a nursing home. However, she soon developed an infection and had to be readmitted to the hospital.

But Judy's condition did not improve. She was placed on a ventilator for nine days. She drifted in and out of consciousness, barely holding on to life. Through the long days and nights, she petitioned Padre Pio to help her. She prayed to him, dialogued with him, entreated him, begged him. For some reason, it was Padre Pio that she addressed her urgent prayers to rather than to the other saints that she had been devoted to for years.

One particular day, as Judy lay silent and immobile in her hospital bed, she heard the nurse supervisor talking to some of the other medical staff. "Before you leave your shift tonight, prepare Judy Hayes' death certificate," the nurse supervisor said. "Make sure you have the doctor sign it before he goes home. I have been observing her throughout the day. She is going to die tonight." Judy was devastated by the words. Everything within her cried out against it. She didn't want to die. She couldn't die! She begged Padre Pio to help her.

People everywhere were praying for Judy Hayes. One of her dear friends, who was in a nursing home, prayed a Rosary for Judy every morning at 2:00 a.m. To the amazement of everyone, Judy's strength slowly returned. She was eventually discharged from the hospital and was able to return to her home.

After Judy's recovery, she had a great desire to promote Padre Pio. She was convinced that she was alive and well because of his intercession. She made it a habit to keep Padre Pio prayer cards in her purse at all times and she found many opportunities to give them to others. People were inspired by her faith and trust in God. Many people were helped, just by meeting Judy.

One day, when Judy was enjoying an afternoon in the Florida sunshine, she happened to see a woman that she felt urged to speak to. The woman was a complete stranger to her. Not knowing what possessed her, Judy went up to the woman and asked her if she was a Catholic. Judy was not in the habit of asking people their religious affiliation, especially not a perfect stranger.

It simply was not an appropriate thing to do. The woman however, did not mind the question at all, and answered in the affirmative. She seemed truly happy that Judy had spoken to her. Judy then gave her a Padre Pio prayer card. She told her a little bit about Padre Pio and showed her the beautiful prayer on the back of the card. "Oh, you are an answer to my prayers!" the woman said to Judy. She then went on to explain her situation. For weeks, the woman had been taking care of her dear husband who had a terminal illness. She had become very depressed as she watched him slowly dying. She had not wanted to leave her husband that day but she had done so at the insistence of a friend. Her friend was adamant that she take a needed break. Her friend was taking care of her husband in her place that afternoon.

The woman explained that she had been praying when Judy came up and spoke to her. "Oh God," she prayed, "Please send me a sign of hope. I need greater faith in You and I need strength to go on. I am so depressed. Please send me someone who will help me!" With her eyes brimming with tears, the woman thanked Judy for the holy card of Padre Pio and assured her that she would pray to him.

For a great part of humanity Padre Pio has been a reference point, a means of find-
ing again the sense of the Divine. To have seen him celebrate Mass has put us in contact
with a world we believed to have vanished, swept away by science. This was his essential
function: to put man in the presence of God, to touch Him.

- Father Domenico Grassi

CHAPTER 28

Mario Bruschi

*T*he testimony that follows is the result of many in depth telephone conversations
we had with Mario Bruschi regarding his trip to San Giovanni Rotondo in 1957.
Mario was very generous with the time he gave to us. He patiently answered our many,
many questions. We also visited him at the annual Padre Pio Celebration at the Fatima
Shrine in Washington, New Jersey and were inspired by the beautiful afternoon dedi-
cated to Padre Pio.

In the summer of 1957, Mario Bruschi and his mother Adele, traveled
from their home in New York City to the town of Ponte Strambo, in northern
Italy, to visit relatives. Mario's mother had just read a biography of Padre Pio
which she had enjoyed immensely. She shared some of the details of Padre
Pio's life with Mario. She decided that she wanted to travel to San Giovanni
Rotondo to attend Padre Pio's Mass and she asked Mario to accompany her.
But to twenty-three-year-old Mario, the prospect did not sound very interest-
ing. He was having a great time in Ponte Strambo, meeting new friends and

going dancing at the local night clubs in the area. At that time in his life, his Catholic faith meant very little to him. To him, there were alot more interesting things to do rather than go to a monastery to see an elderly friar. He declined his mother's invitation.

Mario's aunt Rina spoke to him about Adele's plan to visit San Giovanni Rotondo. "Your mother should not make the trip alone," his aunt said. "It will be much safer if you go with her." Mario realized the truth of his aunt's words and finally agreed to accompany his mother. He thought that they would probably spend one day at Padre Pio's monastery and then be on their way home. He wanted to spend as much of the summer as he could with his new found friends in Ponte Strambo.

Mario was irritated with his mother for not telling him until after they boarded the train, that it would be no less than a twelve-hour trip to get to San Giovanni Rotondo. When they finally arrived at the monastery of Our Lady of Grace, the first order of business was to get a ticket for Padre Pio's confessional. Adele was informed that she would have to wait ten days for her number to be called.

The thought of being stuck in San Giovanni Rotondo for ten long days was very difficult for Mario to accept. There was the monastery and the church and practically nothing else in the area. Adele encouraged Mario to get a ticket for the confessional and told him that she was certain that he would not regret it. It would be a wonderful opportunity. Reluctantly, he asked for a ticket from the Capuchin in the booking office.

As the days passed, Mario and Adele learned the daily routine of the pilgrims in San Giovanni Rotondo. Everything revolved around the small church of Our Lady of Grace. Almost all of the visitors to San Giovanni Rotondo spent their days in the church because that was where they could find Padre Pio. The Capuchins would frequently stand at the front of the church and order everyone to stop talking. "Silencio!" they would repeat, but no one paid any attention to them. However, when Padre Pio called for order in the church, everyone stopped talking at once.

Mario and his mother attended Padre Pio's early morning Mass which began at 5:00 a.m. For the pilgrims, it was the highlight of the day. For Mario, it was a test of patience. It was the longest weekday Mass that he had ever attended in his life. Because Padre Pio became deeply absorbed in prayer during the Holy Sacrifice, there were many extended periods of silence. Mario found himself becoming annoyed with the time it took for Padre Pio to say the Mass. To him, it seemed excessive.

Because the church was too small to accommodate the crowds and because of the summer heat, the Mass was held in an outdoor arcade. Mario made sure to avoid making eye contact with Padre Pio. Having heard that Padre Pio had the gift of reading hearts, the thought of direct eye contact with him made Mario feel uncomfortable.

It was the custom for the Capuchins to invite the pilgrims who had traveled from a distance to serve at Padre Pio's Mass. Mario was asked if he would like to be an altar server but he declined the invitation. Kneeling on the hard stone by the altar for such a long period of time was not something that he wanted to attempt.

As the days passed, the annoyance that Mario had initially felt during Padre Pio's Mass, vanished. Instead, he began to feel greatly uplifted. Although the Mass still lasted the same length of time, for some reason the time no longer seemed to drag, but instead passed quickly. Mario watched Padre Pio's movements closely. Sometimes Padre Pio's eyes would twitch. At times, he would stare upwards in a fixed spot and remain completely motionless. He seemed to be seeing something that no one else could see. His deep communion with God was very evident.

Each day at noon, Mario and his mother attended the public recitation of the Angelus. Daily, Padre Pio blessed religious articles, and on occasion he also blessed automobiles and sometimes even animals. In the late afternoon, Mario and his mother attended the Rosary followed by the Benediction service in the church. In the evening, they joined the other pilgrims who made their way to an open field outside the monastery. With lighted candles, they waited for Padre Pio to come to the little window of his cell. All would wave to him and bid him goodnight.

One afternoon, Mario walked into the monastery church of Our Lady of Grace while a wedding was in progress. Padre Pio happened to be the celebrant that day. Mario had his camera with him at the time and was happy for the opportunity to take some photos. Padre Pio noticed that Mario was taking pictures and motioned for one of the Capuchins to speak to him. He was informed that he was not allowed to take photographs inside the church, so he quickly put his camera away. He was happy that he had been able to take about seven pictures before he was advised to stop. When he went to get the film developed, all of the pictures came out blank. He asked the film developer for an explanation since he had used brand-new film but no reason for the malfunction could be discovered. Later, Mario learned that it was not unusual for photos to come out blank on the occasions when Padre Pio did not want to be photographed.

Another time, Mario happened to be in the sacristy of the church as Padre Pio was putting on his vestments in preparation for Benediction. Padre Pio first wrapped a short, white cloth called an amice, around his neck and shoulders. Next, came the long linen tunic called an alb, then the rope (cincture) which he placed around his waist, and finally the stole which he put around his shoulders, over the alb. The moment that Padre Pio put on the amice, Mario perceived the beautiful fragrance of roses filling the sacristy.

Mario's attitude underwent a change as the days passed. There was a peace and serenity in San Giovanni Rotondo that could be tangibly felt. It seemed to envelop the whole town. Mario described the beautiful church of Our Lady of Grace as "Heaven on earth." The day for Mario to make his confession to Padre Pio finally arrived. He grew increasingly nervous as the time approached. He had heard about Padre Pio's gifts of discernment and dreaded the thought that Padre Pio might be able to read his soul. Mario was afraid that Padre Pio might be able to see the sins in his life of which he was very much ashamed.

Mario was standing near the front of the confessional line when he saw an incident that filled his heart with trepidation. Padre Pio, in a voice full of authority, reprimanded a man and ordered him out of the confessional. Deeply embarrassed, and with his cheeks flushed red, the man had no other recourse but to walk past all the men who were waiting in the line. Everyone saw what had happened.

Upon seeing the unfortunate man leave the church, Mario lost his courage. He began to tremble and to fear the worst. He hoped that it was time for the confessions to end for the morning, but no such luck. "The same thing will probably happen to me, as happened to that poor man," Mario said to himself. "After all, I am not in the best shape spiritually. I have been negligent in the practice of my faith for a long time. I am sure that Padre Pio will see it at once."

Mario told the man who was standing behind him in line that he could go in front of him. "But Padre Pio is pointing at you. He wants to see you," the man replied. Mario looked in Padre Pio's direction and found that it was indeed true. Padre Pio was looking directly at Mario and beckoning him to come into the confessional. The man standing behind Mario in line gave him a shove forward.

At that time, the men's confessions were heard in an open confessional in the sacristy of the church. Padre Pio sat on a chair and a wooden kneeler was placed in front of him for the penitent. A curtain was provided for privacy. Very slowly, Mario walked toward the confessional. Slowly, he reached for the curtain and pulled it closed. He was hoping that by his slow and deliberate movements, he would have at least a few minutes to buy some time to collect himself and to regain his composure.

After Mario closed the curtain and knelt down, Padre Pio patted his hand lovingly and said to him gently, "Be tranquil, my son. Calm yourself." The words seemed to be charged with power for at once Mario felt a great tranquility, a wonderful peace take possession of his soul. The trembling in his body stopped altogether. Padre Pio then asked Mario a number of questions. "Do you say your morning prayers?" Padre Pio asked. "No, I do not," Mario replied. "Do you say your night prayers?" Padre Pio asked. Once again Mario had to say no. "Do you tell lies?" "Yes, I have told lies," Mario replied. It went on like that with more questions, more admissions. Padre Pio seemed to know exactly the right questions to ask. They were all related to Mario's areas of weakness. Mario had the feeling that Padre Pio knew the answers to the questions, even before he asked them. Mario had no need to tell his sins; Padre Pio was naming them for him.

As Padre Pio continued with his questions, Mario could not help but stare at him. Padre Pio's face was beautiful. There was a luminous quality about it, something Mario had never seen before. Mario felt like he was looking at goodness itself. Padre Pio's cheeks were rosy. He looked robust and healthy. Mario stared at Padre Pio in awe and was at a loss for words. He felt himself lifted into a heavenly place. A deep and profound feeling of spiritual joy coursed through his body and his soul. "Padre Pio's eyes were piercing my spirit," Mario said. "I felt that Christ himself was there hearing my confession."

Mario told Padre Pio that he did not know what to do with his life. "I don't know what career to pursue," Mario said. "Could you give me some advice?" "Preghiamo, figiu mi," (Pray, my son) Padre Pio answered. Padre Pio's voice was so sweet, so tender. He spoke Italian in the Pugliese/Neopolitan dialect. Mario felt fortunate that he could understand the dialect. Mario then asked Padre Pio about a personal matter concerning one of his brothers. Padre Pio's response was, "Pray, my son." Lastly, Mario spoke to Padre Pio about his mother. Once again, Padre Pio advised him, "Pray, my son." Padre Pio was so kind, so gentle. "Go in peace, my son," Padre Pio said as Mario kissed his hand. He gave Mario a blessing. The confession was over but Mario did not want to leave the confessional. He wanted to stay with Padre Pio forever.

The thought came to Mario that if Padre Pio had asked him to stay on in San Giovanni Rotondo, he would have agreed to it in an instant. He would gladly be willing to do any work, no matter how small or menial, just to be able to be near Padre Pio. But Mario knew that was just wishful thinking. He and his mother would soon be going back to the northern part of Italy and later they would return to their home in New York City. Mario thought about the long line of men just a few feet away, waiting patiently for the same opportunity, the same blessing that he had just received. He forced himself to get up and walk out of the confessional.

Later on in the afternoon, Mario saw Father Giovanni Battista who asked him how his confession to Padre Pio had gone. Mario shared that it had been a true gift, a truly "heavenly" experience. "Did Padre Pio say the words, *Ego te absolvo?* Father Giovanni Battista asked. "No, he did not," Mario replied. "That means that you received a blessing from Padre Pio but not absolution," Father Giovanni Battista explained. "Don't worry about it, though. Padre Pio on occasion withholds absolution. Believe me. He knows very well what he is doing. He has his own reasons and we trust his judgment completely. He is guided by God. Just follow me into the monastery and I will be able to hear your confession and give you absolution. Padre Pio knows that we Capuchins hear the confessions and give absolution to those who, for one reason or another, have not received absolution from him. That is what we always do in these cases. Everything will be all right." But Mario was disappointed, deeply disappointed. Although Father Giovanni Battista tried to assure him that everything was all right, in his heart, Mario wondered what had gone wrong.

Many people made their confession to Padre Pio but had no real desire to amend their life. They knew that they would continue to commit the same sins; they were not ready to give them up. It became easy for them to go from sinful acts to confession and right back to the sinful acts. Their souls were in grave danger but they remained completely indifferent to their situation. Padre Pio knew that they had to be shaken out of their spiritual lethargy. Something had to grab their attention. Being denied absolution was a definite "attention-grabber." In this way, Padre Pio let the penitents know that by their own decision, they had forfeited the grace of God.

Padre Pio was keenly aware of his responsibility to those who made their confession to him. His greatest desire was to help people draw closer to God. It hurt him to see the way people neglected God, their highest good. He wrote a letter to his spiritual director on one occasion and said, "I am alone in bearing the weight of everyone. And the thought of not being able to give some spiritual relief to those that Jesus sends to me, the thought of seeing so many souls who want to justify their sins and thus spite their highest good - afflicts me, tortures me, makes me a martyr. It wears me out, wracks my brain, and breaks my heart."

Mario followed Father Giovanni Battista into the private quarters of the monastery. He made his confession to Father Giovanni Battista and received absolution. He was assured that he was in a state of grace. As they left the small chapel and walked down the corridor, they passed by Padre Pio's cell and noticed that the door was open. A young altar boy was assisting Padre Pio and helping him put his sandals on. Mario was startled to see that Padre Pio's bed was completely covered with letters. The amount of letters was so great that not even the blankets on his bed could be seen.

"Mario, this is your chance," Father Giovanni Battista said. "Padre Pio is in his cell. Stand right by his door and wait for him. You can ask him for the absolution that he did not give you." But Mario did not think that he had the courage to ask Padre Pio for absolution.

Padre Pio walked out of his cell and saw Mario standing in the hall. For some reason, Father Giovanni Battista was no place to be seen. As Padre Pio drew closer, Mario knelt down. "What is it you want?" Padre Pio asked. "I think that you forgot to give me absolution when I made my confession to you," Mario replied. "If it is possible, I would like to receive it at this time."

Padre Pio placed his hands on Mario's head in a blessing, just as he had done before. Mario once again kissed his hand and waited, but the words, *Ego, te absolvo*, were not spoken. Padre Pio then started to walk down the corridor but before he had gone even ten steps, he stopped and looked back at Mario. He stared at him in silence. Then he raised his eyes upward and remained motionless for some moments. He then turned and continued to walk down the corridor until he disappeared from view.

The next day, Mario and his mother would be leaving San Giovanni Rotondo to take the train back to Ponte Strambo. Father Giovanni Battista knew that Mario wanted to say goodbye to Padre Pio. He told Mario that Padre Pio would be at the monastery stairway at 11:00 a.m. the next morning. If Mario could be there at the same time, he could receive a final blessing from Padre Pio.

At the appointed time, Mario was standing at the stairs where Father Giovanni Battista had indicated. He was able to speak to Padre Pio briefly. Mario told him that he and his mother were leaving that day and he wanted to bid him goodbye. Padre Pio gave him a final blessing and said, "May the angel of God accompany you on your journey."

As Padre Pio started to walk down the stairs, Mario took hold of his arm to assist him. One of the Capuchins held his other arm for support. As they slowly descended the stairs, Mario could tell that Padre Pio was suffering greatly. Mario knew what a privilege it was to be able to help Padre Pio down the stairs. As they made their way toward the landing, many people were reaching out their hands, trying to touch Padre Pio and speak to him.

Before they left San Giovanni Rotondo to return to Ponte Strambo, Mario's mother, Adele, obtained another ticket for Padre Pio's confessional. She explained to Mario that they were going to have to return to the monastery in just a matter of days. She had been so excited about being able to make her confession to Padre Pio that she forgot to kiss his hand, and she had a great desire to do so. When getting her new ticket, she tried to estimate how many days the wait would be before her number was called. She estimated correctly, for she and Mario returned to the monastery on the very day that her name and number were called. She had a chance to see Padre Pio once again and to kiss his hand. To Adele, it was well worth the twelve-hour train trip.

Mario reflected many times on every detail of his trip to San Giovanni Rotondo. It had been a painful experience for him to realize that Padre Pio had not given him absolution. It caused him to do some very deep soul-searching. Mario knew that he had been negligent in the practice of his Catholic faith for a long time. Before visiting Padre Pio, Mario had been fully engrossed in worldly pursuits. He was completely indifferent to the state of his soul. The only reason he went to Mass on Sundays was because his mother expected it of him. Other than that, it meant nothing to him. Although he went to confession on occasion, he knew he would go right back to committing the same sins that he had previously confessed. He did not want to give them up.

Visiting Padre Pio had made Mario aware of the great spiritual distance which separated him from God. He came to understand that he had been offending God by his lifestyle. If Padre Pio had not denied him absolution, he probably would never have realized that his soul was in grave danger. The times that he had made his confession in the past had brought no real change for him. But making his confession to Padre Pio marked a turning point in his life. He would never be indifferent to spiritual matters again.

Mario returned to his home in New York City, but it was not to business as usual. In order to learn more about Padre Pio, he bought a biography of his life and read it with great interest. He prayed for Padre Pio's guidance and intercession. He began to attend daily Mass and he also spent time in church in front of the Blessed Sacrament. He asked his pastor if it would be possible to have an all night prayer vigil at the parish. The pastor thought it was a good idea. Mario organized the prayer vigil which began at 9:00 p.m. and continued until 6:00 a.m. the next morning. It was held on the first Friday of the month and was always well-attended.

Continuing his education, Mario graduated from St. John's University in Queens, New York and went on to get his Master's Degree from John Jay College of Criminal Justice in New York. He felt very fortunate to find a very good job with the state of New York in the field of social service.

It was in the beautiful church of Our Lady of Peace in New York City that Mario met his future wife, Sarojini Kannangara, a native of Sri Lanka. They married in 1972. Their first child, Pia Angeli, was a true blessing from God. In 1973, the Bruschis' traveled to Sri Lanka to visit Sarojini's family.

While in Sri Lanka, a country that is only 7 percent Catholic, Mario gave a talk on Padre Pio and showed a documentary film of his life. The presentation was very well received by both Catholics and non-Catholics alike. Mario had only planned on showing the film once while on his vacation in Sri Lanka. He was surprised to receive many requests for additional showings of the film in other parts of the country. The response to the documentary was so enthusiastic that double showings had to be given on many days. Mario spent almost the entire three weeks of his vacation traveling from one end of Sri Lanka to the other, showing the film. Quite unexpectedly, his first trip to his wife's homeland, turned out to be a "working" vacation. He was filled with joy to be able to share the message of Padre Pio with so many people.

Mario also received many inquiries regarding the Padre Pio prayer groups. Through his assistance, many Padre Pio prayer groups were established in Sri Lanka for the first time. When his three-week vacation was over, Mario knew that his work on the beautiful tropical island of Sri Lanka was not. He returned to Sri Lanka nine more times, sharing the story of Padre Pio from town to town and village to village.

Most Reverend Dominic Athaide, the archbishop of Agra, India invited Mario to show the documentary film of Padre Pio to the people of India. The archbishop had a great devotion to Padre Pio. He had previously visited San Giovanni Rotondo and had met Padre Pio. Mario accepted the archbishop's invitation and traveled to India three times, showing the film of Padre Pio in the cities of Madras, Bombay, Agra, Delhi and many more. Although India is less than 2 percent Catholic, Mario noticed the same interest and receptivity as he found in Sri Lanka. In India, he gave presentations on Padre Pio in schools, seminaries, parishes, private homes, hospitals and cloistered convents.

During his travels, Mario lodged in the Capuchin monasteries of southern India. He came to have great admiration for the Capuchin priests and brothers who lived there. Their lifestyle was simple and austere, true to the spiritual ideals of St. Francis of Assisi. In accord with the monastic custom, Mario slept each night on a straw bed with a hard pillow. He traveled to each new destination, not in an automobile, but in a simple rickshaw. He was able to adapt to the culture of India in all ways, except one. The traditional food, namely the very hot and spicy curry dishes, proved to be more than Mario could handle. He finally settled for boiled vegetables only, with no spices.

While in India, Mario showed the film of Padre Pio's life to the members of a leper colony in the city of Agra. The lepers were very inspired by the presentation. They told Mario that the film on Padre Pio gave them a great sense of hope. Mario was impressed with Archbishop Athaide's important work at the leper colony in Agra. In an effort to help the lepers, the archbishop asked them to list their fifteen most immediate needs. After reviewing their comments, the archbishop finally asked the lepers, "What is your greatest need?" Their answer was, "spiritual consolation." It was the same great need that Mario saw in all of his travels. Everywhere, people were hungry for spirituality and a deeper relationship with God.

Through his public lectures as well as the showing of the documentary film, Mario was able to introduce thousands of people in the Far East to Padre Pio. But Mario thought of a way to reach even more. He contacted one of the executives in charge of television programming in Sri Lanka and asked if it would be possible to have the film of Padre Pio shown on Ceylon television, which broadcast not only to Sri Lanka but also to southern India. The executive viewed the film and approved it. When it was aired, it is estimated that between 17-20 million viewers watched the program and were introduced to Padre Pio in that way.

It was Mario's dream that one day the country of Sri Lanka would have a church named in honor of Padre Pio. He spoke about it to Most Reverend Marcus Fernando, the archbishop of the diocese of Colombo, Sri Lanka. The archbishop was very supportive of the idea. The following year, Mario returned to Sri Lanka. He and his brother-in-law, Gamin Kannangara began making plans for the new church. With the help and guidance of Father Bertram Dabrera and Father Kingsley Jayamanne, the dream began to materialize. However, it was understood that the burden of the fund-raising rested on Mario. He went back to the United States and was able to raise the money for the project.

On September 23, 2007, Most Reverend Oswald Gomis consecrated the beautiful and stately St. Pio Shrine Church in Athurugiriya, Sri Lanka. It is the first church in the Far East dedicated to Padre Pio. Several first class relics of St. Pio have been enshrined there for public veneration. A Padre Pio prayer group has also been established there. Not long after the shrine was erected, several miracles of healing were reported. People now travel from all parts of the Asia to pray at the St. Pio Shrine Church in Athurugiriya.

Back home in New York City, where Mario and his family make their home, Mario has shown the documentary film on Padre Pio's life in more parishes than he can count. A number of people have told Mario through the years that seeing the film on Padre Pio changed their life. For many, it was the wake-up call that brought about their return to the Church and to the Sacraments.

The year 2011 marks Mario's 32nd year as the organizer for the annual Padre Pio Mass and celebration that takes place each August at the shrine of Our Lady of Fatima in Washington, New Jersey. Three thousand people attend the full day of prayer, adoration, holy hour, Mass and procession. In New York City, Mario is the organizer for the annual Mass for St. Pio that is held at St. Patrick's Cathedral.

Mario has started numerous Padre Pio prayer groups throughout the United States. One of the most rewarding of the Padre Pio prayer groups that he has organized and that he leads each Thursday afternoon is held at the Metropolitan Correctional Facility, a branch of the federal prison in New York City. The format for the prayer group includes the recitation of the Rosary, the Divine Mercy chaplet, prayer for the intercession of St. Pio, and a talk on the life and spirituality of St. Pio. One of the inmates who attended the Thursday afternoon Padre Pio prayer group felt the beneficial spiritual effects and wanted to share what she had received with others. When she was released from the Correctional Facility, she returned to her home in Columbia, South America and started a Padre Pio prayer group there.

Mario has also given Padre Pio presentations at the federal prison in Otisville, New York, showing the documentary film on Padre Pio in both English and Spanish. He regularly visits Catholic schools, sharing the story of Padre Pio with children in elementary school and junior high school.

Mario attributes the conversion of his late brother, Dr. Walter Bruschi, to the intercession of Padre Pio. Walter worked as the Chief of Psychiatry at the Menninger Foundation in Topeka, Kansas. Mario frequently had discussions with him about Padre Pio. Walter had a brilliant mind and could hold his own in any conversation. However, whenever Mario talked to Walter about Padre Pio, he felt that his words were falling on deaf ears. Walter had been away from his Catholic faith for most of his adult life. He doubted every word that Mario said about Padre Pio. "It is science that I believe in, not religion," he would say to Mario. But a turning point in Walter's life came when tragedy struck the family. His twenty-three-year-old son died suddenly, leaving the entire family devastated.

Walter visited Mario in New York shortly after his son's death. He told Mario that he wanted to find a spiritual director and asked him if he could recommend a good priest to him. Mario gave him the name of an excellent priest who was gifted in the field of spiritual direction. "I would also like to have a Rosary," Walter said. "Would you happen to have an extra one?" Mario was very surprised at the request. He gave Walter the Rosary that Padre Pio blessed for him when he visited San Giovanni Rotondo in 1957. Walter told Mario that the grief he experienced over the loss of his son, made him aware for the first time in years of his need for God. Walter began attending Mass on Sunday and eventually became a daily communicant.

After Walter's conversion back to his faith, he saw his work as a psychiatrist in a whole new light. For his clients who were Catholics, Walter often recommended to them that they go to confession. He would say, "I am only a man. I want to help you but I am limited in what I can do for you. I am not able to relieve you of the guilt that you feel. But God can. Make a good confession as soon as possible and you will experience the healing power of the sacrament and a great sense of freedom." Later in his life, when Walter was diagnosed with cancer, he united all of his suffering with Christ's sufferings, and offered it in reparation for sins. When Walter passed away, he was at peace with God. He was buried with the Rosary that Padre Pio had blessed.

Mario continues to lead the all night prayer vigils on the first Friday of each month at Our Lady of Peace parish in New York City. This year, 2011, will mark his 42nd year as organizer of the vigils. He is very happy that his son has agreed to continue the prayer vigils and the annual celebration Masses for Padre Pio when Mario is unable to do so. Mario has recently been invited to Africa to speak to the people there about Padre Pio. He is enthusiastic and excited about future possibilities. "Perhaps God has some new work for me to do," he says. "*Preghiamo, figiu mi,*" (Pray, my son), Padre Pio advised Mario each time he asked him for guidance. Mario has learned to entrust all of his plans to the Lord.

Mario, through the years, has learned the supreme importance and value of seeking the deep spiritual realities of life. In his younger days, Mario had little true faith to guide him. His brief encounter with Padre Pio in 1957 changed all of that and set him on a completely new path. Since that time, Mario has seen miracles both great and small. Most importantly, he has seen countless lives transformed and restored through the message and the intercession of Padre Pio.

There is a quotation which says, "I am only one, but still I am one; I cannot do everything, but I can do something; I will not refuse to do the something I can do." Mario Bruschi is only one person. Of course we know that he cannot do everything for the kingdom of God. No one can. But he has never refused to do the work set before him, the work that he has felt especially called to do. And he has done a lot.

I consider what writers say about the kingfishers, little birds who build their nests on the beach near the sea. They build it in a circular form and so tightly compressed that the sea water cannot penetrate it . . . Here these graceful little birds place their young ones, so that when the sea comes upon them by surprise, they can swim with confidence and float on the waves . . . I want your heart to be like this: well compact and closed on all sides, so that if the worries and storms of the world, the evil spirit, and the flesh come upon it, it will not be penetrated. Leave but one opening to your heart, that is toward heaven . . . How I love and am enraptured by those little birds.

- St. Pio of Pietrelcina

CHAPTER 29

Padre Pio - An Extraordinary Intercessor

Some of the Capuchins who lived close to Padre Pio remarked that his magnetism exerted a powerful influence, not only on people, but even at times on animals. It was observed that the monastery dog seemed to be particularly drawn to Padre Pio. If the door to the monks' private quarters was left open, the dog would sometimes go to Padre Pio's cell and wait at his door. It was also observed that when Padre Pio said Mass in the early days, the stray dogs from surrounding areas would come and sit in the square just in front of the church. When Mass was over, they would leave the area. We see by the following story that Padre Pio also had a certain mysterious rapport, even with birds.

The monastery garden at Our Lady of Grace was a quiet and secluded place that was surrounded with fruit trees, a long row of cypress trees and one pine tree. Padre Pio and the other members of his religious community would usually gather there each day. Sometimes, members of the laity were invited to join them. In the summer time, when the weather was hot, Padre Pio would often go to the garden in the early evening. It was a time of fellowship and conversation, a welcome respite from the intensely busy days at the monastery.

Dr. Nicola Centra recalled an extraordinary event that happened on one occasion in the monastery garden. One day when Padre Pio was there with several companions, without warning, a flock of birds flew down and settled on the nearby trees. Blackbirds, sparrows, swallows and more were there in great numbers. Suddenly, one of the birds began to sing loudly, followed by a great flapping of wings from the other birds. Then all of the feathered friends began to sing in unison. It was like a marvelous symphony of chirping, whistling, high-pitched rills and trills. It was indeed beautiful to listen to. However, on that particular day, the birds were so loud that Padre Pio was unable to carry on a conversation with his friends. He could not be heard above the chatter.

Suddenly, Padre Pio looked upward at all the birds in the trees and said with authority, "Quiet, that's enough!" Immediately, the sound of the birds ceased altogether. A great silence descended on the monastery garden. Padre Pio went right on with his conversation as though nothing had happened. But something amazing indeed had happened. Those who were in the garden at the time and witnessed it, were dumbfounded.

———

Nina Villani lived seven miles from the monastery of Our Lady of Grace. Once or twice a week, it was her habit to attend Padre Pio's 5:00 a.m. Mass. She and her two children got up in the middle of the night and walked the seven miles from her home to the monastery. They traveled through the hilly area on a rough and stony dirt path, a goat track. Even the cold of winter could not discourage Nina from attending Padre Pio's Mass.

Nina knew that the journey was dangerous. Wild and rabid dogs were common in the area. Even wolves were known to lurk about and were sometimes spotted by the local people. When the news broke that a man had been robbed and murdered on the same road that she and her children walked on the way to the monastery, Nina became alarmed. She spoke to Padre Pio about it and told him her fears. She asked him for advice. "Continue to come to Mass just like you have always done," Padre Pio said. "You will be protected."

From that time forward, whenever Nina started out for the monastery, she would either see someone walking ahead of her on the road, dispelling all of her fears, or she would see a small animal on the path just ahead of her, almost as if leading the way. Because Nina continued to walk to Padre Pio's early morning Mass, other mothers with their children then had the courage to do the same. None of the women were ever harmed.

While some might have disapproved of Nina for taking her two young children out in the dark of night on such a long journey, there is proof indeed that the children were blessed because of it. Her son Peter became a missionary priest of the Order of the Verona Fathers and her daughter became a nun.

———

Nonce Gargano, who owned a furniture store in Marseilles, France became close friends with one of his customers, Mr. Bossi. Mr. Bossi used to visit Nonce at the shop almost every day. One day, Mr. Bossi asked Nonce if he had ever heard of Padre Pio. He answered that he had not. Mr. Bossi went on to tell him many facts about Padre Pio's life and spirituality. He encouraged him to make a visit to Padre Pio's monastery in San Giovanni Rotondo.

Not long after that, Nonce's twenty-six-year-old daughter Arlette became gravely ill. She was diagnosed with a very serious lung disease and had to be sent to a sanatarium which was almost two hundred miles from Marseilles. Nonce kept Mr. Bossi informed on Arlette's condition.

As the days passed, Nonce became more and more worried about his daughter's health. Mr. Bossi could see the fear in Nonce's face. He gave him a picture of Padre Pio. "Take this picture of Padre Pio to your daughter," Mr. Bossi said. "Have her place it on her chest." Nonce did what his friend suggested. He took the photo to Arlette and encouraged her to pray to Padre Pio.

During Nonce's visit, Arlette's doctor asked him to come into his office. "I have bad news for you," the doctor said. He showed him the x-rays of Arlette's lungs. The cavities within her lungs had become more pronounced and had spread throughout both lungs. The doctor told Nonce that the only solution would be to operate.

When Nonce returned to Marseilles, he was anxious to give Mr. Bossi an update regarding his daughter's condition. He was disappointed when he remembered that Mr. Bossi was not in town. He had made a trip to San Giovanni Rotondo to visit Padre Pio's monastery. However, he had given Nonce the telephone number of the hotel that he was staying at. Nonce called the hotel and soon was able to speak to his friend. He explained to him the distressing news that Arlette's doctor had just told him. "Don't worry," Mr. Bossi said. "We will ask Padre Pio to pray for Arlette."

A few days later, Nonce went back to the sanatarium in order to give his permission for Arlette to have the operation. He was greeted by the doctor and shown a brand-new set of x-rays. The x-rays showed that Arlette's lungs were now completely normal. The doctor told Nonce that there was no explanation for the improvement. It was the doctor's opinion that Arlette had received a miraculous cure. "Your daughter has been healed," the doctor said to Nonce. "We have never before seen a miracle like this at the sanatarium." Nonce was astonished by the news. He realized that it was the supernatural intervention of Padre Pio that had cured his daughter.

In 1966, Nonce took his wife and children to San Giovanni Rotondo. His purpose for the visit was to thank Padre Pio for Arlette's healing. Nonce was happy that Mr. and Mrs. Bossi were able to accompany them on the trip. After they found lodging near the monastery, Nonce learned that Padre Pio celebrated Mass each morning at the early hour of 5:00 a.m. He informed his family that he would not be attending Padre Pio's Mass the next morning. It was just too early. He would wait till later in the day to go to the monastery. But oddly enough, very early the next morning, someone knocked loudly on Nonce's door and woke him up. He never discovered who it was. Since he could not get back to sleep, he decided to attend Padre Pio's Mass with his family.

That morning, the monastery church of Our Lady of Grace was full to overflowing. Nonce and his family were not able to find a seat. They had to stand for the duration of the Mass. Nonce had not been inside a church in many years. He tried to recall how long it had been. He estimated that it had been fifty years since he had received Holy Communion. However, watching the way Padre Pio celebrated Mass made a deep impression on him. Afterward, he asked a man in the church if he knew how he might be able to speak to Padre Pio. The man told Nonce to go up to the first floor of the monastery and wait in the St. Francis room. Padre Pio would soon be going there to greet the visitors.

Nonce and his three sons followed the man's instructions. When they entered the St. Francis room, it was already crowded with men who were hoping to see Padre Pio. As Nonce waited, he silently repeated the only two prayers that he knew by heart - the *Our Father* and the *Hail Mary*. Nonce grew more and more nervous as the time passed. He began to tremble. He had totally neglected the practice of his faith for all of his adult life. He suddenly began to feel very guilty about his actions. He had heard that Padre Pio could be severe with people who were not practicing their faith.

Before long, Padre Pio came out of the elevator with two sturdy Capuchins at his side. When Padre Pio walked into the St. Francis room, Nonce instinctively knelt down. As Padre Pio passed through the crowded hall, his eyes came to rest on Nonce. He paused in front of him and looked at him straight in the eyes. Padre Pio's gaze was so penetrating that Nonce felt overwhelmed. He could not find his words. All he could do was whisper, "Padre Pio." Padre Pio then put his hand on Nonce's head and gave him a blessing. That blessing and touch from Padre Pio changed everything for Nonce. He was never the same again.

When Nonce and his family returned to Marseilles, it was not back to business as usual. They began to attend Mass together every Sunday as a family. In addition, they never missed a Holy Day of Obligation. It was like a completely new beginning. From that time forward, they visited San Giovanni Rotondo every year. They also began to make pilgrimages to the Marian shrine in Lourdes, France.

In 1968, Nonce began to experience many difficulties with his furniture business. His store was impacted in a negative way due to competition from other similar stores which were springing up in the surrounding areas. Nonce decided to take his wife to San Giovanni Rotondo and seek the help of Padre Pio.

In San Giovanni Rotondo, Nonce spoke to Brother Modestino and told him that he and his wife had come from Marseilles, seeking Padre Pio's prayerful intercession. Brother Modestino was very familiar with Padre Pio's schedule and was happy to help Nonce and his wife. He led them to a corridor in the monastery and told them that Padre Pio would be passing through the area in a short time. All along the corridor, women were kneeling. Nonce's wife knelt down with the other women. Nonce soon saw Padre Pio as he came down the corridor. He prayed with great intensity, "Padre Pio, please give my wife a blessing!" Before he had even finished his prayer, Padre Pio walked straight over to his wife and blessed her. Nonce was amazed. When they returned to Marseilles, they both felt that they had received the necessary strength to face up to all their difficulties. Their prayers had been answered.

———

There was a woman who used to go frequently to confession to Padre Pio. She was one of his faithful spiritual daughters. She had a strong, decisive personality and also a hot temper. She was well aware of her impulsive nature and her character weaknesses. She sincerely tried to make progress in overcoming her faults, but it seemed to be an uphill battle.

On one occasion, the woman attended a religious play that was held in the church hall at Our Lady of Grace monastery. Padre Pio was there with all the other Capuchins to watch the performance. The hall was filled to capacity that evening.

When the performance was over, Padre Pio followed the other Capuchins back into the church. The woman happened to be walking right in front of Padre Pio as he was making his way toward the church. Suddenly one of the Capuchins yelled at her in a rude manner, "Get out of the way! Make way for Padre Pio!" The disrespectful way that the Capuchin spoke to her was more than she could bear. The woman felt so insulted that she yelled right back at the Capuchin, "No, I will not do what you say. I am not in the way. You are a bad priest. You are full of bitterness!" The Capuchin became so angry at the woman's words that his face turned red. Padre Pio was standing close by but he seemed to be wrapped in his own thoughts. He did not appear to notice the incident.

A few days later, the woman went to confession to Padre Pio. She confessed that she had lost her temper with the Capuchin priest when he spoke harshly to her. She said words to him that she now regretted and she was truly sorry for her behavior.

Padre Pio listened carefully but remained silent. The woman waited for him to respond, but he did not. "Padre Pio, did you hear what I just confessed? I offended a priest. I yelled back at him and told him that he was a bad priest. I have committed a grave offense. I know that you were there when the incident happened but you seemed to be preoccupied with something else." Again there was silence.

Finally, Padre Pio said to her, "When you lost your temper and said those disrespectful words to the priest, did he answer you back?" "No, he did not," the woman replied. "Did he say even one word?" Padre Pio asked. "No," he said nothing," the woman answered. With those few words, Padre Pio wanted the woman to realize that the priest restrained himself even though he was very angry and even though he could have easily kept the argument going. With very few words, Padre Pio made his point.

On another occasion, Padre Pio taught the woman an important lesson by once again using a few well-chosen words. He shocked her one day by asking her if she would give him a cigarette. She was so taken aback by the request that she could not even find words to answer him. "You know that smoking a cigarette is not a sin," Padre Pio said. "That is true," the woman replied. "It is not a sin, but it is a weakness. I do not want to give you a cigarette because I do not want to see that weakness in you." "Exactly," Padre Pio replied. "And I do not want to see that weakness in you either!" The woman got the message loud and clear. She gave up smoking cigarettes.

Let us confess, my good daughters and sisters, that God is good and that his mercy is eternal. His every will is just, and his decrees are full of lofty mysteries; his pleasure is always holy, and his plans, loveable.

- St. Pio of Pietrelcina

CHAPTER 30

Diana Graves

———————

D iana Graves was an actress by profession who lived and worked in London, England. She suffered from emphysema and bronchiectasis. Both diseases were progressive and incurable and as time passed, she was spending more and more time in the hospital, being treated for her chronic condition. When her health took a turn for the worse, her doctors strongly advised her to move to a milder climate. The damp and cold of London weakened her lungs and aggravated her breathing problems. For the sake of her health, she needed to relocate to a place that had a warm and dry climate.

Diana, who was thirty-five years old, decided to move to Rome where the climate would be more conducive to her health. Diana's cousin, Jenny, lived in Rome which was an added bonus. Rome also had the *Cinecittà*, a large film studio that hosted international movie productions as well as television productions. It was considered to be the hub of Italian cinema. With all of her acting experience, Diana hoped to be able to work there.

Life was not easy for Diana after she moved to Rome. She had some serious financial setbacks which were a cause of great anxiety to her. She also became so ill that she had to be hospitalized on numerous occasions. Her cousin Jenny suggested that they make a trip to San Giovanni Rotondo. Hopefully, they would be able to ask Padre Pio to pray for Diana's recovery. Diana thought it was an excellent idea.

After Diana had regained some of her strength, she and Jenny took a night train to Foggia and then a taxi to San Giovanni Rotondo. They arrived at the church of Our Lady of Grace just as the Mass was concluding. Diana was so weak and exhausted from the journey that she feared she might faint. She needed to get off of her feet but there wasn't a single empty seat available in the church for Diana to sit in.

As Padre Pio made his way toward the confessional, a large group of people crowded around him. He looked ill and he appeared to be fighting for breath in the stifling atmosphere. Diana knew that Padre Pio suffered from the same general health problems that she did. He had chronic bronchitis and asthma which often made it difficult for him to breathe.

Diana was able to speak to one of the Capuchins, Father Dominic Meyer. She explained to him that she was very sick and wondered if it could be arranged for her to receive a blessing from Padre Pio. Father Dominic told Diana that there were people in the church who had been waiting weeks for the same opportunity. However, he said he would try to help.

An hour later, Father Dominic motioned for Diana and Jenny to follow him. Amidst a huge crowd of people who were pushing and shoving, they were able to enter the sacristy. With great effort, Father Dominic managed to close the door. There were about twelve people in the sacristy, and many looked as though they were very ill. When Padre Pio came into the sacristy, Father Dominic whispered in his ear, pointing certain people out to him. Padre Pio would then go to the person that Father Dominic had spoken to him about and give that person an individual blessing. When Father Dominic pointed to Diana, Padre Pio smiled at her. He put his hand on her head and spoke words which she did not understand.

On the last day of their visit, Diana and Jenny went back to the monastery and spent time in the church of Our Lady of Grace. At one point, a woman who was standing directly behind Diana, let out a piercing scream. There was an atmosphere of sheer pandemonium in the church that day. Padre Pio was very upset by the noise. "Silence!" he exclaimed. This is a holy place. No one should be making noise!"

After Diana left San Giovanni Rotondo, she realized what a great impact the visit to Padre Pio had made on her. "It was the only time in my life that I have come in contact with a man of almost perfect goodness and spiritual strength," she said of Padre Pio. After returning to Rome, she felt a great sense of detachment from all earthly concerns. She no longer felt like she must desperately cling to life and she was now prepared to accept death, whenever it came. Seeing Padre Pio face to face gave her the strength to do so. Nothing else seemed to matter. Diana Graves died peacefully shortly after her visit to San Giovanni Rotondo.

I Needed the Quiet

I needed the quiet, so He drew me aside
Into the shadows where we could confide;
Away from the hustle where all the day long
I hurried and worried when active and strong.

I needed the quiet, though at first I rebelled,
But gently, so gently my cross He upheld
And whispered so sweetly of spiritual things,
Though weakened in body my spirit took wings
To heights never dreamed of when strength filled my days
He loved me so gently, he drew me away.

I needed the quiet, no prison my bed
But a beautiful valley of blessing instead;
A place to grow richer, in Jesus to hide
I needed the quiet, so He drew me aside.

Alice Hansche Mortenson

Padre Pio lived in a permanent state of battle fighting his war on three simultaneous fronts, but always with the promised Ally at his side; extreme physical suffering, the constant fear of offending God, and the unceasing battle with the devil and his temptations.

- Father Augustine McGregor, O.C.S.O.

CHAPTER 31

Sister Pia of Jesus Crucified

*O*n one occasion, someone mentioned to me that there was a nun named Sister Pia on the East Coast who had met Padre Pio and that perhaps she would have something to share for our "Pray, Hope, and Don't Worry" quarterly publication. I did not give the statement a second thought. However, several years later I started thinking about Sister Pio and I had a desire to meet her. I decided to call the convents on the East Coast in the hope of locating her. On the very first call I made, Sister Pia answered the telephone. When I asked her if she would share her testimony of Padre Pio with us, she said she would be glad to. Because she is a cloistered nun, our visit with her was through the traditional iron grate of the convent. It separated her from us in body but not in spirit. Sister Pia is a very joyful person, very close to the Lord. We are so thankful that she shared her story with us.

Alexandra (Alix) Brown grew up in a wealthy and socially privileged family in Philadelphia, Pennsylvania. She was raised as an Episcopalian. Although she attended church regularly with her family all throughout her youth, it was not something that she enjoyed doing. At that time, she could describe churchgoing in one simple word, "boring." She believed that people went to church because it was a social custom and an obligation and nothing more. Religion was simply a crutch to try to come to terms with what no one could really understand. And God? God was a "dead word" in Alix's vocabulary. To her, attending church on Sunday was dry and meaningless.

Alix was interested in other things. She enjoyed the wide variety of cultural events that were available in Philadelphia. She found enjoyment in art, music, and the theater. She loved elegant dinner parties, beautiful clothing, and the "good things" that money could buy. In her privileged upbringing, money could buy almost anything she wanted.

After completing high school, Alix enrolled in the prestigious Briarcliff College in Westchester County, New York. There she met many women who, like her, were from wealthy families and who, like her, had been somewhat "spoiled" by an abundance of material advantages.

As the scriptures note, *To everything there is a season, and a time for every purpose under heaven.* The "season" for searching out the deeper meaning of life, came to Alix while attending Briarcliff College. Even though she did not believe in God, in some mysterious way, she was searching for him. She began to spend a lot of time in the college library, reading books on world religions. The Eastern religions of India and Asia attracted her. However, in her study, she found that there were many doctrines in the teachings of Hinduism and Buddhism which she could not accept.

Alix moved to Florence, Italy in her second year of college to study classical art. She had been accepted at the Simi Art Studio in Florence, which was considered to be one of the finest art schools in Italy. One of the students she met at the Simi Studio was a wonderful and gifted man named Antonio Ciccone. Alix enjoyed his friendship and admired him for his remarkable artistic talent.

Antonio, who had grown up in San Giovanni Rotondo, had experienced many hardships throughout his childhood. His father, a widower, was very poor and could barely provide for Antonio and the other children. Antonio tended sheep like many other young boys in the area. As a child, he loved to draw and sketch and it soon became obvious that he possessed an amazing artistic gift.

Throughout Antonio's youth, he had many opportunities to visit Padre Pio and to attend his Mass. Antonio used to try to memorize the fine details of Padre Pio's face in order to draw it. One time, Padre Pio asked Antonio to leave the confessional because he realized that he had come primarily to study his face. Padre Pio had an aversion to being stared at. He made it quite clear to Antonio that he did not appreciate it.

Antonio visited with Padre Pio in the monastery garden on many occasions. It proved to be a wonderful opportunity for Antonio to carefully concentrate on Padre Pio's face. He hoped to capture it as perfectly as possible in his drawings. Padre Pio would notice the way Antonio was staring at him and would say, "Antonio, why are you looking at me like that?" Antonio would simply answer, "I am studying."

Padre Pio used to call Antonio, "Pitturi" (little painter) and he always had Antonio's best interests at heart. He wanted him to lead an exemplary Christian life. Once, in the confessional, Padre Pio took both of Antonio's hands in his own and held them for the duration of Antonio's confession. "Please don't disappoint me," he said to Antonio.

At one time, Antonio thought that he might have a vocation to the religious life and considered joining the Capuchin order. In clear and unmistakable words, Padre Pio said to Antonio, "No, you must paint. That is your path." Years later, Antonio's remarkably beautiful religious paintings would be placed in the Capuchin monastery of Our Lady of Grace as well as in the Home for the Relief of Suffering.

A wonderful opportunity opened up for Antonio when a devout couple from Florence who knew Padre Pio, invited him to live with them and to study art in Florence. They had the financial means to provide for his education and they wanted to help him. Padre Pio was very happy about the arrangement and Antonio left for Florence with Padre Pio's blessing.

Alix Brown considered Antonio to be the most gifted student at the Simi Art Studio in Florence. He used to wear a Rosary around his neck, which always looked very striking to Alix. She admired him for his deep spirituality. Antonio told her many stories of his childhood, and of his experiences of knowing Padre Pio. He encouraged her to visit Padre Pio's monastery in San Giovanni Rotondo.

Because of the example of Antonio, as well as that of other devout Catholics that she had met in Florence, in her private study of world religions, Alix decided to take a closer look at Christianity. The information that Antonio had shared with her about Padre Pio was very meaningful to her. She began to ponder the fact that Padre Pio was a Catholic and she had a desire to learn more about the teachings of the Catholic Church.

Alix Brown's study of Catholicism eventually led her to the decision to enter the Catholic Church, a plan that her family members were opposed to. Her parents would not give their permission and instead told her to delay her decision for two years, until she was twenty-one years old. Alix did what her parents asked of her and waited patiently until her twenty-first birthday. She was received into the Catholic Church in 1961.

After her conversion to Catholicism, Alix received an invitation from a good friend, Louise, to make a visit to San Giovanni Rotondo. Alix remembered the interesting conversations she had with Antonio Ciccone about Padre Pio and was happy to accept the invitation.

It took thirteen hours for Alix and Louise to drive from Florence to San Giovanni Rotondo and it rained heavily for most of the trip. They felt fortunate to find lodging in the one and only hotel in the area. The town was rural and undeveloped and lacked many of the amenities that most people take for granted. For instance, there was very little hot water available in the hotel, something that Alix found surprising.

The next morning, the girls got up very early in order to attend Padre Pio's Mass. The "new" church where the Mass was said had been constructed in 1959, and was built right next door to the older one. San Giovanni Rotondo had outgrown the small but beautiful 16th century church of Our Lady of Grace. The new church was large and spacious compared to the original and could accommodate one thousand people. When Padre Pio was taken to see it for the first time, he spoke prophetically, "It is not big enough." And it was true. Not estimating accurately the crowds that would be coming to San Giovanni Rotondo in the future, those who laid the plans did not make the church large enough. On many occasions Mass had to be said in an outdoor portico, because the church could not contain the people.

Alix had decided that her trip to San Giovanni Rotondo would be an act of thanksgiving for her recent entry into the Catholic Church. Yes, she had come to attend Padre Pio's Mass, but she had also come to thank God for the great gift of faith that she had received and for the blessings of being Catholic. It was easy to pray in San Giovanni Rotondo. It was easy to think about God.

The entire area, though poor and unimpressive outwardly, was pervaded with a sense of the supernatural.

After Louise and Alix attended Padre Pio's early morning Mass, Alix stayed inside the church to pray in silence. It was there that she received the incredible grace of a religious vocation. In an instant, and "deep down in her soul" Alix was suddenly and unmistakably aware that God was calling her to leave everything in the world, and become a nun. It was something she had never even considered as a possibility. She had never felt the slightest attraction to the consecrated life. She had thought at length about her future and was intending to pursue a career in art. For as long as she could remember, she had wanted to marry and raise a family. She assumed that her future husband would probably be Italian, since she loved living in Italy and planned to live there permanently. But in a flash, everything changed.

Alix felt that she had been given an invitation by God to follow the path of religious life. She knew what that meant. The strict vows of poverty, chastity, and obedience were nothing to take lightly. But she was convinced that it was God's will for her and she wanted to follow his will. She knew what a privilege it was to be called to such a vocation. As to which religious order to enter, she did not have the slightest idea. Each order had its own unique charism. There were the Franciscans, the Benedictines, the Cistercians, the Carmelites, and many more. There were missionary nuns, contemplative nuns, teaching nuns, and nursing nuns. She had a great desire to speak to Padre Pio about the matter. She hoped that he would advise her and direct her to a holy religious congregation.

When it was time for Alix and Louise to go back to Florence, Alix knew for certain that she wanted to return again to the monastery of Our Lady of Grace. The visit had been a remarkable experience. She had been able to talk to a number of the residents in the area who shared many stories with her about Padre Pio. The miracles that surrounded his life and his extraordinary spiritual gifts were well known and well documented. They were of course, a part of his spirituality, but to Alix, they were not the most important part. To her, the most significant feature of Padre Pio's life centered on his all-consuming love for God and for the Church. After attending his early morning Mass, Alix came to the conclusion that his Mass was without a doubt, the greatest miracle of all.

Alix returned to San Giovanni Rotondo the following month. She made her confession to Padre Pio and told him what had happened on her first visit to the monastery, when she felt that God was calling her to a vocation in religious life. She asked him to advise her on the next step she should take. "You must pray," Padre Pio said simply.

He gave her no other words of advice on the matter. Alix was hoping that he would make the decision for her as to which religious order to enter, but no such luck. She made many subsequent confessions to Padre Pio and always spoke to him about her vocation, asking for his guidance and direction. His advice was always the same, "You must pray." "Padre Pio made me do all the work in finding the right congregation. He would not do the work for me," Alix said.

Alix returned each month to San Giovanni Rotondo for the next six months - sometimes for a few days and sometimes for weeks at a time. She did not mind the thirteen hour journey from Florence. It was well worth every sacrifice and every inconvenience. Through her many visits to San Giovanni Rotondo, Alix became acquainted with Padre Pio's American secretary, Mary Pyle. Mary had become almost a legend in the town. Everyone either knew Mary or knew of her. When Alix met Mary, she had been living just down the hill from the monastery for more than thirty-five years. Like many others, Alix had a great admiration for Mary and as time passed the two became close friends.

Alix was aware that Mary had a special call, a special vocation to make Padre Pio known to others. Alix noticed that Mary would talk about Padre Pio for hours to the visitors who came to the monastery. She never tired of telling the same stories about Padre Pio, over and over again. Literally thousands of people were introduced to Padre Pio through the years because of Mary Pyle's efforts. Alix described Mary Pyle as having a "beautiful radiance" about her person.

Mary proudly wore the brown habit of the Third Order of St. Francis. On one occasion, she sent one of her new habits over to the monastery to have Padre Pio bless it. However, whether he was jesting or not, for a reason that no one knew, he did not readily bless it. Instead, he voiced a complaint. Mary was told what had happened. "Did he finally bless my habit?" Mary asked. "Yes, he did. He made the sign of the cross over it," the Capuchin replied.

"Where was the habit when he blessed it?" Mary asked. "It was sitting on his lap," the Capuchin answered. "Well, that is good enough for me!" Mary said and she was filled with gratitude. Mary treasured a word, a thought or even a side-glance from Padre Pio. Her dedication to him was total.

Mary Pyle was advanced in years and was beginning to have numerous problems with her health when Alix met her. It became difficult for her to walk. After Mass, Alix used to take Mary's arm and help her down the hill to her home just below the monastery. Mary had a little basket in her home that contained memorial cards with prayer requests for the deceased. Mary referred to the basket as a little "graveyard." If any memorial cards came in, she asked Alix to be sure and put them with the others. Every day without exception, Mary faithfully prayed for the souls of all who had memorial cards in the basket.

It was Mary's habit, especially in her later years, to take a nap every afternoon after her midday meal. Alix used to help her up the stairs to her small bedroom on the second floor of her home. It took a great effort for Mary to get up the stairs. She often asked Alix to read to her until she fell asleep. She always wanted to hear selections from *The Mystical City of God* by Venerable Mary of Agreda. Because Mary Pyle had led an intensely active life, it was very difficult for her to accept her declining health. After Alix moved back to the United States, Mary had a stroke. She wrote several letters to Alix, asking her to pray that she would be able to accept her condition and surrender completely to God's will. Alix assured Mary of her prayers.

Alix knew how fortunate she was to be able to spend so much time in San Giovanni Rotondo, meeting great souls like Mary Pyle, as well as others who had dedicated their lives to assisting Padre Pio's work. Alix savored all of her memories of her times in San Giovanni Rotondo. To Alix, San Giovanni Rotondo, from an architectural and artistic standpoint, was a town that was greatly lacking in style and beauty. It did not have the old world charm of places like Pietrelcina, Assisi, Florence, or Perugia, with their cobblestone streets, interesting structures, quaint buildings, and beautiful churches.

While the architectural style of the town may have left much to be desired, Alix nevertheless felt inspired by its geography. She loved the wide-open expanses, the rocky, barren hills, the heavy rains in the autumn and winter, the strong winds that often howled and whipped down the Gargano mountain, and the cold, bright stars that filled the early morning sky. To Alix, there was a mystical feeling to the landscape and the terrain. And most important of all, Padre Pio lived there.

Alix was also aware of the invisible forces that were at work in San Giovanni Rotondo, the age old battle of good versus evil. Although it was not something that she could see with her eyes, she could sense it and feel it. One recalls that Padre Pio had a vision when he was fifteen years old, of that very battle of good versus evil which takes place within the human soul. His vision was a revelation of the spiritual warfare that he would encounter throughout his life.

In the vision, the young Padre Pio (Francesco Forgione) suddenly saw a majestic and beautiful figure standing beside him. The man had a radiant countenance, similar to the brightness of the sun. He said to Francesco, "I am here to tell you that you are going to have to fight like a courageous warrior." The resplendent figure took Francesco by the hand and led him to an open field. In the field, stood two large groups of men. One group had beautiful and shining faces. They were wearing robes of the purest white. The other group was dressed in black garments. They were ugly and frightening in appearance.

Francesco stood in the middle of the open field with the radiant figure beside him. Suddenly he saw a treacherous and hideous being coming toward him. The gruesome figure was so tall that he appeared to be a giant. "You must fight with this creature," the resplendent man said to Francesco. "But do not worry because I will be with you." Francesco became terrified as the monster like figure advanced toward him. He felt weak and began to tremble uncontrollably. He thought that he was going to faint. Francesco's spiritual guide then took his arm to support him. He felt strengthened by the celestial man's touch. Francesco entered into a violent battle with his dangerous adversary and finally conquered him. The radiant figure placed a magnificent crown on Francesco's head but then quickly removed it. He said to Francesco, "You will receive a crown that is even more beautiful than this one if you will continue to stand up to the dark being whom you just fought. Be strong and do not fear. I will always be near and will always help you."

Shortly after, Francesco had another vision and was given the realization that the beautiful and resplendent man who had stood beside him in the vision was Jesus. In truth, it was Jesus who was always with him, assisting him in the many trials and tribulations of his life. In his fight against evil forces and in his life-long battle against demons, Padre Pio would always remain close to Jesus and would be victorious.

If the demons attacked Padre Pio at times, the angels were always nearby to shield and protect him. The angelic realm was very real and very much alive to Padre Pio. Whenever he spoke about angels, he spoke from his own direct experience.

On one occasion, Alix's friends invited her to go to the shrine of St. Michael the Archangel, Monte Sant' Angelo. They intended to make the twenty-five-mile pilgrimage on foot, as an act of penance and sacrifice. In the confessional, Alix told Padre Pio about her plan to visit the shrine and asked him for his blessing on the trip. Padre Pio made no reply. Thinking that he might not have heard her, Alix repeated her request, this time even louder. Once again, there was no response. As it turned out, on the day of the pilgrimage, Alix became ill and could not make the trip with her friends. Most likely, Padre Pio had known that she would not be able to go on the pilgrimage and so had not given his priestly blessing.

Alix went to confession numerous times to Padre Pio. In the confessional, before Alix could name her sins, Padre Pio often began by asking her a number of direct questions regarding those very sins. "Have you told the truth?" he would say. "Have you exaggerated?" he would inquire. While many people do not consider exaggeration to be a matter of consequence, Padre Pio obviously did. It was something that needed to be addressed and corrected. He was particular and exacting down to the smallest detail. Other than a few simple questions that he might ask, Padre Pio usually said very little to Alix in the confessional. If he was asked a question directly, he often answered by a simple "yes" or "no."

Alix investigated many different religious orders in an effort to find one that would be suitable. As Padre Pio advised her, she spent many hours in prayer, invoking God's intercession. When she read a biography of St. Teresa of Avila, she felt drawn to the Carmelite spirituality. She visited a cloistered Carmelite congregation on the East Coast to inquire about their way of life. The moment she walked through the door, it felt like home. She was accepted into the congregation. Since she chose an enclosed order, there would be no going out into the world, no traveling about. She did not think it would be a difficult adjustment. For Alix, the greatest difficulty that she faced was leaving Padre Pio, knowing that she would never see him again. Before joining the Carmelites, Alix wanted to visit Padre Pio one last time.

In 1963, Alix spent four months in San Giovanni Rotondo. She attended Padre Pio's early Mass every morning and then spent the greater part of the day in the church. At 11:30 a.m. each day, Padre Pio went to the balcony of the church for his private recitation of the Rosary. Most of the pilgrims who visited the monastery were not aware of it. Because Alix had spent so much time in San Giovanni Rotondo, she was very familiar with his daily routine. She made sure that she too was in the church at 11:30 a.m. each day to pray her Rosary and to unite her own prayers with Padre Pio's. It was always a consolation for her to look up into the balcony and see Padre Pio deeply engrossed in prayer. Just to be near him was of great benefit to her soul.

When Padre Pio finished praying his morning Rosary, he would walk across the upper balcony of the church and through a connecting door into the old church. There he would recite the Angelus, the beautiful prayer to the angel of God. All who were gathered joined in prayer with him. Afterward, he would bless the pilgrims. Daily, Alix recited the Angelus with Padre Pio, and then received his blessing.

Alix attended Benediction every afternoon in the church, with Padre Pio presiding. The way Padre Pio held the monstrance for Benediction was something that Alix had never seen before. He was so aware of the true presence of Jesus in the Blessed Sacrament. His face was radiant during the Benediction. Mary Pyle played the organ and directed the choir which sang at Benediction every afternoon. In the evening before retiring, Alix joined the local people who stood at Padre Pio's window and sang their goodnight songs to him. *Buona Notte, Padre Pio* (Goodnight, Padre Pio) was one of the favorites.

Alix entered in the cloistered Carmelite convent in June 1964. After six months as a postulant, she became a novice and took the religious habit. At that time, she was invited to choose a new name. The Carmelite tradition allows the novice to choose two names - a first name and a religious title to follow. The Mother General suggested to her that she take the name, Sister Grace. But Alix had another name in mind and when she told the Mother General, she was given permission to use it. Her new name became Sister Pia of Jesus Crucified. She wanted to stay as close to Padre Pio as she could. Taking his name would be a constant reminder of him.

Of all the memories that Sister Pia has of visiting San Giovanni Rotondo, attending Padre Pio's Mass is the one that she treasures most. The way Padre Pio celebrated Mass was a sermon in itself. One of the pilgrims who attended Padre Pio's Mass once said, "When I saw Padre Pio genuflect, I was deeply edified. It reminded me of Jesus, beneath the Cross. I had never seen a genuflection like it before and I have never seen one since. I will never forget it for as long as I live."

Padre Pio wanted people to make a good preparation before receiving Holy Communion and a thoughtful and prayerful thanksgiving afterward. "The thanksgiving after Mass is something that must never be neglected," he once said. His own thanksgiving after Mass lasted at least forty-five minutes.

Padre Pio strictly observed the fasting rules of the Church before receiving Holy Communion and he insisted that everyone else do the same. Once inside the church, there were to be no conversations, no talking for any reason. Instead, a strict silence was to be observed. Padre Pio and the other Capuchins would frequently call people to task who were talking in church. These considerations are especially important for the times we live in today. Sadly to say, many people have lost a great treasure - a spirit and an attitude of reverence and a sense of the sacred. Many beautiful and devotional Catholic practices and traditions have also been long-abandoned. But in truth, what has been lost can be reclaimed. Let us hope and pray for this intention.

Throughout her many years as a Carmelite nun, Sister Pia has frequently gone back in time to those early days, when she visited Padre Pio. Nothing had been a coincidence. It had all been a God-incidence, leading her step by step to the place where she belonged. She has pondered the fact that she received the grace of a religious vocation, not in Florence where she had studied art, or in New York where she attended college, or in Philadelphia where she had grown up, but on a visit to San Giovanni Rotondo, that small and remote town that seemed so ordinary and unimpressive. There, in the church of Our Lady of Grace, where Padre Pio had said daily Mass for most of his priestly life, where he had spent countless hours in prayer and in hearing confessions, she received the call to offer her life totally to God and to dedicate herself to prayer and reparation, and live hidden from the world.

In 1965, Padre Pio sent a message to Sister Pia through his assistant, Padre Pellegrino Funicelli. The message said, "Tell Sister Pia to keep herself burning ardently like a little lamp before Jesus in the Blessed Sacrament." That is exactly what Sister Pia has been doing for these many years.

Let your desire be to see God; your fear that you may lose him; your sorrow that you are not having fruition of him; your joy that he can bring you to himself. Thus you will live in great peace.

St.Teresa of Avila

We are children of God, and if children, then heirs, heirs of God and joint heirs with Christ, if only we suffer with him so that we may also be glorified with him. I consider that the sufferings of this present time are as nothing compared with the glory to be revealed for us.

Romans 8:16-18

CHAPTER 32

Padre Pio and the Children

L iberato Iannantuoni was just a little boy when Padre Pio and Father Benedetto visited his family's home in San Marco la Catola. The year was 1911. The Iannantuoni family learned that Father Benedetto and Padre Pio were going to be passing through the area on their way to the Capuchin monastery in Venafro. Since Father Benedetto and Liberato's grandfather enjoyed a close friendship, Father Benedetto was glad for the chance to pay him a visit. Liberato's grandfather was delighted to see his good friend and also felt honored to welcome Padre Pio into his home. Liberato's mother too, was very happy to receive the two priests.

Little Liberato was fascinated by the crucifix that hung from the cord of Padre Pio's habit. Over and over again, he kissed it. Padre Pio lovingly took Liberato in his arms and called him by his nickname, "Liberatuccio." Padre Pio had penetrating eyes and a gentle smile. For the rest of his life, the memory of that visit remained vivid in Liberato's memory.

All through his youth, Liberato's grandfather told him stories about Padre Pio. As an adult, Liberato had a desire to go to San Giovanni Rotondo to see Padre Pio once again. He told Capuchin Father Michael Colasanto, his friend and fellow townsman, about his desire. Father Colasanto said that he had close connections with the Capuchins of Our Lady of Grace and could arrange a meeting. He explained that it would not be a private audience with Padre Pio. More than likely, it would be a very brief greeting in the corridor of the monastery. Liberato was very grateful that Father Colasanto was willing to make the arrangements.

In 1966, Liberato made the trip to San Giovanni Rotondo. He was able to speak to Padre Pio briefly in the corridor of the monastery. "You visited our home many years ago," Liberato said. "You called me Liberatuccio, the name my mother always called me. Father Benedetto was with you." Upon hearing the words, a beautiful smile came upon Padre Pio's face. "Pray, hope, and don't worry," he said to Liberato. "God is merciful and he will listen to your prayers."

———

When Elio Leonardi was a little boy, his mother often took him to see Padre Pio. She told Elio that after she put him under the protection of Padre Pio, he was assisted on numerous occasions. She said that at least five or six times, Elio had been miraculously protected by Padre Pio and kept from harm's way. Elio listened to his mother politely but was never really convinced that what she said was true.

One day, when Elio was walking down the road in San Giovanni Rotondo to catch a bus, a car hit him from behind. Elio was thrown into the air from the impact and flew over the top of the car. Elio saw, upside down, the statue of the Virgin Mary which was on top of the church. "Madonna, I beg you to help me!" Elio prayed quickly and with great intensity.

Elio was rushed to the Home of the Relief of Suffering where he had a thorough examination. He knew that he was very lucky to be alive. After he was released from the hospital, he rushed over to the monastery and was surprised to see that all of the monastery doors were open. Padre Pio happened to be praying in the choir loft at the time. Elio burst into tears as he approached Padre Pio. He fell to his knees in front of him and said, "Thank you, Padre Pio! Thank you for saving my life!" "Don't thank me," Padre Pio replied. "Thank the Madonna. It was she who saved you." Padre Pio smiled at Elio and with an expression of immense love he added, "My son, I can never leave you alone for a minute!"

————

Ten-year-old Anna Maria D'Orazi and her mother made a trip to San Giovanni Rotondo in order to attend Padre Pio's Mass. They planned to stay for several days. During the time of their visit, a number of children were getting ready to make their first Holy Communion. Anna had not made her first Communion yet. It was delayed because her mother had many preparations to make for a party in honor of Anna's special day.

The church of Our Lady of Grace looked particularly beautiful on the day that the children were to receive their First Communion. It was decorated with lovely flower bouquets and illuminated with soft candlelight. The girls had on pretty white dresses and the boys were all dressed in suits. Anna had a great desire to join the other children and to receive her first Holy Communion that day from Padre Pio.

Anna's mother did not want her to do so. Being a dress designer, she had been planning to make Anna a beautiful dress for that very important day. She discouraged Anna by saying that there would be no gifts for her, no party, and no beautiful dress. Her mother felt that it would be a great shame for Anna to make her first Holy Communion in her plain green dress, while all of the other girls were dressed up in lovely attire.

Anna explained to her mother that she did not care about the party, the gifts, or a beautiful dress. Finally, her mother told her to speak to Padre Pio about it. If he gave his permission, she would go along with it. However, she did not think he would agree to it.

Anna rushed to the confessional and after making her confession to Padre Pio, she asked him for permission to make her first Holy Communion that day. Padre Pio had a slight smile on his face as Anna spoke to him. She explained to him that she had been preparing for her Communion at her parish and had studied the catechism at her school. She told Padre Pio that there was only one problem. She was wearing a simple green dress. Padre Pio said to her, "It is more pleasing for Jesus to come to you. You may certainly make your First Communion today."

With a great joy in her heart, Anna ran back to her mother and told her she had received Padre Pio's permission. Her mother had no choice then but to relent. She reasoned that she could make up for it at Anna's confirmation and have the desired party then.

Anna told the ladies who were directing the group of children that she had been given permission to make her Communion that day. She moved forward to join the other girls but the ladies rudely pushed her back. The most humiliating incident occurred when Anna was made to stand to the side and then forced to wait until all the boys went ahead of her. She took her place at the end of the line, the very last of all the communicants.

Anna's mother became furious when she saw the way her daughter was being treated. She jumped up and was about to rush up to the sanctuary to get Anna when her friend held her back. She did not want her to make a scene and ruin the day that was so special for Anna.

All of the children were then instructed to kneel down at the altar rail. Anna looked up and saw Padre Pio coming toward her. He smiled at her and told her to follow him. He walked up the altar steps to the very top and she followed behind him. He then gave her Holy Communion in front of the tabernacle. She was the only child to receive such a privilege that day. Everyone in the church watched in silence and awe. Some had tears in their eyes. Anna was overwhelmed by his loving gesture and her mother was also deeply moved. Anna and her mother would never forget the graces they received on that very special day.

———

When Gabby Silsby was a child, she and her family made frequent trips from their home in England to San Giovanni Rotondo to see Padre Pio. Her parents' devotion to Padre Pio was such that they visited the monastery whenever they could. Once, when Gabby was six years old, she was standing with many other pilgrims at the altar rail in the monastery church. As Padre Pio passed by, the people at the altar rail kissed his hand. When he passed in front of Gabby, he stretched out his hand to her. Not knowing any better, she took his hand in hers and shook it. When Padre Pio winced with pain, she immediately realized her mistake and felt terrible about what she had done. Padre Pio spoke to her with great kindness and said, "Yes, these are the wounds of Christ." He then put his hand on her head in a blessing. The moment he touched her, she had the sensation of an enormous weight pressing on her head. It was of such force that it felt like it was pushing her into the ground.

A little boy of five years old, Nunzio Fugaccio, from Naples, had found a way to dodge the doorkeeper at the monastery of Our Lady of Grace. Nunzio would then run directly up to Padre Pio who was usually surrounded by visitors. He enjoyed greeting Padre Pio and receiving his blessing. When it was time for everyone to leave, Nunzio would leave too.

A priest from Bari had often noticed little Nunzio among the group of pilgrims. One evening after everybody had left and Padre Pio was about to go to his cell, the priest said to the boy, "Nunzio, Padre Pio has candy with him. If you ask him for a piece, he will give it to you." He thought he was making a good suggestion but Nunzio did not see it that way. He answered very indignantly, "You ask the saints for graces, not for sweets!" Visibly upset, little Nunzio then turned around and left. Amazed, the priest went to Padre Pio and told him what Nunzio had said. Padre Pio enjoyed the story so much that he could not stop laughing.

Katharina Tangari, who lived in Naples, Italy, was one of Padre Pio's spiritual daughters. One evening, Katharina's neighbor came over to see her. With tears in her eyes, she told Katharina that she was very worried about her daughter, Claretta. Claretta, who was almost a year old, was having trouble walking and had developed a very noticeable limp. Claretta's mother then took her to one doctor after another. Finally, she went to see a specialist in Bologna. It was discovered that Claretta had a congenital defect in her leg. She was put in a plaster cast that went up to her chest. Her mother had to take her to Bologna every six months and have the cast changed. In December of 1951, the third cast was put on her leg. Unfortunately, after a thorough examination, the orthopedic specialist said that he saw no sign of improvement.

The day before Christmas, Katharina made a trip from her home in Naples to San Giovanni Rotondo. Claretta's mother asked her to speak to Padre Pio about her daughter's condition and to request his prayers. Katharina was very happy to do so.

After the Mass, Katharina stood near the sacristy, hoping to say a word to Padre Pio. As he approached the sacristy, Katharina wished him a Merry Christmas. Padre Pio greeted her in a friendly way. Katharina was so excited by the short exchange that she completely forgot to mention Claretta. Just before Padre Pio entered the sacristy, he paused momentarily. Katharina suddenly remembered Claretta and quickly said, "Padre Pio, Claretta's leg!" Padre Pio smiled at Katharina and said, "On St. Joseph's Day!"

When Katharina returned to Naples and told her neighbor what Padre Pio had said, her neighbor was disappointed. St. Joseph's day was on March 19, about three months away. She was hoping that her daughter's condition would improve sooner than that. On the morning of March 18, when Claretta woke up, it was discovered that her plaster cast had fallen off and had broken into many pieces. Her mother took her to Bologna to get a new cast. On March 19, the feast of St. Joseph, x-rays showed that Claretta's leg was finally in the process of healing. She no longer needed to wear a cast.

Claretta's leg was still weak. The specialist in Bologna advised gentle exercise and walking to strengthen her leg. Claretta's mother was afraid to follow the doctor's recommendations. She didn't want Claretta to fall down or to hurt herself. She ignored the doctor's advice and instead carried Claretta in her arms or took her about in a wheelchair. Her fears became almost overwhelming.

During Advent of 1952, Katharina made another trip to San Giovanni Rotondo. While making her confession to Padre Pio, she told him how fearful Claretta's mother had become and she asked for his prayers. Padre Pio gave Katharina a beautiful holy card of the Infant Jesus of Prague. He told Katharina that Christmas was an especially good time to ask for graces from the Lord. "Entrust everything to the Child Jesus," Padre Pio said to Katharina. Claretta's mother attended Mass in Naples on Christmas Eve. When she returned to her home, little Claretta began walking on her own accord. She continued to steadily improve from that time forward.

There was a boy who had a great desire for an electric train. For months he had asked his parents to get him a train. When it was close to the feast of Epiphany, the boy said a heartfelt prayer to Padre Pio, "Padre Pio, if you help me get an electric train, I will bring you a box of candy when I come to visit you."

The boy's father was a policeman. On the feast of the Epiphany, it was the custom at the time to give the police officers gifts. One of the gifts his father received was an electric train and quite naturally, he gave it to his son. Some time later the boy's aunt took him to San Giovanni Rotondo. When Padre Pio saw the boy, he said, "Well, did you bring me the candy?"

Kevin Hopkins was diagnosed with a very rare, aggressive, and lethal type of cancer called Leptomeningeal Sarcoma when he was four years old. All of the doctors were of the opinion that Kevin would not survive. They could not give the family even a ray of hope.

On May 25, a Eucharistic Minister came to Kevin's room in the hospital. She explained to Kevin's mother that she was visiting patients on another floor of the hospital when she suddenly felt strongly compelled to go to room 1065, Kevin's room. She wanted to tell Kevin and his mother that it was a special day. It was Padre Pio's birthday. She had a small book of Padre Pio's sayings in her hand called, *Have a Good Day*. She read the words to Kevin and his mother for May 25 which said, "Science for all its greatness, is nevertheless a small thing, and less than nothing compared to the formidable mystery of the Divinity."

Not long after, Kevin had surgery and chemotherapy. One year later, the tumor had not returned and the doctors declared that Kevin was cancer-free. His oncologist called it "unprecedented." His pediatrician too was very surprised. The family was convinced that Kevin had received a miracle through Padre Pio.

Margaret Cunningham was frail from the time she was born. Her fatigue and weakness was a great concern to her mother. Various doctors were consulted but they could never determine the cause of her problem. The doctors believed that Margaret's condition would probably improve with time.

When Margaret was eleven years old, she was examined by the school doctor. He suspected that Margaret had a problem with her heart and advised her mother to take her to a heart specialist. When the heart specialist's report came back, it was discovered that Margaret had a hole in her heart and that the valves to her heart were smaller than what was normal. She was scheduled for an operation, but was so weak that the doctors had to postpone it. They put her on medication and waited for her strength to build up so that they could proceed with the surgery.

Margaret told her mother that she wanted to write a letter to Padre Pio and request his prayers. After she sent the letter, it wasn't long before she received a reply in the mail. The letter said that Padre Pio was praying for her. It was a great consolation for Margaret and her family to know that she was included in Padre Pio's daily prayers.

When Margaret returned to the doctor, x-rays were taken once again. The doctor came out and said to Margaret's mother, "What have you done to your daughter?" "What do you mean?" her mother replied. "I have not done anything to her." The doctor showed her the two x-rays. The x-ray which had been taken at the time of her diagnosis, showed a large hole in the area of her heart. The x-ray which had just been taken, showed that the hole was almost closed. Margaret did not have to have surgery and her health continued to improve from that time forward.

Kelly Wilkinson was born in Belfast, Ireland in 1976. Shortly before her birth, the doctors discovered that she had an elevated heartbeat. She was born by cesarean section and placed in the special pediatric intensive care unit in Mater Hospital. Tests revealed that Kelly had a congenital heart defect.

Because of her defective heart, she also had an enlarged liver. She was so ill that the doctor feared that she might not last through the night.

The next day, Dr. Fraser came to Mrs. Ann Wilkinson's bedside and gave her a full report. Kelly's heart catheterization test showed that Kelly's heart had not developed properly. She had only one ventricle instead of two ventricles. Dr. Fraser told Ann that there was nothing that could be done to correct the problem. Not even a heart transplant could help Kelly. Medication was given to her to stimulate her heart so that she would have a regular heart beat. Dr. Fraser explained that the strain on Kelly's heart would increase with the passage of time. Eventually, she would have a fatal heart attack. Without coming out and saying how long Kelly could be expected to live, Ann understood from the doctor's words that Kelly would not live very long. She might not even make it to her first birthday.

Jim, Ann's husband, went to see Kelly in the pediatric intensive care unit. There were a number of other babies there, all in incubators. Jim spoke to the doctor about Kelly. Even though Kelly had a life-threatening problem, she did not look sick like some of the other babies. Kelly was so pretty and so perfectly proportioned. Even though she was tiny, she looked healthy. It was hard for Jim to believe that anything was wrong with her. He could not accept the diagnosis. The doctor told Jim that a number of the other babies in the intensive care unit had between a 30 to 50 percent chance of survival. Kelly however did not have even a 1 percent chance.

Ann's mother gave Ann a prayer card of Padre Pio. She told her to pray to Padre Pio and ask for his intercession for Kelly's healing. When she told Ann some of the particulars of Padre Pio's life, Ann knew that she could not pray to him. He seemed too holy, too far above her. When she learned that Padre Pio had the gift of reading hearts, she became even more convinced that she could not pray to him. If Padre Pio looked into her heart, she felt it would prove to be a great disappointment.

It was a great day for Ann and Jim when they finally got to bring Kelly home from the hospital. She had to stay sitting upright rather than lying flat on her back because of her erratic breathing. She had very little energy and seemed to sleep all the time. If she exerted herself in any way, her lips would turn blue. She had to take a number of medications through the day and the night. There were many trips to the doctor for check-ups. Ann's mother faithfully prayed the novena to Padre Pio every day for Kelly's healing.

When Kelly was four years old, the doctor scheduled another heart catheterization in order to see how her heart was functioning. Kelly seemed to be getting weaker all the time. Ann knew that in Kelly's condition, any medical procedure could be dangerous but the doctor insisted that it was necessary.

Ann learned that there was a woman named Kay Thornton who possessed one of Padre Pio's gloves. Kay lived in Skerries, a seaside town in North County Dublin. Ann and her husband took Kelly to Kay's home where she was blessed with the relic. When Ann and her husband were getting ready to leave, Kay gave them some information on Padre Pio, including prayer cards and magazines. They were very grateful to Kay and felt blessed by the visit.

That night after putting Kelly to bed, Ann said a prayer to Padre Pio for the first time, asking for his intercession. No sooner had she finished her prayer, than Kelly got out of bed and came into her room. Kelly said that there was an old man in her bedroom. Ann assured her that it was just a dream but Kelly insisted that it was true. She asked her mother to come into her bedroom and see for herself. Ann followed her daughter into her bedroom. "He is right there!" Kelly exclaimed. Ann looked in the direction that Kelly pointed but could see nothing. She put her daughter back to bed and told her to try to get to sleep. The next day she would be going to the hospital.

The next morning, the family got ready to make the trip to Belfast for Kelly's heart procedure. Before they left the house, Ann asked Kelly to get something out of her purse. When Kelly opened the purse, she saw one of the magazines that Kay Thornton had given her mother. It had a picture of Padre Pio on the cover. Kelly took the magazine to her mother and pointed to the picture of Padre Pio. "Mommie," Kelly said. "That is the old man that I saw in my room last night." The magazine showed Padre Pio wearing his customary dark brown Capuchin habit. Kelly had mentioned to Ann that the old man was wearing a dark coat. For the first time, Ann wondered if it was possible that Padre Pio had actually paid her daughter a visit. When they arrived in Belfast, Ann told her mother about the incident. Her mother was convinced that Padre Pio had visited Kelly and that everything was going to be all right.

After the heart procedure was completed, the cardiologist spoke to Ann about the results. He first showed her the earlier tests, given at Kelly's birth.

Her liver was greatly enlarged and there was only one single ventricle rather than two leading to her heart. He pointed to the test that had been taken that very day. There was no longer any congenital heart defect. Her heart was perfectly normal. The piece that had once been missing was no longer missing. The doctor stated that there was no medical explanation for the change. "Mrs. Wilkinson, all I can say is that you have received a miracle!" the doctor exclaimed.

Immediately Ann thought of Padre Pio. Her mother had prayed to him for Kelly with great faith, day after day, year after year. Ann too had prayed to Padre Pio, but just once. Ann was convinced that Padre Pio had interceded on their behalf and had obtained the miracle for Kelly.

———————

Padre Pio was beatified in Rome by Pope John Paul II on May 2, 1999. That was also a special day for the Egan family, for that was the day that little Joseph Egan made his first Holy Communion. When Joseph woke up that morning, he told his mother and father that he had a beautiful dream of Padre Pio. In his dream, Padre Pio was standing on a grey cloud. He had on a brown robe and held a crucifix in one hand and a book in the other. He spoke to Joseph and said, "Today all will get a blessing in honor of my Beatification."

———————

Joey Finn of Hudson, New York had been coping with severe asthma for most of his childhood. In 2005, when Joey was ten years old, he was diagnosed with cystic fibrosis, an incurable disease that makes it difficult to breathe and eventually destroys the lungs completely. Joey's lungs already showed the damage from the disease and he would have to have breathing treatments twice a day for the rest of his life. The median survival age for those who have the disease is in the early thirties.

Shortly after Joey's diagnosis, his mother, Melissa Finn was introduced to the Make-A-Wish Foundation, a nonprofit organization which offers children with chronic, life threatening diseases, the opportunity to make a wish and have it granted. For those who daily struggle with incurable illnesses, the

chance to have a wish come true is truly a blessing. Suddenly, there is something positive and enjoyable to look forward to in life. The Make-A-Wish
Foundation, in its ministry of compassion, has brought happiness to countless
children.

When Joey said that he would like to submit a wish to the Foundation for
consideration, his mother guessed that he would probably request a trip to
Disney World in Florida. However, when he told his mother what he wished
for, she could not have been more surprised. Joey wanted to travel to San
Giovanni Rotondo to pray at the tomb of Padre Pio. He also wanted to see the
Holy Father in Rome. Where did the desire come from? That is a good question. Joey did not grow up in a particularly religious household. Although the
Finns were Catholics, they did not attend Mass on Sunday. As it turned out,
Joey had seen a documentary on the life of Padre Pio on the History Channel
which had greatly inspired him. He learned about Padre Pio's stigmata, his
prayer life, and his deep faith in God. Like Joey, Padre Pio had suffered most
of his life with poor health. He was afflicted with chronic breathing problems, including asthma and bronchitis. It was an acute case of asthma that was
a contributing cause of Padre Pio's death in September 1968.

In thinking of her son's wish, Melissa had one deep concern. She was
afraid that Joey would be crushed if he expected a miracle from Padre Pio and
did not receive one. She talked to him about it and he assured her that was
not the case. He had a devotion to Padre Pio and wanted to pray at his tomb.
He intended to offer up his prayers for all the people in the world who were
stricken with cystic fibrosis and to pray that there would someday be a cure.

One recalls that Padre Pio felt a great call to help the sick and suffering, not only through his daily intercessory prayers but also through concrete
action. He spoke of the Home for the Relief of Suffering as his "earthly mission." There were many scoffers and detractors who doubted that the project
could ever succeed. But against all odds, the Home grew and prospered and
has helped countless lives.

Joey Finn's wish was certainly one of the most unique that had been submitted to the Make-A-Wish Foundation. Some of the popular requests made
of the Foundation included a shopping spree at the mall, an outdoor play-
ground, and even a trip to the Super Bowl. Occasionally, children requested
a trip to Honolulu or to Hollywood. But the request to visit San Giovanni

Rotondo in southern Italy had to be a first. The Foundation checked with Joey's mother to make sure that it was her son's wish and not hers. She assured them that she was just as surprised as anyone else when she found out the desire of Joey's heart.

Joey's request was finally approved and in June 2007, twelve-year-old Joey along with his mother, father and thirteen-year-old sister made preparations to travel to Italy. Their first surprise came shortly after they boarded the plane. The pilot came over the loud speaker and proposed a question to all the passengers. "Is it true that Joey Finn, who is sponsored by the Make-A-Wish Foundation, is on board the plane?" the pilot asked. Joey's excitement intensified when the pilot asked him if he would like to step to the cockpit and turn the key to start the airplane. His reply was an enthusiastic, "Yes!" It was the beginning of an extraordinary journey for the entire Finn family.

The first stop on the Finns' remarkable pilgrimage was to Rome, where they toured the Vatican. They spent time at the beautiful Sistine Chapel, St. Peter's Basilica, the Catacombs, the Holy Stairs and more. Along with a multitude of others, they were able to see the Holy Father and to receive his papal blessing.

In San Giovanni Rotondo, the Finns stood in line with many other pilgrims in order to make a visit to Padre Pio's tomb. All prayed the Rosary while they waited. They literally just squeezed into the church as it was closing that evening. Melissa was the last person allowed to enter the church before the doors were locked.

Padre Pio's tomb was below the main altar of the church and was surrounded by an iron grating. People were able to draw very close to the tomb but the iron grating prevented anyone from actually touching it. On the evening of the Finns' visit, the little iron gate was wide open. All those who were present were allowed to place their hand on Padre Pio's tomb. Melissa Finn was later told that the iron gate is customarily closed and locked at all times.

The Finn family never imagined the impact the trip to San Giovanni Rotondo would have on their lives. Melissa Finn felt compelled to go to confession while visiting the monastery church of Our Lady of Grace. She had not been to confession in more than twenty-five years. Joey told his mother that when he stood and prayed at Padre Pio's tomb, he had the sense that Padre

Pio had heard his prayers. "Padre Pio has taken our family in as his own," Joey said to his mother.

For the Finns, the time spent at Padre Pio's monastery was a time of spiritual renewal and positive change. After returning home, they began to attend Mass together every Sunday as a family. It was something they had not done for a long time. Joey had a desire to learn more about his Catholic faith and to serve the Church. He soon became an altar server each Sunday at Mass.

Joey had been able to purchase some very meaningful souvenirs of Padre Pio while in Italy. Back in Hudson, New York, he set up his own little shrine dedicated to his patron saint and placed it on display in his home. Quite unexpectedly, he even received a third class relic of the saint. A nurse who had heard about Joey was touched by his story. She sent him a very special gift. It was a Rosary which had been blessed by Padre Pio. One of her elderly patients had given it to her.

"I believe that Joey found something in Italy which is of equal value to finding a cure for his disease," Melissa Finn said. "He found his faith, the strength that he will need in his lifetime to endure the challenges that lie ahead of him. He prayed, he listened, he learned . . . He did this of his own free will and with great determination." In the final analysis, the greatest healings of all are those that take place in the human soul.

Fill up the empty places in your heart with ardent love of God. Humble yourself more and more beneath God's powerful hand and always accept cheerfully and humbly the trials he sends us, so that at the time of his visitation, he may raise us up by his grace. Let us cast all our care upon him, for he is more concerned about us than a mother is for her little child.

- St. Pio of Pietrelcina

Our present life is given only to gain the eternal one and if we don't think about it, we build our affections on what belongs to this world, where our life is transitory. When we have to leave it we are afraid and become agitated. Believe me, to live happily in this pilgrimage, we have to aim at the hope of arriving at our Homeland, where we will stay eternally. Meanwhile we have to believe firmly that God calls us to himself and follows us along the path towards him. He will never permit anything to happen to us that is not for our greater good. He knows who we are and he will hold out his paternal hand to us during difficulties, so that nothing prevents us from running to him swiftly. But to enjoy this grace we must have complete trust in him.

- St. Pio of Pietrelcina

CHAPTER 33

More Remarkable Conversions

A man from Genoa, Italy had been away from the church for most of his life. On one occasion, one of his friends asked him to deliver a letter to Padre Pio. Since he was not too far from San Giovanni Rotondo at the time, he agreed to do so. The letter needed an immediate reply. When the man knocked on the monastery door, one of the Capuchins directed him to the sacristy. "Just wait here. Padre Pio will be down soon to take the letter," the Capuchin said.

When Padre Pio came to the sacristy, he exchanged a few words with the man. Unimpressed by the encounter, the man wanted to leave the monastery as soon as possible. "I just need a reply to this letter and then I will be on my way," the man said. "I understand," Padre Pio replied. "And what about you? Do you want to make your confession while you are here?" "Oh no, I do not care to. I do not even go to church," the man said. "When was the last time you made your confession?" Padre Pio asked. "It was when I was seven years old," the man answered. Padre Pio suddenly became stern, "How long do you plan on living such a worthless and disgusting life?" Suddenly a light seemed to penetrate the man's mind. He realized that Padre Pio was right. He had been living a meaningless existence for years. All at once, he knew that he needed to change. The man made a sincere confession to Padre Pio and left the monastery completely transformed.

Once when Padre Pio was a young priest, he visited a man who was gravely ill. The doctor confided to Padre Pio that the man would not last through the night. Padre Pio prayed at the man's bedside and gave him his priestly blessing. "It would be a good idea if you made your confession now," Padre Pio said to the man. "Oh no, I am not going to do that," the man replied. "Maybe later, when I am feeling better." Padre Pio made a great effort to convince the man of the importance of making his confession. He tried every approach he could think of as he reasoned with him about the matter. However, the man could not be persuaded.

Padre Pio thought to himself that desperate cases needed desperate remedies. This was definitely a desperate case. He said goodbye to the man and walked toward the door to leave. "We will meet again but the next time we meet, it will be at the cemetery," Padre Pio said. The man was shocked at his words and asked for an explanation. "Your doctor has told me that your condition is so serious that you will not last through the night," Padre Pio explained. The man was then able to understand the importance of preparing himself for death and he immediately made his confession. Padre Pio then absolved him and gave him Holy Communion. The man died peacefully that very night.

Aurilio Montalvo of Bolzano, Italy visited San Giovanni Rotondo in order to make his confession to Padre Pio and to attend his Mass. He returned a number of times and felt so inspired that he decided to move there permanently with his wife and four children. He bought a hotel close to the monastery and from the income of the hotel, he was able to provide for his family and take care of all of their needs.

Aurilio had a brother who was a nonbeliever. He had never met Padre Pio. He visited San Giovanni Rotondo right after Padre Pio passed away. Before Padre Pio's funeral, he had a desire to view Padre Pio's body when it was lying in state. However, it was so crowded in the church that the Capuchins decided it would be best to lock the doors. He was never able to see Padre Pio, not even in death.

One day Aurilio and his brother had a talk about Padre Pio. Aurilio's brother told him that he really had no feeling for Padre Pio. He certainly did not believe that he was a saint. All the talk about Padre Pio left him cold and completely indifferent.

Not long after their conversation, Aurilio's brother walked over to the church of Our Lady of Grace and sat alone on one of the back benches. Suddenly he felt a tap on his shoulder and heard a stern voice. He turned to see who it was but there was no one there. He became frightened and immediately got up and moved to another bench the church.

A second time, he heard an authoritative voice and felt someone touch his shoulder. He looked in all directions but there was no one there. He was so frightened that he broke out in a cold sweat. How could he hear someone talking and feel someone touching his shoulder when no one was there?

The next time Aurilio saw his brother, he heard every detail of the unusual story. "How does someone go about making their confession?" his brother asked. Aurilio was happy to talk to him about the sacrament in great detail. "How does one prepare himself to make his first Holy Communion?" his brother asked. Again, Aurilio was very glad to explain it to him.

That night Aurilio's brother had a dream. Padre Pio was standing beside him with a Rosary in his hand and taught him how to pray. The dream marked the beginning of his conversion. Right after that, he asked to be received into the Catholic Church. From that time forward, he lived a very devout life.

———

Raffaele Scalzi invited an elderly friend to go with him to see Padre Pio. The year was 1958. Raffaele and his companion were able to greet Padre Pio in the corridor of the monastery. Padre Pio extended his hand to the elderly man to kiss but not to Raffaele. Padre Pio then continued walking down the hall. Raffaele felt very disappointed by the encounter. He wondered why Padre Pio had rejected him but had been so cordial to his friend.

After Padre Pio had walked a few steps down the hall, he turned around and looked back at Raffaele. He said to him, "May God enlighten you," and then he continued on his way. Raffaele believed that Padre Pio had turned and spoken to him because he had sensed that he had hurt his feelings.

Later, Raffaele saw one of the Capuchins and told him about his encounter with Padre Pio. "Padre Pio spoke to me in the corridor and said, "May God enlighten you." Does he say that very often?" Raffaele asked. "No, he doesn't," the Capuchin replied. "I have never heard him say that to anyone before."

The next day, Raffaele and his friend left San Giovanni Rotondo to return to their homes. Once home, Raffaele could not get the thought of Padre Pio out of his mind. He had been shocked when Padre Pio withheld his hand from him. It caused him to take stock of his life. "May God enlighten you," were the words that kept resounding in Raffaele's mind. Why had Padre Pio said that to him? Raffaele believed that he knew the answer. He admitted to himself that he was in great need of spiritual enlightenment. Raffaele was a non-practicing Catholic. His faith life had withered and died due to long years of neglect. Even though he had been baptized a Catholic, he knew practically nothing about the teachings of the Catholic Church. He had never had the slightest interest in studying his faith.

With great anticipation, Raffaele planned his next visit to San Giovanni Rotondo. The only problem was that he did not have the money to make the trip. It was expensive to travel from his home in Vicenza, in the north of Italy, down to the southern area of San Giovanni Rotondo.

A short time later, one of Raffaele's friends needed 500 lira and asked Raffaele for the money. Raffaele was not in a position to be giving money away. Anyway, he had decided to save any extra money that he could come by so that one day he could return to San Giovanni Rotondo. However, his friend was insistent. Raffaele finally agreed to give him the needed money. Not long after that, his friend returned and handed Raffaele 50,000 lira. He had won a large sum by choosing the correct numbers in a football betting pool. The unexpected money enabled Raffaele to travel to San Giovanni a second time.

Raffaele had to wait five days to make his confession to Padre Pio. When his turn finally came, Padre Pio greeted him and allowed him to kiss his hand. Raffaele's heart soared. "How many years has it been since you have been to Mass?" Padre Pio asked. "It has been ten years," Raffaele replied. Upon hearing Raphael's reply, Padre Pio became stern. He raised his voice and said, "Do not waste my time. Go now!"

There were a number of men standing nearby, waiting in the confessional line. Raffaele was certain that they had heard Padre Pio's strong words. But strangely, Raffaele did not feel the least bit embarrassed or ashamed. He was not offended by what Padre Pio had said to him. Quite the contrary, he felt a great happiness, a "celestial happiness" welling up in his heart. At that moment, he was exactly where he wanted to be. He was kneeling in front of Padre Pio, looking into his eyes, speaking to him. He could hardly contain his joy.

One of the other Capuchins who was in residence at Our Lady of Grace monastery offered to hear Raffaele's confession. Afterwards, Raffaele went out and bought a Rosary and a prayer book. Eleven months later, he returned to San Giovanni Rotondo and knelt before Padre Pio in the confessional once again. "Have you been attending Mass?" Padre Pio asked. "Yes, I have gone to Mass every Sunday since I last saw you," Raffaele replied. "Have you been attending Mass on the Holy Days of Obligation as well?" Padre Pio inquired. "Yes, I have also gone to Mass on every Holy Day of Obligation. I have not missed a single one," Raffaele answered. Three times Padre Pio exclaimed, "Ah." It was as though he was saying, "All is well now. All is very good." For the next ten years, until Padre Pio's death in 1968, Raffaele traveled twice a year to San Giovanni Rotondo to attend Padre Pio's Mass and to make his confession.

————

I grew up in San Giovanni Rotondo and I knew Padre Pio from my childhood. If he had not been so strict with me at times, I would have never corrected myself or made the effort to improve. I will never forget his radical influence over my life.

-*Gherardo Leone*

Remember that we are children of an infinitely merciful Father who is very indulgent toward us.

- St. Pio of Pietrelcina

CHAPTER 34

Antonio Paladino

A ntonio Paladino of Foggia, Italy, earned his living as a day laborer. He had a serious accident on one occasion when he was hit by a car. Due to the accident, he lost most of the movement in his left foot. It became almost completely useless. He also incurred other serious injuries. Finally, he was declared totally disabled and was forced to retire from his job. Due to his disability, he received a small monthly pension.

Eventually, Antonio married and had a large family. As time passed, his health began to decline. He suffered from a heart condition as well as a lung disease. He was hospitalized on many occasions. Instead of improving, he grew steadily worse. The small pension he received was not enough to support his wife and twelve children. Antonio felt a growing sense of anger and frustration regarding the many trials in his life. As a result, he lost his faith in God. His moral life deteriorated as well. He had a deep sense of guilt regarding some of his actions but he did not have the motivation to change.

A number of people urged Antonio to visit the Home for the Relief of Suffering in San Giovanni Rotondo. It was considered to be one of the finest hospitals in Italy. It boasted of an impressive staff of doctors as well as state of the art medical technology. Antonio's failing health caused him to feel desperate. He finally agreed to seek medical help in San Giovanni Rotondo.

Antonio was taken to the Home for the Relief of Suffering on a stretcher on December 6, 1968. He hoped for improved health but he was not confident that the doctors would be able to help him. His health had been deteriorating for years.

Day after day, Antonio lay in bed, immobilized and in great pain. A cane was beside his bed but it was of no use to him. His legs were completely paralyzed. Antonio's anger and depression over his condition was apparent to all who entered his hospital room. He used bad language while speaking to the doctors, the nurses, and even to the nuns who worked at the hospital. He did not care that his profanities offended the hospital staff. It almost seemed as if he enjoyed offending people.

Padre Pio, who had passed away just two months before, was also on the receiving end of Antonio's anger. What did Antonio think of Padre Pio? He believed him to be a deceiver and a charlatan. And Padre Pio's hospital? It had not improved Antonio's condition in any way. As far as he was concerned, the Home for the Relief of Suffering was just another failure. He was convinced that when he was finally discharged, he would be no better off than when he had entered.

On the evening of December 12, Antonio was sleeping soundly in his hospital bed when he suddenly felt someone tapping him on the shoulder. Five times he was tapped on his shoulder. Antonio opened his eyes to find a monk standing beside his bed. "Get up and come with me," the monk said. "But I cannot walk," Antonio replied. "You must get up and follow me," the monk insisted. Antonio looked over at the cane that was in his room, even though he knew it was useless to him. "You will not need that cane," the monk said. Antonio was amazed to find that he could move his legs. He was able to get out of bed without assistance.

Antonio followed behind the monk who walked up and down the hospital corridor. Antonio had been immobile for so long that he was exhausted by the brief exercise. His entire body was sweating profusely. Nevertheless, he followed the monk obediently, like a puppy dog would follow its master. Finally, they returned to Antonio's room. The monk smiled at Antonio and said, "You have done well. Are you convinced now that you can walk just like anyone else? Tomorrow you will feel even better than you do right now. Antonio, I want you to come and visit my tomb." Right after that, the monk vanished. Antonio then understood that his visitor had been Padre Pio.

The next morning, Antonio felt a great happiness in his heart. He was simply bursting with joy. He felt renewed within and without. He realized that the constant pain that had wracked his body for many years was gone. His breathing too felt completely normal. He was certain that he no longer needed to depend on the oxygen tank that was at his bedside. When he got out of bed and walked down the hall, the hospital staff looked at him in disbelief. Antonio explained that Padre Pio had come to him in the night and had healed him. He told the details of his remarkable experience to the doctors, the nurses, and the patients. Everyone listened with great interest. For several days, Antonio did nothing but repeat his story over and over again to the many people who asked him for an explanation.

Dr. Federico Ficola, who worked in the orthopedic and trauma departments at the Home for the Relief of Suffering, listened with great interest to Antonio's story. Dr. Ficola saw the amazing change in Antonio's condition and marveled at it. Dr. Giuseppe Gusso, the chief of staff and medical director of the Home for the Relief of Suffering, also saw the transformation in Antonio's physical condition. Dr. Gusso noted that Antonio's personality seemed to have undergone a complete transformation as well.

Before his remarkable experience, Antonio had been openly hostile to those he came in contact with. His arrogance and sarcasm made him very unpleasant to be with. However, his anger and negativity seemed to have vanished overnight. He now interacted with people in a loving and friendly way. He had previously been a nonbeliever. He now acknowledged God sincerely, with his words and with his actions. It was obvious to everyone who spoke to him that he was a man of deep faith. He began to pray diligently for all of the patients at the Home for the Relief of Suffering. Antonio had truly been healed in body, mind, and spirit.

Soon, Antonio was discharged from the Home for the Relief of Suffering. Upon leaving the hospital, he went to the monastery of Our Lady of Grace. He had an important appointment to keep. When Padre Pio had appeared to him in the hospital, he had asked him to visit his tomb. Antonio walked down to the tomb unaided. He no longer needed to use a wheelchair. He knew that he had Padre Pio to thank for that.

A number of people were gathered at Padre Pio's tomb when Antonio arrived. He knelt down and prayed aloud without any shame. In a strong voice, he named the serious sins in his life, one by one. He asked God to forgive him. He was truly sorry for the many wrongs of his past. All who were at the tomb heard Antonio's public confession and were deeply moved. Many were crying when he finished his prayer. Antonio's family and friends had hoped that he might receive some improvement in his health at the Home for the Relief of Suffering. No one had ever imagined that he would receive so much.

I no sooner begin to pray than my heart is filled with a fire of love. This fire does not represent any fire on this lowly earth. It is a delicate and very gentle flame . . .This is a wonderful thing for me, something I will perhaps never understand until I get to heaven.

- *St. Pio of Pietrelcina*

CHAPTER 35

Alex Quinn

In June of 1998 Alex Quinn's fifteen-year-old son Philip, was sent home from school with a very bad headache. Within hours after coming home, Philip became paralyzed. Alex and his wife Deirdre rushed Philip to the Royal Victoria Hospital in Belfast. They were both terrified that their son was dying. The initial tests that were taken indicated that Philip had a brain tumor. But four days later, after a multitude of tests, Philip was diagnosed with the deadly disease called encephalitis. The virus had attacked the part of Philip's brain that controlled movement, speech and memory.

Alex and his wife Deirdre were devastated. They tried to hide their fear from their son and made every effort to appear upbeat and positive when they visited him in the hospital. Day after day he lay motionless and speechless in his hospital bed, showing no sign of improvement. It was heartbreaking for Alex and Deirdre to witness. Philip still had a slight bit of movement left in his hands. He communicated with his parents by placing his thumb up to say "yes" and placing his thumb down to say "no."

Alex learned that there was a man in Belfast named Brendan Rogers who possessed a relic of Padre Pio, a bandage that had covered his wounded side.

The relic had been given to Brendan by Father Alessio Parente, Padre Pio's secretary. Alex got in touch with Brendan and he kindly agreed to bring the relic to Philip. In the Royal Victoria Hospital, Philip was blessed with the relic of Padre Pio and all who were present prayed for his healing.

Weeks went by but sadly there was no improvement in Philip's condition. Finally, in September, there was a change. When Alex arrived at the hospital to visit his son, Deirdre was in tears. But they were not the usual tears of sadness, they were tears of joy. With great emotion, she told Alex that Philip had spoken a word to her that day. He had said, "mom." Alex cried too, not only because his heart was filled with renewed hope, but also because it happened to be September 23, Padre Pio's feast day. From that day forward, Philip slowly began to improve. He would eventually make a complete recovery.

September 23 marked a turning point in Alex's life as well. He had prayed to Padre Pio for his son's healing and Padre Pio had sent him an unmistakable sign that he had heard his prayers. Alex knew that his life would never be the same. He now felt certain that he had a special calling, a special mission to somehow express his gratitude to Padre Pio. He did not know how he would do so but he was determined to find a way.

In 2002, Alex's wife Deirdre was diagnosed with cancer. The family prayed to Padre Pio for another miracle but on August 15, 2003, on the feast of the Assumption, Deirdre passed away. She was surrounded by her loving family. Alex prayed that he would be able to accept the passing of his dear wife.

The night before Deirdre's funeral, Alex had a vision of his wife. She had a beautiful smile on her face and she was being carried to heaven by an angel. Alex was at peace, knowing that his wife was now free of pain and was happy in heaven. Alex clung to his faith in God and found the strength to go on.

Alex began to regularly attend a Padre Pio prayer group that was held in Belfast. One evening at the prayer group, Father O'Rawe, the spiritual director of the group, said that he would like one of the members of the group to compose a hymn to Padre Pio. As Father O'Rawe said the words, he looked directly at Alex. For many reasons, Alex seemed to be the perfect choice.

In addition to his job as a teacher at a primary school in West Belfast, Alex was also a professional musician and a song writer. He wrote the famous song *Belfast* which had become a big hit throughout the United Kingdom. Alex belonged to a musical group called *Barnbrack*. The group had been on tour through Ireland,

Scotland, England, and Canada and had even sung for the president of Ireland. People everywhere loved listening to the Irish folk ballads that *Barnbrack* sang.

Alex thought that Father O'Rawe had a wonderful idea regarding the song to Padre Pio. He decided to do his best to write a hymn in Padre Pio's honor. He felt that he owed Padre Pio a great debt. Alex was certain that his son's miraculous recovery was due to Padre Pio's intercession.

After Alex finished writing the song to Padre Pio, he went to a recording studio to have it professionally mastered. When the song was released, it became very popular in Ireland where devotion to Padre Pio has always been strong. The CD also featured thirteen other hymns including traditional favorites such as *Our God Reigns* and *Be Not Afraid*. Soon England and other countries as well were listening to the hymn to Padre Pio and buying the CD.

Alex decided to give all of the royalties from his song, *A Hymn to Padre Pio* to the monastery of Our Lady of Grace in San Giovanni Rotondo where Padre Pio had lived for more than fifty years. Alex knew that the Capuchins in residence there depended on the generosity of others to carry on their apostolate. Alex planned to go in person to deliver the check.

When Alex's royalties for his song to Padre Pio reached more than 10,000 Euros, he made preparations for his trip to San Giovanni Rotondo. He felt very insecure about traveling alone. In the past, he had always had his wife at his side whenever he went on a trip. One of Alex's friends was an Italian man. Alex asked him to write a note in Italian explaining that he was traveling to San Giovanni Rotondo. That way, if he got lost or turned around or had any difficulties on the trip, at least he would be able to have the note in hand which explained his destination. Alex's friend was happy to provide him with the note.

When Alex arrived at the airport in Rome, he looked for a taxi to take him to the bus station. It proved to be more difficult than he had imagined. Evidently, Alex's Irish accent made it almost impossible for the taxi driver to understand him. The taxi driver summoned five other taxi drivers in order to see if they could decipher what Alex was saying. Finally, one seemed to understand and motioned for him to get in his taxi.

Once at the bus station, Alex had the same difficulty when trying to communicate with the ticket-taker. When he asked for a round trip ticket to San Giovanni Rotondo, the ticket-taker could not understand his "Irish brogue."

Alex repeated his request a number of times but to no avail. He finally had to settle for a one way ticket.

At one point on the bus trip to San Giovanni Rotondo, the driver made a stop at a convenience store and everyone got off the bus to get something to eat. After Alex had a bite to eat, he stood close to the bus, waiting for the driver to return. By now it had grown dark. He was very tired but he knew that he had to stay alert. He had started his day in Belfast at 4:30 a.m. in preparation for his early flight to Rome. He estimated that he would get to San Giovanni Rotondo about midnight. He had made no hotel reservations and he had no idea where he would be staying for the night.

As Alex stood by the bus, he pondered his immediate situation and tried not to give in to a nagging feeling of anxiety. A stranger approached Alex and spoke to him in Italian but unfortunately he did not understand a single word of what was said. Alex then spoke to the man in English but the man was not able to understand him. Finally, because of the communication problem, the man simply stared at Alex. He was so friendly and engaging that it seemed a shame to Alex that they could not talk to each other. Alex then remembered the note in his wallet. He handed it to the man who read it with interest.

Soon everyone got back on the bus. Alex noticed that the kind man who had just spoken to him also boarded the bus. During the journey, Alex observed that the man was constantly on his cell phone, making one call after another. The bus driver made many stops along the way, letting people out at one small town after another. Every time the bus pulled to the side of the road to let people off, Alex would ask the bus driver if they were in San Giovanni Rotondo. He couldn't relax because he was afraid of missing his stop.

When the bus arrived in the town of Foggia, the kind man communicated to Alex by way of hand signals that he was to get off the bus with him. Alex was confused. He was not traveling to Foggia but to San Giovanni Rotondo. But for some reason, Alex trusted the man completely. He did as instructed. They were the only two passengers who got off at the Foggia stop.

In Foggia, Alex and his new found friend boarded another bus. Alex learned that it was the bus that went to San Giovanni Rotondo. Alex couldn't believe it. He had no idea that he needed to transfer to a second bus in order to reach his destination. If he had not been assisted by the man, who knows where he might have ended up that night.

When the bus arrived in San Giovanni Rotondo, the man motioned to Alex to follow him. They walked for about twenty minutes until they arrived at the man's house. The man then drove Alex to a beautiful hotel. To Alex's great surprise, it was right next to the monastery of Our Lady of Grace. Alex learned that the man had been using his cell phone on the bus, making one call after another, in order to make a hotel reservation for him.

The man went into the hotel and spoke to the manager. Alex was then given one of the finest hotel rooms available. After the man bid him farewell, Alex never saw him again. Unfortunately, he never even got his name. He had been a true "guardian angel" to Alex.

Once in his hotel room, Alex was able to let his guard down. Due to his excitement, his exhaustion, and feelings of loneliness, he began to cry. Thoughts of his late wife and of his children flooded his mind. Even so, in his heart he knew that he was not alone. He had received many signs of the Lord's watchful care.

The next day at the monastery of Our Lady of Grace, Alex received a warm welcome from the Capuchin community. They were very grateful to accept his generous donation and they were truly happy about the success of his song to Padre Pio. They invited him to eat with them in the monastery refectory, the same refectory where Padre Pio had taken all of his meals.

The Capuchins also took Alex to the private chapel where Padre Pio used to say his Mass during the 1930's when he was segregated from the public. Alex prayed in thanksgiving for the healing of his son. He also prayed for his wife Deirdre. He knew that she was with God now. He had the great consolation of seeing that she was at peace and that she was happy.

There would be many more occasions in Alex's life to give thanks to God for blessings received. He was now able to see that much good had come out of the painful experiences of the past. He would continue to see the hand of God working in miraculous ways in his life.

————

For more information on the CD by Alex Quinn *A Hymn to Padre Pio* as well as his newest CD which was made to benefit the Children's Hospice in Belfast, Northern Ireland, visit his website at www.barnbrack.bandcamp. com or contact Alex at: alexquinn1@yahoo.co.uk

To everything there is a season, a time for every purpose under heaven: A time to be born, and a time to die; a time to plant, and a time to uproot . . . a time to break down, and a time to build up, a time to weep, and a time to laugh; a time to mourn and a time to dance; a time to cast away stones, and a time to gather stones.

- Ecclesiastes 3:1-4

CHAPTER 36

Father Louis Solcia, C.R.S.P.

Father Louis Solcia has been the spiritual director for our Padre Pio prayer group at Our Lady of the Rosary parish in San Diego for almost 20 years. This is his testimony:

Amalie Gonzales was a little girl at our parish who taught me many things. She taught me much about both life and death. Her short life was a blessing to her family and to all those who knew her. It certainly was a blessing to me.

Amalie's mother, Amata, and her grandmother Marlene, regularly attended our Padre Pio prayer group at Our Lady of the Rosary parish. The family was very devout. Amelie, who followed the good example of her mother and grandmother, was a very spiritual child. Amata told me that when she took Amelie to the store each week, Amelie always wanted to buy a bouquet of roses to place in front of the statue of the Blessed Virgin Mary.

Amelie was diagnosed with a rare form of lung cancer called Pluropulmonary Blastoma. It is a cancer that occurs most often in infants and children but has also been reported in adults. The doctors hoped that chemotherapy treatments would stop the cancer. They used every modern medical means at their disposal. Finally, the doctors told the family that they had done everything in their power to save Amelie but the treatments had not arrested the cancer.

Amelie grew weaker as her disease progressed but strangely enough, she never looked sick. She had a desire to receive Holy Communion. Children ordinarily do not receive their first Holy Communion before the age of seven and Amelie was just five years old. But because she had a spiritual maturity beyond her years and because of her terminal diagnosis, I was able to give her Holy Communion.

Amelie told her mother that Padre Pio had come to her and had given her a blessing. One day, near the end of her life, she was lying in her bed, looking up at the ceiling in her room. Suddenly, the ceiling disappeared, and in its place she saw the evening sky, studded with brilliant stars. Jesus and Mary were there in the sky and they were smiling at her. Later, her mother showed her a holy card of Jesus. "Amelie, did Jesus look like this?" she asked. "No, he didn't," she replied. "He was so bright!"

Our Padre Pio prayer group had prayed for many weeks for Amelie. We all hoped in our hearts that she would be healed. But it was not to be. Amelie died peacefully in her mother's arms on December 14, 2009. On the day that she died, she saw a white butterfly. "Mommy, don't you see the butterfly?" she asked. But her mother could not see it. No one saw it but Amelie. After her death, Amelie truly looked like a little angel.

I had a desire to visit the cemetery where Amelie was buried and I went there on several occasions to pray. Beautiful red roses in a heart-shaped pattern had been placed on her grave by her mother. In my heart, I felt a great sadness. I wondered why God had taken such a beautiful little girl and left us all with such heavy hearts. I especially felt sorry for Amelie's family because of their grief. But then I reasoned to myself that God never allows something bad to happen unless He can draw good out of it. I have been a priest for more than fifty years and I have always believed that. But in this situation, I struggled with God. At the time, I could not see past the pain of the situation, but soon I would see the good that God would draw out of Amelie's death.

Amelie's best friend was her eight-year-old cousin, Alexis. The two girls were inseparable. After Amelie's death, Alexis' sister, Cassandra, had a vivid dream. In her dream, Amelie was looking everywhere for Alexis. "Where is Alexis?" she asked. "I want to find Alexis!" It was shortly after Cassandra's dream that Alexis announced that she wanted to take instructions in the Catholic faith and she wanted to be baptized. Everyone in the family was surprised. Alexis' desire seemed to come out of nowhere. There was certainly no one in her family encouraging her to take that step. It occurred to me that perhaps Amelie was now able to help her loved ones from heaven.

Alexis' mother had no religious affiliation and she never took the family to church on Sunday. However, she was willing to let Alexis take instruction in the Catholic faith. Amalie's mother now brings Alexis to our parish once a week. I am giving her the instructions myself and preparing her for baptism, confirmation and for her first Holy Communion. God can and does draw good out of the hard and painful situations in life. We only have to look and we will see.

I waited patiently for the Lord. He turned to me and heard my cry. He lifted me out of the pit. . .He set my feet on a rock and gave me a firm place to stand. He put a new song in my mouth, a hymn of praise to our God. Many will see it and fear, and put their trust in the Lord.

- Psalm 40:1-3

CHAPTER 37

Bill Gleason

*A*t one of our Padre Pio prayer group meetings, Father Louis Solcia asked Bill Gleason, one of our members, to step forward and share his testimony. Bill had received a beautiful grace from Padre Pio. Later, we met with Bill at the rectory of Our Lady of the Rosary parish in San Diego and learned even more of the details. This is Bill's story:

Bill Gleason was getting ready to have shoulder surgery in the winter of 2008. The night before the surgery, Bill decided to go to the rectory at Our Lady of the Rosary parish and ask one of the priests for a blessing. Father Louis Solcia answered the rectory door that evening. He blessed Bill with the holy oil of St. Pio and gave him a prayer card. It had St. Pio's picture on one side and the novena to the Sacred Heart of Jesus on the other. Bill was happy to accept it even though he didn't know anything about St. Pio. Father Louis told him to put it in the pocket of his hospital gown and to keep it there during the surgery.

Bill was not too concerned about the surgery. It was going to be a routine operation, a rotator cuff repair. Nevertheless, he was going to have to go under general anesthesia and he knew that when doing so, risks were always involved. He was glad that Father Solcia had prayed for him. Bill had been praying quite a lot in recent months. Due to budget cuts in the state of California, he had been laid off from his supervisory position at the County Office of Education. Ever since the lay off, he had prayed to God for guidance. "Lord, show me what you want me to do with my life and lead me in the path you have marked out for me," he frequently prayed.

Bill had the shoulder surgery and was supposed to be discharged from the hospital that very afternoon. However, during the surgery Bill's breathing became erratic. He had to stay overnight in the hospital and receive breathing treatments throughout the night. Late that evening, his wife Mary Ann called his nurse to see how he was doing. She told the nurse that Bill had a Padre Pio prayer card in the pocket of his hospital gown and she wanted to make sure that he still had it with him. The nurse explained to Mary Ann that Bill had put on a new gown and his other gown had already been sent to the hospital laundry room. The nurse was sorry, but it was too late to recover it.

The next morning, Bill was very surprised to see his Padre Pio prayer card in his room. Bill's nurse told him that she could sense Mary Ann's disappointment upon learning that the prayer card was gone. The nurse realized that it must have been important. About two o'clock in the morning, she felt a strong urge to go in search of it. She went to the hospital laundry room and looked through the many bins of dirty clothes until she found it.

After Bill was released from the hospital, he told Mary Ann that he thought they should start attending the Padre Pio prayer group at Our Lady of the Rosary parish. Neither of them had ever attended it before. He also wanted to make a commitment to pray the novena to the Sacred Heart of Jesus every day. Father Solcia had told him that it was the prayer that Padre Pio had said daily throughout his life. Bill had thought a lot about the fact that his nurse at the hospital had taken it upon herself to search for his Padre Pio prayer card. No one had asked her to do so. Bill was amazed, not only that she went in search of it, but also that she had found it. He felt for certain that the odds were against recovering it. He believed that it was a sign that he should start attending the Padre Pio devotions.

Toward the end of the year, Bill began to feel ill. He had chronic pain which seemed to intensify with each passing day. Finally, he was hospitalized. Tests revealed that he had Crohn's Disease. His condition continued to deteriorate. Further tests were taken which indicated that the first diagnosis had been wrong. Bill did not have Crohn's disease. Doctors were still trying to discover the cause of illness but it remained undiagnosed.

During his hospital stay, Bill contracted pneumonia as well as the potentially deadly bacterial staph infection called MRSA. His condition became critical. He drifted in and out of consciousness. He had difficulty breathing, his heartbeat became irregular, and his blood pressure could not be stabilized. As a last resort, his doctor put him into a medically induced coma.

Finally, after Bill had been in a coma for many days, the doctor told Mary Ann that he could offer no hope for her husband. He had done everything that he could for Bill. Bill was dying. The doctor told Mary Ann to take care of any arrangements that she needed to. Mary Ann called Father Solcia and told him the news. He immediately came down to the hospital and gave Bill the Last Rites and the blessing for the dying.

To his family's great relief, the doctor's prediction did not come true. Bill came back to consciousness after being in a coma for eighteen days. He told Mary Ann that while he was in a comatose state, he had a remarkable experience. He found himself in a place of pitch darkness. There he saw the faces of frightful demons. It was truly a place of pain and suffering. An angel came to Bill and tried to lead him out of the dark ravine that he was caught in. "We have to climb the mountain, Bill. We have to go toward the light," his good angel would say to him. No matter how hard Bill tried, he was always pulled back down toward the darkness. More than anything in the world, Bill wanted to get to the place of light.

At one point, Bill saw a saintly man dressed in robes of pure white. Looking closer, he realized that it was St. Benedict. "Save me!" Bill entreated St. Benedict. St. Benedict pointed toward his right, indicating the way that Bill was to go. Bill went in the direction that St. Benedict indicated and soon saw a figure standing close by. It was Padre Pio. "Stop right there, Bill," Padre Pio said, in a voice full of authority. "You must go back. Your work is not finished." "But what work?" Bill asked. Padre Pio made no reply.

Bill knew that the light was up ahead, but he only had a faint glimpse of it. He was never able to reach it. He never saw the angel again either. Instead, when he finally opened his eyes, he saw his earthly angel, Mary Ann, at his hospital bedside. How happy his family was to know that Bill had returned to the land of the living!

All together, Bill spent a total of seventy-eight days in the hospital. He weighed 223 lbs. when he was admitted and he weighed 139 lbs. on the day he was sent home. Bill's recovery took many months. His family took expert care of him. They were just glad that he was alive.

Bill's experience in the hospital gave him a whole new perspective on life. Since that time, his priorities have changed completely. Before his illness, he had often attended Mass simply to fulfill his Sunday obligation. Not anymore. Today, he looks forward to going to Mass on Sundays. He knows what a privilege it is. He now sets aside time so that he can pray the Rosary each day. His relationship with God has become much deeper and much more real. He has peace of mind and peace of heart. His faith is stronger now than it has ever been in his life.

These days, Bill assists Mary Ann in *Our Lady's Catholic Gift Shop* on the grounds of Our Lady of the Rosary parish. He sees his work there as a ministry. He always wears a little pin of St. Pio and a medal of St. Benedict. People often ask him about the pin and the medal. It has become an opportunity for him to share his faith with others. He keeps prayer cards of St. Pio with him and often gives them to the customers at the shop.

At the Padre Pio prayer group one evening, Father Solcia surprised Bill by asking him to step forward and share his testimony with the prayer group. He was happy to do so. Since that time, many people have asked Bill to relate his story of how Padre Pio helped him in the hospital, after his doctors had informed his family that there was no hope of recovery. A number of people have told Bill that his words have strengthened their faith.

Bill feels that he has been given a second chance at life. His family was certain that they were losing him. His own doctor confirmed it. But as our faith teaches us, God always has the final word. Indeed, our lives are in His hands. Bill knows for certain now that he has work left to do. He feels that each new day is truly a gift from God and an opportunity to share his faith and to serve. Today Bill is alive and well and working in the service the Lord.

No matter what may happen, I feel at peace. May Jesus do with me what he wills. Just having his help is enough.

- St. Pio of Pietrelcina

Teach everyone the spirit of St. Francis which is the spirit of Jesus Christ.

- St. Pio of Pietrelcina

CHAPTER 38

Padre Pio's Seraphic Father - St. Francis of Assisi

St. Francis of Assisi, the founder of the Order of Friars Minor, more commonly known as the Franciscans, is one of the most beloved saints in the history of Christianity. Padre Pio's mother Giuseppa Forgione had a great devotion to St. Francis of Assisi. When Padre Pio (Francesco Forgione) was born, Giuseppa chose to name him Francesco because of her love for St. Francis.

Like his mother, Padre Pio too, had a lifelong devotion to St. Francis of Assisi. He joined the Capuchin branch of the Franciscan Order when he was fifteen years old. Padre Pio's vocational choice was Franciscan, his spiritual discipline was Franciscan, his message to those who sought his spiritual counsel was a Franciscan message.

Padre Pio observed the Rule of St. Francis with exactitude. In 1922, he reflected on his calling to the Franciscan way of life and wrote, "Where could I serve thee better, O Lord, than in the cloister, under the banner of the Poor Man of Assisi?" Padre Pio, along with all the members of his religious community, felt a profound happiness when St. Francis of Assisi was officially proclaimed the patron saint of Italy in 1939.

When looking at the lives of Padre Pio and St. Francis, we find that there are many similarities. Both St. Francis and Padre Pio suffered from poor health throughout their adult life. Both had a great compassion for others. St Francis and his followers provided free service to the sick, especially lepers and the sick poor. Padre Pio founded the hospital, the Home for the Relief of Suffering, in order to bring relief and assistance to the sick and the suffering. Padre Pio founded the Prayer Groups; St. Francis founded the Order of Friars Minor and the Third Order. The goal of each was the same: to help the members grow in prayer and holiness. For many years, Padre Pio was the spiritual director of the Third Order of St. Francis in San Giovanni Rotondo.

St. Francis was the first known stigmatist in the history of the church, receiving the stigmata on September 14, 1224. On September 20, 1918, Padre Pio received the stigmata, making him the first stigmatized priest in the history of the church. Both St. Francis and Padre Pio were mystics. Both preached love. Both demonstrated great spiritual power. Both talked about the vanity of material goods. Like St. Francis, Padre Pio practiced Christian penance and mortification in all things.

During a difficult period in Padre Pio's life, St. Francis let him know that he was very near. The Minister General of the Capuchin Order was considering Padre Pio's dismissal from his religious congregation because of his poor health. Padre Pio felt a great fear in his heart at the thought of it. St. Francis appeared to him and spoke words of consolation. He assured Padre Pio that he would never be dismissed from his religious congregation. He reminded him that God's will was being accomplished and that he had nothing to fear.

Like St. Francis, who practiced simplicity of life and detachment from material possessions, Padre Pio tried to follow in his founder's footsteps by being frugal in all things. He was scrupulous to avoid medicines that were too expensive and was sparing in all things, even in his use of water.

On one occasion, the superior of the monastery, Father Carmelo, decided to have an air conditioner installed in Padre Pio's cell. He hoped that it would bring him some relief during the stifling heat of the summer months and also help to ease his chronic asthma and bronchitis. Knowing that Padre Pio would not be in favor of such a luxury, it was installed in his cell on a day when he was in the church hearing confessions. When Padre Pio returned to his cell and saw the air conditioner, he became upset. Upon learning the cost, he became even more upset. He felt that it was an offense against the vow of Franciscan poverty that he had taken when he was fifteen years old. "What will the Seraphic Father, St. Francis say about such a luxury?" Padre Pio asked his fellow Capuchins.

Padre Pio was so concerned about the air conditioner that he talked at length about it to two of his close friends - Dr. Sanguinetti and Father Tarcisio of Cervinara. Father Tarcisio assured Padre Pio that he had done nothing wrong. He had not requested the air conditioner and it certainly would not be wrong for him to accept it. Somewhat relieved of his anxiety, Padre Pio allowed the air conditioner to stay in his cell, but he never turned it on, not even once. He only used it as a shelf to place some of his personal belongings on.

At the end of Padre Pio's life, when he learned that a large and elaborate granite crypt was being constructed for his burial, he was not pleased. His desire was to be buried in a simple and unadorned grave. He always sought to be conformed to the ideals of his teacher, St. Francis.

Padre Pio wore the habit of St. Francis with great devotion, from the time he received it in 1903 until his death in 1968. He used to say that he wanted to "live and die" in the habit of St. Francis. And so he did. Several hours before his death, he told the priest who was assisting him, Father Pelligrino Funicelli, that he wished to renew his vows to his religious profession. Father Pellegrino listened respectfully as Padre Pio repeated his vows of poverty, chastity and obedience.

Padre Pio died a holy death, after a life spent in total dedication to the Lord. St. Francis too, died as he had lived, close to God and completely conformed to His will. One author compared St. Francis' death to the "close of a beautiful day" like the setting sun which shed its last splendor on the world.

St. Francis, who had lived 700 years before Padre Pio, was revered as a saint in his lifetime and was canonized less than two years after his death. Thomas of Celano, who had been received into the Franciscan Order by Francis himself, wrote the first biography of Francis' life at the request of Pope Gregory IX. His writings on St. Francis are important because they are an eyewitness account of the saint's life.

Padre Pio's allegiance to St. Francis never wavered in the fifty-one years of his priesthood. He used to call St. Francis his "Seraphic (Angelic) Father." We must meditate on the fact that he is our Seraphic Father too.

———————

The mission that God entrusted to Francis of Assisi, was made known to him gradually, and often in mysterious ways. When Francis was in Puglia on a military assignment, he heard the voice of God telling him to return to Assisi and he would then be told what to do. He returned to Assisi at once. One day, while Francis was praying at a wayside church in front of an ancient icon of Christ crucified, the image of Christ suddenly became alive and said to him, "Go and repair my Church, which you see is falling into ruin." Francis interpreted the words in a literal way, and began repairing the church buildings in Assisi. Later, Christ revealed to Francis that he wanted him to restore the Church, not from without, but from within, that is, in the hearts and minds of the people. Francis' obedience to the voice of grace within him, enabled him to follow the promptings of the Holy Spirit and to do untold good for the Church and for the world.

I heard the voice of the Lord saying, "Whom shall I send, and who will go for us?"
Then I said, "Here I am, Lord; send me."
- Isaiah 6:8

Francis had a vision of a little black hen, whose feathers and feet were those of a dove. She had so many chicks that she couldn't gather them under her wings, and so they ran all around her, beyond her reach. When Francis woke up, he began to think about the dream. The Holy Spirit revealed to him that the hen symbolized Francis himself. "I am that hen," Francis said, "because I am small in stature and dark, and because I am to be simple like a dove and fly heavenward on wings of virtue. The Lord, in his mercy, has given and will give me more children, which I could never care for by myself. I need, therefore, to surrender them to Mother Church, who will protect them and gather them under the shade of her wings."

We know the love God has for us and we trust that love.
- 1 John 4:16

After Francis had abandoned all of his earthly possessions, he began to preach in the streets and in the wayside churches of Assisi. In the beginning, many of the townspeople scoffed at Francis' message. However, as time passed, the people had a change of heart and began to greatly admire him. Bernard of Quintavalle, a wealthy and highly-educated man, was the first to join Francis. Peter of Cattaneo, a clergyman, was the second.

When Francis and his followers numbered twelve, Francis wrote a short and simple Rule of life based on the Gospel teachings. Francis decided to name his congregation, the *Friars Minor* (Little Brothers), because it expressed his desire that the Brothers would always remain humble and never seek positions above others.

Francis then took the Rule to Pope Innocent III in Rome, requesting approval. Pope Innocent III, who had great religious, social and political power, listened with interest to Francis and took note of his request. However, he was not convinced that the small and insignificant looking Francis would have the ability to breathe new life into the Church through his Rule. He did not grant his approval.

Shortly after his meeting with Francis, the pope had a vivid dream in which he saw the huge Roman basilica of St. John Lateran going to ruin. It was about to topple over. Francis, the little poor man to whom he had just granted an interview, was holding up the entire basilica on his shoulder. The dream caused the pope to reconsider his decision. Finally, he decided to give Francis the approval he sought for his Rule. Step by step, God was leading Francis and opening the doors to the great mission that he had been chosen to fulfill.

Morning by morning, he wakens me and opens my understanding to his will.
- Isaiah 50:4

When Francis was assailed by temptations, he would sometimes throw himself naked into a snow-filled ditch or roll in a thorny briar patch. He called his body, "brother donkey," and denied himself many legitimate physical comforts. In later life, he would apologize to "brother donkey" for treating him so harshly. But God enlightened Francis to see the great value in a life of penance and reparation and his example has helped the whole world. He never proceeded in Holy Orders beyond the diaconate because he did not feel worthy of the honors of the priesthood. One of his outstanding virtues was his compassion, which reached out to all, but especially to the marginalized and the underprivileged. It was said of Francis, "Among the saints, he was the most saintly, and among sinners, he looked like one of them."

Strive for peace with everyone and for that holiness, without which no one will see the Lord.
- Hebrews 12:14

According to witnesses, Francis' ability to preach was truly remarkable. It frequently happened that people who had no religious inclination whatsoever, experienced a sudden and dramatic conversion, simply by listening to Francis proclaim the word of God. On one occasion, when he was preaching in the village of Cannara, the people were so moved by his words that the entire congregation approached him and begged to be admitted to his Order. It was because of such requests that Francis began to think about plans for forming a Third Order.

Brothers, I want to remind you of the gospel I preached to you, which you received and in which you stand firm. You are being saved by it at this very moment.
- 1 Corinthians 15:1-2

A chronicler, who witnessed one of Francis' sermons at Bologna, left this account: "In 1222, on the feast of the Assumption (August 15) as I was a student in Bologna, I saw Francis preach in the marketplace in front of the courthouse, where nearly all the townspeople were gathered. His sermon was titled, *Angels, Men, and Devils*. He treated his theme so wisely that many learned men who were present, were filled with admiration when they heard such words from the lips of an untutored friar. The whole matter of his discourse was directed to the quenching of hatred and the establishment of peace. His clothing was unattractive, his appearance insignificant, his face without beauty. But God inspired his words with such power that many noble families, torn apart by ancient blood feuds, were reconciled forever. And all felt such great devotion and reverence for him that men and women in crowds, prevailed upon him, and tried to tear off bits of his habit or even to touch the hem of his garment."

My prayer is that your love may more and more abound, so that you may learn to value the things that really matter, up to the very day of Christ.
- Philippians 1:9-10

On a certain occasion when St. Francis was suffering extraordinary physical pain, one of his religious brothers meaning to sympathize with him, said in his simplicity, "My father, pray to God that He treat you a little more gently, for His hand seems heavy upon you just now." Hearing this, St. Francis strongly resented the unhappy remark of his well-meaning brother, saying, "My good brother, did I not know that what you have just said was spoken in all simplicity, without realizing the implication of your words, I should never see you again because of your rashness in passing judgment on the dispositions of Divine Providence." Whereupon, weak and wasted as he was by his illness, St. Francis got out of bed, knelt down, kissed the floor and prayed thus, "Lord, I thank Thee for the sufferings Thou art sending me. Send me more, if it be Thy good pleasure. My pleasure is that You afflict me and spare me not, for the fulfillment of Thy holy will is the greatest consolation of my life."
- St. Bonaventure

Lord, make me to know my end, and what is the measure of my days, that I may know how frail I am.
- Psalm 39:5

There were many people who witnessed Francis' extraordinary and supernatural rapport with the animal kingdom. It is recorded that he befriended a falcon, a lamb, a crow, a nest of robins, a pheasant, a cricket, and more. During the winter time it was his habit to put honey into beehives to provide food for the half-frozen bees. He would always stoop to remove earthworms from his path so as not to crush them. At Lake Trasymene, he made friends with a wild rabbit who would not leave his side. He wrought a miracle in the town of Gubbio by taming a wolf that had been terrorizing the citizens there and it was for the turtle-doves that Francis built nests with his own hands. Francis found a reflection of the Divine in all created things, and his love embraced even the most humble of creatures.

He has made everything beautiful in its time. Also, he has put eternity in their hearts, except that no one can fathom the work that God does from beginning to end. I know that nothing is better for them than to rejoice, and to do good in their lives.
- Ecclesiastes 3:11-12

Francis had a special love and tenderness for birds, whom he called his "sisters." On one occasion, he preached a sermon to a number of birds who gathered on the roadside near the town of Bavagna, and they listened to his words with attention. On another occasion, a nightingale responded to his great magnetism and sang with him in an evergreen grove. Francis loved robins and swallows and doves and sparrows, but his favorite bird by far, was the lark. The lark was a humble bird. She was satisfied with a few small kernels and seeds, found by the wayside. Her clothing of feathers was humble, the color of the earth. The lark gave the Brothers a good example not to wear showy or fine garments but to dress in a simple and unassuming way. Francis loved the sweetness of the song of the lark, as she soared heavenward. He told the Brothers that they too, should always sing praise to God, and have their conversation in heaven. The love that Francis showed these humble creatures was reciprocated, for it was the larks that paid a special tribute to him when he was dying.

Your words are very pure, and your servant loves them.
- Psalm 119:140

"He (Francis) overflowed with a spirit of love, not only for men who suffered, but also for dumb animals, reptiles, birds, and any other creature with or without consciousness. Above all, he loved little lambs with a special affection and love, for they showed forth the humility of our Lord Jesus Christ, since the scriptures used the image of a lamb in describing him."
- Thomas of Celano

The next day John saw Jesus coming unto him, and said, "Behold, the Lamb of God who takes away the sin of the world."
- John 1:29

Once when Francis was traveling from Siena to the Spoleto Valley, he passed a large field where a number of sheep were grazing. When he greeted the sheep, they all ran over to him and began to bleat and raise their heads, communicating in their own way with him. The Vicar General of the Order and several of the Friars Minors were walking a short distance behind Francis and witnessed the scene. The Vicar General said to the Friars who were with him, "Look at how the sheep respond to our holy father, Francis. Truly he is a man of God, that even insensible animals revere him and feel his love."

Blessed are the pure in heart for they shall see God.
- Matthew 5:8

In addition to the animal kingdom, Francis felt a strong kinship with the earth and with all of creation. He called the moon his "sister," and the sun, his "brother."

When I consider your heavens, the work of your hands, the moon and the stars, which you have ordained, what is man that you are mindful of him, and the son of man that you visit him? For you have made him a little lower than the angels, and you have crowned him with glory and honor.
- Psalm 8:3-5

On one occasion, Francis was traveling in Tuscany with Brother Masseo. As they were walking, they came to a crossroad where three roads met. They could go to Siena, to Florence or to Arezzo. When Brother Masseo asked which road they should take, Francis replied that they would take the road that God willed. "But how will we know God's will in the matter?" Brother Masseo asked. "By the sign I will show you," Francis replied. He told Brother Masseo to twirl around in a circle, and not to stop until he was told to. He did as Francis asked. As he twirled in a circle, he became very dizzy. Finally, Francis told him to stop. What direction are you facing?" Francis asked his companion. "Toward Siena," Brother Masseo replied. "That is the road God wants us to take," Francis said.

While they were walking down the road, Brother Masseo thought about the instructions Francis had given him, to twirl around in a circle the way children do. Brother Masseo considered it to be a ridiculous order. However, because he had such great esteem for Francis, whom he revered as a saint, he did not dare ask him for an explanation. Many of Francis' actions seemed absurd, but those who knew him well were aware of his close union with God. It was the Holy Spirit, guiding and enlightening Francis that made his ministry to souls so fruitful. The time that Francis and Brother Masseo spent in Siena proved to be a great blessing to the citizens of the town and many people received extraordinary graces through their visit.

Consider your own calling brothers and sisters. Not many of you were wise by human standards; not many were powerful; not many were of noble birth. But God has chosen the foolish things of the world to confound the wise; and God has chosen the weak things of the world to confound the strong. God has chosen the lowly things of this world and the despised things, and the things that are not, to bring to nothing things that are, so that no one may boast before him. It is because of him that you are in Christ Jesus, who has become for us wisdom from God, that is, our righteousness, holiness and redemption. Therefore, as it is written, "Let him who boasts, boast in the Lord."
 - 1 Corinthians 1:26-31

There was a woman from a village near Arezzo who was pregnant. When the time came for her baby to be born, she was in labor for several days but unable to deliver the baby. She was hanging between life and death. Her relatives heard that Francis was going to pass through the village. They were aware of his reputation of holiness and had great faith in his prayers. They were told that he would be riding a horse because he was too weak and ill at the time to walk. They waited for him with great expectancy but he did not appear. They learned that he had taken another route and they were deeply disappointed. They did however see his companion Brother Peter, who was bringing the horse back that Francis had used for his journey.

The townspeople wondered if they might be able to find something that the saint had touched that could be of help to the dying woman. They realized that Francis had held the reins of the horse in his hands. Taking the reins, they laid them on the woman and she immediately was freed from the crisis and gave birth.

I turned every way, but there was no one to help me, I looked for one to sustain me, but could find no one. But then I remembered the mercies of the Lord, his kindness through ages past; For he saves those who take refuge in him, and rescues them from every evil.

- Sirach 51:8-9

When Cardinal Hugolin of Ostia first met Francis and the Friars Minor, he admired the great simplicity and humility of their lives. They lived in huts made of wood and clay and slept without pillows on mounds of straw and broken pallets. They ate sparingly and only of very plain food. They spent their time in prayer, penance, manual labor, and preaching. They were always at the service of their neighbor, particularly the sick and destitute. Francis chose the undyed and rough woolen tunics of the poorest peasants in Assisi to be the clothing of the Friars Minor. When Cardinal Hugolin saw how poorly the Brothers lived, he was so overcome with emotion that he began to cry. "How will it go with us," he said, "who live in luxury day after day, having so much more than these humble Brothers." Eventually, Cardinal Hugolin had the privilege of being named Special Protector of the Order of Friars Minor.

Because the first must be the last
And only little ones may pass
Beyond the gate, narrow and small
Where God is waiting for us all.
Saint Francis, lift my spirit up
I raise to you my empty cup.
As I approach the narrow way
Make me a little one today.

When Francis was preparing for an important audience he was to have with Pope Honorius III, Cardinal Hugolin gave him some words of advice. Cardinal Hugolin, who venerated Francis as a saint, wanted him to make a good impression on the Holy Father. He was aware that at times, Francis exhibited behavior that was unconventional, to say the least. To Cardinal Hugolin, this was a cause for concern. He told Francis to prepare a speech and study it thoroughly, using it as a framework for all that he would say, and not to deviate from it.

Francis did what Cardinal Hugolin recommended but when the time came for him to stand before the Pope and the entire Roman Curia of Cardinals, he could not remember a single word of the speech he had intended to make. Instead, he spoke from his heart to the powerful and highly esteemed religious prelates. As he was speaking, he felt a great devotion to God welling up from within and he started to tap his feet. Unable to contain his spiritual joy, other parts of his body began to move and finally, he began to dance "in the Lord." The Pope and the Cardinals did not find his actions objectionable or indiscreet. Quite the opposite, their encounter with Francis left them deeply edified.

We have not received the spirit of the world but the Spirit that is from God.
- 1 Corinthians 2:12

Due to his many chronic illnesses and increasing weakness, Francis decided to appoint Peter of Catana to be the head of the Order of Friars Minor. In addition, Francis let it be known that he no longer wanted to have a Brother assigned to assist him in his needs or accompany him when he traveled. He said that once he saw a blind man who had just a little puppy to guide him on his way. He did not want to have more than that or to appear singular in any way.

Not to us, O Lord, not to us, but to your name be the glory.
- Psalm 115:1

Francis spent the Christmas of 1223 at Greccio, in the valley of Rieti. Before the Holy Day of Christmas arrived, Francis told his friend, John Velita, that he wished to celebrate the birth of the Savior in a special way. He wanted to honor the Nativity of Jesus by setting up a poor stable with live oxen and donkeys and a small creche (crib). There, everyone could meditate on the humble birth of the Infant Jesus in Bethlehem.

John Velita possessed some property that was bordered by a wooded area and he was more than happy to let Francis use the land that he owned. Francis obtained permission from the Holy Father, Pope Honorius, for the Christmas memorial. At midnight, the townspeople came from surrounding areas, bearing torches and candles to light their way. Francis, wearing the vestments of deacon, assisted at the Mass and preached on the Christmas mysteries. Some of the hay that had been placed in the manger was later distributed to people who were ill. It was also given to animals that were sick. The blessings of God were showered down upon everyone on that cold and dark Christmas night. Many of the sick were healed. Francis' Christmas creche of 1223 began the tradition which has spread throughout the entire Christian world.

O Lord God of all, hear our prayer . . . for if we can be with you even one day, it is better than a thousand without you.
- Psalm 84:8-10

After the feast of Christmas, Francis, who was weak and ill at the time, stayed on in Greccio for several more months. He spent much of his time there in prayer and seclusion. Brother Leo, who was his secretary and closest friend, stayed with him in Greccio. During that time, Francis entered such a deep state of prayer, that Brother Leo often saw him elevated above the ground.

To be near God is my happiness. I have made the Lord God my refuge.
- Psalm 73:28

While most people try to hide their defects and shortcomings from others, Francis would accuse himself of his faults openly and make a public confession of his errors. He once said that some of the problems he encountered in the Order of Friars Minor were the result of his own sins. He always made an effort to hide the abundant graces that he was receiving from the Lord because he did not want to appear singular in any way. "I can still have sons and daughters," he once said to his admirers. "Do not be too quick to praise me, for my future is not certain," he added. He felt unworthy of the many blessings that the Lord had showered on him. He once stated, "If the Lord had shown the favors that he has shown me, to a criminal, he would have made better use of them."

I had no gifts to offer You
No talent that I could profess
And yet you called me by my name
And used my brokenness.
And knowing what I could not be
Your mercy reached to cover me
Because I was a broken thing, and small
You lifted me.

Once when Francis was on his way to Riete, he stopped at the church of San Fabiano. When the townspeople heard that he was visiting the church, they came in great numbers to see him. The crowd was so large that the vineyard that belonged to the parish priest was completely ruined. To make matters worse, it was vintage time and the grapes were to be harvested soon. When the priest saw the damage that had been done to his vineyard he was greatly distressed and regretted that he had allowed Francis to visit his church. He complained to Francis about the destruction. Francis asked him how many measures of wine the vineyard produced in one year. "Thirteen measures," the priest answered. Francis promised him that the vineyard would indeed have a plentiful production that season. That year, the vines produced twenty measures of wine, which was greater than ever before.

I will bless them. There will be showers of blessing.
- Ezekiel 34:26

One of the spiritual gifts that the Lord had given Francis was the gift of reading hearts. This was made very clear to Brother Leonard on one occasion when he and Francis were traveling together. Francis was very tired from the journey, and so had mounted a horse at the advice of his companions. Brother Leonard, who was walking beside him, began to think to himself, "It isn't fair that Francis should ride on a horse while I have to walk. After all, he is the son of Peter Bernardone where as I am descended from a family of much greater nobility. I am tired as well." At that moment, Francis dismounted from his horse and said to Brother Leonard, "I don't think it is right that I should be riding this horse while you have to walk. After all, I am only the son of Peter

Bernardone while you are of much more important ancestry. I know that you are tired like I am. Please change places with me." Deeply embarrassed, Brother Leonard helped Francis back on the horse and determined to keep a careful guard on his thoughts for the rest of the journey.

Lord, deliver me from my distress. See my hardship and my poverty and pardon all my sins.
- Psalm 25:17-18

Once a woman spoke to Francis about the suffering she endured at the hands of her husband. Not only was her husband cruel to her, he also made every effort to stand in the way of the good works that she attempted to do for the Lord. She asked Francis to pray for her unhappy situation and he assured her that he would. Francis said to her, "Give a message to your husband. Tell him that now is the day of mercy and that hereafter is the day of justice." Then Francis gave the woman a blessing. When she spoke the words to her husband, it brought about a great spiritual change within him. He began to serve the Lord with her and their marriage was blessed with happiness for the rest of their lives.

Every morning he brings his justice to light. He never fails.
- Zephaniah 3:5

Brother Rufino was greatly loved by Francis and was considered to be one of the holiest of the Friars Minor. Francis once said that God had revealed to him that Brother Rufino's soul had already been canonized in heaven. His esteem for Brother Rufino was so great that he told the Brothers not to hesitate to call him St. Rufino, even while he was living, for he had found great favor with God. Brother Rufino, of the Scifi family, had been born of the nobility in Assisi. He was shy by nature and was a man of few words.

Once, Francis told Brother Rufino to go to Assisi and preach a sermon in the cathedral. Brother Rufino begged him to send someone else, saying that he did not have the ability to speak before a crowd. Unhappy with his answer, Francis told him to go anyway, but to strip off his tunic and wear only his breeches when he spoke to the congregation. Brother Rufino obeyed Francis' instructions. When he went up to the pulpit and began preaching without a shirt on, all the people who were in the church burst into laughter. Although embarrassed and humiliated, Brother Rufino did his best to preach the sermon, according to his spiritual father's wishes.

Francis deeply regretted his harsh treatment of Brother Rufino. In order to make amends, he walked into the church dressed in the very same way. Francis preached with such spiritual power and conviction that the men and women who were present began to weep. There were many conversions that day. He preached on the kingdom of heaven and the passion of Jesus Christ.

Accept whatever befalls you, and in times of humiliation be patient. For gold is tested in the fire, and those found acceptable, in the furnace of humiliation.
- Sirach 2:4-5

One time, Brother Leo, one of Francis' closest companions, was suffering a grievous temptation. He longed to have something written in Francis' own hand but he could not bring himself to ask for the favor. During that time, Francis asked Brother Leo to bring him a piece of parchment and a pen. On one side he wrote praises to God, and on the other side he wrote a special blessing for Brother Leo. When he gave the letter to Brother Leo, Brother Leo was instantly freed from the temptation which had oppressed him. He kept the letter with him at all times for the rest of his life.

Remember your compassion and love, O Lord; for they are ages old. Remember no more the sins of my youth; remember me only in the light of your love.
- Psalm 25:7

Once, while in San Severino, Francis preached at a convent where a novice was making her religious profession. The famous poet, William of Lisciano, who was a relative of the novice, was present for the occasion. William had the honor of being crowned Poet Laureate by the Emperor. William was a worldly man who traveled in worldly circles. He had no interest in spirituality. He had never met Francis before but he listened carefully to his sermon that day and was profoundly moved by it. While Francis was preaching, William saw two glittering crosses extending from Francis' body. One of the crosses went across Francis' chest and the other went from his head to his feet. William was deeply convicted by what he saw and he began to reflect on the state of his soul. He knew that he needed to amend his life, and seek a better way. Afterward, Francis singled William out and spoke to him. William became the first poet to join the Order of Friars Minor. Because of the great peace that filled William's heart at the time of his conversion, Francis gave him the name Brother Pacifico (peace).

I ask the Father in his great glory to give you the power to be strong inwardly through his Spirit.
- Ephesians 3:16

Francis meditated on the poverty of Christ's birth and the poverty of his death, stripped of his garments and nailed to a Cross. This became the model for his own life. He would be poor because Christ was poor. The Friars Minor had no land, no income, no possessions beyond what was needed for daily life and the Brothers were forbidden to accept money under any conditions. On these points, Francis was uncompromising. He called the spirit of holy poverty, the foundation of the Order.

For the gate is small and the way is narrow that leads to life, and there are few who find it.
- Matthew 7:14

"Francis desired no house, no safe stronghold, no cloister, no possessions, no privileges; all these things he saw as fetters, links with the affairs of the world. His brotherhood was to be defenseless, exposed . . . Christ's friends and disciples on earth should remain in complete poverty, without possessions and without legal protection . . . He (St. Francis) did not waver from his position. "I strictly command all the brethren on obedience that . . . they shall not dare to ask for any letter from the Roman court . . . neither for purposes of preaching nor because of any persecution of their bodies."
- Friedrich Heer

They were longing for a better country, that is, a heavenly one. Therefore God is not ashamed to be called their God, for he has prepared a city for them.
- Hebrews 11:16

Francis was guided by divine wisdom in his relationship with those who had joined his Order of Friars Minor. Often just a look or a word from him to a Brother who was discouraged or depressed was enough to bring relief. Francis understood human weakness and was the first to admit weaknesses of his own. He consoled one Brother by saying, "The more you are tempted, the more I will love you." Regarding the Brothers who left the Order, Francis said that those who renounced their religious vows and abandoned their vocation should be treated with a special mercy since the difficulties and temptations which caused them to leave must have been overwhelming.

When we were unable to help ourselves, at the moment of our need, Christ died for us.
- Romans 5:6

As time passed, more and more people came to know of Francis' reputation for holiness, and during his lifetime, he was venerated as a saint. The church bells would be rung when he entered a town, and with great joy, all of the townspeople would go out to meet him. Children would wait for him with anticipation, holding gifts of flowers in their hands. One of the Brothers who observed the people's devotion to Francis, found it to be excessive. He told Francis, "It is not good for the people to display their love for you in the way that they do. It is not good for them and it is not good for you." Francis said to the Brother, "This reverence that the people pay me, I never take to myself. I pass it all on to God."

We do not preach ourselves, but Christ Jesus the Lord.
- 2 Corinthians 4:5

Two years before his death, Francis retreated with three of his companions to the mountainous region of La Verna, in the Tuscan Apennines. His great desire was to spend his time at La Verna in prayer and seclusion and to make a forty day preparation for the feast of St. Michael the Archangel. Francis stayed in a tiny hut that had been provided for his use.

One morning while he was praying, he had a vision in which he saw a Christlike figure in the sky, moving toward him. As the figure came closer, he saw that it was suspended on a cross and that it had six shining wings, like the wings of an angel. The angelic being was suffused with a fiery light. As Francis gazed at it, he felt both a great joy and a great sorrow - joy because of the beauty of the apparition, and sorrow because the figure was crucified. As Francis looked in wonder, the wounds that Christ suffered in his Passion, suddenly appeared on his own hands, feet, and side. It was September 14, 1224, the feast of the Exaltation of the Cross. Francis became the first known person in history to receive the stigmata.

> It is no longer I who live, but Christ who lives in me.
> - Galatians 2:20

After the feast of St. Michael the Archangel, Francis left La Verna. Greatly weakened by the wounds of the stigmata, he rode down the mountain on a horse. There were people waiting to see him in the plain below, and a number of the sick who were brought to Francis that day, were healed of their infirmities.

> I love the Lord because he heard my voice; he heard my cry for mercy.
> - Psalm 116:1

Francis made every effort to conceal his stigmata, by pulling the sleeves of his habit down over his hands and by wearing shoes and woolen socks to cover his feet. It was very difficult for him to walk, with wounds that pierced his feet clear through. Some of the Brothers who were closest to him, on occasion, saw the wounds of the stigmata in his hands and feet. Only one of the Brothers had the privilege of seeing the wound in his side. One day, when Francis was taking off his habit so that it could be cleaned, the Brother caught a glimpse of his side wound. All of the others saw the wound in his side only after his death.

> Christ's love is greater than anyone can ever know but I pray that you will be able to know that love.
> - Ephesians 3:19

"Though he (St. Francis of Assisi) exhibited the greatest esteem for all men and rendered each man every possible deference, he looked upon himself as a sinner, considering himself as only one among many sinners. In fact, he believed himself the greatest of all sinners. He was accustomed to say that if the mercy shown him by God had been given to any other sinner, the latter would have become ten times holier than he, and that to God alone must be attributed whatever was found in him of goodness and beauty, for from God only was it derived. For this reason he tried in every possible way to hide those privileges and graces, especially the stigmata of Our Lord, imprinted on his body, which might have gained for him the esteem and praise of men. When at times he was praised, either in public or in private, he not only refused to accept such praise but protested that he was worthy only of contempt and abuse and was really saddened thereby. Finally, what must we say about the fact that he thought so humbly of himself that he did not consider himself worthy to be ordained a priest?"

- Pope Pius XI - from his 1926 Encyclical on St. Francis - *Rite Expiatis*

God forbid that I should glory, save in the cross of our Lord Jesus Christ by whom the world is crucified to me and I to the world.
- *Galatians 6:14*

It was Francis' practice, whenever he felt he had done wrong, to confess his fault openly and to all. Once when Francis was suffering from a long and painful illness, one of the Brothers convinced him to eat a bowl of stew. It had been specially prepared for him, in hopes that his body would be strengthened. Afterward, Francis regretted eating the meal and felt like a hypocrite since he was ever encouraging people to practice penance and self-denial. He went to the town square and said to the people who were gathered there, "You think I am a holy man but you are wrong. I confess to you and to God that during my illness I indulged in eating chicken and some stew." On that winter's day, Francis had a fever and was extremely weak. A number of people who heard his words began to weep, seeing him exposed to the cold weather, and knowing how ill he was. The people said to themselves, "This man has done nothing wrong. He accuses himself of a fault but all he did was to try to care for his health. What will happen to us, we who satisfy our every desire and enjoy so many pleasures?"

God does not withdraw his mercy, nor permit even one of his promises to fail.
- *Sirach 47:22*

"O how beautiful, how splendid, how glorious did he (St. Francis) appear in the innocence of his life, in the simplicity of his words, in the purity of his heart, in his love for God, in his fraternal charity, in his ardent obedience, in his peaceful submission, in his angelic countenance."
- Thomas of Celano

The trust you have shown shall not pass from the memories of men, but shall ever remind them of the power of God.
- *Judith 13:25*

Cardinal Hugolin of Ostia said that whenever he looked at Francis, he always felt uplifted in spirit. The Cardinal testified that whenever he was upset by problems of any kind, he had only to speak to Francis briefly or glance at him, and his peace of mind would return at once. He considered Francis an apostle of Christ, and in his reverence for him, the Cardinal would often take his hand and kiss it. Knowing the great amount of good that Francis was doing for the Church and for the world, Hugolin begged him to take better care of his health.

You know how we lived among you for your sake. You became imitators of us and of the Lord; in spite of severe suffering, you welcomed the message with the joy given by the Holy Spirit. And so you became a model to all the believers.
- *1 Thessalonians 1:5-7*

Francis never enjoyed good health and his physical infirmities increased as time went by. On one of his missionary journeys to the Middle East, he con-tracted trachoma, an eye disease which was prevalent in Egypt at the time, and which caused his eyes to be painfully inflamed and swollen. Francis kept the hood of his habit pulled down over his eyes because the light of day caused him great discomfort. Cardinal Hugolin of Ostia, concerned about Francis' failing eyesight, persuaded him to travel to Reite and consult the pope's physician.

The agonizing treatment that was prescribed consisted of cauterizing his forehead from his temple to his ear with a red-hot iron and the use of plasters to keep the wound open. How did Francis respond to this trial? The same way he responded to all the other trials in his life. He accepted it without a trace of bitterness or self-pity and maintained his spiritual joy throughout. He regarded his sufferings as a purification and always spoke of them as such. He composed the beautiful and triumphant poem, *Canticle of the Sun*, a hymn of praise to God, toward the end of his life, when he was blind and undergoing intense and unrelenting physical pain.

Hope in God, for I will yet praise him.
- Psalm 42:5

In his final illness, Francis remained united to God and to the spirit of joy that had so characterized his life. Although his body was wracked with pain, he felt a greater need to sing than ever before. He asked the Brothers to sing the psalms to him. Brother Elias, who had been appointed the Vicar General of the Order, was worried about public opinion. He did not think it was appropriate to have songs of praise being sung when Francis was so close to death.

A large crowd had assembled outside, knowing that Francis was dying. Brother Elias feared that they would have a poor opinion of Francis. He went to Francis' bedside and warned him not to give scandal to the people. He said, "There is a watch set down below. A crowd is gathered there, knowing how serious your condition is. They will not think you are a holy man if they hear music coming from your cell. They will assume that you are not taking your death seriously. What will the faithful think of your sainthood, if you do nothing but sing?" Francis answered the superior of his Order, "Suffer me, Brother, to rejoice in my Lord, both in his glory and in my infirmities, since by the grace of his Spirit, I feel so united to him."

You are a hiding place for me; You preserve me from trouble; You surround me with songs of deliverance.
- Psalm 32:17

"St. Francis spent the few days that remained before his death in praise, teaching his companions whom he loved so much to praise Christ with him. He also invited all creatures to praise God."

- Thomas of Celano

My presence will go with you and I will give you rest.
- Exodus 33:14

When Francis was dying, a large number of larks perched on the roof of his cell and began singing. The lark had always been Francis' favorite bird. Although it was evening, when the larks characteristically do not come out, they were all there, making their voices heard. The city watchman who guarded the area and a number of other witnesses were astonished by the sight and considered it a miracle.

I will bless you as long as I live; I will lift up my hands and call on your name.
- Psalm 63:5

Francis told the Brothers that when his last hour came, he wanted to be laid naked on the bare earth, in imitation of the Lord. In his final moments, his habit was removed and he was laid on the ground and covered with a cloth. The Lord's Passion, according to the gospel of St. John, was read to him at his request. He said to his companions, "I have done what was mine to do; may Christ teach you what you are to do."

I want to know Christ and the power flowing from his resurrection; likewise to know how to share in his sufferings, becoming like him in his death. Thus do I hope that I may arrive at the resurrection from the dead.
- Philippians 3:10-11

"Nothing was to be lacking in the life of the Poverello (St. Francis) to make it a perfect masterpiece, and his death was the harmonious culmination of his life. His last weeks on earth were like the close of a beautiful day, wherein the setting sun seems to shed on the world, all its remaining splendor. Thus, before leaving his friars, Francis expressed to them once more, his most intimate thoughts, poured out upon them all his tenderness, and then, serene and filled with gratitude, went home to God."

\- Omer Englebert

Stand firm and see the deliverance the Lord will give you.
- 2 Chronicles 20:17

After suffering through a long illness, Francis welcomed with love, his entrance into eternal life and what he came to call, "sister death." He passed away on October 3, 1226. He died painfully and he died singing.

For to me, to live is Christ, and to die is gain.
- Philippians 1:21

Francis had asked to be buried in the criminals' cemetery in the Colle d'Inferno. Instead, his body was taken in procession to the church of St. George in Assisi, where he had first preached. The marks of the stigmata on his body, which he had been so careful to keep hidden during his life, were now visible to all.

None of us lives as his own master and none of us dies as his own master. While we live we are responsible to the Lord, and when we die, we die as his servants. Both in life and death, we are the Lord's.
- Romans 14:7-8

"While St. Francis embraces death as a sister, he in no way sentimentalizes death. He sees death as an inevitable finale to life; the fate of every person. His mind however, immediately turns to something worse than death, dying outside the grace of God . . . Death for St. Francis had an eschatological meaning. It was a transit either to God or away from God."

\- Lawrence Cunningham

Fear not for I have redeemed you. I have called you by your name. You are mine.
- Isaiah 43:1

Holy Father, give us today our daily bread. Give us Jesus always during our brief stay in this land of exile. Give him to us and grant that we may be increasingly worthy to welcome him into our hearts.

- St Pio of Pietrelcina

CHAPTER 39

Letters Received

---

*T*he following testimonies are from those who have shared their stories with us through email, telephone calls, letters, and by writing to us at our Padre Pio Devotions website at www.saintpio.org :

Padre Pio Put His Hand on my Head and Prayed for Me When I was just a toddler, I was diagnosed with an inoperable malignant brain tumor on the left side of my brain. My father's best friend, Charles Mandina (Uncle Charlie) encouraged him to take me to Italy to see Padre Pio and to request his prayers. My Uncle Charlie had a great devotion to Padre Pio. My father took me to Italy and was able to see Padre Pio. Padre Pio put his hand on my head and prayed for me. My condition began to improve while I was in San Giovanni Rotondo and I made a full recovery.

Through the years, Uncle Charlie often spoke to me about Padre Pio. For a long time he worked at Padre Pio's side at the monastery of Our Lady of Grace. He translated for Padre Pio when English-speaking pilgrims visited him and wanted to speak to him. He also assisted at his Mass. Uncle Charlie told me that during the Mass, he saw Padre Pio's hands and they were bleeding. Uncle Charlie was so moved that his entire body would tremble at Padre Pio's Mass. He also told me that during the Mass, Padre Pio sometimes spoke to someone that Uncle Charlie could not see. He asked Padre Pio about it and Padre Pio told him that he was speaking to the souls in purgatory who were on their way to heaven. They had come to thank him his prayers.

In 1968 when Padre Pio died, Father Alessio, Padre Pio's personal secretary, gave Uncle Charlie a very precious relic, Padre Pio's shawl. Uncle Charlie did not keep that precious relic to himself. He allowed others to venerate it, often those who were sick or in need. I remember when I was sixteen years old and in the hospital, Uncle Charlie brought the shawl to me. I still remember that I slept so good and so soundly that night. When Uncle Charlie passed away, he left the shawl to me.

In 2008, when I was 47 years old, I was diagnosed with three brain tumors on the right side of my brain. At this very difficult time in my life, my family was there for me. I believe that Padre Pio was there for me, too. My Aunt Margaret who is 93 years old, told me that she prayed, "Padre Pio you helped my nephew when he was just a little boy, please help him now!"

I had two surgeries at Loma Linda Medical Center in Loma Linda, California. The first surgery lasted 8 hours and the second surgery lasted 20 hours. Before my second surgery, my sister Christine dreamed that she saw me on the operating room table. The surgeon walked in the room, and as he rolled up his sleeves, Christine realized that it was actually Padre Pio. He was wearing a hospital gown. A sense of peace came over Christine and it was certainly a consolation to me to learn of her dream.

After six weeks in the hospital and rehab, I was finally able to go home. My relatives were kind enough to make the 80 mile round trip to bring me Holy Communion every Sunday. But the illness proved to be a real test of my faith, for many times during the many months of my recuperation, I felt abandoned by God.

For 25 years I have taught CCD to 2nd graders at St. Pius V Catholic Church in Buena Park, California. During the time I was sick, it was a great consolation to know that my students were all praying for me. I was able to return to teaching after a one year absence. We always spend the last fifteen minutes of our class, praying for those in need. I know that the prayers of children are very powerful. I have talked to my students on many occasions about Padre Pio. I have also brought his shawl to class. Together, we have witnessed many graces and even miracles that have come through the intercession of Padre Pio.

- *Rocky Falatico*

Padre Pio Said to My Mother, "You are Healed" I was raised in the Catholic Church but after a time, I lapsed. I lost interest in seeking God. I was not an atheist, for I never denied God's existence, but I lacked faith. By profession, I am a medical doctor and also a scientist. I used to say that I was a Catholic but I did not experience an authentic spiritual life until recently, when my mother, Telma Ferrari became ill.

In 2008, my mother was diagnosed with an inoperable brain tumor. After I received news of the diagnosis, I began to pray two novenas each day for my mother - a novena to Padre Pio and a novena to Our Lady of the Rosary. It was the first time in my life that I had ever prayed a novena. I chose to pray to Padre Pio because I had heard a testimonial of someone who had received a grace through his intercession and I was impressed by the story. After a time, my mother and father joined me in praying the two novenas each day.

My mother received chemotherapy and radiation at the MD Anderson Cancer Center in Houston, Texas. She had an incredible response to the treatment and all traces of the tumor vanished. On one occasion, when I visited my parents at their home, we watched a movie about the life of Padre Pio. During the movie, a strong and exquisite fragrance of violets suddenly came from my mother's Rosary. I had never experienced anything like that in my life. At that moment, we all had a sense of inner peace.

This year, my mother developed cancer of the bone and although we did not lose our faith, we were very concerned. We prayed once again for the intercession of Padre Pio.

After the first round of treatments, my mother heard a voice in her home. It was the voice of Padre Pio. He spoke to her in Italian and said, "You are healed." My mother understood the words easily for she speaks both English and Italian. After that, the bone pain that she was experiencing in her lower back went away. She was then able to walk by herself again without using her walker.

We went to San Giovanni Rotondo in June of this year, 2010, to express our gratitude for the graces that my mother (and all of us) received from Christ and Our Blessed Mother through the intercession of Padre Pio. I attended Mass with my parents at the church of Santa Maria delle Grazie and I felt moved to tears while I was at this church. They were not tears of sorrow but of joy and peace. While my mother was in the church, she noticed an intense fragrance of violets that lasted about 20 minutes. She felt a great peace in her heart. My mother's second tumor is now in remission. We are planning to visit San Giovanni Rotondo again this year, December 2010 in order to give thanks.

- Dr. Fernando Scaglia

Father John brought Padre Pio's Glove to Children's Hospital My daughter Elizabeth was eight years old when she was diagnosed with Hodgkin's disease, a type of cancer. She stayed at Our Lady's Children's Hospital in Dublin for a number of weeks. I used to visit her on my lunch break from work every day and also at the end of my work day before going home. Her throat was affected by the disease and she lost the ability to speak. One day a nun, who was the head nurse on my daughter's ward, pulled me aside to speak to me privately. She did not want my wife to overhear our conversation as she said that my wife seemed to be a very emotional person. She told me that Elizabeth was not going to survive the cancer. After she told me that, I went to the Capuchin Friary at St. Mary of the Angels in Dublin.

One of the Capuchins at St. Mary of the Angels, Father John, had a glove of Padre Pio's. I asked him to visit Elizabeth and bless her with it. I have had a devotion to Padre Pio for many years. I have also attended daily Mass for almost 50 years, since the year of my marriage in 1960.

Father John came to the hospital and blessed Elizabeth with the glove as well as all of the other children who were there. Not long after, I was having a meal at the Fish and Chips restaurant on Kimmage Road in Dublin. Suddenly, the whole area was pervaded with the fragrance of roses. I instantly knew that it was Padre Pio. I also thought to myself that it was an odd place for him to make his presence known.

A few days later, I spoke to the head nurse again. She told me that she had astounding news for me - all of Elizabeth's tests were normal. My daughter recovered rapidly and completely and her voice came back full strength. When she got older, she sang professionally throughout Europe. I believe that through the intercession of Padre Pio, my daughter was healed.

- Michael Gormley

A Very Important Day I recently had a very vivid dream in which I was walking with a man who was carrying a lantern. He was limping slightly as he walked and his posture was somewhat bent. He had a serious demeanor and I noticed that he seemed to be in a hurry. He spoke to me in Italian and said that a very important day was coming soon. I understood the Italian words in my dream even though I do not speak the language. Then the dream ended.

I told my good friend Tony Fajardo about the dream and he then showed me a picture of Padre Pio. There was no doubt about it. He was the man I had seen in my dream. I knew practically nothing about Padre Pio. Tony had told me on a previous occasion that he had the stigmata. That was the extent of my knowledge. I had never seen a photo of Padre Pio before. I did not even know that he was from Italy.

In my dream, I felt that Padre Pio was proud of me for finally realizing that the Catholic faith was destined to be a part of my life. This month I am going to begin to take classes so that I can be confirmed. In the dream, when Padre Pio said that an important date was coming up, I thought that he might be talking about his birthday. But since then, I have learned that he received the Stigmata on Sept 20 and that his feast day is September 23. I had the dream on September 6.

- Nicholas Beattie

Padre Pio said, "There will be Victory" I was born near Bagdad, Iraq and baptized in the parish of the Virgin Mary of the Holy Heart. When I was still a baby, my parents decided to move the family to the United States to escape the dangers of the country and so that my brothers and sisters and I might have a better life. It was a great sacrifice for my parents to leave their country and all that was dear to them but they knew it was for the best.

I learned about Padre Pio in 2006 and started attending the Padre Pio prayer group in San Diego. On occasion, I brought my mother with me and she liked it very much. 2007 was a devastating year for the Chaldean Catholic community in Bagdad. My mother became very distraught over the tragedies that were occurring there. Chaldean Catholic bishops, priests, and deacons were being threatened daily. Extremist terrorist groups warned them that they would be killed if they continued to have Mass in their churches.

My mother watched the news on television one day and saw several of the Catholic churches in Bagdad that were destroyed by roadside bombings. She was filled with anxiety and wept over the tragic events. She had a great love for the parish she had attended when she lived in Iraq and feared that it would also be leveled just like the others.

One evening when my mother was very sad, I took her to the Padre Pio prayer group with me. When we came home, I placed a picture of Padre Pio next to my parents' bed. That night she had a vivid dream. In her dream, she was praying and pleading that God would protect her parish in Bagdad. Padre Pio suddenly appeared in her dream. He raised his hands and she could see the marks of the stigmata. He said to her in Aramaic, "Do not worry. There will be victory." When my mother woke up, she was filled with a great sense of peace. My parents' parish in Bagdad is still standing today. Although one window was shattered and an outer wall was damaged by an act of violence, the church was repaired and Mass is said there regularly. My parents have remained very devoted to Padre Pio.

- *Zina Hallak*

I Prayed to St. Pio and Asked Him to Help My Friend   Recently I was praying in the side chapel in our local Cathedral of St. Monica's here in Cairns, North Queensland, Australia. I was praying for a friend of mine who is an atheist and an alcoholic. She also has several diagnosed mental health problems including bipolar disorder and anxiety disorder. I prayed to St. Pio and asked him to help her.

There was only one other man in the chapel at the time and as he was leaving, I noticed that he paused to touch the statue of Our Lady. At the moment he touched the statue, I perceived the sweetest fragrance of flowers. I believed it must have come from the man but after he left the chapel, the fragrance remained. I trusted then that St. Pio had heard my prayer. Shortly afterward, I received a message from my friend. She said that quite suddenly she had come to the conclusion that she must do something positive with her life. She has since applied for a good job and with Our Lord's help and mercy and St. Pio's intercession, I believe she is now on a new and positive path.

- *Name Withheld*

Padre Pio's Hand was So Warm I live in Belfast, Ireland and one cold and windy winter morning, I went to pray in the chapel at the parish of St. Agnes. It was raining heavily that day. Outside it felt colder than the coldness of my heart and home. The night before had been a bitter night with family problems and I was broken-hearted. I entered the chapel of St. Agnes and kept the hood of my coat up hoping that no one would notice my tears.

When I finished my prayers, I left the chapel by the side door. I was amazed to see a life-size bronze statue of Padre Pio at the foot of the grotto of Our Lady of Lourdes. I had never noticed it before as St. Agnes is not my regular parish. Still crying, I went over and put my hand in Padre Pio's and begged for his help. Because it was such a cold day, I was taken aback by the warmth of the statue's hand. I wondered how it was possible that it could feel so warm.

A few days later I returned to pray but also to see if the hand was still warm. The hand was stone cold. Over the last few years, I have visited the grotto a number of times and have touched the statue's hand. It has been cold ever since. It is my belief that Padre Pio personally comforted me on that Saturday morning. My mind was in such turmoil and my heart was so cold that he gave me some of his warmth. I love Padre Pio and I know he has helped me in many ways over the years.

- *Name Withheld*

My Mother Brought Me a Medal of Padre Pio I had lived in England for many years and to be honest, I did not live a good or holy life. I began seeing a man and I became pregnant. From that point on, the man no longer wanted anything to do with me. I moved back to Ireland to live with my parents as they said they would help support me and my baby. It was a very dark and painful time in my life. My son was born in November, 2006. It was a long and difficult labor and there were some serious complications. A few days after the birth of my son, I became quite ill, both physically and emotionally. The wound in my abdomen from the cesarean section deliver had opened and was bleeding.

My mother brought a medal of Padre Pio to the hospital and told me to put it under my pillow. I thought that my mother was very silly to suggest such a thing. I had never heard of Padre Pio before and I had no interest in learning about him either. I assumed he was a biblical figure and it annoyed me that my mother believed that Padre Pio could save me. I thought no more about the matter.

I was finally discharged from the hospital but my wound was still open and bleeding after ten days. My parents took care of my son so that I could sleep at night. One night I had a dream in which I was a little girl again, maybe seven or eight years old. I was standing in a field. I could see trees at the top of a hill. They were not like any of the trees I have ever seen in either England or Ireland but seemed to be from a foreign country. They looked like orange trees. Underneath the trees was a man dressed in a long brown cloak. He had a beard. I felt full of happiness just to be with him. He placed his hand on my head and then he hugged me. In my dream, I saw myself with a big smile on my face.

When I woke up, I did not think too much about the dream but as I was changing the dressing on my wound, I discovered that it had healed. It was not even bleeding. It was still painful but all the signs of the open wound had disappeared. I felt like a new person. I did not tell my mother about the dream, but when I showed her how the wound had healed, she could not believe it. Later, I came across a book on Padre Pio and saw a picture of him on the cover. Sure enough, he was the man I saw in my dream. I then told my mother. My eyes still fill with tears whenever I think about it. My mother told me how lucky I was that Padre Pio chose to help me.

- C. Tobin

They Drove Back to the Monastery to Thank Padre Pio My uncle, Eugene (Gene) Grimes, told me of a miracle that occurred through his contact with Padre Pio. Uncle Gene enlisted in the Army Air Corp during World War II and was stationed at the air base in Foggia, Italy assigned to the 347 Bombardment Squadron. As a sargeant, he worked on the ground crew as a munitions inspector. Uncle Gene had been a devout Catholic all of his life, and he used to attend Padre Pio's Mass in San Giovanni Rotondo which was not a great distance from the air base. He and the other GI's would take a two and a half-ton truck, called a deuce and a half, up the steep road that led to Padre Pio's monastery. He described Padre Pio as a very humble priest and he was awed by his stigmata. He felt blessed whenever he was in his presence. Uncle Gene had the honor of being an altar server at Padre Pio's Mass. He knew what a great privilege it was.

One day after Mass, Padre Pio said to my uncle, "Gino, I want you to be very careful when you go back down the mountain today." He warned him about the brakes on the truck. Uncle Gene assured Padre Pio that he and the other soldiers would all be fine. Before they left, Padre Pio gave them a blessing. On the way down the mountain, the truck lost its brakes and began to pick up speed. The driver fought to keep it on the road. Uncle Gene was sitting in the front passenger's side of the truck. As they came around a blind curve on the narrow and winding road, they saw a massive five ton wrecker directly in front of them. It was about to hit them head-on. Suddenly Uncle Gene's whole life flashed before his eyes, and he believed that he was going to die. Their truck then started to go off the side of the mountain. In an instant, their truck was back on the road but going in the opposite direction, now headed up the mountain. There was no accident, no head-on collision.

Uncle Gene and the other soldiers were awed by what had happened and knew that it was a miracle. They returned to the monastery to thank Padre Pio for saving them. They decided not to tell anyone because they were convinced that no one would believe them. In 1945, Uncle Gene received an honorable discharge from the Army and returned to the U.S. and made his home in Worcester, Massachusetts. His was very active in the parish of St. Peter located in Worcester. At that time, very few people in the U.S. had heard of Padre Pio. Uncle Gene remained very devoted to Padre Pio for the rest of his life.

- *Charles T. Grimes*

My Father Returned to Mass after an Absence of 30 Years My father, Sylvester Gentile had a brilliant mind and worked in the field of electrical engineering. He was a published author and the book that he wrote was a best-seller in the world of engineering and was translated into several languages. He was a good man and he was very kind but he was not religious. He felt that religion was something for women who needed emotional comfort. Personally, he had no use for religion.

After my mother died at the young age of 52 years, my father fell into a depression. I gave him two books on Padre Pio which he read with interest. My father knew that Padre Pio's stigmata as well as the miracles that surrounded his life, were scientifically inexplicable. That fact convinced him of the existence of God.

The graces that my father received after reading the books on Padre Pio caused him to return to Mass after an absence of 30 years. He began to attend Mass regularly at St. Dorothea's parish in Eatontown, New Jersey. My father then joined the Catholic prayer group that I belonged to. On one occasion, he gave a full presentation at our prayer group on Padre Pio, sharing many stories about his life as well as the scientific studies of his stigmata. It makes sense that God would use science to attract my father and bring him back to the faith!

- Pat Hulick

Padre Pio's Glove was Placed on my Husband In 1994, my husband became very ill with Crohn's Disease. He was not responding to the medical treatment that he was given. He became sicker and sicker and was in the Maine General Hospital in Waterville, Maine for 45 days. He had lost so much weight that he looked like a skeleton. There was a Padre Pio prayer group that met at St. Mary's parish in Augusta and my friend contacted them and told them about my husband's condition. They gave her their relic to borrow. It was a part of Padre Pio's glove encased in glass. They promised to pray for my husband.

I brought the relic to the hospital that night and placed it on my husband's stomach and he and I prayed the novena to the Sacred Heart of Jesus. That was the prayer that Padre Pio had always prayed. My husband called me from the hospital at 4:00 a.m. the next morning. I was surprised that he was able to use the telephone to call me since he was so weak that he could barely lift his hand. He told me that something had happened when the glove was placed on his stomach. He felt a warmth go all the way through his body.

When the doctors came in to examine him the next morning, they were astounded. The swelling in his stomach had disappeared. They decided to go ahead and do surgery. The surgery went beautifully and he has never been bothered with this dread disease since. I know Padre Pio's powerful intercession healed my husband and it was after that experience that I became a spiritual child of Padre Pio.

- *Ann Douglass*

In Quezon City, Philippines, I Found a Prayer Pamphlet of Padre Pio In the year 2000, three months after our wedding, we learned that my wife was pregnant. Like other newly-wed couples, we were extremely delighted with the news. Thursday of that week, my wife went to the doctor. That day was a most difficult day for us as the doctor told us that she suspected an ectopic pregnancy. A sonogram revealed that it was indeed true. The baby was growing in the fallopian tube instead of the uterus. We were devastated by the news. We decided to go to another clinic and have another sonogram done, just to be sure. The second sonogram revealed the same. We returned to my wife's doctor who informed us that the pregnancy had to be terminated. The baby could not survive and my wife's life was endangered as well. The doctor wanted to schedule the procedure for Monday.

Before we went home that day, we visited the Our Lady of Lourdes Church in Quezon City, Philippines. We prayed so hard hoping that a miracle would happen. As I was praying, I noticed a little prayer pamphlet in the church. It was a pamphlet about Padre Pio, with prayers and devotions. I had never heard of Padre Pio before. I showed the pamphlet to my wife and told her that we should pray and seek Padre Pio's intercession. We prayed to Padre Pio for the safety of our little one. We prayed that the baby would move towards the uterus. I began to feel confident that everything would be fine.

Monday came and we postponed the procedure to terminate the pregnancy. I went to work and shared our predicament with close friends. My Godmother told me to seek another opinion. We went to the doctor she recommended to us. He told us to postpone the procedure for one month and to continue to pray. After a prayerful month, we learned that the baby had moved towards the uterus. We received an answer to our prayers through the intercession of Padre Pio! Our first born child is a healthy nine-year-old boy now. He is doing very well in school and is turning out to be a fine boy. His name is Pio. I thank God for letting us experience his presence in our family through St. Padre Pio. Today, we continue to pray and seek Padre Pio's intercession for guidance.

- *Mike Cunanan*

The Doctor was Perplexed I have a friend named Glenda who is a Protestant and belongs to the Presbyterian denomination. I shared the prayers of Padre Pio with her and told her about his life and his familiar saying, "Pray, Hope, and Don't Worry." I gave her a Padre Pio Rosary. I also gave her a pamphlet on how to pray the Rosary and suggested that she pray it each day. Glenda thought it was a good idea and began to pray the Rosary every morning. She told me that whenever she had entered a Catholic Church in the past, she always had a special feeling. I told her that she was feeling the real presence of Jesus in the Blessed Sacrament.

Glenda had to go to the hospital for quadruple bypass heart surgery. Her sister called me to let me know that she came through the surgery just fine. However, her sister said that the doctor had come to her room the next day and he was perplexed. He told Glenda that she was repeating some initials during the operation, and he, as well as all of the doctors and nurses who were attending her, were curious as to what she was saying. He said that none of his patients had ever murmured even one word during open heart surgery. The anesthetic they are given is so strong, that they do not utter a sound in their unconscious state. But Glenda, for some reason, was different. "What was I saying?" Glenda asked him. "You were constantly repeating the initials, P. H. D. W." the doctor answered. "We would like to know what it stands for. Then Glenda understood and told him, "It stands for "Pray, Hope, and

Don't Worry." The doctor has since shared the phrase with his patients who are preparing for surgery.

- *Tom Thurston*

Mr. Warner, Your Hearing is Perfect Two years ago I was offered a job which required a complete physical examination, including a hearing test. I passed the physical but I failed the hearing test twice. I was told to get another hearing test at my own expense. If I failed that test, I would lose my chance for the new job.

I felt very anxious about the situation. Three years before I had been diagnosed with a form of degenerative hearing loss. It also produced symptoms such as vertigo and nausea. I was certain that I would fail the next hearing test.

On the day of my appointment with the specialist for my last attempt to pass the hearing test, I had taken my daughter to a Catholic bookstore in Hampton, New Hampshire. While there, I noticed a dvd about Padre Pio. I did not know very much about him. As I read the words on the cover of the dvd, I felt an itching sensation deep inside both of my ears. I also felt as though my ears were being tickled. I did not pay too much attention to it because I had become absorbed in reading the information about Padre Pio on the dvd cover.

Later that afternoon, I had my hearing test. I was tested twice. They also looked at the paperwork I gave them with the results of my two previous tests. "Mr. Warner," the doctor said. "Your hearing is perfect. There is nothing wrong." I was so happy that I shouted for joy and I was very surprised as I noticed that for the first time in years I could hear everything. Also, the pain in my ears was gone.

I told my parish priest the whole story and he told me that I had received a healing through Padre Pio's intercession. I was hired for the job and my hearing has continued to be perfect.

- *Bruce Warner*

I Prayed to Padre Pio that My Mother Would Receive the Last Rites My mother was diagnosed with Parkinson's disease. The most painful part of the illness for her was the awareness that she was losing her independence and her sharpness of mind. After four years, my sisters and I realized that she could no longer remain in her own home, even with 24-hour care. We found a lovely care facility for her. Mom's condition rapidly worsened.

During this time, I prayed daily to Padre Pio that mom would have a priest to assist her and give her the Last Rites before she passed away. I begged Padre Pio to help her in this way. After a fall, she was moved to a hospital and her condition worsened. However, when Fr. Don came to see her, she recognized him and was able to receive the sacraments of Anointing of the Sick and the Eucharist. Two days later, I received a call that I needed to come to her bedside to say goodbye. I called her and told her I was on my way. She had not been able to have a phone conversation for 6 months. But she was able to take my call and to understand what I was saying to her. As I hung up the phone, the scent of roses filled the car. I thanked Padre Pio for obtaining these favors for me and for my mother. She passed away peacefully two days later. Glory to God for his tremendous prayer warrior, Padre Pio.

- *Kayte Russell*

I Asked Padre Pio to Send Me a Sign A few years ago I was praying to St. Pio and I asked him to send me a sign that he was listening to my prayers. Well, about a week later I received a package in the mail from Italy. The package came from San Giovanni Rotondo. A letter inside the package informed me that I had won the "Epiphany Raffle." I had never even heard of the Epiphany Raffle. I won books on St. Pio, a number of beautiful photographs of St. Pio, a St. Pio hat and many other St. Pio items. Padre Pio had given me his sign that he was definitely listening to my prayers.

- *Josie Grossi*

Brenda, You Had Better Get Up! Once, while on a job-hunting trip, I checked into a motel for the night. Several people who were at the motel made me feel uneasy. I began to feel a concern for the safety of my car and I hoped that it would not be vandalized in the night. Before I went to bed, I prayed and asked Padre Pio to watch over me and protect me and also my car.

That night, I had a dream. In the dream, I was laying on my right side, and Padre Pio came and shook me awake saying, "Brenda, I think you'd better get up now." When I woke up, I was laying on my right side, just like in my dream. I looked at the clock and saw that it was 3:00 a.m. I was so groggy, that I fell asleep again. I then had a second dream in which Padre Pio shook me once again, saying with greater emphasis, "Brenda! You had better get up now!" At that, I got up and looked out the window. Sure enough, the two fellows who had concerned me after I checked into the motel, were at my car. One of them was under it! They left hastily when that saw me at the window. I am convinced that Padre Pio heard my prayer that night and came to my rescue.

- *Brenda Zizzo*

Lord, Send Padre Pio to Help my Parents In my younger years, when I was on a quest to grow in spiritual understanding, I found a used book, a biography of Padre Pio. After I read the book, I knew that I wanted Padre Pio to be my spiritual father for the rest of my life. Many years later, I read another book on his life and my dedication to him grew even greater.

When my mother and father were in their early 80's, they were having some financial difficulties. One night I knelt by my bed and prayed, "Lord, send Padre Pio to my parents to help them." Two weeks later, I was visiting my parents when my mother said, "I had a most unusual experience a few nights ago. I woke up at 3:00 a.m. and there was a monk standing right next to me. The hood of his habit was pulled up on his head." I asked my mother if she was afraid and she told me that she had no fear at all. On the contrary, she said that she felt very peaceful. When the monk appeared at her bedside, she looked over at my father because she intended to wake him up, and when she looked back, the monk was gone. I then told her that I had prayed to Padre Pio and I had asked him to help both her and my father. Right after that, my parents' financial difficulties became resolved and they had no more worries.

I believe that my parents realized that Padre Pio's visit was an answer to my prayers. But because they were both Protestants, and because the idea of saints was not in their religious tradition, I feel that they had some difficulty comprehending what had happened. Through the years, the blessings that I have received from Padre Pio continue to help me and to strengthen my faith in God.

- *Dr. Ron Cobb - Retired Colonel, U.S. Army*

My Father's Dream My father, Italo Francia, had not been feeling well. When he went to the doctor for tests, it was found that he had a large cancerous tumor. In order to shrink the tumor, he was given radiation and chemotherapy at the Metropolitan Hospital's Windsor Cancer Center in Windsor, Ontario, Canada. After that, he had surgery. He had to continue with the chemotherapy treatments after his surgery. The treatments made him so ill that he said that he would rather die than endure any more of them. He told his doctor that he had decided to discontinue the treatments.

My mother and I resigned ourselves to my father's decision. Throughout my father's illness, my mother had been praying to Padre Pio for a cure. I too prayed for Padre Pio's intercession. I pulled out an old prayer card of Padre Pio that my mother had given me years before. I prayed to Padre Pio that my father would be healed and that he would be able to walk me, his only daughter, down the aisle some day. If however, it was his time to die, I prayed that he would not suffer. During this time, I learned more about Padre Pio and the miracles that he performed, even after his death.

The night before my father's next doctor's appointment, he had a dream. In his dream, he was at the doctor's office. Two images of Padre Pio's face appeared on the screen of the monitor in the place where the tumor had been. After my father woke up, he felt secure that all would be well. A few days later we got the joyous news that my father was cancer-free. My parents are planning to go on a pilgrimage to Padre Pio's monastery to thank him for this miracle.

- *Mary Francia*

Padre Pio Rescued Me in Vienna I have had a difficult marriage due to my husband's struggle with mental illness. In 2008, in the middle of a personal crisis, my husband left home. I felt into a deep depression and was unable to find a way to get out of the gloom and sadness that had engulfed my life. I had to make a business trip to Vienna which I could in no way postpone. I did not want to make the trip and was in no shape to be alone in a foreign city. I found strength in prayer and the Eucharist.

When my Rosary broke, I went to a shop to buy a new one. A gentleman in the shop gave me a prayer card, with a third class relic of a saint that I had never heard of, St. Pio. The prayer card had the Novena to the Sacred Heart of Jesus and the prayer for the intercession of St. Pio. I prayed the Novena and the prayer for St. Pio's intercession every day, and I slowly started feeling better.

I went to my mother's house for the holidays. One night, my mother and I were watching T.V. As she was changing the channels, I told her to stop on one particular channel. "That man looks like the saint on the prayer card I was given in Vienna," I said to my mother. I went to get the prayer card to look at it closer. The television program was a movie about the life of Padre Pio. The next day, I went to a Catholic bookstore and bought a book on Padre Pio. I found out that his feast day is September 23, the day of my wedding anniversary.

My husband came back home and is now taking care of his illness. Today is our 15th wedding anniversary. I am very thankful to St. Pio because I know he made it possible for me to accept what I have to live with and for my husband to return home and take care of his illness. I tell people that St. Pio rescued me. He found me in Vienna, there is no doubt about it. He reached out through that gentleman who gave me the prayer card. He touched my life and my heart and brought me closer to Jesus. We know the road is not easy, but I have confidence that I have Padre Pio's help to walk as Jesus would want me to walk. Every night I pray to St. Pio for all the people I know who are sick, including my husband.

- *Name Withheld*

I Prayed for a Forgiving Heart From the time I was a little girl, my mother and my grandmother told me stories about Padre Pio. They both had a great devotion to him and used to go to the public library and check out books about him. I turned to Padre Pio in prayer and received help from him during the most painful time in my life, when my husband of twelve years left me.

I came home from a work convention and discovered that my husband had moved out of the house. I was soon to learn that my husband was in a great deal of debt. He had taken out large loans and had kept the information a secret from me. Before long I was getting threatening letters and telephone calls from creditors, demanding payment. I was deeply saddened to see that my eighty-year-old parents were suffering too. The bill collectors were calling and harassing them as well, demanding money. They were frightened by the calls.

I was seething with anger whenever I thought about the desperate financial straits that my husband had put me in. At the time, I had eighty-five cents in my checking account. I was also filled with fear, trying to figure out how I would be able to survive. I began to feel a deep hatred for my husband and all that he had done to me. Even after the divorce became final, his financial problems continued to pursue me. I knew that it was wrong for me to feel hatred in my heart, but I did not know how to change.

One day I was waiting in the confessional line at Our Lady of the Rosary parish. As I stood in the line, I looked at a picture of Padre Pio that was hanging just outside the confessional. I prayed with all my heart to Padre Pio and begged him, "Please take this hatred away from my heart. Help me to forgive my former husband. Please give me peace of heart and peace of mind." The moment I finished the prayer, I could smell the wonderful scent of roses. It appeared to have been coming from the picture of Padre Pio. The hatred I felt in my heart vanished. I was instantly healed of my resentment and bitterness.

I still had to deal with the terrible financial devastation that my former spouse had left me in. I had just read a story in one of the Padre Pio newsletters about a young girl named Yvette who lived in Paris. She made a trip to San Giovanni Rotondo in order to ask Padre Pio for his advice regarding the financial hardship she was in. I prayed, "Padre Pio, I am not quite as desperate as Yvette was when you helped her, but I am almost there. You have got to help me!" As soon as I ended that prayer, the anxiety regarding my finances left me completely. It has never returned.

That same day I attended Mass at my home parish of St. Anne's. As I sat quietly in the pew, I thought I heard someone calling my name. I turned around but there was no one calling for me. Something compelled me to look up in the choir loft. There I saw a beautiful banner of Padre Pio. I had never seen one there before and I have never seen one there since. I knew then and there that Padre Pio had confirmed twice in one day that he was with me and that he was helping me.

I know that we must forgive all who have harmed us. It is what Jesus asks us to do. If we cannot bring ourselves to do this, we will never have peace. I am making a trip to San Giovanni Rotondo in April 2011. I am not going there to ask for anything for myself. I am going in order to give thanks to Padre Pio for all that he has done for me. I also feel privileged that I will be carrying the prayer petitions of my family and friends to his shrine.

- *Name Withheld*

Padre Pio was Carrying Me I have a great devotion to Padre Pio. It began in 2002 when I visited Italy. In the past six years, my family has had many problems. My granddaughter was diagnosed with a rare blood cancer. My daughter was also diagnosed with cancer. My stepdaughter had a hole in heard heart and was in very serious condition. Also, my son suffered a heart attack. To each one of them, I gave either a Padre Pio medal or a Padre Pio statue and told them to pray to Padre Pio and ask for his help. I thank God and Padre Pio that they are all doing well now.

In January 2008, I was diagnosed with lung cancer. I am seventy-eight years old and have other serious health problems. I have a pacemaker and defibrillator and also a bad heart. I needed surgery but my doctor was not optimistic about my chances of surviving an operation. I gave my doctor a medal of Padre Pio and told him that I had complete confidence that Padre Pio would see me through. I was operated on at Sloan-Kettering Hospital in New York City and my left lung was removed. I developed an infection after the surgery and spent three months in the hospital. After that I was transferred to Burke Rehabilitation Hospital in White Plains, New York.

One day, one of the nurses' aides came in my room and told me that she had a dream about me. "I have never had a dream about one of my patients before," she said. I asked her about the dream. She looked at the Padre Pio statue that I had in my room and pointed at it. "I dreamed that he was carrying you," she said.

I am recovering slowly from the surgery. I continue my devotion to Padre Pio and the Blessed Mother and urge everyone to pray the Rosary daily.

- *John Giumarra*

My Son's Life was Out Of Control My son Ken is an alcoholic. When I shared my worries about Ken with a friend, he said that he would write to Padre Pio's monastery in San Giovanni Rotondo and ask for prayers on my son's behalf. Ken would drink every single day and he drank throughout the day, consuming large quantities of beer and tequila. He had no appetite for food. His memory was short and he could not hold down a job. He was a chain smoker and was also addicted to TV. He had stopped going to church. His life was out of control.

About two weeks before Easter, Ken and I started praying together and we have continued to do so ever since. Each day we have been praying three Hail Mary's. After each Hail Mary we pray, "By thy holy and Immaculate Conception, O Mary, make my body pure and my soul holy," and "O my Mother, preserve me this day from mortal sin." We then pray the prayer to St. Michael the Archangel, the Act of Contrition and finally the prayer for Padre Pio's intercession.

Ken went to Mass with me on Holy Thursday. During the service, Ken was kneeling next to me. At that time, I prayed and asked Padre Pio to heal my son of his addictions. As I prayed, I felt a great sense of peace come over me. That night when Ken returned home, he happened to find ten patches to help him stop smoking.

Since Easter Sunday, all of Ken's addictions have been lifted. He has not had a drink and has not smoked a cigarette. He has had only minor withdrawal symptoms. He has a good appetite now and is working most every day. He is making an effort to pay off his debts. He has decided that he does not want to indulge in frivolous things or buy anything until he can afford to do so. He has also canceled certain TV programs. He tries to keep busy so that he will not waste his time watching TV. He has decided to go back to church and is preparing to make a good confession. He calls me every day so that we can pray together over the telephone. He is trying to regain his health with exercise and healthy eating. I feel confident that Padre Pio was instrumental in lifting the chains of vice that Ken was bound to.

- Gloria

Padre Pio Went all the Way for Me! About 20 years ago I attended a seminar given by a priest who had returned from a trip to San Giovanni Rotondo. His testimony about Padre Pio was very inspiring and since that time I have developed a very close relationship with Padre Pio. I keep a small Padre Pio prayer card in the left pocket of my shirt at all times. Every night I place it on my night table before I go to bed.

I obtained a Master's Degree in Theology and Pastoral Ministry from Barry University and I am also a Certified Public Accountant. My wife and I have been active parishioners at St. Timothy Catholic Church in Miami where we head the Evangelization Ministry. I also teach Bible classes on Tuesdays.

In 2010, I was diagnosed with severe aorta stenosis. My aorta valve should have had an opening of 3 cms and mine showed only .75. To confirm the findings, my cardiologist, Dr. Hugo Garcia ordered a transesophageal echo test. The test showed the same results. My doctor explained to me that I was going to have to have open heart surgery. I met the doctor who was going to perform the surgery, Dr. Nirberto Moreno, at Baptist Hospital of Miami. When he saw the results of the echo test, he characterized the aorta stenosis as "critical."

Before the surgery, I had to have one other procedure, a heart catheterization. The procedure would take a close look at my arteries in order to determine the entry point for the open heart surgery. It my arteries were in good shape, the surgeon would go through the side of my chest. If the coronary arteries were obstructed, the center of my chest would have to be opened for the surgery.

The heart catheterization procedure was performed at South Miami Hospital on April 12, 2011. As I was coming out of the sedation, my cardiologist, Dr. Garcia, said to me, "Mr. Contreras, what have you done?" I did not understand what he meant and was afraid that he had bad news for me. "I have not done anything. But I have prayed a lot," I replied. "Well, keep praying," my doctor said. "Your aorta valve now shows a 1.44 cm. opening. You do not need heart surgery." I had been praying to Padre Pio since January, asking only that my coronary arteries would be healthy. Well, Padre Pio went all the way for me!

- *Jorge Contreras*

May the Lord confirm with his blessings these wishes of mine, for your happiness is very close to my heart and I work and pray continuously for this end.

- *St. Pio of Pietrelcina*

Efficacious Novena
To The Sacred Heart Of Jesus

(This novena prayer was recited every day by
Padre Pio for all those who asked for his prayers)

I.   O my Jesus, You have said, "Truly I say to you, ask and it will be given you, seek and you will find, knock and it will be opened to you." Behold, I knock, I seek and ask for the grace of...
Our Father...Hail Mary...Glory be to the Father...
Sacred Heart of Jesus, I place all my trust in You.

II.   O my Jesus, You have said, "Truly I say to you, if you ask anything of the Father in my name, he will give it to you." Behold, in Your name, I ask the Father for the grace of...
Our Father...Hail Mary...Glory be to the Father...
Sacred Heart of Jesus, I place all my trust in You.

III. O my Jesus, You have said, "Truly I say to you, heaven and earth will pass away but my words will not pass away." Encouraged by Your infallible words, I now ask for the grace of...
Our Father...Hail Mary...Glory be to the Father...
Sacred Heart of Jesus, I place all my trust in You.

O Sacred Heart of Jesus, for whom it is impossible not to have compassion on the afflicted, have pity on us poor sinners and grant us the grace which we ask of You, through the Sorrowful and Immaculate heart of Mary, Your tender mother and ours.

Hail, Holy Queen, Mother of Mercy, our life, our sweetness and our hope. To thee do we cry, poor banished children of Eve. To thee do we send up our sighs, mourning and weeping in this vale of tears. Turn, then, most gracious Advocate, thine eyes of mercy upon us; and after this our exile, show unto us the blessed fruit of thy womb, Jesus. O clement, O loving, O sweet Virgin Mary,

Pray for us, Holy Mother of God;
That we may be made worthy of the promises of Christ.

St. Joseph, foster father of Jesus, pray for us.

Stay With Me, Lord

————————————————

by St. Pio of Pietrelcina

Stay with me, Lord, for it is necessary to have You present
    so that I do not forget You. You know how easily I abandon You.

Stay with me, Lord, because I am weak
    and I need Your strength, that I may not fall so often.

Stay with me, Lord, for You are my life,
    and without You, I am without fervor.

Stay with me, Lord, for You are my light,
    and without You, I am in darkness.

Stay with me, Lord, to show me Your will.

Stay with me, Lord, so that I may hear Your voice and follow You.

Stay with me, Lord, for I desire to love You very much,
    and always be in Your company.

Stay with me, Lord, if You wish me to be faithful to You.

Stay with me, Lord, for as poor as my soul is,
    I want it to be a place of consolation for You, a nest of love.

Stay with me, Jesus, for it is getting late and the day is coming to a close, and life passes; death, judgment, eternity approaches. It is necessary to renew my strength, so that I will not stop along the way and for that, I need You. It is getting late and death approaches, I fear the darkness, the temptations, the dryness, the cross, the sorrows. O how I need You, my Jesus, in this night of exile.

Stay with me tonight, Jesus, in life with all it's dangers. I need You.

Let me recognize You as Your disciples did at the breaking of the bread,
    so that the Eucharistic Communion be the Light which disperses
    the darkness, the force which sustains me, the unique joy of my heart.

Stay with me, Lord, because at the hour of my death, I want to remain
    united to You, if not by communion, at least by grace and love.

Stay with me, Jesus, I do not ask for divine consolation, because I do not
    merit it, but the gift of Your Presence, oh yes, I ask this of You.

Stay with me, Lord, for it is You alone I look for,
    Your Love, Your Grace, Your Will, Your Heart, Your Spirit,
    because I love You, and ask no other reward but to love You more
    and more. With a firm love, I will love You with all my heart while
    on earth, and continue to love You perfectly during all eternity.

Amen.

Litany of St. Pio of Pietrelcina

Lord, have mercy.   *Christ, have mercy.*

Lord, have mercy.
Christ hear us.   *Christ, graciously hear us.*

God the Father of Heaven,   *have mercy on us.*

God the Son,
Redeemer of the World,   *have mercy on us.*

God the Holy Spirit,   *have mercy on us.*

Holy Trinity, One God,   *have mercy on us.*

Holy Mary, Virgin Immaculate,   *pray for us.*
St. Pio of Pietrelcina,   *pray for us.*
Beloved of God,   *pray for us.*
Imitator of Jesus Christ,   *pray for us.*
Good shepherd of the people,   *pray for us.*
Model for priests,   *pray for us.*
Light of the Church,   *pray for us.*
Adorer of the Blessed Sacrament,   *pray for us.*
Faithful son of St. Francis,   *pray for us.*
Marked with the stigmata of Jesus,   *pray for us.*
Patient in suffering,   *pray for us.*
Helper of the dying,   *pray for us.*
Director of souls,   *pray for us.*
Heart of gold,   *pray for us.*

Apostle of mercy,	*pray for us.*
Worker of miracles,	*pray for us.*
Consoler of the afflicted,	*pray for us.*
Lover of the Most Holy Rosary,	*pray for us.*
Helper of souls in doubt and darkness,	*pray for us.*
Comforter of the sick,	*pray for us.*
Example of humility,	*pray for us.*
Source of wisdom,	*pray for us.*
Mirror of the divine life,	*pray for us.*
Lover of Jesus Crucified,	*pray for us.*
Resigned to the will of God,	*pray for us.*
Doing good upon earth,	*pray for us.*
Filled with the spirit of self-sacrifice,	*pray for us.*
Our help and hope in all our needs,	*pray for us.*
Vessel of the Holy Spirit,	*pray for us.*
Leading us to Christ,	*pray for us.*
Our spiritual father and advocate,	*pray for us.*
Crowned with glory in Heaven,	*pray for us.*

Lamb of God, Who takes away the sins of the world,
    spare us, O Lord.
Lamb of God, Who takes away the sins of the world,
    graciously hear us, O Lord.
Lamb of God, Who takes away the sins of the world,
    have mercy on us.

Pray for us, St. Pio of Pietrelcina,
    That we may be made worthy of the promises of Christ.

Let us pray:
God our Father, You helped St. Pio to reflect the
image of Christ through a life of charity and self-sacrifice.
May we follow your Son by walking in the footsteps of
St. Pio of Pietrelcina and by imitating his selfless love.
Amen.

Prayer for the Intercession of
St. Pio of Pietrelcina

O God, You gave St. Pio of Pietrelcina, Capuchin priest, the great privilege of participating in a unique way in the Passion of Your Son. Grant me through his intercession the grace of...(Here mention your petition) which I ardently desire; And above all, grant me the grace of living in conformity with the death of Jesus, to arrive at the glory of the resurrection.

Glory be to the Father...(three times)

Recommended Reading

Allegri, Renzo, *Padre Pio: Man of Hope*, Ann Arbor, MI, Servant Publications, 2000.

Ball, Ann, *Modern Saints: Their Lives and Faces - Book One*, Rockford, IL, TAN Books and Publishers, 1983.

Ball, Ann, *Modern Saints: Their Lives and Faces - Book Two*, Rockford, IL, TAN Books and Publishers, 1990.

Brown, Raphael, *The Little Flowers of St. Francis*, New York, Image Books, 1958.

Capobianco, Costantino, *Words and Anecdotes of Saint Pio*, San Giovanni Rotondo, Edizioni Padre Pio da Pietrelcina, 2006.

Carty, Charles Mortimer, *Padre Pio: The Stigmatist*, Rockford, IL, TAN Books and Publishers, 1973.

Castello, Nello, ed., *Padre Pio Teaches Us*, San Giovanni Rotondo, La Casa Sollievo Della Sofferenza Editions, 1981.

Cataneo, Pascal, *Padre Pio Gleanings*, Sherbrooke, Quebec, Editions Paulines, 1991.

Contessa, Fabrizio, *Padre Pio*, New York, Alba House, 1999.

Cruz, Joan Carroll, *The Incorruptibles*, Rockford, IL, TAN Books and Publishers, 1977.

D'Apolito, Alberto, *Padre Pio of Pietrelcina: Memories, Experiences, Testimonials*, San Giovanni Rotondo, Editions: Padre Pio of Pietrelcina, 1986.

D'Ascanio, Andrea, *Padre Pio's Smile*, Edizioni "PATER", L'Aquila, Italy, 1972.

Daws, Gavin, *Holy Man: Father Damien of Molokai*, University of Hawaii Press, 1989.

Delaney, John J. *A Woman Clothed with the Sun: Eight Great Appearances of Our Lady in Modern Times,* New York, Doubleday, 1961.

De Robeck, Nesta, *Padre Pio*, Milwaukee, Bruce Publishing, 1958.

Di Flumeri, Gerardo, ed., *Acts of the First Congress of Studies on Padre Pio's Spirituality*, San Giovanni Rotondo, Edizioni "Padre Pio da Pietrelcina", Our Lady of Grace Capuchin Friary, 1978.

Di Flumeri, Gerardo, *The Apparitions of the Child Jesus to Padre Pio*, San Giovanni Rotondo, Edizioni Padre Pio da Pietrelcina, Our Lady of Grace Capuchin Friary.

Di Flumeri, Gerardo, *Homage to the Blessed Padre Pio*, San Giovanni Rotondo, Our Lady of Grace Capuchin Friary, 1999.

Di Flumeri, Gerardo, *The Mystery of the Cross in Padre Pio of Pietrelcina*, San Giovanni Rotondo, Edizioni Padre Pio da Pietrelcina, Our Lady of Grace Capuchin Friary, 1983.

Di Flumeri, Gerardo, ed., *Padre Pio's Prayer Life*, San Giovanni Rotondo, Edizioni Padre Pio da Pietrelcina, 1999.

Duchess of St. Albans, *Magic of a Mystic: Stories of Padre Pio*, New York, Clarkson N. Potter, 1983.

Edizioni Publicolor, *Blessed Father Pio - Life, Miracles, Beatification - Thoughts and Prayers*, Pescara, Italy, Publicolor Publishing, 2000.

Freze, Michael, *They Bore the Wounds of Christ: The Mystery of the Sacred Stigmata*, Huntington, Indiana, Our Sunday Visitor, 1989.

Funicelli, Pellegrino, *Padre Pio's Jack of All Trades*, San Giovanni Rotondo, Padre Pio da Pietrelcina Editions, Our Lady of Grace Capuchin Friary, 1991.

Gaeta, Saverio, ed., *The Stigmata of Faith - Thoughts of Padre Pio*, Sherbrooke, QC, Canada, Médiaspaul, 2000.

Gallagher, Jim, *Padre Pio: The Pierced Priest*, London, Harper Collins, 1995.

Gaudiose, Dorothy M., *Mary's House - Mary Pyle: Under the Spiritual Guidance of Padre Pio*, New York, Alba House, 1993.

Gaudiose, Dorothy M., *Prophet of the People: A Biography of Padre Pio*, New York, Alba House, 1992.

Gigliozzi, Giovanni, *Padre Pio: A Pictorial Biography*, New York, Phaedra Publishers, 1965.

Hanley, Bonifice O.F.M., *Ten Christians*, Notre Dame, Indiana, Ave Maria Press, 1979.

IasenzaNiro, Marcellino, *The Padre - Saint Pio of Pietrelcina - Charismatic Priest - Testimonies*, San Giovanni Rotondo, Edizioni Padre Pio da Pietrelcina, Our Lady of Grace Capuchin Friary, 2007.

IasenzaNiro, Marcellino, *The Padre - Saint Pio of Pietrelcina - His Mission to Save Souls - Testimonies*, San Giovanni Rotondo, Edizioni Padre Pio da Pietrelcina, Our Lady of Grace Capuchin Friary, 2006.

Ingoldsby, Mary F., *Padre Pio: His Life and Mission*, Dublin, Veritas Publications, 1988.

Kalvelage, Francis Mary, ed., *Padre Pio: The Wonder Worker*, New Bedford, MA, Franciscan Friars of the Immaculate, 1999.

Keane, Colm, *Padre Pio: The Irish Connection*, Edinburgh, Mainstream Publishing Company, 2007.

Lappin, Peter, *Give Me Souls: Life of Don Bosco,* New York, Don Bosco Publications, 1986.

Laurentin, Rene, *Bernedette Speaks: A Life of Saint Bernadette Soubirous in Her Own Words,* Boston, MA, Pauline Book and Media, 2000.

Leone, Gherardo, *Padre Pio and His Work*, San Giovanni Rotondo, Editions Casa Sollievo Della Sofferenza, 1986.

Leone, Gherardo, *Padre Pio: Childhood and Adolescence*, San Giovanni Rotondo, La Casa Sollievo Della Sofferenza Editions, 1986.

Lilley, Stella Maris, *On the Road with Padre Pio*, San Giovanni Rotondo, Edizioni Padre Pio da Pietrelcina.

Luce, Clare Boothe, ed., *Saints for Now*, New York, Sheed & Ward, 1952.

Mandato, Graziella DeNunzio, *Padre Pio: Encounters with a Spiritual Daughter from Pietrelcina*, Sea Bright, New Jersey, Angelus Media Distribution Group, 2002.

Manelli, Stefano, *Padre Pio of Pietrelcina*, New Bedford, MA, Franciscans of the Immaculate, 1999.

Massa, Bonaventura, *Mary Pyle: She Lived Doing Good to All*, San Giovanni Rotondo, Our Lady of Grace Capuchin Friary, 1986.

McCaffery, John, *The Friar of San Giovanni: Tales of Padre Pio*, London, Darton, Longman & Todd, 1978.

McGregor, Augustine, *Padre Pio: His Early Years*, San Giovanni Rotondo, Editions: Padre Pio da Pietrelcina, Our Lady of Grace Capuchin Friary, 1985.

Miscio, Anacleto, *Mary Pyle*, Foggia, The Capuchin Friars, Vinelli Press, 1985.

Nolan, Geraldine, *A View of Padre Pio from Mary's House*, San Giovanni Rotondo, Our Lady of Grace Capuchin Friary, 1993.

Padre Pio of Pietrelcina, *Letters Volume I: Correspondence with his Spiritual Directors (1910-1922)*, San Giovanni Rotondo, Editions: Voce di Padre Pio, 1980.

Padre Pio of Pietrelcina, *Letters Volume II: Correspondence with Raffaelina Cerase, Noblewoman (1914-1915)*, San Giovanni Rotondo, Editions: Padre Pio da Pietrelcina, 1987.

Padre Pio of Pietrelcina, *Letters Volume III: Correspondence with His Spiritual Daughters (1915-1923)*, San Giovanni Rotondo, Editions: Padre Pio da Pietrelcina, 1994.

Parente, Alessio, ed., *Have a Good Day*, San Giovanni Rotondo, Edizioni Padre Pio da Pietrelcina, 1975.

Parente, Alessio, *The Holy Souls: Viva Padre Pio*, San Giovanni Rotondo, Padre Pio of Pietrelcina Editions, Our Lady of Grace Capuchin Friary, 1994.

Parente, Alessio, ed., *Padre Pio Counsels*, Dublin: Padre Pio Office, 1982.

Parente, Alessio, *Send Me Your Guardian Angel*, Naples, Editions Carlo Tozza, 1984.

Parente, Pascal P., *A City on a Mountain: Padre Pio of Pietrelcina*, St. Meinrad, IN, Grail Publications, 1956.

Pasquale, Gianluigi, *Secrets of a Soul: Padre Pio's Letters to His Spiritual Director*, Boston, MA, Pauline Books & Media, 2003.

Peyret, Raymond, *Marthe Robin: The Cross and the Joy*, Alba House, New York, 1983.

Preziuso, Gennaro, *The Life of Padre Pio: Between the Altar and the Confessional*, Alba House, New York, 2002.

Rega, Frank M., *Padre Pio and America*, Rockford, IL, TAN Books and Publishers, 2004.

Ripabottoni, Alessandro da, *Padre Pio of Pietrelcina: Everybody's Cyrenean*, San Giovanni Rotondo, Our Lady of Grace Capuchin Friary, 1987.

Ruffin, C. Bernard, *Padre Pio: The True Story (Revised and Expanded)*, Huntington, IN, Our Sunday Visitor, 1991.

Ruffin, C. Bernard, *The Life of Brother Andre: The Miracle Worker of St. Joseph*, Huntington, IN, Our Sunday Visitor, 1988.

Schug, John, *A Padre Pio Profile*, Petersham, MA, St. Bede's Publications, 1987.

Schug, John, *Padre Pio*, Chicago, Franciscan Herald Press, 1983.

Six, Jean-Francois, *The Spiritual Autobiography of Charles De Foucauld*, Ijamsville, MD, The Word Among Us Press, 2003.

Steiner, Johannes, *Therese Neumann*, New York, Alba House, 1967.

Tangari, Katharina, *Stories of Padre Pio*, Rockford, IL, TAN Books and Publishers, 1996.

Tarcisio of Cervinara., *The Devil in the Life of Padre Pio*, San Giovanni Rotondo, Padre Pio of Pietrelcina Editions, Our Lady of Grace Capuchin Friary, 1998.

Tarcisio of Cervinara., *Padre Pio's Mass*, San Giovanni Rotondo, Padre Pio da Pietrelcina Editions, Our Lady of Grace Capuchin Friary, 1992.

Treece, Patricia, *A Man for Others: Maximilian Kolbe Saint of Auschwitz*, Libertyville, IL, Franciscan Marytown Press, 1993.

Treece, Patricia, *Nothing Short of a Miracle,* Huntington, IN, Our Sunday Visitor, 1988.

Trochu, Abbe Francis, *The Cure D'Ars: St. John-Marie-Baptiste Vianney,* Rockford, IL, TAN Books and Publishers, 1977.

Vogl, Adalbert Albert, *Therese Neumann: Mystic and Stigmatist*, Rockford, IL, TAN Books and Publishers, 1987.

Wilson, Anne, ed., *Padre Pio of Pietrelcina: Walking in the Footsteps of Jesus Christ*, St. Paul, MN, Leaflet Missal Co., 1993.

Wright, Cathy, *Charles de Foucauld - Journey of the Spirit*, Boston, MA, Pauline Books and Media, 2005.

10147061R00305

Made in the USA
Charleston, SC
10 November 2011